ROD MACQUEEN 'There is more to li by Macqueen to give his players a mor... there is much more to Rod Macqueen t... sented.

Married with two children, Macqueen was born and raised on Sydney's northern beaches. He won numerous awards rowing surfboats with the Collaroy Surf Lifesaving Club and captained an undefeated state team on three occasions. At the same time, he played almost two hundred first grade games with the local Warringah Rugby Club, before achieving spectacular success coaching the NSW Waratahs and then the ACT Brumbies.

During the same period he took over part of the family business and transformed it into a multimillion dollar point-of-sale merchandising company with a long list of multinational clients.

As Wallaby coach Macqueen clinched not only the 1999 World Cup but every international rugby trophy available, including an historic series victory over the British and Irish Lions.

KEVIN HITCHCOCK is an award-winning journalist with thirty years' experience in newspapers, radio and television. A keen sportsman, he played rugby for several clubs, including Warringah where he played first grade alongside Rod Macqueen, an association which developed into a strong and lasting friendship.

In 1991, not long after being promoted to Director of News at Channel Ten, Kevin broke his neck in a diving accident and he was told he would be a quadriplegic for the rest of his life. With the help of family and friends, he undertook a unique and demanding exercise program that enabled him to regain the use of his body, including the ability to walk. He documented his extraordinary struggle in his bestselling autobiography *Walk With Me*, also published by Random House.

Kevin now works from home as a freelance writer and television producer.

ONE STEP AHEAD

ON THE FIELD AND IN THE BOARDROOM

ROD MACQUEEN

WITH KEVIN HITCHCOCK

RANDOM HOUSE AUSTRALIA

Random House Australia Pty Ltd
20 Alfred Street, Milsons Point, NSW 2061
http://www.randomhouse.com.au

Sydney   New York   Toronto
London   Auckland   Johannesburg

First published by Random House Australia 2001

National Library of Australia
Cataloguing-in-Publication Entry

Macqueen, Rod, 1949-.
One Step Ahead: on the field and in the boardroom.

ISBN 1 74051 173 5

Macqueen, Rod. 2. Teams in the workplace. 3. Business.
4. Success. I. Macqueen, Rod. II. Title

796.333092

Cover photograph by Gayna Murphy
Cover design by Greendot Design
Typeset in 12 pt Adobe Garamond by Midland Typesetters,
Maryborough, Victoria
Printed and bound by Griffin Press, Netley, South Australia

10 9 8 7 6 5 4 3 2 1

Lyrics from the song 'A Number on my Back' composed by John Williamson
(www.johnwilliamson.com.au) and published by Emusic Pty Ltd from the CD
Anthems distributed by EMI Music Aust.

Permission to reproduce lines from 'The Battle of Christchurch' kindly granted by
Rupert McCall.

Thanks to Doug Watson, Creative Director, Fame Advertising, and to Ian McIntosh
for the forewords.

I dedicate this book to my wife Liz
'the heart and soul of the Macqueen team'.

Foreword

Others are better qualified to explore the rugby side of Rod Macqueen. It's the businessman I know best—a devoted, creative, self-made individual who brings his calm, thoughtful and focused counsel to every exchange; an accomplished, modest and effective man whose attributes became immediately apparent when we first met at his company conference some years ago on the shores of Sydney harbour.

So what was so special about that day? It happened every year. Maybe it was the change of venue from the building he and partner Frank created for their merchandising company. But there was something more—there always was, every year. Every storeman, secretary, designer and executive attending knew that they'd be in for mental gymnastics with pike. It was the annual think tank where people would break off into small groups and concentrate on the company's issues—everyone knew to expect the unexpected.

The coach walks into the room cheerfully. Those who haven't seen him for a while smile for recognition. Those who haven't been doing so well smile, but defensively cross their arms. Everyone is awed by his presence, even though they work with him every day.

For those of us familiar with the culture of business conferences and used to sporting celebrity presenters, the opening address is somewhat different. No words like 'team'. No sporting analogies. Straight facts mostly, about how it's going and how everyone here should say what they think.

When the staff break out into groups of six or eight they all have one leg of the elephant to consume around their tribal fire. Fifteen minutes later they take turns to deliver their summary of the issues that face the company. The problems are arrayed on the white board and then subjects for discussion are set and assignments given.

Rod isn't a member of any one group. He shuffles, kicks dust, ponders the sky, admires the view of turn-of-the-century buildings and the luminescent harbour. He's awaiting the verdict of the jury he appointed to determine the program for the upcoming year.

Sometimes he visits the vocal group and slips back into the shadow unseen. However, the stilted, shy group will be invaded by a beaming Macqueen reassuring them that anything is valid and, 'hey, have some fun'.

He is the first person in the room to spot the problem and the last to offer his advice. He actively encourages discussion and the first to recognise the solution from another. Perhaps he is the perfect business coach without the platitudes that sports' lesser mortals are forced to rely on.

I've never been in the Wallabies dressing room at half-time. But I've always imagined the same real world facilitation from the coach. What do you think is wrong? What do you think we should do? Let me tell you what I saw from the grandstand. What do you think? Do we think that's right? Okay. So what if we tried this? I reckon it would go something like an Advantage Line get-together.

Management, like coaching, is a day-to-day thing with the same focus: people. 'How's her pregnancy going?'; 'I hear your son's teething?'; 'What happened to your hot date the other night?' Rod asks all those questions as he circles like a rudderless surfboat around the office. When he has to deliver bad news it's taken without argument. Perhaps because he's built up so many points in heaven.

Those who work with Rod will tell you he is the smartest designer and business person. However, his greatest attribute is his desire to see those around him do better than he ever did. Is it the skills developed as a coach that make him such a great businessman? Or is it the other way around?

Doug Watson

If ever a person epitomised the philosophy that rugby coaching and running a business go hand in hand it is Rod Macqueen. Over the years I have met many brilliant coaches but Rod was the first to impress on me the importance of thorough preparation through meticulously organised team management.

Of course, such management structures are now run-of-the-mill in every modern coaching set-up, but Rod Macqueen was the first coach that I came across that was so systemised and thorough in this department. He left nothing to chance. He chose his management team carefully and he ensured that each individual was hard-working and loyal. It was no wonder that only one try was scored against the Wallabies in the 1999 World Cup. Rod had employed a specialised defensive coach some two years before the event. Today, of course, other teams are scrambling to catch up and are now also using defensive coaches.

He was the first coach I saw introduce the famous angled running, with numerous variations of runners and dummy runners operating off the ball carrier to break up defences. He did it initially with New South Wales, then the Brumbies and later the Wallabies. I have met many coaches, especially from the southern hemisphere, who claim that they introduced angled running before Rod. It's strange though that we never saw their teams producing that fresh, effective attacking style before it was a feature of Macqueen's successful approach. Who will ever forget the scores rattled up by New South Wales against their opponents, many of them international teams, when Rod was in charge; or how he transformed the Brumbies, a team of rejects, into one of the most exciting and enterprising teams in the Super 12.

He was also responsible for showing me the importance of ball retention; the drills involved in keeping possession and the principle of runners becoming fetchers and fetchers becoming runners. It was an aspect of the game unheard-of in our part of the world and in the northern hemisphere at the time Rod was pioneering this new style in Australia. It is therefore not surprising that Rod's track record will show that every team he has coached has set the standard in their respective competitions culminating with the Wallabies winning the 1999 World Cup.

Those enjoying the privilege of an intimate rugby coaching discussion for the first time with Rod will be bewildered at his instinctive perception of the game and his innovative ideas. There are many coaches who have helped me enormously during my rugby life but the man who not only enhanced my coaching career, but saved it, was Rod Macqueen.

I will always be indebted to him for his inspiration and his example. That is why I waited for him in the tunnel after the World Cup final in 1999. I was filled with emotion as I warmly congratulated him on achieving the ultimate goal in rugby. Originators in life are those who become the legends, masters and pacesetters—Rod was such a person. Just as a champion chess player is always two moves ahead of his opponents so has Rod Macqueen always been several steps ahead of his fellow rugby coaches.

Ian McIntosh
Coach of provincial side, Natal, South Africa 1986–1999.
National Coach, South Africa 1993, 1994.

Contents

Preface

Not long after Australia won the World Cup in 1999, I was approached by several people who asked whether I had ever considered writing a book. It was certainly not something I had seriously thought about, however some of the questions that were being asked, and some of the stories that were being told, made me think that it mightn't be such a bad idea.

Because I haven't made a point of going public on my thoughts, there seemed to be some mystery and a great number of misconceptions about my life, business and coaching philosophies. After discussing the options with Liz as to who would help me document my thoughts, I decided to call on an old friend, someone who knew me more than any other across all walks of life.

Kevin Hitchcock and I have been mates for over twenty-six years. We've shared many great times on and off the rugby field, and with our respective families. We've also shared some incredibly tough times, experiences often made easier by a similar offbeat sense of humour. A true friend, 'Hitchie' was always there when I needed him.

An award-winning journalist, Hitchie had not long been promoted to the position of news director at the Channel Ten television network in Sydney when, early in 1991, he broke his neck in a freak accident on his farm. Doctors told him he would be a quadriplegic for life. His incredible determination to survive and walk again is an example of the strength of the man.

Although he suffers from spasticity and constant nerve pain, he related his experience in a best-selling book called Walk with Me. So I knew my mate had the talent to write. I phoned him and asked if he would help me document my own journey through life. Fortunately, he readily agreed.

This book is not just about winning the World Cup. It also explains how we got there and how it involved every aspect of my life. While my father was my mentor and best mate, there are many other people who have had a great influence on me and contributed along the way. My journey through life has been an accumulation of experiences and lessons. Some *have been bad, most have been good. And I have always tried to apply this knowledge to everything I've done.*

Through my experiences in everyday life, business and sport I have found that the same philosophies generally apply. For me, sport has been the common theme throughout and I have learnt the importance of a fine balance of fun, standards and hard work.

In putting this book together, I've been reminded of just how many people have been involved. And I would like to thank all those, especially family and friends, who have shared in and contributed to my journey. I have no doubt that without them I would not have enjoyed the success I have managed to achieve. In particular, my children Jacqui and Scott whose love and constant support have helped all of us through some very difficult times. And to my long-suffering mother who, for the past fifty years, has always been there for me with a reassuring word and a ready smile.

I would also like to thank Hitchie, not only for agreeing to take on this project in the first place, but for his tolerance over the last eighteen months, especially considering his physical limitations. And to rugby journalist Jim Webster for helping with the final finishing touches. Special mention must be made of course, of the role of Liz. I'm sure it would not have been completed without her. She made an enormous contribution helping with the content of the book and managing, as always, to keep everything on track during our hectic day-to-day schedule.

Hopefully some of the experiences I have rencountered in this book will be of value in the future to others in their life's endeavours.

Rod Macqueen

As a close friend of Rod's, I was happy to agree to his suggestion that I co-author this book. More than most, I know and have seen the complexities of character that have made Rod so successful. But because he chooses a low profile path, few of his many achievements have been documented. Apart from a circle of close friends, to most people he remains an enigma. Here was the chance to share knowledge and perceptions accrued through some extraordinary circumstances.

Since our first meeting more than twenty-six years ago, our lives seem to have been running in parallel, occasionally becoming inexplicably entwined. We shared experiences that changed our innermost characters and dramatically altered the course of our lives. From the mutual respect. These essential seeds of friendship were first sown on the field of rugby.

'Do you know the game plan Hitchy?'

The unexpected question from Rod Macqueen interrupted my private psyching-up session in the Warringah Rugby Club dressing room. I glanced at the man sitting next to me and saw a youngish face set hard with intensity. We were about to run onto the field in our first game together for the Warringah first grade, playing on either side of the scrum as the two breakaways. Macqueen had just returned to the club after rowing surfboats during the summer season and was immediately back in the top team after one training run. Having recently moved from the Hunter's Hill sub-district side, I knew little about him except that he was a long-term member and stalwart of the young emerging club and was respected throughout the competition as a 'tough nut', an enforcer.

'What game plan?' was my puzzled reply. We had already run through our various moves and tactics with the coach during a short warm-up session. The team we were about to take on was one of the competition favourites and as relative newcomers to the top division, and short of experienced players, we were expected to cop a hiding.

Macqueen leant forward and enlightened me, 'Kill the five-eighth.'

I was still taking this in when he grunted out further information.

'Their backs are much better than ours so we have to stop them getting the ball. I'll take care of their open side breakaway who's a real mongrel. He'll be offside all day and will try and get on top of us by kicking in the rucks and belting people in backplay.'

He gave me a quizzical look, 'Are you right?'

The rest of the team was up and surging toward the door when I gave the obvious reply, 'Of course, let's stick it right up 'em.'

The game unfolded as expected. We were struggling to be competitive but the highlight was a ferocious ongoing brawl between Macqueen and his opposite number. Not only was our opponent playing permanently and deliberately offside to spoil play he was using fists, elbows and feet at every opportunity. Macqueen was almost oblivious to the fact we were playing a game of football and carried out his own private war against the mad dog running wild with no interference from the referee. The battle ended halfway through the second half when his battered and bloodied antagonist was carried from the field. On the report of a shaken local linesman Macqueen received a severe caution and was penalised. We went on to lose the game by a narrow margin.

'He won't try that against us next time,' was Macqueen's quiet summary of events in the dressing room afterwards. While disappointed, like everyone else, by the defeat he was obviously pleased with his prediction of a problem, his determination to do something about it and his execution of a solution.

That was my first real introduction and insight into the straightforward yet complex character of Rod Macqueen. It was also the beginning of a strong friendship that would generate numerous happy occasions, spark unusual adventures, and by tragic coincidence, help us through heart-rending, life-threatening situations.

When Rod contracted a near-fatal illness, I broke hospital rules by pretending I was his brother to spend time at his bedside in intensive care. Not long afterwards, his life was threatened once more. Again, like any good friend, I was there to help him through a frightening personal crisis. His brush with death on this occasion brought about a dramatic change in personality and his approach to life, a change I appreciated but didn't fully understand—at least not until eighteen months later when I found myself in the same hospital intensive care unit. I had broken my neck in a diving accident and was told by doctors I would be a quadriplegic for the rest of my life. Even in my drugged state I wasn't surprised when Macqueen broke the rules by pretending he was my brother to be at my side. Our lives seemed to be running in parallel and for some reason our understanding of ourselves and of each other was further deepened by personal crises.

Rod Macqueen is a man who has achieved much despite great personal adversity; success which, he is quick to acknowledge, is due in no small part to the wonderful support and personal contribution from his wife, Liz. He is a man who could be described as a student of life in the truest sense, someone who learns valuable lessons from his own experiences and of those around him. He combines them with his natural determination and lateral thinking skills to achieve success in a wide variety of endeavours. This book documents and highlights the many lessons, observations and insights which helped mould Rod Macqueen's unique character. I am pleased to be in the position to share yet another part of his personal journey.

Kevin Hitchcock

Chapter 1

A Circle of Wallabies

We've done it.

The voice was hushed and broken as the words spilled out,

Thank you. We've done it, we've done it.

Australian rugby coach, Rod Macqueen, was fighting back tears as the relief and euphoria of winning the 1999 World Cup finally overwhelmed him. The short emotional statement wasn't addressed to the two assistant coaches or management who had helped throughout the long campaign. Nor was it directed at the players: the Wallabies were still on the field. But with just three minutes remaining in the historic match, Macqueen had left his seat in Cardiff's Millenium Stadium, and was waiting outside the lifts to go down and join his team.

As the barracking of 72,000 fans reverberated around the stadium, Macqueen was, for a moment, in a quiet personal world, locked in a lengthy embrace with his wife and childhood sweetheart, Liz, and their son, Scott. He was oblivious to the pushing and shoving of those around them and the prying lens of a television camera. It was a brief but almost sacred union as the husband and father thanked his family for their support during a long and difficult campaign. Daughter Jacqui was there too, at least in spirit: the twenty-six-year-old was at home, speechless on the other end of Rod's mobile phone.

Spending that time together was extremely emotional and probably my strongest memory of the occasion. It was something really special.

Perhaps even more special because it wasn't pre-arranged. Seated some distance apart, it was pure coincidence that the family members started looking for each other at almost exactly the same time.

That unique moment, outside the lifts leading down to the dressing rooms, was soon followed by an overwhelming series of emotional scenes. Macqueen was joined in the lift by the rest of the management team, who like him, had left their seats when Wallaby lock, Owen Finegan, scored a try in the dying minutes of the game which put the result beyond doubt. When the doors re-opened the trio was confronted by rows of beaming, applauding officials who lined the bare concrete tunnel that led to the playing field.

As they emerged Macqueen first saw a group of team members completely beside themselves with excitement. He had barely stepped onto the edge of the arena when the game ended. He didn't hear the final whistle: he didn't have to. The Australian players' arms suddenly shot skywards, their clenched fists symbolically grasping the victory that was emphatically theirs. Seeing the look of euphoria on their faces was something he'd never forget.

I just stood back for quite some time watching the team embracing each other. It's impossible to describe the feeling of satisfaction, of being part of a team that achieves success after so much planning, commitment and sacrifice.

The on-field celebration suddenly exploded as all of Macqueen's extended family joined in. Not just players but trainers, managers, assistant coaches—the whole squad of forty-two members running from one to another, hugging and shouting, all joining as one in victory as they had in so many months of preparation.

Macqueen walked slowly through his jubilant, cavorting band of warriors, laughing and congratulating them in their moment of triumph. He eventually reached the towering figure of captain and good friend, John Eales. They embraced and Eales repeated vaguely familiar words with a grin, and a mischievous twist: 'We've done it, Roddy.' Macqueen particularly disliked the nickname but for once didn't mind.

After lengthy and genuine congratulations from the defeated French players and officials, it was time for the formalities which for most would be the highlight of success—the presentation of individual medals by Her Majesty the Queen and finally presentation of the gleaming gold William Webb Ellis Trophy to John Eales. But even this was surpassed, according to Macqueen, by individual personal scenes.

The emotional moments just kept building. Holding up the trophy with my two assistants, Tim Lane and Jeff Miller, was fantastic because we had worked so well together all the way through.

Then as other members of the squad continually raised the coveted trophy amid a swarm of television crews and flashing newspaper photographers, a remarkable sequence of events unfolded. The entire Wallaby contingent found themselves forming a circle which slowly tightened and, by sheer accident, trapped Macqueen in the centre holding the trophy.

Without even thinking, he slowly placed it on the ground like some sort of ritual and they all linked arms and spontaneously sang the Australian national anthem. It was incredible, uplifting, almost spiritual.

With the huge crowd still roaring, the group began a lap of honour. Waves of shining tickertape almost obscured the players, adding a surreal feeling to an already extraordinary experience. The all-Australian atmosphere was complete moments later when the stadium sound system thundered into life with a stirring song written for the team by entertainer John Williamson, 'A Number On My Back'. It was immediately followed by the Men at Work classic, 'Downunder', which years earlier had become synonymous with Australia's historic victory at the America's Cup.

Surely the emotional mix was complete. But no, for Macqueen there was still more to come. As they toured the perimeter of the ground he looked around the almost sheer wall of applauding humanity and in an instant recognised his family. He saw Liz and Scott standing together, arms raised, hands clasped together. Beside them were his sister, Katy, with her husband, Coleman Jenkins, along with old friends, Del and John Nolan. He experienced a strange instant of quiet solitude. He was the only person standing in the centre of the Cardiff cauldron.

Waving and making contact at that time just widened the whole sharing experience even further. There were the people I had shared so many things with in the past now joining in this special moment together.

Many would be surprised by Macqueen's ability or willingness to look further than the celebration with team members on the field. But not those who know him well. Family and close friends who have watched him develop over many years through different fields of endeavour know he is not a one-dimensional rugby man.

The momentous victory at Cardiff was just reward for a man about whom so many people know so little.

Chapter 2

Leading by Example

Rod Macqueen moves effortlessly through several worlds of sport and business. He is recognised and respected for an unusual mix of skills. A lateral thinker and innovator, he has demonstrated throughout his life an ability to unite people to a common cause and create an environment to help them realise their potential to achieve maximum success. Influential too have been the experiences and lessons he has learnt in sport and business along the way. All this was combined and applied at the right time and in the right place to win the 1999 Rugby Union World Cup.

Macqueen's ability to surprise everyone by doing the unexpected began when he decided to enter the world a week early on 31 December 1949. His sudden arrival ruined any plans his mother may have had for New Year's Eve, but gave his father double reason to celebrate.

Right from the beginning it was obvious to all those around him that Macqueen's determination to succeed would overcome any setbacks along the way. He not only conquered a debilitating illness in his early childhood, but also overcame the after-effects with a rigorous and imaginative exercise regime. Every aspect of life was a challenge to be met head on and conquered by his constant urge to try something new, something out of the ordinary. His involvement with surfboat rowing brought success at the highest level. It was the result of organisation and leadership skills which left nothing to chance, and where different training methods and rowing techniques were tried and perfected.

His playing career with the Warringah Rugby Club was not only highlighted by regular Man of the Match awards but also by his contributions to club morale and culture; these revealed his early management skills and an ability to recognise the importance of a harmonious working environment. But Macqueen was never one to pause and boast about his achievements. He led by example, achieved his personal goals, and moved on.

He showed equal enthusiasm and similar standards when he took over part of the family business. A commercial artist by profession,

Macqueen displayed a gift for lateral thinking and innovation, while his ability to think three-dimensionally constantly astounded clients and business partners alike. He designed revolutionary point-of-sale merchandising concepts and systems for multinational companies; his designs carried contracts worth millions of dollars, were widely acclaimed, and would later be copied throughout the world.

The same principles Macqueen used in business were those he later applied to rugby coaching. In his first year of representative coaching he guided the NSW Waratahs through the season undefeated. It was an unheard-of performance, built on the foundations of discipline, meticulous planning and a new, creative approach to the game. In the face of ignorant amateurism, he established professional style structures which are still being duplicated by international management teams in the new professional era, almost fifteen years later.

In 1996 Macqueen had the daunting task of creating a brand new side to represent the ACT in the prestigious Super 12 competition. Within a matter of months, Macqueen moulded a collection of rejects and unknowns into a team which played a radically different and exciting style of football that took them to within a point of the semi-finals. In their second year the ACT Brumbies played an even more creative and unpredictable brand of rugby which took them to the final. What few people realised was that behind the impressive on-field sporting performances was a salutary lesson in sound business management. Everything about the Brumbies—from their name, distinctive jersey, club logo, training camp, personal accommodation and even the team song—was a product of Macqueen's personal vision; the innovative ideas and meticulous planning had been taken straight from his company boardroom.

When Macqueen was appointed coach of the Australian Wallabies in 1997 many observers were doubtful of his ability to turn a dispirited and disjointed team into world champions in less than two years. But the crucial ingredients had been slowly blended over a long period to produce a person capable of such a feat. The man now recognised as having revolutionised rugby worldwide was a lifetime in the making.

Macqueen's personal development began with two other key ingredients—stubborn independence and a devilish sense of humour. During his formative years, his parents at times wondered what they had done to deserve such a child.

Chapter 3
Determination to Succeed

Wave after wave, the attack is repetitive, relentless. The blue-green rollers of the Pacific Ocean sweep in and crash onto the golden sand, only to retreat slowly, reform, and attack the beach once more. The waves and the sand of Collaroy Beach were the early playground of Rod Macqueen. A long open beach about fifteen kilometres north of Sydney's world famous harbour, it is one of many popular surfing spots in a string of oceanside suburbs locally referred to as the 'northern peninsula' or the 'northern beaches'. The family home in Beach Road was a short walk from the ocean in a tiny suburb called Collaroy Basin, named after a small bay at the southern end of the beach. It nestles almost secretly between the rocky end of the beach and the towering cliffs of Long Reef Headland, the area's most notable geographical feature.

In respect of learning

Macqueen's earliest memories here reflect a happy childhood with parents Ian and Marjorie and an especially close relationship with his father. Macqueen remembers most clearly things like early morning wrestles, which inevitably began with a surprise attack by an overzealous child. It was no-holds barred with super-headlocks, leg-locks and flailing arms turning the parental bed into a battlefield.

The effect this may have had on the start of Marj Macqueen's day was never considered. Fortunately Marj was, and still is, a woman with a great sense of humour and apparently endless patience. But Macqueen's closeness to his father provided much more than early morning fun and games.

Dad had very high standards and was very well thought of in the community. To me he was someone I could have fun with but at the same time someone I could also confide in. He was never someone to tell me what

I should do or how I should do it, but there was always an expectation of the type of standards he himself set and demonstrated. He would always remind me if I did something wrong but he would always do it in a quiet way. It was coming from someone who I always respected and because of that I always wanted my father to respect me. It was very important to me. We had a great relationship and a lot of fun together.

What I didn't realise then was that I was actually learning something that was to become an important part of my business and coaching philosophies. The importance of winning and maintaining the respect of those around you to encourage them to work together efficiently. Once you've lost that respect it makes it very hard to be effective as a leader.

Fun is infectious

Marj Macqueen has fond memories of her son's close bond with his father but also remembers some disciplinary problems with a boy who was determined to do things his own way and in his own time. In the days when troublesome children were dealt with in the traditional manner it meant some hefty smacks on the backside. Unfortunately for Marj and Ian, it didn't always produce the desired result. 'Rod never seemed to be bothered by punishment so long as he achieved what he set out to do,' Mrs Macqueen recalls.

It was a similar situation during his early years at school. Macqueen readily admits that his academic achievements bore a direct relationship to his connection with the teacher. A liking and a healthy respect for the person in charge meant good behaviour and good results: dislike brought the opposite. One teacher complained to Mrs Macqueen about a frustrating year of total time-wasting. Rod's talking and disruptive behaviour had included fighting and throwing things about the room. However, the teacher did make one positive observation: 'I think he is the most honest boy in the class because if I try to find out who is the cause of any trouble he is the first to own up and accept any punishment.'

Macqueen admits he had a reputation for being a 'naughty, rebellious kid', but his memories of canings and detention have dimmed with time. His recollection, though, of trying to learn from people he believed to be incompetent or uninterested in what they were doing has remained crystal clear.

There's no doubt I wasn't an easy kid to teach in those days, probably because I always found it difficult to learn anything from people who were either not interested in teaching or unable to get their message across clearly. Those who taught straight from the textbook unfortunately lost my interest and the lessons became just ink on paper to me rather than a learning experience.

However, when I had a teacher who understood, enjoyed and believed in their work, it generated the enthusiasm for me to want to learn. The more enthusiastic the teacher, the more I wanted to learn and the harder I worked.

I know I am not alone in this experience but it's incredible to think back and realise the long-term effects of either good or poor teaching.

Macqueen's overall memory of early life is of a warm, loving family with supportive, forgiving parents—memories supported by elder sister, Shaen, and young sister, Katy, who happily toss into any conversation numerous anecdotes of brotherly games and practical jokes. Although some aren't remembered all that fondly. Not everyone finds it amusing to be locked in the hallway cupboard or 'accidentally' tipped fully clothed into a bathtub full of water. On one occasion, a day-long frantic search for the family cat ended when it was discovered locked in the family car, much to the amusement of the six-year-old boy watching from the bedroom window.

Crawl before you walk

The fun and games suddenly ended at the age of eight when Macqueen started to have trouble sleeping and complained of increasing pain in his ankles and knees. The medical diagnosis, when it finally came, was a shock to the whole family—rheumatic fever, a debilitating condition which restricted natural growth and caused painful swelling of the joints. The cure in those times was not only primitive but also devastating for a young active boy. He was ordered to stay in bed for at least six months. To save pressure on his leg joints he was carried everywhere—up and down the stairs of the small house, even to and from the outside toilet. The only medication was twelve Disprin tablets a day. They were difficult times for everyone, especially the parents. Mrs Macqueen was struggling to keep her young charge in his bedroom, let alone in bed.

She remembers how difficult it was to keep him up-to-date with his schoolwork but how he took to reading and to creative drawing, where he showed a natural talent. Also, how his father came up with what he thought was an ingenious incentive scheme to keep the young tearaway in his bed. Lining up a long row of pennies on the bedhead, he promised that for everything he did right one penny would be pushed to one side and saved. But if he did something wrong then one would be taken away for good. The young Macqueen took a long hard look at the row of shiny pennies and weighed up the plan which threatened to keep him under control. With a sweep of one hand he scattered them across the room saying: 'You can keep all your stupid pennies.'

They were difficult times indeed.

It was seven months before they were told he could get out of bed and walk around and resume a normal life. But it wasn't that simple. Over that long period he had not been given any regular exercise or physiotherapy and consequently his body had wasted away.

When I first tried to stand up I just fell over. I basically had to learn to walk all over again. It came as a total shock to me. I never even thought about the possibility that I wouldn't be able to walk. Mentally, I set myself a program that I had to improve on every day. We had a pool table in the family room and I soon discovered that by leaning over onto my chest and gripping the sides, I could drag my legs along the floor. Every day I'd get up and slowly pull myself around and around the table. It became a sort of rehabilitation area and after several weeks I eventually started to regain the use of my legs. I also learned to play pool pretty well.

As the days passed by, my standing times doubled. When I could stand, I started to walk. When I could walk, I started to run. When I could run I wanted to run faster.

Coming to grips with confrontation

There were several other consequences arising from the bout of rheumatic fever.

It seems odd now, but at the time the Macqueen family was advised to move from their home close to the beach because the constant breezes could be detrimental to his struggling respiratory system. So, at the age of ten, Rod moved a short distance inland to Collaroy Plateau. By now, he was smaller and more frail than most children his age. He'd lost muscle bulk in all parts of his body. In fact it was obvious to everyone he had virtually stopped growing. Being so small and skinny soon created a problem. By moving from one suburb to another Macqueen had to change schools, and in the new playground at Collaroy Plateau Primary he immediately became the target of the local bully. He in turn was a big boy for his age and told Macqueen he was going to 'bash him up' during lunchtime. The word soon spread and excited all the other kids who could hardly wait for the confrontation. The hostile atmosphere and the thought of what was going to happen frightened Macqueen who went home before lunchtime worrying about what to do.

I sat on the back steps of the house staring out at the backyard, staring into space for what seemed to be a long period of time. I was pretty scared and had all sorts of things going through my head, but the big issue came down to a simple fact: Do I front up or not? I realised there was no way I was going to solve any other problem until I had sorted that out.

So front up he did. When he arrived in a corner of the playground a large circle of laughing, jabbering schoolboys jostled for position to see the show. Realising that the other boy had the advantage of size, Macqueen hoped that he would have the advantage of speed. After careful thought he devised a strategy that included the all-important element of surprise. To the astonishment of all concerned, as soon as the smiling bully appeared the small skinny kid rushed in, took a mighty leap into the air and grabbed him in a headlock. It was a bizarre scene with the fat bully staggering blindly around the playground with the scrawny kid wrapped tightly around his thick neck. Exhausted and disorientated, the bully eventually slumped to the ground and, with eyes bulging and face bright red, finally gave up.

Macqueen now admits that he, like all the other boys in the playground, was surprised at his sudden victory. As a result, from then on he was treated with respect by the different gangs that roamed the playground and sought his membership, although he generally remained on his own.

I held on for as long and as hard as I could. I knew that once I let go I'd be in big trouble. This was probably the first time I actually had to confront an issue. Since then I have discovered there are always different ways of confronting a problem but the main point is to confront it rather than try to ignore it. I realised that I was just wasting time worrying by trying to avoid an issue that inevitably had to be resolved at some stage. Once I had accepted this, I could then set about identifying the different options to overcome the problem.

The other interesting thing I found was that by confronting the issues, I've been able to discover what my limitations are. To know what I am and am not capable of doing has proved extremely important. Being aware of my limitations helps me figure out how I'm going to overcome them.

Reflections on water

Despite his family move inland, the nearby Collaroy Basin remained the personal playground for Macqueen and his young friends. Hopping from one rock pool to another searching for marine life was paradise for a group of ten-year-olds—gouging out fresh oysters from rock ledges, herding shimmering schools of tiny fish into make-shift nets and luring vicious green eels from their secret hiding places. If the weather was unsuitable for swimming or terrorising the inhabitants of the rocky foreshore, there was always makeshift tobogganing. This involved sliding down the grassy slopes of the headland on scraps of thin plywood or cardboard boxes pilfered from the rear of the local corner shop. For Macqueen there were quiet times too.

I've always enjoyed fishing. Dad and I had some great times when I was very young. I'd often bring home a catch of reef fish and the occasional bream. I enjoyed the tranquillity and solitude of time alone and would spend hours sitting on my favourite rocky outcrop in the Basin, gazing out at the ocean, or wondering what mysteries might be lurking in the caves and crevices hidden beneath the water. I liked to spend a lot of time by myself in that type of environment. Just thinking. It is something I've done all my life and still do today, whenever I have a problem to resolve. These days I usually go running or swimming. It helps clear my mind, allowing me to make better judgements.

Then there was Freddie. Often while Macqueen was fishing off his rocky outcrop, an old fisherman would come ashore, his small boat laden with prized jewfish and kingfish. Freddie was a weatherbeaten sinewy old man of the sea in his early sixties. A special bond developed between the young boy and the shy old man who always fished alone and refused to divulge the whereabouts of his special fishing spots. It was rumoured that if anyone followed him out to sea he would anchor far away from his prized territory, all day if necessary, to keep his private fishing grounds a secret. He was also rumoured to be crazy and reclusive, but although shunning the company of others, he would let the youngster help clean the large valuable fish and invariably give him some to take home. Macqueen appreciated their close relationship and once decided to confront him about the constant rumours.

I had heard the rumours that Freddie was a 'crazy, angry old recluse'. When I questioned him about it, he told me the only person who could make judgement on such matters was myself, based on my own beliefs and instincts. It's what you think, not what others tell you.

It was a fairly profound response and one that later took on a particular significance once I became involved with the hearsay and politics of business and sport.

There's always a way

Macqueen's dislike of bullies continued, generating numerous scrapes in primary school and after-hours sport. However, it also created an unusual problem not long after he started high school. His parents sent him to a private school, St Andrew's Cathedral School, in the centre of Sydney, where he was expected to benefit from a higher quality, albeit more expensive, form of education.

St Andrew's also nurtured another side to Macqueen's life—his relationship with religion. He always had a strong Christian ethic, even if it was his own denomination. His older sister Shaen, a devout Christian, was also a huge influence in this area. She was his passage to God. The strong emphasis on religion at the school rekindled and strengthened Rod's Christianity.

Within the first week, Macqueen was confronted with some unusual problems. Having caught a bus from his home to the edge of the city, he then had to travel by train to get to the school in the city centre. Unfortunately, some of the older schoolboys weren't altogether forthcoming when Macqueen asked for directions. In fact, as the train approached the designated station, they remained in conversation with one another, until the train began to leave the platform. At this stage, they all turned and jumped off, leaving the panic-stricken Macqueen riding around the city circle. It was embarrassing for the young boy in his new straw boater, walking the streets of the city asking directions to his new school. He also quickly learnt one of the downsides of being in a private school: the old-fashioned headwear.

After my first day I arrived home with my new boater topless and hanging around my ears, courtesy of some unsympathetic, older state school boys. It certainly wasn't the best way to start my new school, but it forced me to become more determined and resilient. I studied the train system, drew a map on the palm of my hand and fibreglassed my boater hat to make it unbreakable. Basically the idea worked very well.

Macqueen's dislike of standover tactics remained and he freely admits that at times it became somewhat of an obsession, one that was to cause pain and suffering for a great many bullies in different walks of life in years to come.

Do it well or it's not worth doing at all

During his schooldays at Collaroy Plateau, Rod's father encouraged him to take up rugby with the local Collaroy Plateau under tens' side. It was a game Maqueen took to immediately and he showed early potential with aggressive and punishing defence. At the time he was still suffering the disadvantages caused by his bout of rheumatic fever—relative slightness of stature and a lack of muscular development. Macqueen had another disadvantage which was to plague him in all junior sports graded by age. He was born on the last day of the year, 31 December, and as a result was always the youngest and often the smallest in any team or competition. Others are quick to point out that this was usually overcome by his fierce determination to be the best. This relentless drive meant a passion for training which, over time, dramatically increased his physical build, fitness and strength. One of his young teammates was Paul Booth, or Boothie, once the almost obligatory nickname was created. He was to become a lifelong friend and still remembers being impressed by the performance of the new kid in the team: 'Macca always gave one hundred per cent whenever we played, and because we weren't a particularly strong side there was plenty of tackling to do. I was one of the bigger kids in our team and I think between the two of us we did most of the defending. Because of that we discovered a natural bond which developed into a close friendship.'

Once at St Andrew's, Macqueen's love of rugby suffered a major setback. His new school was not part of a regular competition and did not train or play on a regular basis. As a result they were inevitably thrashed by the opposition, which upset the super-competitive Macqueen. Not only that, the school played their matches on weekends which prevented him from continuing with the Collaroy side. This frustration was compounded by the difficulty of being one of only a few students travelling the long distance from Sydney's northern beaches to the centre of the city, which involved two buses and a train. It created a dilemma because he quite enjoyed the school itself and two other sports not readily available at other schools, fencing and boxing. In his second year he came fourth in the state fencing tournament and won his weight division in the school boxing competition.

It was a very difficult decision because I was basically very happy with St Andrew's and all the other activities it had to offer. But it was frustrating to be playing rugby against sides who were in a regular competition and fully prepared.

It seemed to me at the time, if we were going to compete against these teams, we should give ourselves the best possible opportunities to be competitive. As good as the school was, I realised that I would never enjoy the sport I loved under these circumstances. But I had no choice, I was obliged to play for the school, with little incentive. Also, I didn't enjoy the long weekend trips into town, they left me very little time to spend at home with friends.

Tough times are the trigger for effort

After a long discussion with his ever-sympathetic father, Macqueen changed schools at the age of fourteen, enrolling in the nearby Manly High School. It meant yet another fresh start and playground initiation, this time in an environment known in the local region as a 'tough school'. His first day was either forgettable or memorable depending on your point of view. He played a trial match for the junior football side and was promptly knocked unconscious. Under the school's first aid policy this meant no sport at all for the next week, not a promising start for someone trying to establish some sort of reputation at a new school.

There is no doubt that the development of Macqueen's character was greatly influenced by the many problems he had along the way. The fact that his physical growth was delayed by rheumatic fever, the fact that his date of birth made him the youngest and often the smallest in any competition and the fact that the changes of school seemed to continually make him the new kid on the block.

Looking back on those early years, I think my character was toughened by the many problems and setbacks. I believe they were all part of my learning experiences. It was these experiences that I think in later years helped to increase my determination to succeed.

Whenever I find myself confronted by adversity in any situation, my first thoughts are to fight back. I now believe that I can overcome the majority of adverse situations by focusing and intensifying my determination to succeed. Even something as simple as running. Whenever I come to steps or a steep hill my first reaction is to attack and push myself harder.

A fresh start

The other major sport worth pursuing in the beachside suburbs north of Sydney was of course surfing. Macqueen and Boothie, now his best friend, became avid surfboard riders and with half a dozen mates, formed their own club called 'Surf and Sand' or 'S & S'. This was a rather presumptuous attempt to set themselves apart from several well-established board-riding clubs in the area dominated by accomplished surfers like Nat Young and Midget Farrelly, who were soon to become world famous on the emerging professional circuit.

During these developing years, Ian Macqueen was running his own company, Exhibition Displays, which specialised in large exhibitions for commercial events such as motor shows. To set his young board-riding club apart from the others, Macqueen designed a stylish logo for 'Surf and Sand'. He took the finished sketch to his father's work to be reproduced as emblems for club members' clothing, and adhesive labels for their surfboards.

One brisk Sunday morning, when he was sixteen, Macqueen and his father were fishing, their long rods flexing with the tug of the waves against lightly weighted lines. These fishing expeditions were a regular shared activity, strengthening an already close bond. The solitude, quiet and harmony of nature were a far better catalyst for friendship than any fireside man-to-man chat and offered memorable moments where the catch of the day was more often than not a better understanding of each other. Problems were resolved and agreements reached over hours of relaxed exchange.

We were knee-deep in water in my favourite spot at the Basin. I always enjoyed these quiet fishing times with Dad when we could talk as mates, solving the problems of the world and discussing life in general.

I explained to him that I was disillusioned with where I was heading at school and that I had a new goal. It seemed to me that additional time in school was not going to satisfy me or help me achieve that goal. My best option was to establish a career as a commercial artist. This would mean getting into the workforce as soon as possible and pursuing a tertiary education.

Young Macqueen's argument proved successful. It was agreed: no more school! With this all-important parental blessing, Macqueen successfully applied for a position as an advertising designer for the Empisal Sewing Machine Company in Sydney. Pleased at achieving the first job he tried for, he was only slightly disappointed when he discovered that working in the advertising department as a junior meant there was more wrapping and delivering of parcels than there was in using his creative talents as an artist.

One thing he did know was that despite his impressive title he had an equally good relationship with the workmen on the loading dock. While half his lunchtime was spent in deep discussions with media sales people and advertising executives, the other half was spent in arm wrestling competitions with the knockabout labourers out the back. In this type of school he learnt quickly, and by combining his natural determination and strength with a variety of tips from his experienced opponents, he developed a successful technique that turned his bemused workmates into disgruntled losers. His regular winnings at the time were a valuable addition to his meagre salary.

Still, there was more traditional learning to be done. Working five days a week, he enrolled in night study courses to help further his career. At the East Sydney Technical College in Darlinghurst he studied commercial art, advertising and design. These courses were spread over three nights each week for three years.

During this time, he once again fell out with someone who he believed had no rapport with the students he was teaching. A lecturer who specialised in advertising copy for television commercials insisted there were only two ways to get a message across—his way and the wrong way. The young student from Collaroy openly disagreed, insisting that in creative areas people should have an open mind on the different ways that things could be done. When the discussion turned into a heated argument, Macqueen made the observation which lecturers everywhere hate to hear: 'If you're such an expert on this subject, why aren't you running your own advertising business making lots of money?'

In amongst the verbal barrage that came back was a guarantee that there was one particular student who wouldn't pass copy writing in the next examinations. The threat triggered a characteristic streak of determination in the disruptive student who studied so hard for that particular topic he was begrudgingly awarded an A-level pass.

There is no doubt that I was in the wrong and deserved to be considered an obnoxious student. However, it still surprises me that so many people in positions of authority refuse to listen to differing points of view. In all my experiences the best results have come from having an open mind and considering input from everyone involved.

Soul is something special

One family member made an especially important contribution to Macqueen's life from an early age. His father's sister-in-law, June Macqueen, or Junie, as all the family called her, had a small farm in a picturesque little valley at Wollombi, 300 kilometres north of Sydney. The home, situated on a riverbank, was an old timber convict-built house with the typically Australian bullnose verandahs. June had lovingly restored it, and with her artistic touch had created a charming and comfortable cottage surrounded by magnificent gardens. A large orchard boasted a variety of fruit trees. Close by, the paddocks were studded with horses and cows. Kangaroos and wombats were constant visitors, their nocturnal activities also an occasional disturbance to the evening silence of the surrounding bush. It was, and still is, a place where Macqueen would visit when needing to use his creativity or develop new visions for the future.

June Macqueen is one of those special people capable of seeing the beauty and the good in anything and anyone. She bought a place that was old, bare and uninteresting and with very little to work with, transformed it into something with warmth and character. She gave it soul.

The tranquillity and beauty of the farm has brought me back regularly over the years, and still remains a special place for our whole family to visit. Although the environment is quite different to that of the ocean, the solitude I experience at the farm has the same effect. I have confronted many problems and made many important decisions there and it is also a great place to rekindle family values. Liz, our children Jacqui, Scott and I have spent many weeks there enjoying quality time together and on occasions Mum and Dad would join us.

June had watched the development of young Rod with great interest. Like other family members she agrees he was a determined, troublesome child but one with a compassionate and creative streak. During his teenage years she saw him as aggressive and non-conformist, 'like most kids that age', but she also recognised attributes that would be a key to future success. 'He was always building and designing strange contraptions and showed remarkable artistic talent for his age. He was also very thorough. He really did his homework before tackling any project.'

Don't worry, be happy

While in the city, Macqueen would often visit June's office. She ran her own small company importing and selling homewares. Her business employed five or six women who had all become friends and enjoyed working together as equals. June herself described it as a friendly, family atmosphere where constant banter and spontaneous laughter made for a pleasant and very efficient workplace. 'Rod would come in and sit with us for a while and often comment on the benefit of having a relaxed place of business,' she says. 'I thought it quite unusual for a young man of his age, only sixteen or seventeen, to recognise that.'

It was not only a pleasant working environment, but one which left a lasting impression.

My strongest recollection of June's office is one of excitement. The enjoyable atmosphere was infectious. You could almost smell success in the office. The easy interaction and enthusiasm were obviously a catalyst for a thriving business. If there was a problem, they would set about sorting it out together. There was always a joke along the way and very soon there was no problem. The place was always so positive, you couldn't help but get wrapped up in the enthusiasm. I have no doubt that when clients came into the small showroom-cum-warehouse they would buy, just so they could be part of the buzz. This culminated in a hugely successful business that grew immensely in a very short period of time.

I think it was a shining example for any business to follow. It's an example I have been conscious of during all my business and sporting endeavours. By creating a happy and positive working atmosphere, it automatically promoted productivity and ultimately success.

Dancing with destiny

While working at Empisal, Macqueen enjoyed the busy lifestyle of any teenager living near the beach. On weekends, he and Boothie played rugby league in the local junior competition. The rest of his time was spent riding a surfboard and taking in all the other attractions the beachside culture had to offer. At night there were regular church and youth club dances, where he was usually accompanied by an attractive, dark-haired girl called Elizabeth Meyer. The pair had met at a youth club night several years earlier. According to Boothie and other mates of that time, Macqueen was very outgoing and the first to ask one of the young girls for a dance at the start of any evening. But Macqueen remembers this occasion differently, insisting he approached Elizabeth for a dance with the real intention of asking her to introduce him to a blonde girl he was attracted to but afraid to approach. Miss Meyer had other ideas, and the two remained together for most of the night, dancing and talking. During their conversation they discovered that because of a tragic coincidence they desperately needed to share each other's company.

A few days earlier, a very good friend of mine had been knocked down by a car and killed while walking along a roadside. It wasn't long before I realised that Liz had actually been walking next to him at the time of the accident. She was still very upset by everything she'd seen and needed to talk about it. At the sáme time I needed to know how it all happened. It was an extraordinary coincidence and one which brought us close together. It was the start of a lifelong friendship.

This chance meeting at the dance and their common bond in tragedy prompted a relationship that was to develop intermittently over the next five years.

In his last few years as a teenager Macqueen entered three totally different worlds. At the age of seventeen he was invited to join his father's company and enter the high-pressure environment of advertising, exhibitions and design. In the same year, almost by accident, he found himself involved in the highly regimented surf lifesaving movement. Twelve months later, he joined the Warringah Rugby Club in the second division competition, where he was immediately drafted into the top grade.

All three areas demanded determination, commitment and lateral thinking. At the same time, all three provided Rod Macqueen with an outlet for his natural aggression, competitive nature, creativity and larrikinism. They slowly intertwined and began to change and mould his character, setting a course for the rest of his life. But as much as they changed him, he changed them. Each world is now different in many ways because of his unique involvement.

Chapter 4

A Good Crew

It was a beautiful sunny Sunday afternoon on Collaroy beach when the unthinkable happened. Rod Macqueen and two of his board-riding mates joined a group of lifesavers outside the local clubhouse for an organised game. By all the laws of nature, it shouldn't have happened. Every board-rider hated members of surf lifesaving clubs, or 'clubbies', and the feeling was mutual.

In the mid 1960s the battle-lines had been drawn by beachside suburban councils who passed regulations setting aside one section of the beach for surfboards and another section for swimmers. If a surfboard-rider rode a wave and ended up amongst swimmers inside, or even close to, the safety flags set up on the beach, they would be targeted by the surf club patrol members and their board confiscated. Likewise if one of the unwieldy three-metre plus surfboards was lost on a wave and accidentally washed into the swimming area, it was immediately confiscated and locked in the clubhouse. The board riders would then have to pay a fine before their surfboard was returned.

To make it easier for the lifesavers, administrators came up with the ingenious idea of charging all board-riders an annual registration fee and insisting they display stickers on their boards so ownership could be traced. The registration system was introduced on all Sydney beaches to the dismay of the free-spirited board riders known colloquially as 'waxheads'. The system was inflexible and regimented, the lifesavers were dedicated and rigorous, the board-riders were outraged and defiant. It was war.

Responsibility helps

Like other 'waxheads', the fifteen-year-old Macqueen was contemptuous of the volunteer lifesavers who seemed intent on making their free-flowing lifestyle a thing of the past. The board-riders disliked the culture of having to wear silly, red and yellow caps and skimpy nylon costumes, instead of trendy knee-length board shorts. They believed the lifesavers were constantly blowing their annoying whistles and yelling at people in the surf who may have been swimming illegally outside the flags but were just trying to have fun. The surfers abused them at every opportunity and deliberately flouted the laws if they thought they could get away with it.

The common interest which at last brought some members of the two warring sides together was football. Some of the lifesavers were aware that Macqueen and his group were highly regarded in the district as talented players and so invited them to join in a game to bolster their team. They played a form of rugby league, barefoot on the beach. The board riders had already seen a few games in progress. It was hard, it was fast and Macqueen was impressed. Together with other board-riders he jumped at the chance to get involved.

The group went right through that winter not realising until later that their team was officially representing the Collaroy Surf Club. In effect they were unofficial 'clubbies'. At the end of the season the team coach put forward a proposal which was to change Macqueen's life. He suggested they turn up early the following Sunday when he would arrange for them to have a trial session rowing one of the club's surf-boats.

Although it meant officially being a part of the surf club, Macqueen saw it from a different perspective. He'd already noticed that the boat rowers were a different breed of people who seemed to be separate from the other lifesavers on the beach and at the regular carnivals. The great majority were also footballers which meant they would have a lot in common. Their first session in a surfboat proved to be physically demanding but challenging and enjoyable. Over the following weeks they were coached and moulded into a promising junior crew.

However, there was a downside which created a problem for the former board-riders, especially Macqueen. Rowing boats meant you actually had to do all the traditional surf club things like training for a bronze medallion, learning to do mouth-to-mouth resuscitation and, perhaps worst of all, turning up for rostered patrols on the beach wearing the silly red and yellow caps. For the first season the embarrassed group pretended they weren't lifesavers at all.

When they were on patrol they slid their caps off as soon as the patrol captain was out of sight or alternatively covered them with large straw sun-hats that, luckily, were the fashion of the day. The biggest problem was what to do when board-riders actually surfed into the restricted swimming areas which was their responsibility to patrol. The new clubbies were embarrassed and couldn't bring themselves to run down to the water's edge, blow whistles and order their mates out.

For that season at least the local board-riders at Collaroy had an unexpectedly free run of the surf.

I wasn't to know that this was going to be one of the most positive influences in my life. There were two distinctive cultures in the surf club movement, the competitive side and the community service side. In order to enjoy the competition I was forced to educate myself in the lifesaving skills and fulfil my community responsibilities. To compete you had to carry out your rostered beach patrols. Looking back, I realise that the competitiveness, camaraderie and sacrifices that needed to be made, successfully combined to create responsibility and discipline. While at times I hated doing a lot of the patrols and didn't take it seriously, I now realise what an important element this was in personal development.

Teamwork conquers crisis

What really irked the super-competitive Macqueen was that at the time Collaroy performed so badly in the surfboat competitions that they were regarded as somewhat of a joke. However, attitudes began to change when a senior 'boatie' from the North Bondi club moved into the local area and joined Collaroy. John Brown had been an integral member of a seasoned North Bondi crew, which won gold medals at the Australian titles under a legendary captain and sweep named 'Spaz' Hurst. Now as a new member of Collaroy, Brown was keen to select and develop a young crew.

In each crew there are five members, all with a distinct role to play. The sweep is the crewman who stands at the rear of the boat directing its progress with the long steering oar. He calls out instructions to the rest of the crew who are facing him, unable to see where they are going or what conditions lie ahead. It is up to the sweep to call the action. He tells the four rowers when to pull hard on their oars or when to ease off when heading out from the beach through breaking waves. Once out in open water he determines the pace, or rate, of the crew's oarstroking, depending on the conditions or their place in a field of racing boats. At a crucial moment the sweep must assess when the boat is on the wave and when to call out 'come aft'. All members then quickly scramble to the stern being careful not to unbalance the unstable craft. It's an important manoeuvre because without the rapid and controlled transfer of bodyweight from the bow to the stern, the boat will either nosedive or slew sideways across the face of the waves.

The stroke is seated in the stern just in front of the sweep. The other rowers sitting in staggered formation behind take their timing from him, copying his speed and rhythm. The stroke, with advice from the sweep, generally sets the pace for the rest of the crew. The long, traditionally wooden boats can be flipped completely backwards when struck by a steep oncoming wave when heading out to sea, or buried nose first and rolled over when hit from behind while making a run for the beach. When a boat is dumped or rolled in heavy surf the crew members are at the mercy of the churning water which tumbles them against each other and their craft. There is also the danger of being belted and battered by loose oars and rowlocks.

Like Hawaiian outriggers that still race today, there are strict guidelines in place to retain the many traditional aspects of the surfboats. Despite this there have been many dramatic changes. Boats are now made of more modern materials such as fibreglass. They also have oars made from lightweight carbon fibre, and feature pumps to drain out water quickly to help them refloat when swamped by big seas. In recent times rowing techniques have also been refined and perfected but the same principles remain.

It is not a sport for the faint of heart. In fact, surfboat racing is regarded as the most dangerous sport in Australian surfing. An often quoted surf club legend has it that surfboat rowers are selected in a very methodical way. All lifesavers are lined up against a wall and have house bricks thrown at them. Those who don't take evasive action are chosen to row in the boats.

There's no doubt it can be a dangerous sport but the more proficient you become and the better your teamwork is, the less danger is involved. A good crew learns to react together instinctively in pressure situations, avoiding personal injury and damage to the equipment. There's nothing more exhilarating than all working together as a team and catching a big wave and riding it into shore. It's the same in most team environments. The better the teamwork, the easier you handle critical situations and the more satisfying the experiences are.

When John Brown went looking for new crew members he was given a long list of likely candidates. When Macqueen's name came up, club officials described him as a troublemaker who'd be too hard to control. But that only tweaked the interest of Brown who said he'd like to make his own judgement. When he met the young 'troublemaker' he discovered the critics were pretty close to the mark but, nevertheless, he decided to follow his own instinct. His assessment was typically frank and to the point: 'I thought he looked a likely prospect, just waiting for an opportunity to get somewhere in a team environment. I thought, well, bugger this, I'll give him a trial.'

Brown found the young Macqueen to be 'a bit moody,' but very self-assured: 'He was a confident young man, a bit hot-headed, but I had strong discipline with young blokes in those days and I found he reacted to that quite favourably. He had a good physique, was very fit and enjoyed the training. We got off to a great start.'

Brain over brawn

Once out on the water Macqueen soon developed a respect for his new mentor. Brown insisted on total commitment and obedience from the young men who were keen to learn from someone superior in knowledge but equal in competitive spirit. He taught them a style of rowing different from the traditional method. They would dip the oars and pull long and hard, holding onto the stroke until they were lying almost flat in the boat. It was slow, powerful and almost clinical in the way it forced the boat to surge through the water. To everyone's surprise the crew started to get results and soon came first in a district carnival, the first win by a Collaroy boat crew in many years. Macqueen noticed a difference immediately in the reaction of other club members on the beach, and the respect they were suddenly awarded not only inside, but outside the Collaroy ranks.

Soon afterwards came another victory which, although it didn't go down in the record books, was more important to the young rowers still trying to prove themselves. They were training well off-shore when the senior crew rowed to within shouting distance and challenged them to a race. At the time it was common for older members to exert their superiority over juniors whenever possible. This behaviour was generally accepted as part of the training and toughening up process in most club movements of the day.

Both crews started level with the juniors rowing their new style, pulling long and slow while the seniors were alongside sitting upright, rowing at almost three times the rate. After only about fifteen strokes the young crew was pulling away. The unexpected win brought instant respect from the senior boat crew and other older members of the club, and the new rowing style was introduced to all boat crews at Collaroy the following year.

The senior rowers were more experienced and stronger than our crew and at least as fit. But we appeared to have the edge in timing and attention to technique. In this particular case the result was a clear advantage in performance and it proved to us how good teamwork can overcome almost anything. It was a tremendous feeling when we finished first. It confirmed to us that the hard work was worth it.

Soul-searching rewarded

On training days, Macqueen found the hard physical effort of rowing with four close mates exhausting but rewarding. He revelled in the jokes, the laughter, the camaraderie. He also discovered something else—a new, strangely rewarding experience.

Rowing way out to sea in the soft warm light of an early Sunday morning generated memories for me that would last: the serenity, where the only sound was that of oars dipping in the water; the sensation of having the whole world to ourselves; the sharp salt air mixing with the smell of the wooden boat, the sweet, earthiness of cedar. It also brought an early love for the old-fashioned style boats and what they represented.

I understood how some of the ancient whalers would have felt, how they would have had an affinity with their craft. That's one of my earliest and strongest memories of rowing. Catching perfectly formed waves all morning in the boat, in that atmosphere, was great fun and really good for the soul.

Something else equally good or even better for Macqueen's soul occurred in the spring of 1971. It was a beautiful wedding which caught no-one by surprise. After a two-year engagement, Rod Macqueen and Elizabeth Meyer walked down the aisle of their small local church. Before the bride-to-be had left home for the church she was surprised to receive a dozen roses. The young knockabout character she was about to marry had revealed a little-known, romantic side of his personality. This symbolic gesture was to recur throughout their married life. In the name of tradition Macqueen had earlier sought a meeting with Mr Meyer to formally seek the hand of his daughter in marriage.

Liz's parents, Herman and Jane, came from a Dutch background and as their culture demanded, things were a little more formal than the laid-back Australian way of doing things. Both had been interned by the Japanese during the war. Herman spent much of his time working on the infamous Burma Railway and he was one of three men who helped build the Changi Chapel which has now been restored on the barracks of Duntroon in Canberra.

Parental blessing was given but with a suggestion that the young man stop playing the game of rugby which seemed to take up so much of his time. Maqueen accepted the advice but gave no firm undertaking in return—thankfully for rugby enthusiasts and the direction of Australian rugby many years later. For some reason, Mr Meyer made no mention of surfboat rowing which continued to be the other great influence on both their lives and was probably a more demanding one in terms of their relationship.

Light at the end of the tunnel vision

During the rugby season players trained two nights a week and played one game on the weekend. The six-month surf club season was far more intensive. Carnivals sometimes went over two days and the boat rowers trained most days of the week. Not only that, but girlfriends, wives and families weren't exactly welcome when the competition was on. In particular they were excluded from the large tent set up on the beach for the competitors. At the time Macqueen and his fellow rowers accepted the situation, which was totally opposite to today's way of thinking.

The culture of the Collaroy boat crews at the time was one of total focus. Girls were not allowed in the tent and wives and partners were discouraged from having any participation in the sport other than as spectators on the beach. Fortunately this has now changed, to the extent that women are not only allowed in the competitors' tent but are lifesavers in their own right and compete in boat races. An integral part of success is for the team members to be relaxed and happy and to be in the best possible personal environment. That usually means being close to their families, or at least to their partner. It really is a matter of individual choice and one which professional people can be relied on to make for themselves. What I failed to realise at the time was how important it was to have a balance between family life and competition.

Headhunting

When John Brown was promoted to sweep a senior crew, the young errant Macqueen was elevated along with him. Brown soon discovered a number of attributes he could use to advantage.

'He was extremely competitive and also showed leadership skills among the other young rowers. He had a strong head on his shoulders and could listen and define tactics,' Brown says. 'That's why I finished up rowing him in the stroke position so he could lead the other blokes in the boat. And that's where he stayed, right throughout his rowing career. He couldn't row anywhere else really.'

Brown also noted something else. 'He was different to all the other guys. Although he liked to go out and enjoy himself, he was a very deep thinker. He had a way of sitting down and resolving things by thinking them through.'

With different changes of personnel and Brown's work commitments the Collaroy 'A' crew competed with mixed results for several years before Macqueen decided to try a different approach. Why persevere with the same limited resources? In business terminology it was time to go headhunting. He would build a new crew from scratch.

Over a few beers at the local hotel, Boothie and I considered the attributes of all the rowers we knew. We were looking not just for talented individuals, but for people who could develop camaraderie and put in the extra effort to forge a committed team. The first person we contacted was Peter Bott, a rower from the nearby South Narrabeen club. He had the imaginative nickname of Gannet, after the local sea birds which swoop on any morsel of food left lying about. Although older and with one glass eye courtesy of a teenage accident, he was extremely fit, skilled and had the dedication we believed would be necessary. To our surprise he agreed straight away. In seeking out a fourth rower we turned to the rugby field, looking for someone with similar values and attributes. We finally decided on Barry Cox, a tough young prop from the Eastwood club. Coxie also rowed with a rival surf club, but like Gannet agreed to change allegiance to Collaroy. We all agreed to the stipulation that we stay together for at least two seasons and during that time be 'dedicated to boat rowing only'.

According to Coxie, Macqueen was immediately recognised as the leader of the crew. 'He put us together and the game plan was pretty clear. We were going to hit the beach fitter, tougher, and more competitive than the other crews,' he says. 'We trained three to four times a week. By the time we finished that three-month period before the start of the season, we had unity as a crew that I think was a foundation for success. Rod promoted the drive, the training in the boat, and the discipline. We had a lot of fun and we really played hard and trained hard, but out of it came a camaraderie that I have never experienced since.'

Coxie also remembers the effect Macqueen's attitude had on those around him. It didn't seem to matter whether they were training in the gym or in the boat, he was always the one that had to try and lift the heaviest weight, do the most repetitions or row the hardest. He was always there challenging. He'd never take a backward step. There was more to it than simply leading by example.

The newly formed crew performed remarkably well in its first season, making fourteen finals from nineteen starts but was eliminated early from the 1976 State Titles after a difficult start in the heats due to rough seas.

When we were beaten we were loudly cheered by other competitors on the beach. This was a typical reaction by rival crews to show their delight at seeing one of their adversaries eliminated. I suddenly realised that we were finally being considered as serious contenders. Boat rowing took on a new perspective. The crew developed a camaraderie because we knew the sacrifices we were making were bringing the enjoyment of success. On the other hand, the more competitive we became the easier it was to put in all the hard work.

Laughs and larrikinism

In the training sessions, Macqueen was ruthless in pushing everyone to the limit. But what those around him found most exasperating was his ability to switch off immediately the hard work was over. While others struggled to regain their breath, relax and gather their thoughts, Macqueen seemed to have the uncanny ability to change his mood almost immediately. It was a similar situation in business when he and his associates were involved in tense negotiations or company planning sessions. Once the moment of intense concentration was over his mind automatically switched to another level. It usually meant it was time for games and jokes which prompted his trademark giggle, a combination of a stifled chuckle and a wheezing laugh which, unfortunately, was almost identical to the sound made by a popular cartoon character of the time, 'Muttley the Dog'. As a result Macqueen was widely referred to as 'Muttley'. In years to come his ability to switch off would remain, so would his readiness to laugh, though thankfully, for his sake, in a different form.

Macqueen's boat crew came to be remembered for more than their success. An almost essential part of the boat-rowing culture was an ongoing series of pranks, practical jokes and all-round larrikinism between the competing crews. At that time virtually everyone going to the beach wore slip-on rubber thongs. Both Macqueen and Coxie discovered they could sink their teeth into a thong and remove a full, bite-sized piece. This soon became a regular prank during post-carnival celebrations. During the carnivals, as the various crews completed their race they would retire to their tent area for a rest only to discover that their much-loved old thongs had large serrated pieces missing. This became a calling card of the Collaroy boat crew and, in some instances, an annoying form of intimidation.

Sometimes it is just the simple little messages that lead to your competitors' perception of you. The more their perception is of a team with camaraderie and confidence, the harder it is for them to seek out and perceive weaknesses. Sometimes it is hard for people to understand the importance of these little things but in the overall persona of a team, these little things can take on an enormous importance, psychologically.

Teams within teams

The following year the crew again rowed consistently and this time went all the way to win the state championships, the first state boat title for Collaroy in more than thirty years. As a result they were chosen to represent NSW in the interstate championships in Victoria. It was a memorable achievement. For Macqueen, it rewarded and justified his almost obsessive attention to detail and discipline. But it opened up yet another dimension of experience and learning, one that wouldn't be wasted.

The coach and manager took me aside to spell out the importance of representing the state. The side consisted of elite athletes in their field and included Olympian swimmers, board paddlers, sprinters, iron men and rowers, but we were told we weren't there as individual champions. We had been selected for winning individual boat races or swimming events but now we were also expected to put the team first and work together for New South Wales. From day one the manager and coach impressed on us the winning traditions of the New South Wales side and encouraged us to have pride in our state and, perhaps more significantly, pride in each other. Up until now our crews placed their own needs before anything or anyone else. Now our focus had to change to conform with a bigger team. I was impressed that so many individuals with widely different skills and personal aspirations could be motivated to perform with a common purpose. Winning our own event was just one part. Supporting and encouraging our teammates at all times was crucial to the common goal. The more support and encouragement the team was given the more confident and united we became. And ultimately the more successful.

Team-building in rags

However the Collaroy boat crew soon made a special contribution of their own. Although outfitted in expensive uniforms by the team sponsors, the Collaroy rowers found the traditional tracksuits and blazers no match for the freezing Victorian weather.

We headed off to a St Vincent de Paul charity shop and bought as many old overcoats, hats and scarves as we could. It wasn't long before the entire New South Wales team was strutting about in shabby but warm second-hand coats. Although unintended at the time, the simple act of all wearing the same outrageous clothing brought an extra dimension of bonding to the team. Simple innovations and changes can sometimes be the catalyst to make special things happen. Interestingly enough, a photograph of our team of Olympians and other elite athletes skylarking in their hand-me-down rags still adorns the offices of the Surf Lifesaving Association of New South Wales.

Their attire certainly set them apart from everyone else, leaving perhaps an even more lasting impression after the other team members also learnt the gentlemanly art of thong chewing.

When it came down to business the NSW state team secured first place in the Interstate Titles. Team administrators later attributed much of the victory to the team's strong camaraderie.

True to their original agreement, the crew stayed together the following year and successfully defended their title, winning the NSW championship a second time, and again being called on to represent the state. Following his memorable introduction to the Interstate Titles the previous year, Macqueen in particular regarded state representation as a serious commitment. While there was always time for the usual pranks and skylarking, he insisted on total dedication by all team members in the lead-up to any event.

Warren Rennie, a senior administrator in the surf lifesaving movement at the time, was immediately impressed by Macqueen for a number of reasons. He remembers a young man physically strong and extremely fit who was a fierce and determined competitor, a bit wild and unruly at times, but paradoxically, also quiet and reserved. Rennie, who went on to become the president of the Australian Surf Lifesaving Movement, believes that from a relatively young age Macqueen had developed a special quality. 'At that high level of competition he never lost his nerve no matter how adverse the conditions. Other people falter or question themselves. This bloke never did. Not once. He had a steely determination to achieve against all odds and others in the team looked up to him and gained strength from it.'

Yet, Rennie points out, at the same time Macqueen respected discipline and authority. 'He might have had his own point of view but, as the team coach, when I wanted something done he didn't argue. He just did it.'

Rennie was also impressed by other achievements. 'I was amazed to find out that while he was rowing at the top level he was also captain of the Collaroy club, playing first grade rugby and running his own successful merchandising business. He was obviously intelligent and able to focus his talents to win through at everything he took on.'

Life's jigsaw

Now in his twenties Macqueen was indeed a very busy young man. Apart from his almost fanatical commitment to sport, he was also preparing to take over a section of his father's business in the competitive area of exhibitions and merchandising. When not rowing, playing rugby, running, swimming or sweating through heavy weight sessions in a gym, he was dressed in a suit and tie dealing with marketing executives from some of Australia's leading companies.

I was leading a very hectic life but that's the way it has always been. I was trying to mix the different areas that were important to me in such a way that they complemented each other. In retrospect I should have been devoting more time to Liz at that stage, and in the few years that followed, to our young family. I look back now and realise how much quality time I missed with my young family. If I could have my time over, I would have spent much more time with them. The ideal situation is to combine the things in life you love doing most, without one detracting from the other, then you can create something very special.

Lateral leadership

Intent on enjoying himself while at the same time striving to win at all costs, Macqueen, without really knowing it, was setting an example. His contributions were often unusual and invariably a talking point. The night before one interstate competition in Queensland he used his skill as a commercial artist to draw up giant posters depicting steamrollers running over cane toads, the unflattering image for Queenslanders. Competitors unaware of his artistic talent were dumbstruck by the dramatic images plastered around the walls of their common room. According to Warren Rennie, this typically unexpected action created enormous interest and stirred up the team spirit. He says it was inspirational behaviour supported by all members of the Collaroy boat crew.

'I was woken at 6.30 one morning by a crunching sound outside my hotel window. When I looked out I saw the boat crew marching in formation around and around the motel's gravel driveway. Although rowers they were also part of the senior march past team and were up early practising for that day's competition. There was a limited number of members in the state team and everyone had to double up and compete in several events. These guys tried out for absolutely everything. Marching, sprinting, rescue drill, board paddling, the lot. As far as I was concerned they were the backbone of every state team I coached.'

As captain of the NSW team, Macqueen was constantly looking for any way to upset their arch rivals, Queensland. This intensified when Queensland newspapers predicted that after many years the local team was talented enough to comprehensively defeat their southern rivals. An opportunity arose in 1978 when the NSW squad arrived at the site of the championships, Kingscliff, and noticed the main opposition team training at the other end of the beach. The Queensland tent was unattended and the team thongs, complete with sponsors' logos, were piled enticingly in one corner. Without hesitation Macqueen and the rest of the Collaroy crew rushed in and took a large bite from the toe of every single one.

At the time it was a spontaneous thing to do. The entire NSW team stood back on the sand dunes and watched the Queensland surf team come back to their tent. We broke out in laughter when we saw the reactions of the Queenslanders as they discovered that every one of their team thongs had a bite out of it. It was really only a silly prank that was taken in good spirits. But quite often it's the simple little things that can give you a winning advantage. I suspect it probably had a bit of a psychological effect on the Queensland competitors as well.

Apart from Macqueen's determination and innovative leadership qualities, something else about him struck Warren Rennie. At crucial times, like the intensity of a competition, he became ill, usually with flu. It concerned his close friends, in both lifesaving and rugby. Whenever the pressure was really on before a big carnival or important football match Macqueen would get sick. But typically, he never let it get on top of him. Somehow he always managed to fight through without letting it affect his performance. The mystery of these recurring bouts of flu would not be resolved for many years to come and not before they threatened his life.

Keep searching or you'll never find it

Macqueen's determination to do anything possible to gain an advantage over the opposition might have impressed his mates, but it drove others to distraction. When the Collaroy club ordered a new boat for the senior crew Macqueen immediately visited the local boat-builder and insisted he build the lightest boat possible. The bemused craftsman said the only way that could be done was if he selected different pieces of timber for each section, and then someone would have to have the time and patience to choose the lightest individual piece required. He didn't expect to hear anything more about such a pedantic and time-consuming idea. He was wrong. Paul Booth recalls the following routine: 'Every day at lunchtime, Rod insisted I join him on a trip to the boat-builder's workshop. We'd go in and weigh every bit of timber the guy had selected as being suitable for our boat. We'd get up to ten similar pieces of timber, put them on the scales and say, "Use this piece", and put it in a special pile.'

There is no doubt the boat-builder thought they were madmen but he went along with it. It turned out there was a big difference between the weight of the individual pieces of wood. Overall the new boat was ten or fifteen per cent lighter and extremely fast.

By now Booth was accustomed to Macqueen's constant search for perfection. 'That's just the way he was. If there was any way of improving the boat or getting outside help Rod would look for it.'

Of course there is often a downside. Having a lightweight, more competitive boat did prove to have one disadvantage.

Although it was lighter and faster than all the other boats, unfortunately it wasn't as strong. A few months later it suffered a most unceremonious exit from competition much to the great amusement of the opposition crews. In the middle of a race the boat was rolled by a big wave, and it promptly disintegrated. Hundreds of small pieces slowly washed onto the shore where they were collected by the amused rowers from rival crews.

Not everything works exactly as you'd like it, however there is nothing to lose by experimenting with new methods. If the results aren't satisfactory you can always revert to the tried and true while at the same time continuing the search for a winning edge. In my case, I never stop trying to come up with new ideas.

Learn why you lose before you start to win

The now well-established Collaroy crew made it through to their first Australian Titles final in 1979 in Perth. They had a neck-and-neck tussle with the race favourites, a seasoned senior crew from Warriewood, another club on Sydney's northern beaches. The Collaroy crew gave it everything and turned the marker buoys first and headed for the beach with a good lead.

Unfortunately for us, the Warriewood crew had kept something in reserve and in the flat conditions had more energy to row past us and catch a small wave to the finish.

We were devastated to come so close only to be beaten into second place. Later when we calmed down we realised we had been beaten by a better, more composed crew. If we had been good enough we could have won. Our enthusiasm, strength and technique were good but in the final analysis their composure under pressure gave them the winning edge. It was to be another learning curve for me. The formula for success is made of many components, the aim is to get the right balance.

The following year, 1980, both crews again made the final at Maroochydore in Queensland. Once more it became a virtual match race between the two with Collaroy holding their own to make a controversial finish. Both boats crossed the line simultaneously, causing confusion amongst the judges standing in the water at flags marking either end of the imaginary finish line. Two officials closest to the Collaroy crew declared them winners but, after a drawn-out conference with three judges at the other end, victory was officially awarded to Warriewood. Later examination of television footage showed the Collaroy boat appeared to cross in front, but the decision had already been made. The Collaroy crew were devastated at having come so close.

At the end of the day, as the sun began to fade, Macqueen sat alone on the sandhills overlooking the beach. As the last remaining competitors gathered their belongings in the distance, he took time to reflect. It was something he usually did at the end of each National Championship series, but this time was different. The traditional closing tune was playing over the loudspeakers. The haunting and aptly named 'The Carnival is Over' by Australian folk group The Seekers invariably made him pensive and sad. This time he was angry.

I sat there thinking and cursing the judges and wondering why it had to be me. It was probably my last real chance at winning an Australian title. After all the hard work we had put in I felt cheated. It was as though the prize had been won and then taken away. I sat there for a long time listening to the music, looking out to sea and reflecting on what could have been. It was some time before I was able to walk back and rejoin the crew. In hindsight it was probably another good lesson for me. I've often looked back and wondered what difference it would have made to me if we had won the gold medal on that day. I think quite honestly I wouldn't have tried so hard in all my endeavours since. It takes a while to put things into perspective. At the time victory was a matter of life and death. I subsequently realised that life goes on. There are other goals to set and strive for. I believe now that learning to cope with those disappointments helped me achieve other things in life. It proved to me the importance of being in control of our own destiny in whatever we do. We only get chances at great achievement every so often and we have to make sure we are fully prepared to take advantage of the opportunities as they arise.

To other members of the crew the pursuit of perfection, of leaving nothing to chance, seemed never-ending and at times literally exhausting. The simple act of carrying the boat from its trailer to the water's edge became a test of endurance. During a carnival half a dozen crews could be moving their boats onto the beach at the same time. Evenly spaced along each side, straining to carry the heavy weight up to fifty or sixty metres to the water, the rowers would stop and rest several times. Not the Collaroy crew. Boothie remembers that at major events Macqueen would urge them on, grunting and groaning with the enormous effort. No stopping, no hesitating, no looking ahead, just keeping on until they reached the water. It was a matter of putting on a show for the opposition. A chance to go one better, to intimidate, to seize an opportunity to gain yet another advantage.

Chapter 5

Challenge and Controversy

Buckets of pride

What does it feel like to have a plastic bucket jammed over your head then have someone punch the bucket as hard as they can? Unless you are silly enough to try the experience with a friend, the only way to find out would be to ask a select group of highly regarded Australian surfboat rowers.

As the successes of the Collaroy senior crew continued to mount, so did their notoriety. Some of their antics, which began as good-hearted fun, eventually became traditional behaviour and even recognised 'boatie events'. Following their second place in Perth the crew organised a buck's party for Coxie who was due to be married on his return to Sydney. They knew that any organised party would attract a variety of other lifesavers they didn't know and also non-competitors just looking for a drink and a good time. Many of the post-carnivals' celebrations ended up in an absolute debacle with guys getting drunk and breaking glasses and destroying furniture. Generally these were the 'hangers on' who had little respect for the boaties and their culture. The boat crews were determined that this was not going to happen. Their new sweep, Craig Cunningham, was a well-known identity who had rowed for several years with John Brown at the North Bondi surf club. After discussing the problem with several other senior crews he came up with the idea of calling it a boat rowers' convention. They expected only the most serious rowers would bother attending a convention. They assumed these would be other crews they knew well and got on with. To their surprise nearly every crew in town turned up. Not only that, many of them were carrying pads and pencils expecting a serious conference on all aspects of surfboat competition. If it weren't so funny it would have been embarrassing. To save face they actually started proceedings with a wide-ranging discussion and exchange of ideas.

As it turned out it was a worthwhile and enjoyable get-together. Then the serious business started.

When word spread that Coxie was about to get married the heavy drinking was accompanied by the inevitable hijinks. The tradition for any buck's party is for the prospective groom to wear a ball and chain but without one available they tied a plastic bucket around his neck with a piece of rope. Later, when the partying intensified, the bucket proved to have another, unusual purpose. One group arrived late, already well-inebriated, and began breaking glasses and causing problems. Macqueen and Cox decided to confront the biggest member of the group. His aggressive reaction led Cox to ask politely if he would stand still so he could place the bucket on his head.

'While he was still looking confused I put it over his head and before I knew it Macca had punched the bucket,' Cox explained.

The pair then went to two others in the group and did the same thing, taking it in turns to punch the bucket. Macqueen then pointed out that obnoxious behaviour wasn't welcome at the convention. This bizarre form of punishment was loudly cheered by all the onlookers, a reaction which almost certainly saved the incorrigible Cox and Macqueen from being set upon by the humiliated group. The idea of 'bucket belting' was immediately adopted as an amusing and harmless way of dealing with troublemakers during the rest of the night. The hotel manager was astonished by what he saw. Not only was a bucket being used to knock sense into people, but members within the group were also ensuring that bad behaviour was not tolerated, and that any breakages were cleaned up and paid for.

In the midst of all the revelry the get together had a special feeling about it. The mates standing around drinking together had been fierce competitors all year. All the rivalry was put aside and replaced with genuine goodwill and friendship. We had a lot of laughs and a lot of fun. Unfortunately there was a small group there who were determined to cause trouble and that annoyed the rest of us. However, we were able to overcome that during the day by setting our own standards. It was significant they came from within the group and were supported and enforced by the majority of athletes that were present. In the end it was a long and enjoyable day, enhanced by the sense of pride at being able to maintain the 'code of conduct'. Even the bar staff and hotel owner enjoyed themselves.

Toward the end of the night a collection was taken up and the barmaids tipped more than 600 dollars—the hotel owner was so impressed he put on a free keg for the rest of the evening.

The sense of pride and a high level of standards was common practice within the boaties' culture throughout the surf clubs, and it fostered a mentor system for the young and new boat rowers. This system mirrors the ethics of the surf lifesaving movement, a system of standards set by tradition and existing club members. It varies from club to club, but the principles are the same. I know the experiences and the lessons I have learnt were invaluable to me and I am pleased to see my son Scott experiencing the same benefits I was able to enjoy. Unfortunately, like most fathers, I find I have a selective memory when it comes to some of the shenanigans the boys get up to.

The 'Boaties' Convention' became an annual event and over many years evolved into a far more sophisticated occasion. In the late 1990s, with the National Titles being held each year on the beaches of Queensland's famous Gold Coast, it became a semi-formal occasion held in the Grand Ballroom of the nearby Jupiters Casino. The winning boats from each category are suspended from the ceiling and video replays of decisive races are shown on giant screens around the room. A variety of achievement awards are presented and outstanding individual contributions recognised by induction into the boat rowers' 'Hall of Fame'. The convention now attracts between 800 and 1200 boaties, including beautifully dressed and coiffed representatives from the many female crews. Much has changed. But not the original traditions and standards set so many years before in the hot and noisy saloon bar of a pub in Perth.

Singing in harmony

In the lead-up to each season the Collaroy boat crews practised rowing in the still waters of Little Manly Cove, a corner of Sydney harbour just inside the northern headland. At the end of one year, in the week before Christmas, the crews decided to meet at the local pub and share the spirit of the season with fellow drinkers. After all, there's nothing like a good old-fashioned singalong to bring people together. Macqueen asked each member of the crew to bring along an item representing Christmas—a small Christmas tree, some bon-bons, an angel, carol books, whistles and party hats. It was a smoke-filled, crowded working man's pub, where the majority of rowdy patrons were enjoying a few drinks on their way home from work. In one corner of the pub, on the bar, sat a Christmas tree, surrounded by a small group of merry carol singers wearing party hats.

They were all enjoying themselves but some of the locals were less than impressed. One large, regular drinker headed for the bar and began pushing at the rowers on the way through. The situation was beginning to look ugly until Macqueen quickly seized him in a headlock, thrust a carol book under his nose and laughingly urged him to sing along. After a few tense moments a couple of strangled verses came out and the laughter of everyone in the room broke the tension. The Collaroy carollers then moved as a group to other individuals and encouraged them to also take part. By the end of the night everyone had joined in.

It was an amazing scene! One of the toughest pubs in town, with truckies, labourers and five boat rowers arm in arm, singing Christmas carols and wearing party hats.

This common theme brought everyone together and it was a memorable and funny night. One of the most satisfying things was seeing the antagonism and differences between the two factions disappear temporarily as the spirit of Christmas set in. It was also interesting to see that a number of locals remained friends and were always keen to catch up with us after our training sessions.

The Christmas party and singalong has become an annual tradition with some rowers going to the extreme of wearing fancy dress. Each year one is nominated as the shepherd. He gets to carry a staff in case any revellers get out of line. A 'gentle' tap on the shoulder was the only warning needed, a practice Macqueen qualifies. 'Only boat rowers are allowed to be hit with the staff, no outside people. That wouldn't be in the true spirit of Christmas.'

Don't underestimate underestimation

The many lunch breaks that young Macqueen had spent arm-wrestling with workmen back at the Empisal Sewing Machine offices

Rugby became Macqueen's favourite sport at an early age.

Early leadership.
Captain of the under 10s rugby side, Macqueen shakes hands with friend Greg Bray before the game.

Junior cricket was one of the many sports played by the young Macqueen.

Learning the simple pleasures. One of many special moments with father, Ian.

An early message. Ian Macqueen brought back this photograph signed by the Fijian football star Apakuki Tuitavua which was inscribed with 'play hard, have fun'.

School day memories.

Rod aged 12 taken at Collaroy Plateau School.

A premonition of things to come.

```
        COLLAROY PLATEAU YOUTH CLUB


                                    40 Essilia Street,
                                    COLLAROY PLATEAU.


                                    20th April, 1960



Dear Rod,

        The committee of your Youth Club are very proud
to have a boy who is able to take such a sincere interest in
his Club.  We feel that you are to be congratualted on your
fine effort and club spirit and hope you will keep this letter,
that you may look back in later years and gain pleasure from one of
your youthful events.

        Thanking you on behalf of the Youth Club,

                        Yours faithfully,



                        Hon. Secretary.
```

Macqueen, sporting attractive footwear, grooves with sister Shaen.

Rod's mother and father, Ian and Marjorie Macqueen.

Surfboard-riding with
friends.

Board-riding was one of
Rod's favourite pastimes
in his early years.

Early courtship centred
on beachside activities.

Rod and Liz at Collaroy,
1965.

Sunday recreation.

Beach football—a hard ten-a-side game played on sand.

Warringah Rugby Club 1st XV second division premiers, 1970.

This victory promoted Warringah into first division.

Rod and Liz's wedding.

Both aged 21, Rod and Liz walked down the aisle in 1971.

Rod's pencil sketch of June Macqueen's farm.

Junie's farm was an early source of inspiration for Macqueen, the artist.

One of many family visits to Junie's farm which later became a welcome retreat from rugby and business.

proved not to be hours of idle time-wasting. During that period he had perfected a technique, which allowed him to lock his arm in such a fashion it couldn't be bent over by the largest or strongest of opponents. As he progressed in the sporting worlds of rugby and surfboat rowing his unique ability to win arm-wrestling bouts against seemingly impossible odds proved invaluable in settling disputes, winning bets and making friends.

The results were always favourable and the winnings often paid for the crew's travelling expenses and dinner bills. Boothie admits, though, that on many occasions Macqueen didn't see the cash. 'He was so hell-bent on beating everybody he usually didn't worry about the betting. It was just incredible. He always won no matter how big the other guy was. Certainly none of us could ever beat him, which was really annoying.'

According to his crewmates, Macqueen's arm-wrestling prowess became a highlight of the celebrations, which followed each year's state and national titles. His successful run almost ended thanks to the promotional aspirations of his close mate, Coxie. It came at the end of a long day when some of the NSW team and the Collaroy boat crew had been involved in a television advertisement for a new brand of beer. Needless to say, they were well-primed by the time they adjourned to the nearest hotel. Everyone was in a jovial mood, trying to outdo each other as they recounted the events of the day. Macqueen and John Brown became alarmed when they heard noise coming from the rear of the hotel and they realised Coxie was missing. Apparently he had wandered into the public bar and stirred up a large group of drinkers visiting from western Queensland. Coxie had heard one of the visitors was an arm-wrestling champion who'd just won a major competition. He was belittling the man's achievements and talking up the prowess of his mate. By the time Macqueen and Brown arrived at the bar there was a table already set up with a huge chanting group of spectators calling for the challenger. Brown was stunned when he saw the opponent Coxie had managed to line up. 'He was a massive guy, a big truckie originally from the outback mining town of Mt Isa. My first reaction was, "If Macca doesn't beat this bloke we're going to get belted from one end of the pub to the other."'

State team coach Warren Rennie was also involved in the advertising shoot and entered the rear bar just as the contest was about to start. He too was worried.

'Local drinkers told me the other bloke was unbeaten in professional competitions right round Australia. He sure had the size and another advantage. Like the rest of us, Macqueen had plenty to drink during the photo shoot. I didn't like his chances and the general mood was pretty ugly.'

Once they engaged and put on the pressure, Macqueen appeared to be in trouble. The man was almost twice his size and Macqueen was struggling just to hold him. Almost a hundred people in the bar were trying to crowd the small table shouting and laughing, urging their hero to teach the young upstart a lesson. The tension and the noise continued to rise as the struggle continued for almost five minutes. Momentarily, Macqueen felt his opponent's arm relax slightly as he glanced over to one of his mates.

Suddenly there was stunned silence as Macqueen crashed the giant's arm to the table. There were murmurs of disbelief as the crowd began to disperse to try to comprehend what they had just witnessed. There was at least forty kilos' difference between the two combatants. But there was more to it than just physical technique. Mind over matter and a touch of amateur psychology also played a part. Unknown to the spectators, Macqueen had devised different tactics for different people.

I think I saw it as a type of game and I enjoyed the challenge. Each contest became a tactical battle in itself. I believe my greatest asset then was being aware of my strengths and weaknesses.

In the majority of situations, I have found there is a definite advantage in being underestimated by your opposition. There is no doubt that it can increase your chances of winning immeasurably.

Mind your body

When new sweep Craig Cunningham first came to the club he was an extremely fit policeman who trained regularly with George Daldry. George was famous for his unique type of fitness training and was responsible for a silver medal-winning performance by the Australian rowing eight at the Mexico Olympics. After a short period Cunningham convinced every crew at Collaroy to join him at the Daldry training sessions held at the City Tattersall's Club gym in the centre of Sydney. It became the experience of a lifetime for all concerned, but for many different reasons. Daldry's methods were undoubtedly effective but certainly didn't appear in any book on sports physiology. For instance, during an hour and a half of extraordinary exercise, the intake of any fluid was banned.

Tattersall's was an old-fashioned gym located in the bowels of the club with an internal set of concrete fire stairs. These were one of Daldry's favourite pieces of gym equipment and the cause of much pain and suffering to the rowers who were ordered to sprint up and down each flight, more often than not carrying someone on their back. His routines were based on competitiveness. The Collaroy rowers soon discovered they were being pitted against each other, forced to train harder and harder or suffer the indignity of giving in before someone else.

One of Daldry's specialties was 'the log', a huge piece of hardwood with six handles on it. He would direct six people through a series of exercises which ended with the hefty length of timber being held above our heads while we jogged on the spot. When everyone was exhausted Daldry would call out 'A minute to go' and then count out the minute in his own time. In real time it was inevitably more like three minutes. We found ourselves in a situation where our bodies were crying out to lower the log but our minds were forcing us to hold on for just a few more seconds. Don't be the first to give up, don't let your mates down. When Daldry finally called out 'Time!' we would collapse on the floor, totally spent. I had a healthy respect for the super-fit Daldry and revelled in the tough training sessions. It was an amazing feeling, a cross between exhilaration and exhaustion with your mind continually pushing your body to the limit. The feeling afterwards was quite incredible. It showed me how much you could push your body and endure pain, much further than I could possibly imagine. It also showed me just how much influence your mind has on your performance. However, today many of these oppressive techniques would certainly not be accepted. In fact, I am sure that some of the old school methods have left me with the legacy of a suspect back. Despite this, it gave me a fierce determination to train hard and I have continued to enjoy keeping fit, running or swimming on most days no matter where I am or what I'm doing.

Level playing fields

During his surfboat rowing career Macqueen was involved in a number of controversial events which led to changes in official procedure. After representing NSW at the 1979 Interstate Championships, the Collaroy crew was told that like all other crews they would have to represent their club in the early elimination heats for the National Surfboat Titles in races scheduled to be held late the same day. They were all exhausted, not only from rowing, but from contesting a variety of other events for the state team as well. Collaroy drew a particularly tough heat against several of the other leading boats and failed to win through. They were hot favourites to win the event and were understandably distraught at being eliminated in round one. The obvious inequity of the system was recognised by the officials in charge. The most senior official present was the new chief superintendent of Surf Lifesaving Australia, Warren Rennie. As the person in charge of all technical matters, he immediately changed the regulations so that all state representatives were given a break until competition the following day.

Following their defeat by Warriewood back in the 1980 National Titles in Queensland, the crew had been supported by other clubs in demanding that close finishes be decided with photo or video assistance. This policy was subsequently adopted.

Now, in 1982 the Collaroy club found it had two senior boat crews of equally high standard but it was confronted by a regulation that stipulated that each club could enter only one senior crew in championship competitions. This led to a five-race row-off between the crews, which divided the club and caused acrimony between the 'boaties'. They had all been good mates up until that time but the competition for the prestigious position of top senior crew saw them refusing to talk or have anything to do with one another. The opposing Collaroy crew won 3–2 and went on to become the club's 'A' crew. Both crews later performed exceptionally well in their respective competitions, but the bitterness remained. After representations by Collaroy, and other clubs, the regulations were later changed to allow each club to have more than one 'A' crew. Macqueen welcomed the important changes.

I've always argued against situations which give competitors an unfair advantage or deprive someone else of a fair result. I believe that it's important for each competitor to be given an equal opportunity to perform to the best of their ability. There's no point having rules and regulations in place if they don't ensure you have a level playing field. Any advantages should ultimately come from those created by the competitor himself.

For Macqueen there was another positive element, which was to come about some time later. Two members of the fiercely competitive opposing crew, Steve Nance and Brendan Mockford, would become important allies in years to come.

Inside focus fixes failure

'You're never too old to learn', is one popular adage. 'You can never know too much', is another. After winning a third NSW Championship, this time with a revamped crew, Macqueen organised some specialist coaching. In his mind it was time to learn something new, to further improve the skills which had already brought them so much success. He approached senior members of the Mosman Rowing Club, one of the bastions of traditional rowing in Sydney. While still-water rowing in narrow racing shells requires a slightly different technique, he was, as usual, searching for anything that would give his crew an advantage over the opposition. Their first instruction came from former Olympic rower and coach, Michael Morgan. He ordered them into a 'tub' or training shell. Although well-rounded and twice the beam of a racing shell, it was only a quarter the width of a surfboat and a new experience for all but one of the four bulky lifesavers. There were two new rowers, both strapping young rugby players from the Eastwood club, brothers Scott and Angus Reid. Only Scott had some previous experience in still water rowing. All were over 1.8 metres tall and Macqueen was the lightest at 90 kilograms. The others were all 100 kilos plus. Once seated they pushed off from the clubhouse pontoon and promptly tipped over, much to the delight of the several dozen oarsmen who had gathered in expectation of such a display. After they had mastered the art of actually staying in the boat, a number of sessions under tuition soon improved their balance, timing and stroke technique.

However, something unusual happened in a novice race several weeks later. Macqueen was rowing in the all-important stroke position, pumped up with excitement and straining to give maximum effort. The voice of experienced coxswain, Terry O'Hanlon, finally cut through the fog of adrenalin-charged racing emotion.

We were struggling to stay with the other boats when I suddenly became aware of this quiet voice issuing instructions from the rear of the boat. He told me to forget the race and concentrate on catching the water correctly with the blade, to focus on balance and timing, to set a different style for the three crewmates following my lead. It was new for me to hear someone talk so calmly and authoritatively during a race. Then his orders changed, calling for a brighter catch and a cleaner finish. I concentrated as hard as I could, ignoring everything outside. I could feel the run of the boat and the water against the oar. It was in the middle of the race and I remember being really focused.

As O'Hanlon continued with his quiet instructions the fragile racing shell sat firmly upright and moved quickly and smoothly through the glassy, green water of Sydney's Middle Harbour. It was some time before Macqueen looked around. He was surprised to see a line of boats strung out behind them. They were close to the finish line, then across it, winning the race by several boat lengths. It was an experience Macqueen wasn't to forget.

I was amazed that you could have this inner focus—as one with the boat with no outside influences. One person was able to take control. It was a huge learning experience for me. I was worrying too much about what was happening outside the boat rather than concentrating on the real issues, inside the boat. It taught me several things: stay calm under pressure; assess the different options; and take action accordingly. Identify the problem and give the team something to work on.

The value of traditions

During two years as Collaroy Club captain, Macqueen was noted for many efforts to boost morale, increase club spirit and improve efficiency. In consultation with club president John Bradford, he designed a separate lounge area, dividing the single large hall with a partition and pulling down the ageing collection of photographs and plaques from the walls. New and old photographs were hung along with historic memorabilia, honour boards and regularly updated photographs of emerging champions. Macqueen hoped the mixture of new and old would help bridge past glories with new achievements and give some inspiration to younger members.

One of the things that always impressed me was older members of the club talking about the great exploits of the past champions. The people that brought honour and character to the club were so important, yet all of this would be lost if we didn't make a conscious effort to cement the memories and keep them as part of the passion and soul that made the club what it was. They were heroes to look up to, characters to aspire to be—that's why it seemed so important to rejuvenate the honour rolls and renovate the club. I realised we needed an area, not only where members could relax and remember good times with their mates, but also where new members could walk into and feel the tradition around them. I wanted people to be able to look at the photos and honour boards on the walls and think about what went into such achievements and feel proud to be associated with the club.

Recognition and reward

Although the surf club movement was an integral part of Macqueen's life, it was still only one of his three dedicated pursuits. He continued rowing competitively at the senior level during the summer months, playing and coaching rugby union during winter, while he was aggressively building his own business all year round. Despite this hectic schedule, there was always time to take advantage of the beautiful local environment and to spend time with Liz, and their young family. There were pursuits all could enjoy from surfing and fishing to just lazing on the beach.

Macqueen's commitment to Collaroy and rowing brought satisfaction, recognition and rewards. He won four state titles, five interstate, came second in the national titles twice and later won the Australian Masters rowing competition in 1989 and 1990. During his career he represented the state five times, on three occasions as captain, with the team winning each time. Following a NSW tour of the UK and America, the team manager's report describes Macqueen's selection as captain as a most successful choice. He was 'An ideal leader who carried out all his duties most ably.'

A comment on his insistence of strict team discipline and demeanour was perhaps a portent of things to come for Australian rugby: 'I cannot speak too highly of the excellent behaviour . . . at all times they were a credit to their state and country.'

It was a description of a man far different to the young 'troublemaker' introduced to John Brown many years before.

Macqueen's association with the Collaroy club has never ended. It has continued at different levels, both as a competitor and administrator. After twenty-five years he was awarded the honour of life membership. His involvement with the Warringah Rugby Club was no less competitive, successful or eventful. The same parallels that can be drawn here, involving personal development and transformation, are quite remarkable.

If early rugby officials were asked who they believed would guide the club to its first senior club championship victory and two grand finals, would any have nominated the young, long-haired breakaway who enjoyed a drink and a good time as much as playing the 'gentleman's game'? Not likely!

Chapter 6
Serious Rugby

Focus on vision

If it wasn't for his success at surfboat rowing, Rod Macqueen may well have played professional rugby league for the rest of his football career. At the age of eighteen both he and Paul Booth had been invited to try out for a grade position with the Manly Warringah Rugby League Club, one of the most successful Sydney clubs at the time. Strangely enough, the offer came because of their experiment with beach football. Encouraged by fellow surf club members, they had subsequently played numerous games in the local C-grade rugby league competition. Their performances had obviously been noticed. But while football training and completion of the final trials for grade selection was underway, they had rowing commitments and were unable to make a training day until after the trials were over and the team gradings had already been announced.

They knew they would get a cold reception at the very strict, professional rugby league outfit, so they decided to join a training run with the Manly Rugby Union fifth grade side. For some reason no-one showed much interest so, the following week, they tried their luck at Warringah, a young emerging club formed four years earlier in the second division competition.

After training, everyone retired to the local pub where, according to Macqueen they met Elly Bennett, a typical club stalwart, who went out of his way to see they were welcome. It was the way they were welcomed and the way football was discussed that convinced them that with Warringah they were in the right place.

Macqueen and Booth were both put straight into the first grade side. Warringah was performing well in the competition but desperately needed some younger, more aggressive players. The new, extremely fit pair came made to order. Macqueen especially is well remembered by former players and officials. The descriptions offered are remarkably similar: 'An extremely fit, strong young man. More driven than skilful. Very focused and very physical.'

According to the coach, John Anderson, Macqueen stood out in the very first game: 'He was an extremely talented player with pace and size, and tackled everything that moved. He was a bit of a wild man and wouldn't be intimidated by anyone. I must admit he was hard to discipline and keep under control, but he certainly showed the way for everyone else.'

In short, he was an ideal aggressive and highly mobile young break-away or flanker. Of course not everyone is perfect: Macqueen has always admitted, and regretted, not having great ball skills, something about which he accepted a fair amount of good-natured ribbing throughout his playing career. But it was more than compensated for by the rest of his play. There was no question that he and Booth added a new edge to an already accomplished side. They revelled in the free-flowing style of play promoted both by Anderson, and especially club president Bill Simpson, a former player with one of Sydney's premier clubs. Macqueen was impressed by the efforts made to teach new players all the skills. Extra training runs were regularly called on Sunday mornings where for several hours the emphasis was on ball-handling, running angles, attacking moves and defensive patterns.

Bill Simpson had a vision that he constantly espoused to the players. At the Sunday sessions he would take individuals and explain to them what it was that he thought each position required. It is a great thing to have a vision but the real talent is being able to communicate those thoughts to others.

Plan A needs a Plan B

Perhaps understandably, Macqueen and Booth were drawn to some of the other more competitive players including five-eighth John Nolan, and the fullback, John Ogilvie. Although small in stature Ogilvie, or Ogie as he was universally known, was an inspirational player, constantly joining backline play and outstanding in defence. Nolan was highly regarded as a gifted ball player and was one of only a few ever to be selected from the second division ranks to play representa-tive matches in the higher grade. Both were several years older and long-term players from local junior clubs. They were more than happy to provide guidance to the two superfit tearaways keen to take on the world. All enjoyed the football and associated activities, although perhaps in different measures of intensity. They were to become lifetime friends.

By any definition, Macqueen's first season with Warringah in 1969 was a memorable one. He was awarded the trophy for Best and Fairest player; the first grade team made it to the grand final only to lose narrowly. Then the club was set a goal, which motivated all the top players. If they won the following year Warringah would be promoted as a new team in first division. At the end of the year Warringah again made the grand final and this time carried through for a win securing the prize of elevation to the top division.

Young and enthusiastic Macqueen, like other members of the team, didn't fully appreciate what they were in for. They didn't understand it was time to step up a level and play really serious rugby. The side was pitched against clubs with decades of experience, hefty financial resources, and most daunting of all, teams studded with seasoned international players.

It wasn't going to be easy for the fun-loving enthusiasts who lived in the almost holiday-like environment of the picturesque northern beaches. What made it harder was the fact they suffered not only from a lack of experienced players but a lack of players, full stop. They just didn't have the numbers or the replacements to be truly competitive.

According to John Nolan the first two seasons were a real struggle not just physically, but psychologically: 'After being the top team in one competition it was hard to accept not only losing every week, but losing by big margins. It took a lot of character for many of the guys to keep turning up knowing what the result was going to be.'

Macqueen found himself in familiar territory. Once again he was starting at the bottom of the ladder, needing to re-establish his position.

Looking back to those days I realise we were playing a fast-flowing predictable game without variation, attempting to run the ball from every- where. Although I believe the sentiments and principles were right and that it's a good thing to be positive, in reality we became our own worst enemy. We had fallen into the trap of constantly practising and playing a game without taking into account what the opposition would do.

It wasn't until later when I became more involved in my business and sporting commitments that I realised how predictability made winning so much easier for the opposition.

Know what you want—to get what you want

As for his own style of play, Macqueen had learnt quickly and was regularly voted Man of the Match. He was noted for his speed around the paddock, harassing the opposition backs and using his strength to secure a loose ball against usually greater numbers. His aggressive and uncompromising defence quickly promoted him to another role. At a relatively young age he became the unofficial team enforcer. In a young club sometimes regarded by the opposition as 'easybeats' the forward pack was often involved in torrid exchanges up front.

The memories of Macqueen's retaliation to violent play bring a wry smile to the faces of former teammates who now follow his coaching career with keen interest. During that time, almost thirty years ago, rough play was commonplace. Now 'the enforcer' of former years is seen as the quietly spoken coach who promotes discipline and self-control. Few would have predicted such a radical change to the game. Fewer would have foreseen the personal transformation.

Macqueen may have lacked some of the finer ball-handling skills, but he was relentless in taking the ball forward and breaking the first line of defence. He admitted he was reluctant to pass the ball, was not an elusive sidestepping runner, and preferred to run over the top of opponents rather than run past them. It may not have been the epitome of classic attacking rugby, but the fact that he was a consistent try-scorer proved that, at least for him, it was reasonably effective.

Because of his inspirational style of play Macqueen was soon voted captain, a role that came naturally according to Anderson. 'He was a leader because others would always follow. Some people have it—most don't. Macqueen was the best player on the field and he always had the full respect and support of his teammates.'

As captain, Macqueen dictated tactics and called all the basic moves but, in some notable instances did not always follow the coach's instructions. At training Anderson drilled the back row to perform only in a defensive and support role. Out on the field Macqueen quite often used them to instigate attacking moves from set play and from phase ball, passing between each other and linking with the inside backs. It became a constant source of argument between captain and coach. In later years it would become a successful trademark of Macqueen's own coaching philosophy.

Another matter for concern was a lack of commitment by some of the Warringah players. Despite stepping up into the higher division, many still turned out each week apparently happy to play a social style of rugby. This didn't impress their ever-competitive captain. Macqueen was in a unique position to compare how difference in attitude affected a team performance.

I was coming from a summer season of rowing in a five-man surfboat crew where each member was dedicated to giving 100 per cent effort and could rely on the support of those alongside. In a rugby team of fifteen players the difference in fitness, ability and dedication was extreme. I found the transition from one world to the other incredibly frustrating. If every player had a similar level of fitness and shared the same determination to succeed the level of achievement would be so much greater. What I didn't take into consideration at the time was that there was nothing wrong with a lot of those players wanting to have fun and not train as hard or make the sacrifices. When the club was in second division, there was a much more social theme. Perhaps the administrators should have impressed upon the teams more strongly the different type of commitment needed to play first division.

Family and friends forever

Unlike the surfboat culture, the rugby fraternity strenuously promoted family involvement. Most girlfriends and wives spent their share of time on the inevitable canteen roster but also socialising together during the games and at the traditional post match functions. Because it was a young club everyone helped out when there were jobs to be done. Liz Macqueen recalls being involved in working parties as the club expanded and built better facilities. 'Everyone helped out whenever there was extra work to be done. Whether it was just being there in support when building work was underway or painting fences around the oval, there was always something we could do.'

Perhaps more than any other club, Warringah encouraged family activities. With extensive park-like grounds, barbecues and picnics were extremely popular as the club developed.

Although Warringah had problems on the field in the early days, the culture and environment developed by the club had a significant impact on me. There was always a strong emphasis on family participation which made life a lot more balanced and easier for us at the time. Being able to play the sport that I loved and involve Liz, and later Jacqui and Scott, was a new experience for me.

The frame of mind is the big picture

Early in the 1973 season Macqueen's consistent performances were finally recognised and he was selected to play for a Barbarian side against an Invitational team from the Central Coast, north of Sydney. The Barbarian concept is to put together a team of internationals and up-and-coming players. It's a tradition which gives the younger players the chance to learn from those with greater experience. The Barbarian sides also play against junior teams to give them the opportunity of stepping up a level. In this instance Macqueen was the only member playing his first senior representative game.

The Barbarians gave me a totally new perspective on rugby. For a player who had only played at senior level with one club side it was a huge awakening. To meet and play alongside players with international experience broadened my on-the-field, and off-the-field, perception of the game. I learned far more than I ever would have just on the training paddock or in club rugby. The concept of the Barbarians brings together the real ethos of rugby and hopefully will continue despite the advent of professionalism.

Once noticed, Macqueen was selected to play in a number of Barbarian matches during the season. One of them was against a side from the town of Cowra in western NSW. The team was studded with Wallaby stars such as Ken Catchpole, Barry Stumbles and Reg Smith. He was also joined in the scrum by the legendary hard man of Australian rugby, Tony 'Slaggy' Miller. A former Wallaby number eight, second-rower and prop, Miller had played forty-one Tests during a fifteen-year international career. At the time it was the second highest number of Test matches for Australia by any player. Aged forty-four, the grizzled veteran was remarkably fit and, although retired from club rugby, was still more than a match for most forwards who reluctantly lined up against him. Macqueen was a great admirer of the man and his achievements. Their meeting as teammates was to bring about a mutual respect and close friendship. But not without a difficult start.

It was near the end of the game and I received the ball close to the try line with two players to beat. I looked inside and saw Slaggy screaming out for the ball. Instead of passing to him I put my head down, crashed through the defence, and managed to score the try myself. Unfortunately, my left leg twisted sideways and wrapped around the goal post. I was holding my knee and writhing in agony, waiting to be carried from the field, when Slaggy wandered over and gave me a long hard look. He leant over and said quietly, 'Serves you right for not passing the ball.'

It was a comment they would laugh about in years to come but at the time it didn't amuse Rod Macqueen. He was flown back to Sydney where a diagnosis of extensive medial and cruciate ligament damage meant a full knee reconstruction.

The priorities of problems

Lying on a trolley in the corridors of the old dilapidated Sydney Hospital, Macqueen was upset by the brusque attitude of the anaesthetist preparing him for surgery. That immediately prompted a battle of wills that watching nurses later described to a concerned Liz.

'They said the anaesthetist gave Rod an injection and told him that by the time he had counted to ten he would be unconscious,' she says. 'By the time Rod had counted to forty the anaesthetist apparently gave him a second injection. When he reached seventy he gave him a third and Rod eventually passed out after counting to one hundred.'

Macqueen's incredible willpower impressed the nursing staff, annoyed the anaesthetist, and did nothing to help his own medical condition. When he eventually recovered after the operation he suffered extensive and painful hardening of the veins in his arms which took days to abate. The experience also affected Liz who was heavily pregnant at the time with their first child.

Only days after I arrived home from hospital Liz went into labour two weeks before time. She carried her own bags into hospital while I followed on crutches with my knee in plaster. When our daughter, Jacqui, was born shortly after I was in the delivery room holding Liz's hand. Here I was, one of the first new age husbands following the latest trend to be present during childbirth. But whether it was by accident or design I'm not sure. Shortly before Liz gave birth, one of the nurses took my crutches out of the room because they were obstructing the doorway. I had no way to escape, whether I wanted to or not.

Finally reality set in and I realised I was with the woman I loved. Watching all the pain she had to endure and sharing the moment as Liz gave birth to our first child, I realised what a wonderful and memorable experience it was. I made sure I was present at the birth of our son Scott, two years later.

'Unfortunately the damage you sustained was so extensive you will never be able to play football again.' That was the knowledgeable prediction of the surgeon who assisted in the reconstruction of Rod Macqueen's smashed left knee.

Wrong. Within seven months the crippled patient was back playing with Warringah and later in the year was selected to represent Sydney.

Macqueen's recovery was typical of an extraordinary single-minded determination to achieve what 'experts' believed was impossible. After leaving hospital with his leg in plaster he had immediately begun a strenuous course of weights to keep his upper left leg in shape. Once the plaster was removed he even devised a complicated system of ropes and pulleys under his desk at work so that he could constantly exercise the damaged knee throughout the day. As a result of his unique fitness program he eventually joined regular training and was able to lead Warringah out onto the paddock at the start of the year, although he wasn't exactly in the same physical shape. Because of the constant lifting of heavy weights his previously crippled left leg was now noticeably bigger and stronger than the right, the opposite to the normal situation of a damaged limb that's been in plaster.

Creative cooking

The wide variety of characters in both rowing and rugby circles provided an interesting round of social activities. Soon there was an undertaking that the men would cook dinner for their wives or partners at the end of each month, using each other's homes in turn. Strong friendships were forged between young couples over the years as they progressed from backyard barbecues to candlelit dinners.

I clearly remember one specific dinner where John Ogilvie and I were put in charge of the main course at my home and I almost murdered the family dog.

We went to enormous trouble, spending four hours preparing, seasoning and stuffing two giant-sized fish which were to be cooked on the barbeque. That evening while the fish were cooking outside, we were all sipping cocktails and spinning the usual yarns inside.

When Ogie and I went out to check on our masterpiece we were horrified at what we saw—or at least I was. Our pet labrador, Benny, had discovered the fish and taken more than just a few bites. Enraged at the sight, I started to chase the dog around the yard in an attempt first to 'kill' him, then try and retrieve what was left of our seafood feast. Unfortunately, I got little help from Ogie who was suffering from an uncontrollable fit of laughter.

When I finally collared the dog I realised that the situation called for some ingenuity and a code of silence from my co-conspirator. We collected the undamaged head of one fish and the tail of the other and placed them on the serving platter almost half a metre apart with a gaping hole in the middle. We then filled this with what could be salvaged from the barbeque and yard and garnished it with the remains of the stuffing and parsley, which we quickly picked from the garden. When we finally presented the exotic arrangement at the dinner table, our other guests were highly complimentary of our talents and fortunately, didn't notice that both Ogie and I ate far more salad than fish that night.

Making things happen

The first major change to the Warringah club since its promotion to first division came when coach John Anderson offered to step down if they could find a suitable replacement. Macqueen had a lot of respect for Anderson and his achievements with the club and was sad to see him go. Without consulting club administrators or other players, Macqueen then took it upon himself to find the person he believed could further lift standards without upsetting the club's harmonious environment. He approached former Randwick player and Wallaby centre, John Francis, who had just coached a sub-district side to two consecutive premierships. Macqueen believed that Francis would bring tougher discipline and the expertise of running the ball which, at the time, was in line with Warringah's vision. As Macqueen had hoped, Francis settled in easily and brought a new enthusiasm and a more professional attitude to activities at the struggling club. However there was one major disappointment. When Francis arrived he discovered that the club captain and key player who had sought him out had himself been lured elsewhere: Macqueen had left.

Answering the challenge

During the rowing season Macqueen had been courted by the rival Eastwood Rugby Club, one of Sydney's original clubs with a strong tradition and a team sprinkled with representative players. Although a hard decision, it was a chance to find out just how good he really was, how far he could go.

It was an agonising decision for me. At the time I was captain of a rugby side drawn from a community where I had spent the whole of my sporting, business and social life. But I was now in my seventh year with Warringah and I hadn't seen the other side. If I was going to make a move it had to be then. If I hadn't gone I always would have wondered what it would have been like in another club, and questioned if I could have gained top representative honours. No matter what my motives were, I knew any move would certainly be questioned and I was worried about losing some valuable friendships. It was only after some long and difficult discussions with family and friends that I decided to take the opportunity.

As it turned out, I believe it was the right decision. Although I didn't achieve my aim to play for Australia during my time at Eastwood, it opened up a new dimension in my life which I would have never experienced had I not made the change.

Macqueen decided to commit himself for one year only. He fitted in well at Eastwood and became a regular in the first grade side. Both he and Liz enjoyed the social life. They developed a number of strong lifelong friendships, which he believed was an important and enjoyable part of playing rugby. It was here that he first met the three young players who he would later recruit for surfboat rowing—Barry Cox, and brothers Scott and Angus Reid. This was Coxie's first introduction to Macqueen and they quickly developed the friendship which strengthened in the surf lifesaving movement. They shared a similar, quiet sense of humour and a love of practical jokes. On the playing field it was a different matter. He remembers Macqueen as a strong and committed player, someone who could always be relied upon when the going got tough.

'He played the game really hard and probably a bit rough, but I don't know of anyone from that time who didn't respect him or like him. As hard a man as he was, there was never any hatred. There was no malice in what he did and people respected him for that.'

During the season Macqueen learnt a great deal playing alongside state and national representative players. The club had a professional attitude and he more than held his own playing at a higher level. But despite his strong performance, and selection once again in the Sydney team, higher representative honours eluded him. Although he had thoroughly enjoyed his time at Eastwood, he decided to abide by his original decision to make it a commitment for one year only.

The news of his return to Warringah was welcomed by everyone, especially coach John Francis, who was happy to forgive his sudden disappearance twelve months before. According to Francis, Macqueen had been sorely missed, not just because of his playing ability but because of the influence he had on teammates. 'Rod was a quietly spoken guy who had the ability and willingness to help any of the other club members, irrespective of their playing standard. On the paddock he was an excellent leader and immediately made his presence felt.'

With the recruitment of several experienced players from other clubs, Warringah established itself as a stronger, more competitive outfit. But the changes continued. Because of family and business reasons John Francis retired at the end of the year and once again Macqueen took it upon himself to find a replacement and to tackle another problem: team performances had continued to improve but there was still something missing. Players had become more dedicated and committed to the club but there was not much recognition in return. It was a situation Macqueen had encountered before in the surf club and he took a similar course of action. Warringah was a club with a history dating back only thirteen years but its achievements still deserved to be recognised. He was prompted into action when Paul Booth retired. Although Boothie had played well over one hundred first grade games, there was no record of his achievement, and subsequently no recognition.

Macqueen outlined his concerns in a detailed letter to the club secretary. He said it appeared no attempt was being made to establish 'tradition and team spirit', elements which he believed were essential to promote performance on the field and an overall 'will to win' attitude. He suggested the clubhouse be decorated with team photos and plaques recognising award winners and representative players; he pointed out that accurate records were not being kept of the number of games being played by individuals. Subsequently there was no honour board to show who had reached the revered milestone of one hundred games or more. Macqueen pulled no punches, saying former players were upset at the lack of recognition and contribution and were dropping out of all club activities: 'While the committees have been effectively active in most club functions they have neglected to communicate with, or look after, the players themselves.'

The response was swift and appropriate. A group of officials ventured into the NSW Rugby Union headquarters to research game and player details. Old and new photographs were enlarged, framed and hung on the clubhouse walls. Sponsors were organised to provide impressive wooden display panels that soon boasted the names of player details in traditional gold lettering.

To me the clubhouse always looked empty. The Warringah Rugby Club already had a growing tradition and it deserved to be on show for all to see and share. Having memorabilia and club records on display gave the place 'soul'. Something you were proud to be part of. It gave young players an extra purpose to achieve so that one day they too would form part of the club's tradition.

Loyalties tested

By now, at the age of twenty-seven, Macqueen was a partner in the company he had bought from his father and well knew the importance of leadership. Still looking for a new first grade coach, he approached the coach of their nearest neighbours and fierce rivals, Manly.

The Manly coach happened to be a teammate in the Barbarian side, none other than Slaggy Miller, the legendary Wallaby warhorse, who several years earlier had made it plain to Macqueen he believed a smashed knee was just punishment for scoring a selfish try. Slaggy was initially reluctant to leave his club and take over leadership of the young rival side. Some members of the Warringah committee were also reticent about embracing a traditional foe. However, political infighting at the Manly club made Slaggy's position untenable and he decided not to reapply for the top coaching job. He was suddenly free to take up any new challenges in the game to which he had devoted most of his life. Further encouragement came from Warringah president Bill Simpson, himself a former Manly player and who many years before had actually coached Slaggy in junior football. After several more formal discussions Slaggy and the Warringah committee soon reached an amicable agreement.

With his imposing physical presence and likeable personality, Slaggy had an immediate impact. When training began in late summer the Warringah players often found themselves struggling to keep up with a coach almost twice their age. They were being led, rather than pushed, to a higher level. But as summer drifted into winter and the surf lifesaving season finished, Macqueen was confronted by an unexpected dilemma. For the first time ever there was conflict between his two sporting passions. His friend and rowing partner Barry Cox would agree to remain with the boat crew only if Macqueen rejoined him at the Eastwood Rugby Club. Once more he was torn between loyalties. But he was determined to keep the successful rowing crew together and so he eventually returned to Eastwood.

United by dignity

The season began badly for Warringah. One of their early games ended in total demolition by a low-placed team they expected to beat easily. Newspaper reporters quickly flooded the change room. Several key players had played appallingly and they wanted to know why. Would they be dropped? Would there be mass sackings? Were enough Warringah players good enough to play first division quality football?

I have never forgotten that morning, waking up in bed and reading the Sunday papers. The headlines read, 'Warringah sinks to a new low'. Warringah had just lost to the worst side in the competition. Someone of Slaggy's standing in the rugby community could easily and justifiably have distanced himself from the result by saying, 'They played very badly.'

Instead he said, 'We didn't play well but we will be putting a great deal of time into seeing that we improve.' It was a simple twist of words yet a significant one and a defining moment in the history of the club. Slaggy had given his name and soul. With it came dignity, pride and character. This attitude was the catalyst of the future, and I have attempted to apply it in most things I have done, whether in general life, business or sport. We work together as a team. We achieve together as a team. We lose together as a team. The 'we' or 'they' option taken by an individual at crucial times can often be a telling insight into their character.

And so, the next season Macqueen was back at his 'rugby home' under the uncompromising guidance of the respected Wallaby veteran. The pair had a lot in common. For a start they had the same attitude to commitment. Put in one hundred per cent every time or don't bother turning up. When Slaggy barked instructions, players jumped. There was no grumbling or argument. Likewise the importance of team spirit, and having pride in the club jumper, in yourself and fellow players. There was no place for shirking or hiding on the field. If play got violent the call was, 'One in, all in'. God help any player who didn't give his all or support his mates.

With Slaggy in charge a new steel emerged in the Warringah club. Warringah rapidly climbed the ranks with Macqueen still leading by example. No longer the easybeats of the competition, the club enjoyed record crowds as the first grade side challenged to make the semi-finals. At last Warringah came of age when, in 1982, Slaggy Miller coached his team into the grand final. Victory would not be theirs but the club was now an established and respected force in the Sydney competition.

Knowing the time

Sadly, Macqueen wasn't playing in the side. The previous year, at the age of thirty-one, he had announced his retirement. Because of his numerous achievements it was perhaps fitting that he was the last remaining player from the original Warringah first division side.

I had now been playing rugby for over twenty years. It was a hard decision to make but when I felt I was no longer capable of competing at the top level I knew, that for me, it was time to stop playing. I had achieved all I possibly could as a player and rather than keep playing socially in the lower grades I thought it wiser to bow out. My playing days with rugby were extremely rewarding. Both on and off the field I have made lifelong friendships and gained the special camaraderie of a team sport. The only regret that I carry with me to this day is that I concentrated too much on the physical side rather than working more on developing my skills when I had the opportunity in my younger years.

During his career Macqueen had played more than two hundred first grade games. With Warringah he captained the first grade for five years, won the team Best and Fairest award on four occasions and served as club captain. His representative career also saw him play for the Australian Possible/Probables and the Australian Barbarians and Sydney.

While welcoming the decision, Liz was quietly sceptical. She knew her husband only too well and wondered what new challenges he would undertake. He was still committed to rowing with Collaroy during the summer months, and his business was demanding more and more time. But she had every reason to have doubts. While his business was expanding rapidly it had always been intertwined with his two main sporting pursuits. Over the years rugby, rowing and business had seemed to inexplicably merge into one highly charged successful entity. Would it be the same with one of the key ingredients missing?

Chapter 7

Work and Play

Back in 1968, the question of whether the eighteen-year-old Rod Macqueen would become successful at advertising each shiny new range of sewing machines had become academic. After eighteen months at Empisal, a position had become available for a young designer in the Macqueen family company, Exhibition Displays. Ian Macqueen had invited his son to join the company and placed him under the guidance of his business partner, a commerical artist; at the same time he was studying commercial art three nights a week. Being on the bottom rung of the ladder once again meant running errands and making deliveries across the city, which took him away from the creative area.

It was a difficult decision for me to change my direction at that stage, because at Empisal I had progressed to a position where I was able to use my own creativity and be quite independent. However I knew to further my ambitions I'd have to make the change. Once at Exhibition Displays, I realised the expected standards were much higher than I had been used to. This effectively meant that no matter how much I achieved it didn't seem to be good enough. At times this was very depressing but in the long run it turned out to be very beneficial because it lifted my work ethic and made me more determined.

I realised Dad was also aware of the potential disruption my working there could have in the workplace. He made sure that he was never directly involved in my work and it was quite clear to me that if I was going to progress I'd be doing so on my own merits.

Business friends

Later, when given the opportunity in the design area of the company, Macqueen's natural creativity flourished.

A few years after he joined the company, another position became available, this time requiring bookkeeping and marketing experience. On Rod's recommendation, and after some interviews, they took on a young insurance executive already familiar to those in the office, Paul Booth.

A major turning point arrived for Macqueen some years later when the opportunity arose for the company to diversify. They received an opportunity to move into the warehousing and delivery of merchandise to fill the display fixtures they'd been making for a major oil company.

When the company split in two Macqueen was keen to continue and expand the current side of the business and so he and Booth bought that division. Ian Macqueen who was now running the new division called 'Stentor' was delighted with this decision. Like other senior people in the industry he was impressed by a confident display of young, natural talent. His son was already highly regarded not just for artistic creativity, but the ability to come up with radical new concepts in design. He displayed a regular source of lateral thinking which overcame everyday constraints and stumbling blocks in a business where companies too often recycled their same tired ideas or fed off those of the opposition.

Now settled into married life with Liz, perhaps this was the time for an energetic young man to put aside the many distractions of a hectic sporting life and concentrate solely on developing his own business.

Then again, perhaps not. The new head of Exhibition Displays needed something else—additional staff. When the time came for a salesman the first person Macqueen hired was another football friend who also happened to row in a rival surfboat crew. Ed Ifould had worked in several jobs but from Macqueen's early observations could sell anything to anybody, and was an extremely dedicated and hard worker. To help the company expand, Macqueen also needed a financial advisor. John Ogilvie was consulting to him at the time and Macqueen suggested that he join the company. While they were playing rugby together, Ogilvie had progressed from being a young accountant to the position of a troubleshooting auditor with an international company.

Perhaps to outsiders it appeared that I was hiring my mates because I would be more comfortable working with people I knew and with whom I could have some fun. That wasn't the case.

Even though I seemed to be ignoring the conventional wisdom that 'there are no friends in business', I knew these people well and the specific attributes and qualities they had to offer. Each one had different strengths and skills that complemented the others. I also knew them well enough to know they were good team men who got on well together. These combinations resulted in a great problem-solving unit that for the most part worked smoothly throughout all facets of the business. Admittedly having friends in your own business doesn't always work—when something goes wrong you can also lose a lifelong friend. There can also be other drawbacks, because when you are faced with a major decision you can be caught between your emotion and reality.

All four became partners in the company, which slowly expanded against hefty competition. This unique combination of sporting people coming together rocketed the company to new heights. Nor were their individual sporting activities curtailed. Rugby and rowing were the main topics of office conversation. Training and competition commitments were not just fitted in but integrated into business planning. It seemed every problem could be overcome by their individual talent, hard work, and the common bond of mateship, which helped them to open up new opportunities.

Macqueen drew not only associates from the sporting arena but much more besides. Key principles and tactics became interchangeable, then almost imperceptibly blended, as he instinctively created a formula for success. As in sport, here again he was the undisputed leader, his competitive nature dragging others along with him. He showed a remarkable ability to be able to read people and then motivate them. He treated people differently, depending on their personalities, strengths, weaknesses, fears and foibles. If there was a setback he would lift himself up and improve his own performance next time round. Those about him automatically followed. Macqueen didn't make a fuss about what he was doing to try and incite others into action. He didn't have to. It was just like a football team or boat crew working together for success. They had different attributes but the same team spirit, the same team ethos and the will to succeed.

Macqueen provided the extra drive and the vision to bring it all together. It was this ability to look forward and see the big picture that, according to John Ogilvie, pushed their small company forward. 'Rod always seemed to know what had to be done. If he couldn't see a solution to a problem he'd seek out someone who did or someone who could find out. Then it was he who would put it into practice.'

Right from the beginning the team of four didn't sit back with an executive style, but kept a 'hands on' approach. If there was manual work to be done late at night or on weekends everyone pitched in, from loading and carrying raw materials to bolting together exhibitions in deserted show pavilions in the early hours of the morning. If a job was struggling to reach completion it was a familiar story—one in all in. It was a formula that worked, and the company continued to grow. The business world looked on with admiration and amazement at what these sporting people had achieved.

It was becoming obvious to me that there was no difference between everyday life, sport or business. The same philosophies applied and the more I compared and integrated what I had learnt between the three, the more problems we were solving and the more successful we were. The similarity between the workings of a rugby side and a business were strong. A rugby team comprises the same ingredients as any business, and the key to success in both is bringing these different elements together and uniting them to a common cause. I found that to obtain harmony each element needed to respect the role played by the other members and to some extent also understand their role. The team should always come first. Treating one section or person more favourably than others can lead to internal division and ultimate failure.

Behind the goalposts

Like any business things didn't always go well. During some of these times they still found rugby analogies useful. When they were sitting around in a boardroom confronted by a major problem, a depressing situation could be turned into a positive.

One simple phrase could break the feeling of gloom around the boardroom table. Since our promotion to first division, we were experiencing many losses and after tries had been scored against us we became used to standing behind our goal line. Each time we stood there we would talk about what we had to do to get back into the game. It was exactly the same feeling when we had a major problem at work. We'd look at each other and say, 'Well, we're behind the goalposts again. There's nothing for it but to go back out and get stuck into it.' We knew there was always time, always a chance, to do something to sort it out and fix it, and inevitably we did.

The 80–20 principle

By now Exhibition Displays was an established and successful company but everything changed when Macqueen commissioned a facilitator and called a management meeting to discuss future directions. The meeting was a revelation when it became obvious that most of their capital was tied up in designing and staging exhibitions. However, their most lucrative source of income was in point of sale merchandising, the design and manufacturing of product display units. Macqueen knew the ramifications.

We knew we had to change direction to make the most of our limited resources. It was amazing to think we had been working together in the business for almost four years without really understanding what our business was all about. By sitting down and analysing all aspects, it was clear that our strengths and consequently our profits lay in our creative merchandising ability. The exhibition side of our business was highly labour-intensive, mainly 'one off' situations taking up the majority of our time. It was a classic example of the 80–20 business principle: too much effort for too little return. We had to redefine the equation by ensuring we allocated 80 per cent of our resources to the 20 per cent that was the most profitable. The easy thing was identifying the situation and acknowledging it, the hard thing was making the decision to make the necessary changes.

The next day Macqueen reluctantly walked into the boardroom of their largest client and announced they would no longer be able to handle the account. He felt strange, a mixture of uncertainty and expectation, as he watched the stunned looks on the faces in front of him. The account, worth well in excess of one million dollars a year, involved designing and setting up exhibitions all over Australia. Although their client was a large multinational company, their research showed the profit return was minimal. The account simply wasn't worth the effort.

Instead, they steadily built a client base that included international household names such as Revlon, Qantas, Taubmans and Wedgwood.

Macqueen was the creative drive behind their success. He had the vision required to satisfy the client and indeed the vision to improve on it. After taking the brief he would start with rough pencil sketches, which became detailed plans to scale, then full mock-up display units. He insisted on perfection. Their talented in-house craftsmen were driven to distraction building dummy units out of virtually any material they could find to ensure the prototype emulated the promised design. Paul Booth says he was constantly amused by the surprised reaction from company representatives. 'A team of marketing executives would walk into our boardroom for a presentation and be completely dumbfounded. They often thought we had gone into full production making the special, expensive, moulded plastic components. But the extra trouble certainly paid off when it came to winning contracts.'

What happens next

Fired by enthusiasm, the company continued to surge ahead. Macqueen was the creative mainstay, conjuring up concepts and thinking three or four steps ahead of clients, and his partners. During casual discussions with potential clients in the boardroom he would suddenly produce detailed sketches of products about which they themselves had only a vague idea, if any. According to Ogilvie, people were constantly amazed at the variety of ideas and especially the detail. 'Not many people can think three dimensionally. Rod could visualise a product in every minute detail and then reproduce it on paper in minutes. He was far ahead of everyone else and they had trouble keeping up.'

Macqueen was instinctively applying principles he would only read and 'learn' many years later when studying a wide variety of texts on business principles and motivation.

In any decisions I make I always ask the question, 'What happens next?'. This usually opens up many different opportunities and often leads to unexpected solutions and results. It can often highlight possible problems which can be addressed and solved before they are actually created. It's a catchcry that I apply on a daily basis to every situation and problem I am faced with. In looking back I am sure many of the correct decisions I have made started from asking the simple question, 'What happens next?'

Funny business

To clients, the new EDs—as Exhibition Displays had come to be known—looked exactly what it was: a creative, professional young company on the move. It was also a company run by a group of young men still zealously involved in rugby and surfboat rowing, still enjoying the camaraderie and sometimes crazy antics that were part of the competitive sporting life.

The constant pressure of an increased workload and longer hours was relieved by a seemingly endless round of practical jokes between the four partners. Paul Booth probably suffered the most. He had a mice phobia, which the others played on constantly for amusement. Unfortunately for Boothie, regular infestations of mice in the different storage areas provided a ready source of ammunition, especially for Macqueen whose pranks became more and more inventive as Boothie became more and more cautious. One day a courier arrived with an express parcel requiring his signature. It was obviously important. When he opened the long narrow cylinder he was horrified when a small mouse jumped into his lap. By then Boothie believed every possible trick had been tried.

Macqueen pleads innocence to that prank, claiming he wouldn't subject a mouse to such a frightening experience. However, other stunts bore the hallmark of a distinctive, creative mind and were harder to disown.

What do you do if you sit down at your desk and see a small wooden lever attached to one side bearing a note saying, 'Pull me'? After looking around for any possible consequences each partner in the business eventually did just that. They were immediately hit in the chest by a raw egg that had been suspended from the ceiling on a loop of superfine nylon thread. A Macqueen special! The pranks continued back and forth as each tried to square up with the other. Fortunately, the female employees were all noted for their own good sense of humour, and always appreciated the fun. However, they were also clever enough to stay away from the boardroom where some of the more dangerous activities occurred.

As the business grew and became more intense so too did the regular meetings in the boardroom. Sometimes they were too intense for Macqueen's liking. To lighten the moment he would occasionally disappear and suddenly return with a fire extinguisher. The amazing scene that followed was a room of white foamy bodies, yelling and abusing their attacker as they ran for cover behind upturned chairs. The sequel came after an inspection by the local fire brigade captain who then demanded to see the managing director. He warned that most of the extinguishers in the building were half empty and demanded to find out who was playing silly games.

In the presence of a bemused receptionist an embarrassed Macqueen promised personally to find who was responsible and deal with them. The receptionist duly made out an 'action' reminder for his diary.

Macqueen remains a strong advocate of encouraging a certain amount of fun. Early in his career, he went for a routine medical check with his insurance company. If he had been looking for more than just a physical check-up Macqueen couldn't have gone to a better person. By some strange twist of fate he entered the consulting room of someone far more qualified than most to make judgements about the real importance of life. Then in his early sixties, Dr Rowland Richards, 'Please call me Rowley', had already been an inspiration to many through words and deeds. In his mid-twenties he was serving as a doctor in the Australian Army in World War II when captured by the Japanese and sent to the Changi prisoner-of-war camp. He spent three-and-a-half years helping others in horrific conditions, including time on the infamous Burma Railway. Eventually Rowley and other survivors from the camp were loaded onto a Japanese freighter headed for Japan, only to be torpedoed by an Allied submarine. Along with a lucky few he was rescued by another Japanese vessel and eventually spent the last twelve months of the war incarcerated in Japan. Around the time he gave advice to Macqueen he accepted the position of honorary medical director of Sydney's famous 'City to Surf' fun run and became a prominent identity promoting better community health standards.

During one of my routine check-ups Rowley Richards casually asked me if I was enjoying my work. My answer was yes, but I was curious to know why he had asked the question. He explained that the majority of his patients didn't enjoy their work, and many of them had stress-related symptoms. He said that 60 per cent of your life is dedicated to work and therefore you should enjoy what you are doing. If you're not then you should change jobs. It was something that really hit home to me. Remembering the friendly atmosphere in my Aunt June's office and the comments made by Dr Rowley Richards, I became much more conscious of the need to enjoy my work and, in turn, to encourage others to enjoy theirs.

I've generally found that in a more relaxed atmosphere you are able to bounce thoughts off each other more constructively, resulting in better decision-making and more innovative ideas. Therefore, whenever the meetings became intense, I would try to find something new to diffuse the tension and sometimes the best way to do it was the unorthodox and unexpected.

But it wasn't all fun and games. The company quickly developed as more and more creative designs and innovations became their trade. Clients were greeted and treated in a courteous and professional manner. No trouble or expense was spared to ensure that advantage was taken of every business opportunity. In fact clients well remember the thorough, professional approach, even during the early days. The unusually friendly, high-spirited relationship between staff was also often noted, and admired.

Lateral concepts

When the chance came to pick up a large contract with Revlon, Macqueen knew the project was a big challenge for their small company. He decided to bid for it anyway, it was not in his nature to let something like this pass by. The giant multinational cosmetics firm wanted something special—a presentation unit that would give them dominance in a crowded marketplace. In the words of the trade it meant, 'Owning your piece of real estate within a store'. What they were presented with was certainly something special, and EDs won the contract.

To oversee the commencement of the program, Revlon New York sent over one of their top marketing executives to work with Macqueen. To the surprise of all concerned, the two men from totally different backgrounds developed a close working relationship. Together they bounced ideas off each other and within two weeks came up with a design that was totally revolutionary.

The units were an immediate success and helped consolidate Revlon as the leader in cosmetics. The design was so advanced that now, more than twenty years later, many of the original models, although now upgraded, are still in place. Determined to repeat the

A fast synchronised entry into the boat required constant practice.
The Collaroy boat crew in action.

Timing the row out through big seas is crucial.

Surfboat rowing is not for the faint of heart.
The Collaroy boat crew about to be engulfed.

The original boat crew receiving their first open state medal in 1977.
Barry Cox, Paul Booth, Rod Macqueen, Peter Bott, John Brown.

The Collaroy boat crew representing Manly Warringah at the branch championships, 1978. The crew had mixed feelings about wearing the traditional lifesaving costumes to compete in the march past.

Barry Cox, John Brown, Paul Booth (rear) Peter Bott and Rod Macqueen (front).

Boat crew in Hawaii World Championships.
Fun always remained an important ingredient for Macqueen and his teammates.
Rod Macqueen, Angus Reid, Scott Reid, Craig Cunningham, Brendan Mockford.

The Collaroy Boat Crew with new member Steve Scott receive their
first-place medals at the 1984 NSW State Titles.

The state surf team, outfitting themselves in old clothes, forged new bonds.
Victoria, 1977.

The Collaroy crew receiving their gold medals at the Australian Masters Championship
in 1990, less than twelve months after Macqueen survived a life-threatening operation to
remove a tumour close to his brain.

The final game.

Rod leads Warringah out for the last time at Manly oval, 1981.

Taking over as Warringah coach in 1986 from good friend and Wallaby legend Tony 'Slaggy' Miller, who put standards and dignity above all else.

A media interview in the dressing sheds after winning the club championship in 1988. Rod Macqueen, Jim Webster, Peter Jenkins.

The chefs at Exhibition Display's famous barbecues.

Clarrie Cox, Rod Macqueen, Paul Booth.

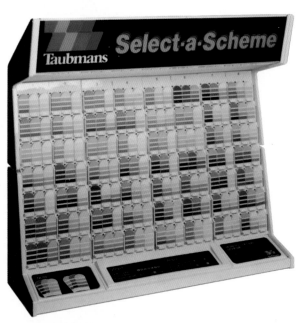

The Taubmans' Select-a-Scheme: Macqueen's computerised answer to colour co-ordination.

Macqueen's winning entry in the *Sunday Telegraph* competition in 1983.

same success overseas, Revlon sent Macqueen to South Africa and the UK to oversee the production of similar designs. It was a stunning recognition of his creative talents. Particularly impressed was the then deputy managing director of Revlon in Australia, Paul Cummings. Although on the surface he appeared to be dealing with a bunch of surf club guys having a good time he recognised a refreshing, innovative line of thought. In his mind Macqueen stood out. 'He was incredibly focused and was immediately tossing forward original thoughts and concepts. He showed discipline and the constant desire to get every detail exactly right. I'm sure we would have accepted a much earlier model if he hadn't persevered striving for the best. He showed a tremendous vision and thought outside the square to come up with the final concept.'

Paul Cummings, who is now the managing director of Hanimex, continued to follow Macqueen's career with interest.

Selecting the colour scheme for painting a house can be a nightmare, not only for the householder but also the long-suffering paint salesperson in the local hardware store. The Taubmans paint company wanted a new display that would try to solve this age-old problem. Macqueen was given a brief to design a unit which manually offered colour combinations. However, he took it a step further and came up with a revolutionary concept: he mixed paint with electronics.

Macqueen devised the Taubmans-Selecta-Scheme which revolutionised the retail area of the paint industry. Consumers were able to look at an extensive wall display of matching and contrasting colour cards electronically coded to offer contrast, harmony and highlights at the press of a button. Macqueen designed the display and keyboard presentation then found a local computer programmer who made it all work. The rights to the design concept were bought by Taubmans and sold worldwide.

Even people in the hard-nosed world of advertising were taken aback by the radical concept. The television commercials advertising the display unit were produced by Mojo, one of the hottest Australian agencies of the time. The creative director, Doug Watson, describes Macqueen's concept as a marketing dream.

'I didn't know it was Rod's idea until we discussed it years later, but it certainly was a breakthrough. Then as now, paint is generally a generic product with only trust in the brand dictating market leadership. By creating Select-a-Scheme, Rod added style to the product without the manufacturer having to spend one additional cent on reformulation. The fact that this innovation came from someone only charged with building a display stand says a lot about Rod's mental processes.

'The computer system would be considered a kid's hobby piece today, but then it was extraordinary. Pick the wall colour, press a button and lights illuminate over matching, contrasting and complimentary colours. His idea was so hi-tech that it seemed like magic in the pre-home computer area.

'It was also unique that the merchandising idea actually wrote the commercial. As an average couple discussed colours, the walls changed hues and the skirting boards and ceiling tranformed to match. Oh, if only other less important domestic disputes could be settled so easily!

'I think the appeal of the Select-a-Scheme would still be huge today if only the manufacturer had maintained their support. Just drop by any paint store, visit the racks of paint brochures and you'll understand why Rod's idea was so ahead of its time *and still is.*'

The point of difference

Early in 1983 argument was raging over the Australian republican issue and whether the country should have a new flag. Sydney's *Daily Telegraph* newspaper ran a competition seeking designs for a new distinctive flag. Over several weeks thousands of entries flooded in from members of the public, offering a variety of colours, stars and native wildlife in some startling combinations. The winner was eventually decided by a public vote. First prize went to a design featuring a gold kangaroo in full stride accompanied by the stars of the Southern Cross set on a green background. The winner—Mr Rod Macqueen of Collaroy. Although his design was by far the most popular, the national referendum needed to change the country's flag was never held. If it had been, the future Australian rugby team may have been playing under a flag designed by their coach.

Whenever I had an idea, I always wanted to act on it immediately. I actually liked the design of the existing flag because it represented our heritage, a little like a surname. However, if a new flag was to be considered then I believed it should display things that were synonymous to Australia, in particular the Southern Cross and the kangaroo.

Fun and professionalism

Macqueen's ability to think differently also showed in other areas. An important part of most business is having a good social relationship with clients. Convivial lunches and dinners, often including Liz, established strong and lasting relationships. But sometimes it was a case of expect the unexpected, as the senior vice-president of another multinational company discovered when he arrived from New York. Keen to meet the young Australian team responsible for their innovative concepts, he inspected their small but well-appointed premises and was told they would all be dining at Sydney's best restaurant. After drinks in the board-room he was led out onto the balcony with distant ocean views. Without further explanation he was offered sausages stuffed with fresh oysters and cooked on a portable barbecue. At first he was dumbfounded, then slightly amused, and then, fortunately for the waiting staff, delighted. The team at EDs figured they were dealing with someone who constantly travelled the world staying in the best hotels and eating in all the best restaurants. They decided to try something different. It had the desired effect and EDs had secured another client.

The senior executives from all their client companies came to appreciate the offbeat humour and entertainment from the four partners. The company Christmas party soon became a must because it meant much more than standing around sipping drinks and having a polite chat. An invitation which said 'Join us dressed for a Xmas Cricket Game', meant the building's underground car park had been turned into a small playing field with a synthetic pitch, a mini-grand-stand and a members bar. Of course everyone had to join a team and play. A 'Xmas Beach Party', meant the car park was filled with twenty tonnes of sand and surrounded by plywood panels painted with beach scenes, while a 'German Xmas Party' meant the car park had been converted into a traditional beer hall complete with German brass band and a bar serving German beer in souvenir steins.

All the parties were remembered and talked about for months to come but the German event had the greatest impact thanks to the unusual invitations. Each invitation card was tied to a large and extremely odorous Bratwurst sausage. After upsetting the clean air of the delivery van, and spending time on the receptionist's desk, the sausage would make its way through the offices to the appropriate recipient leaving its smell in its wake. As usual it was Macqueen's idea, but even he didn't realise it would be such a success and still be talked about years later.

The designs, the parties, the decision-making, were all looked at in the same manner. In everything we did we always tried to think outside the square. If we were confronted with 'That's the way it is' the first question would always be, 'Why?'. If it had been done before, 'How could it be changed?'. If it hadn't been done before, 'Why couldn't it be done?'. It seems to me that there are always other ways of doing things. We are only ever restricted by our minds. I have always found that people are enthusiastic about new ideas, change and innovation. The more we incorporated this logic in everything we did, the more enthusiastic and exciting things became for everyone involved. I believe this way of thinking will always increase productivity and achievement.

Over a period of ten years EDs grew to employ more than fifty staff and boasted an annual turnover of close to ten million dollars. The company had developed a blue ribbon client list and was recognised as one of the most innovative and creative companies in the country.

The senior executives were no longer the wild young rowers and rugby players of the early years. But they had not changed much. Ifould and Booth were still committed to surf lifesaving, Ogilvie continued his involvement with Warringah Rugby, while Macqueen remained devoted to both sports. Through it all EDs continued to grow and prosper despite the numerous distractions which, Macqueen believes, probably maintained the balance of fun and professionalism.

The mixture of business and football coaching was to become the successful pattern of Rod Macqueen's future life. It began with some tough lessons on rugby politics.

Chapter 8

A Coach's Vision

Support and succeed

In 1985, at the age of thirty-five, Macqueen was still super fit, still rowing surfboats competitively and still heavily involved in rugby. He had returned to the Warringah ranks several years earlier, this time as a fitness trainer. It was an opportunity to stay in touch with the footballers and at the same time pass on the fitness skills which had brought success in his rowing career. At the request of club coach 'Slaggy' Miller, Macqueen stood for and accepted the position of second grade coach. At the very first selection meeting Macqueen saw a side to rugby he didn't know existed.

'Is everybody happy with tonight's selection decisions?' Slaggy Miller glared around the room, his brow furrowed and battered, waiting for an answer. When he received a general chorus of approval, the clatter and scraping of chairs signalled an automatic move to the bar. Macqueen was impressed with the way coaches from each grade readily agreed on the movement of players from one team to another. Any disagreement was usually settled quickly and amicably. The only really contentious decisions concerned the first and second grade, but here, the opinion of the softly spoken but formidable Slaggy generally went unchallenged. Of course, any movement of top players because of injury or change in form, resulted in a trickle-down effect to the lower grades, but this was inevitable and supposedly accepted. If only it were true. Within minutes of a selection meeting, private conversations would soon commence over a few beers. Many of the decisions so happily agreed to during the meeting were roundly condemned and individual coaches were criticised.

I must have been very naive at the time. I found it quite amazing that officials who had openly supported decisions during public discussion would later voice totally different opinions to their mates in private. I found it negative, disruptive and divisive. But that was my introduction to the politics of coaching. It's a good thing to be ambitious but to use undermining tactics to achieve advancement totally destroys the system. You're either part of a team or you're not. Once you're part of a team and you make decisions together you should support that decision. Everyone should aspire to reach higher levels and their actions should reflect this.

Personal goals can be achieved, and are more likely to be achieved, by being supportive of the system. People who can work within these boundaries as a team member should always be the first choice for higher honours.

As second grade coach, Macqueen put together his own management team of people he not only knew were capable but people he knew personally and could work with. He brought in John Ogilvie as coach of the backs. A good friend from surfboat rowing, Colin Scully, was appointed fitness trainer with a brief to devise a rigorous but innovative and interesting exercise program. The onerous position of team manager and assistant coach of forward play was allocated to Kevin Hitchcock (the author), with a brief that other retired first grade forwards should also make themselves available for additional support and to provide physical opposition during training sessions.

There was no shortage of volunteers and training often escalated into an aggressive ruck and maul contest between the young guns and the struggling, puffing old 'hard-heads'.

If we were going to put the time in, I decided it should be fun for all concerned. Both management and players developed a strong bond by joining together in the fitness and skills training. I also believed it was important to have a number of former senior players involved, not only to pass on their knowledge and experience, but to add a sense of tradition.

This concept of combining the old with the new to establish tradition would become a feature of his future coaching. Macqueen would expand it even further to help create new standards for the Wallabies.

Long-term thinking produces long-term success

With an increased level of fitness, a wide range of new attacking moves and plenty of enthusiasm, hopes were high for a place in the grand final. The team performed strongly throughout the year and just failed to reach their goal, being defeated in the final. It was the highest level ever reached by a second grade side even though they'd been disrupted by injuries and the shuffling of players to the higher grade. Macqueen always stressed the honour of being elevated to first grade, and was annoyed by the attitude of some lower grade coaches who complained when their key players were promoted. Near the end of the club competition selectors made a major tactical change by lifting the second grade five-eighth into firsts. It was the young player's first selection in the top side, something he'd been striving for since joining the club the previous year. After the selection meeting Macqueen went straight to his house to give him the news and offer his personal congratulations.

To be honest, losing my key play-maker going into the semi-finals hurt, but as it turned out it was the start of his representative career. Any club is judged by the performance of their top side and all the structures that are put in place should support that. Although there were five senior teams, with five separate coaches, I thought the goals should be to advance the prospects of the players and the club as a whole.

At the end of the season and after nine years as the club, coach Slaggy Miller stood aside. He had lifted the first grade side into its first grand final in 1982 and won the minor premiership in 1984. During his term Slaggy had brought greater strength and respectability to the club. Macqueen was then given the opportunity to take over his position. At a packed general meeting he was elected with a massive vote of support coming from players through all grades. Afterwards Miller offered his full support saying he would be happy to assist in any way possible. It was a typical response from a man who, although regarded as one of the toughest players in Australian rugby, was also widely respected as a true gentleman off the field by friend and foe alike.

Innovation is the fuel for going forward

Macqueen moved quickly. Only four days before Christmas, 1985, he called a special coaches' meeting in the single-storey brick club-house at Warringah. He presented them with a 'vision statement' of several pages divided into seven points. It outlined the philosophy he wanted adopted throughout all grades the following year. Macqueen already knew his plans would be readily accepted and implemented. The five coaches joining him were personally selected, and included old friends and playing colleagues, John Ogilvie and John Nolan. The most important part of Macqueen's vision for the club was consistency.

I suggested we put a system in place that would encourage all teams to use the same basic moves and tactics. The individual coaches, who would be part of developing this 'pattern of play', would then be encouraged to develop their own game plan based on this principle. This would allow for an easy transition between teams during the season where players are constantly moving around either due to injuries or the fact that they have improved and warrant promotion.

I also thought there needed to be more attention to teaching players the basic skills, to developing links between forwards and backs, and a formalisation of defensive and attacking patterns.

Putting all these pieces in place gave us a structure and a platform to start from. The fine line was making sure that it didn't impede innovation, individualism and spontaneity by the players and coaches.

It was also agreed that every team, including the colts, would have an assistant coach and manager as well as their own full-time conditioner and support runner. Every effort would be made to make the Warringah club as competitive as possible. The team of nine conditioners would be recruited by Brendan Mockford. Players would also be advised on diet and personal exercise. Special weight-training sessions would be arranged, at the nearby Collaroy Surf Club. Two sprint coaches would be available on training nights and, on match days, two physiotherapists on duty in the change rooms. Another Macqueen proposal was that players should receive up-to-date written information on all relevant matters, such as training times, trial matches, club policy and club goals for the season. All coaches also agreed to attend a two-day coaching seminar, recently set up by the NSW Rugby Union, in late January.

At the end of the meeting, they worked out a detailed program for skills training and conditioning which would start at the end of January, a month earlier than usual. Before adjourning there was a lengthy argument about a time and place for the last item on the program. It was another Macqueen innovation, one which he stressed was all-important—a golf day for the coaches.

The room was abuzz with ideas and enthusiasm. It was a professional business plan, the likes of which had almost certainly never been put to any local rugby club. Those present were surprised, despite the fact they had all either worked and or played rugby with Macqueen. They were familiar with his sometimes annoying search for perfection but even they were impressed by the amount of thought and attention to detail. Macqueen had suddenly raised the approach to winning a football competition to a whole new level. In fact, it was something he'd been considering for a while.

During all the competitions in which I'd been involved I always thought about how much better we could be, how we could give athletes the best possible preparation so they could perform to the utmost of their ability. To do this I needed to call on everything I'd learnt in business and sport to develop the structures I believed necessary to bring it about. As it turned out I knew a lot of people who had the type of skills we required. Others I sought out. Once we started to get organised the level of enthusiasm lifted and once this happened new ideas started coming.

An essential part of the Macqueen plan was his management team. Like the coaches, they were chosen not only because he thought they would be the best for the job but because each person was self-employed and therefore able to determine his own availability and level of commitment. John Ogilvie was again the assistant coach, Mockford was the conditioner and the team manager was another old friend, Bill James. To help with selection and offer an outside view on coaching methods he approached Barry Meredith, a former coach and stalwart of the northern suburbs club. Already knowing Macqueen, they should have realised this was not going to be a part-time tilt at success requiring only limited involvement. If they didn't they soon found out, as did everyone else involved with the club.

Without a goal you've got nothing to kick at

Senior players and colts turning up for their first training session under the new regime were surprised to receive a document entitled 'Warringah Rugby Club—Players' Manual 1986.' Macqueen had taken the seven-point plan and with the help of his management team had expanded it to produce a detailed 12-page players' guide. The first page was a letter from Macqueen beginning with the club's goal for the season: 'To Win the Club Championship'. While the performance of the first grade team would always be paramount, a serious attempt at winning the club championship could be mounted by performing well in all grade and colts' teams.

His message at the front of the manual went on to explain the philosophy discussed at the coaches' meeting. Players were urged to work hard in their own time, to overcome personal weaknesses and improve their strengths. His note concluded with a reminder that all players should make every effort to attend club social functions, stressing that club spirit was an important part of achieving any goal. Macqueen also pointed out what to many might seem obvious, but is often forgotten in grade rugby: 'The whole idea of rugby is to enjoy ourselves and this is easy to do if we are fit and winning games.'

The manual reflected Macqueen's approach to business—an insistence on meticulous planning. It was divided into sections covering all topics discussed at the coaches' meeting: conditioning and training; concentration and positive thinking; injury management; nutrition; advice on communicating personal problems to officials; and a tongue-in-cheek reminder to pay all fees on registration, or face the club secretary with an explanation. After carefully studying the document players knew they were expected to give a far more serious commitment to their sport than ever before. They also knew they would be receiving unprecedented professional support and advice in all areas.

Like a commander-in-chief preparing his army for war, Macqueen presented separate orders to his generals. Each coach was given a document of four pages detailing patterns of defence and attack, listing the field positions players should take up in any given situation, and outlining the different options players should take when moving up in defence or the lines and angles they should run when launching an attack. He stressed that the notes were guidelines only.

It was always much easier to outline my thoughts in writing. This showed me the step-by-step process I was taking to achieve a specific goal. It also gave me a basis to work from and improve on. If things remained the same for two successive years then we were not going forward at all. Having everything written down also gave the team members the necessary guidelines and a clear indication of what was expected and where we were going.

These guidelines were not intended to restrict a player's or coach's individuality. Rather, they were intended to create a common base of play for the club, on which all players and coaches could expand.

It was the first time I had produced any type of coaching manual but I saw it as a necessity in bringing the club together and to have a clearly defined goal. It's similar in business, where there is no point in a senior executive, or team of executives, working to a detailed plan if key staff are unaware of the goals and procedures.

It was also probably the first time that anyone had produced such a professional style of business plan for the game of rugby union. The vision and attention to detail would become the hallmark of Macqueen's future coaching career. It would be widely copied and adopted by others, but not until the advent of the professional era more than ten years later.

The club was looking to the future with a new confidence. Could anything else be done to improve their chances? With Rod Macqueen involved the answer would inevitably be yes.

Know your opposition

As the first grade players prepared to run out onto the pitch for the first game of the season a small group of spectators in the highest seats of the ground was being jostled to one side by a young man setting up the tripod for his video camera and small television monitor. He wasn't there to record the game for his own viewing pleasure. He was recording the match for later analysis—this match and every other game for the rest of the season. On the other side of town another cameraman was also setting up his equipment. He was about to record the performance of the team scheduled to play Warringah the following week. Both tapes would be delivered to Macqueen's home early the next morning ready to be played, replayed and dissected in time for the first training session the following week. In 1986, when home video cameras were still a novelty, going to the trouble and expense of recording your team's performance was regarded as an interesting innovation. Recording the performance of next week's opposition was seen as being 'a bit serious' or even eccentric. After all this was rugby, the gentleman's game, a game for amateurs. Not for Macqueen. As in business, he wanted to know all the strengths and weaknesses of his own team and those of the enemy.

Interestingly enough Macqueen's appointment of John Nolan as second grade coach had been somewhat contentious. Although recognised as a very good player, unlike other candidates he had no coaching experience whatsoever, not even with junior sides. But Macqueen's typical logic was that, because Nolan was a successful businessman, he would combine those attributes with his playing experience to success-fully guide a football side; Macqueen also quietly sought information from his old friend and teammate regarding player relations off the paddock. At the time Nolan was managing a large manufacturing complex. He remembers long and involved discussions with Macqueen over his handling of industrial relations.

'Macca was very interested in man-management. He constantly wanted to know how we resolved disputes and kept people working together in a constructive environment. In an industrial situation it was important that the goals and objectives of the organisation were clearly understood by all parties. Issues that arose could generally be resolved without conflict and in a manner that strengthened the organisation. Outright confrontation, with its potential to destabilise, was a last resort.

This philosophy was reflected in Macqueen's handling of conflict between players or with club administration.

Sometimes you lose short term to gain long term

With the Macqueen innovations in place, team performances through-out the grades lifted noticeably. However, the ultimate prize of reaching the first grade grand final remained elusive. Their all-round style of play improved and at different times during the year they defeated all the other top teams. But by the end of the season they were inconsistent and finished a disappointing fifth, just failing to make the semi-finals. However, successes throughout the rest of the club proved the new united approach was having the desired effect and at the end of the season, rugby followers throughout Sydney were surprised to see the 'new look' Warringah had come a close second in the Club Championship, narrowly failing to topple the Randwick club. The most pleasing result was an unexpected premiership victory for the second grade. If there were still any doubts about John Nolan's businesslike approach to coaching they were effectively drowned by the team's noisy celebration.

Club officials were pleased with the result, making special mention of the consistent coaching policies throughout the grades, and reappointed Macqueen for the following season.

It was very pleasing and encouraging to me to see that the new structures had produced results, but I was also inwardly frustrated by the inconsistency at the end of the season. Losses to lower-placed sides we had expected to beat easily had cost us dearly.

Obviously I was disappointed with the fifth placing, but on reflection the major focus and long-term goal was to win the Club Championship. The effect this focus had on the entire club was extremely encouraging. Across the board we improved 75 per cent in our overall standing. Sometimes some of the most significant things are missed because they are less obvious. In fact what had happened was that the skills throughout the club had lifted, giving us greater player depth and potential for the future. It was with this in mind that I realised the need to stress the importance of the big picture, winning the Club Championship. I decided to make this a personal quest for each and every player.

Focus and passion

As the young third grade breakaway pushed his chair back and slowly rose to his feet, the general chatter in the packed Warringah clubhouse stuttered to a halt. The room full of players and officials listened intently as the young man began a short nervous speech: 'I'd like to win the Club Championship because it would mean other clubs would have more respect for us when we run onto the field,' he said. As he continued, there were several hidden smiles in the crowd, and the odd muffled laugh, but the majority of those present were attentive and appreciative. They knew it could be their turn next week. This was another Macqueen innovation: after training on Thursday nights all players were asked to gather in the clubhouse where one would be chosen at random to stand up and say what winning the championship meant to him. Given only fifteen or twenty minutes' notice, some of the speeches were short and stilted, others were passionate and inspiring. On the wall behind each speaker was a huge whiteboard which would carry the details of all points accrued by the club during the season.

The initiative had the desired effect. All players were soon very much aware of the importance of striving for the goal, and many, particularly in the lower and junior ranks, were taking their football far more seriously than ever before. As an exercise in focusing attention and performance the idea was an outstanding success. It gave many players a new perspective on the club as a whole. Everyone was involved, from the first graders right down to the fourth grade colts. It brought everyone together and the camaraderie it developed was exceptional. The club had a new life.

Away from the long hours and high pressure of coaching and running his business Macqueen showed a different side to his own life. Quiet days or weekends with family and close friends often brought out another side of the otherwise highly charged authority figure. During the football season he took the opportunity to spend several days at a friend's holiday house at Tea Gardens on the mid north coast of NSW. After dinner, with the children in bed, the adults sat around on the floor sharing jokes and after dinner drinks. Macqueen unexpectedly picked up an old battered guitar and began playing, quite badly. Jokes about his lack of musical skill flew thick and fast and continued as he began singing 'Mull of Kintyre', the popular Beatles ballad which was one of his favourite tunes. As the laughter and joking gradually subsided, everyone in the room slowly realised Macqueen was genuinely lost in the haunting melody and lyrics which evoked images of distant mountains, green valleys and of course the romantic mist which rolled in from the sea. Soon everyone joined in. They sang 'Mull of Kintyre' spontaneously over and over again until everyone discovered the same feeling of peace and serenity that Macqueen obviously had.

Doing simple things perfectly

At the beginning of the next season, every player was again given a manual, similar to the previous year's, but in a much expanded form.

At the start of the manual, Macqueen reminded players of their goals.

It was important that we consolidated and developed the patterns and guidelines that were initiated the previous year. The more I got involved in the upper levels of rugby the more it became obvious to me that the simple things were the most important. In this case winning the ball. Quite simply, if you've got the ball how can the opposition win? I tried then to take it a step further by developing drills that taught players skills on how to retain possession. Like the 80–20 business principle I'd used with my business, I realised we were spending too much of our precious training time on what I regarded to be the 80 per cent trivial part of the game. We needed to develop our skills to win possession and more importantly retain it.

This was an important insight into a game that was traditionally dominated by clubs with recognised superior players. There were other ways to win. Macqueen also believed that success on the field would only come if player bonding and team spirit were continually boosted. He also recognised the need for a Players' Committee to assist in the organisation of social activities including the club ball, presentation night, after game functions and social outings. Its primary aim would be to instil and maintain the 'Warringah Spirit' throughout the season. Macqueen knew it was imperative to keep the momentum going if their major goals were to be achieved. Improvements and adjustments to the coaching program were one thing but he also wanted to further the feeling of unity and sense of a common purpose. It was a technique he already used in business and one he would use extensively when coaching in the years to come.

Rats of Tobruk

Rod Macqueen added something else to help boost morale—a new club song. The father of one of the players, Doug Leslie, had served during World War II with the Australian Army 9th Division known as the 'Desert Rats'. He compared the courage of the Warringah team to that shown by his comrades. Macqueen helped write lyrics inspired by the exploits of the Australian troops who became famous as the 'Rats of Tobruk' defending the North African seaport of Tobruk against overwhelming odds. With the help of good friend Kent Sheldon, an advertising executive, Macqueen arranged for a professional recording and presented the finished song to the club president. It was another addition to the spirit and emotional mix he thought was required to give the club a united purpose.

Soon there was a string of crushing victories against all the leading clubs. Warringah officials acknowledged the new professional business approach was taking effect. Players were moving smoothly from one grade to the next in an atmosphere of unity and cooperation.

The booby prize for audience motivation

Not all Macqueen's initiatives were successful. One day he brought in a training film that was meant to depict the coming together of different groups to achieve success. Macqueen brought all the players into one room and then without explanation rolled the tape. The video showed the different sections of an orchestra coming to rehearsals in everyday clothes. They tuned up and played in groups of individual instruments, practising for opening night. The big day eventually arrived. All clothed in evening wear, the musicians at last began playing together. The haunting strains of Ravel's classic orchestral piece 'Bolero' slowly filled the room as the different sections of the orchestra slowly joined in one after another. Each group of instruments added a new strength and quality until at last they were united, complementing each other in a powerful booming crescendo which shook the room. When the tape finished Macqueen switched on the lights and waited for a reaction.

There was silence. I was very pleased with myself and I thought the video brought the message across well. It displayed simply and vividly how vastly different cultures could be brought together for a common purpose. I thought there was an obvious comparison to how the varied skills of different cultures and elements of the team could combine to produce a powerful force. Looking around the room I could see enthusiasm from some of the forwards. I walked over and asked them what they learnt from the presentation. One of the older forwards, Steve Temple, looked up and with a big grin on his face said words to the effect, 'The blonde woman playing the violin had extremely attractive breasts.' As you can imagine that brought a riotous end to proceedings.

I learnt that at times it is better to be more direct in trying to get a message across.

Combined commitment conquers challenges

Successes continued as the season progressed. With four matches remaining in the competition the atmosphere in the club was electric. Warringah first grade were equal leaders, and the 'Green Rats' had an almost unbeatable lead in the Club Championship. Leading media commentators were looking for reasons behind the Warringah success story. Most pinpointed the Macqueen policy of insisting the same pattern of play be followed through all grades. In his regular newspaper column, former Wallaby Mark Ella went further, praising the style of play: 'In his second year at the helm Macqueen has turned the club into a formidable and consistent outfit. He has blended one of the best packs in the competition with an adventurous backline, with speed to burn.'

With one game remaining, Macqueen walked to the centre of the clubhouse and was almost flattened by a wave of ecstatic players and officials. Results just tallied showed Warringah first grade was unbeatable as minor premiers, and a strong performance through all grades had clinched the Club Championship. After fifteen years in the top division the club had finally come of age. The party was on. Some still have vivid memories of the biggest and noisiest celebration in the club's history. Macqueen's recollection of the night is perhaps understandably vague.

You might say it was a big night. It was also a milestone in the history of the Warringah Club and one that deserved celebrating. It was achieved not by one team of players or even all the players combined. It was the result of hard work and commitment by everyone with any involvement in the club. Enjoying the fruits of success together is a great way to acknowledge an achievement and clear the way for you to prepare for the next challenge.

The next challenge for Warringah came the following week in an entirely different form: resisting media attempts to make Macqueen a star. At the end of the playing season all ten teams fielded by the club had qualified for the semi-finals. The battle was on for grand final positions and ultimate glory. Once again the media went searching for reasons and attempted to pin the success on Macqueen. As usual their efforts were turned aside as Greg Growden from the *Sydney Morning Herald* explained: 'Warringah, always a harmonious outfit, have kept mostly to themselves this year. Talk to club officials and they explain that their club coach should receive all the credit for the memorable year. As can be expected from the determined Macqueen he argues otherwise, in his usual unassuming way.'

It was a period when coaches of several high-profile teams were termed 'colourful' for the way they ranted about poor performances and raved about the good. It made life easy for journalists seeking to brighten reports with more than the usual description of play. But Macqueen gave them little to work with. He was invariably dubbed 'quiet' and 'restrained'. They deduced it was a ploy to keep pressure off his team, which it was in part, thanks to the influence of the reserved Slaggy Miller. But there was another side. Macqueen felt uncomfortable dealing with the intrusiveness of the media. As a player he was almost shy in avoiding publicity about his achievements. The laughing, joke-playing larrikin known to family and friends was not for public display. He seemed to regard the media almost as another adversary to be kept at bay or occasionally used to praise those working around him. But as there were plenty of noteworthy characters from other clubs willing to provide juicy quotes Macqueen was happy to remain in the background.

What began as a natural tendency would, in later years, be developed as a deliberate policy. He would become adept at delivering thoughtful and constructive comments that would be listened to and appreciated. In the meantime it was a frustrating time for the media. It was finals time and they wanted all the excitement and colourful news they could get. Strangely enough they would soon get a terrific story to run in the weeks leading up to the grand final, and Macqueen would provide it.

Chapter 9

Life in the Balance

The 1987 grand final was only weeks away. The weather was particularly bleak, the heavy rain and bitter cold worsened by the howling winds that swept across the grounds from the nearby ocean beaches. Travelling straight from his office to football training, Macqueen continually pushed his side in the miserable conditions, focused only on the ultimate goal. Liz Macqueen was concerned that her husband was pushing himself too hard. She decided the time had come to have one of their 'little chats'. Choosing the right time over a candlelit dinner, she would discuss her concerns and frustrations.

'I found it was a good way of dealing with any problems. We were always able to talk about whatever the issues were and resolve them within this environment. At that stage I thought Rod had become too focused with the combination of football, surf lifesaving and his work. He just needed a wake-up call. And this wake-up call was to be a very serious one.'

However, before Liz had a chance to have their 'little chat' Macqueen finally succumbed to a particularly severe case of influenza. Racked with pain and suffering high temperatures and fever, he called in the local GP who prescribed a course of general antibiotics and advised him to stay in bed for a few days. Liz was concerned that her husband's tendency to fall ill when under stress was now becoming consistent and the symptoms more chronic. Frequent visits from close friend, Bill James, were the only outside contact over the next few days other than family. When his condition worsened Macqueen himself sensed he was in serious trouble and suggested Liz call another local GP, Dr Graeme MacDougall, who was also a surfboat rower for the nearby Warriewood club and a long time friend. MacDougall agreed that Macqueen's condition was worsening. He changed the type of antibiotics, then told Liz to call him immediately if she was starting to panic. Frustrated by the situation Liz replied, 'How do I know when it's time to panic, he's struggling to breathe now?'

By that evening Macqueen's temperature, already high, started climbing further. When Liz made her panic phone call, Dr MacDougall arranged for immediate admission to the local Mona Vale Hospital and contacted the senior specialist who organised emergency x-rays. An anxious Liz overheard the specialist analysing the report say, 'I don't know how this guy is still alive.'

Seeing the real picture

Macqueen was later diagnosed as having chronic atypical pneumonia that refused to respond to normal antibiotics. He was transferred to the intensive care unit where he was given intravenous medication and oxygen. Liz sat quietly by his side. 'He was the only person in the ward and because his condition was so serious the medical staff refused all visitors other than close family. At one stage Hitchie came in by pretending to be his brother. There wasn't much to be said because the doctors couldn't tell us how long it would take for Rod to recover. Or even if he would recover. It was a matter of waiting and hoping for the medication to take effect.'

His life in the balance, Macqueen remained in intensive care for several days until his condition stabilised. As he slowly recuperated, he had time to take in the magnificent view which stretched across the neighbouring Mona Vale golf course, the beach and out to sea. He had time to reflect on many memories that would sink deep and force subtle but important changes to his outlook and personal emotional state.

From my bed I had a clear view of the steeply undulating golf course with the ocean just behind. I remembered the countless early evenings I had trained on the fringes of the course. The many repetitive sprints up and down the steep hills that overlooked the beach. Running back and forth carrying a heavy medicine ball above my head, piggy-backing other players up and down the slope and relay racing across the top of the sand dunes. I remembered all the exercises in perfect detail but I gradually realised something I didn't remember—the surroundings. Not once had I stopped to look at how beautiful it was. How great the ocean was and just what a wonderful area we were sharing. I was so preoccupied with what we were doing I'd lost the perspective of what it was really all about. That really came home to me, lying there for the first twelve hours or so, not knowing whether I was going to live or die.

The game of life

Once transferred to a recovery ward, and with Liz constantly by his side, Macqueen quickly improved. Within days the Warringah team captain, Steve Lidbury, and several other players came to visit and, at Macqueen's request, went over tactics for the final matches. Other important visitors during that time included his father who had initially struggled emotionally to come to terms with his son's illness. His mother and other members of the close knit family were by now spending many hours at his bedside.

On his return home Macqueen underwent daily physiotherapy to help break up the remaining congestion in his chest. Usually it was performed by the Warringah first grade physiotherapist, Louise, or alternatively by Liz who was shown what to do. Now on the mend, Macqueen's thoughts were focused only on rugby. With coaching advice from his bedside the team had won through to the grand final.

He was well enough to supervise one final training session before the premiership decider. But at the final whistle there was no fairy-tale happy ending to this period of personal trauma. The Warringah Green Rats were defeated 19–16 by the polished Randwick side. It was a committed and disciplined effort by the Rats who were desperate to win the first major premiership for their club. It was a game which media commentators agreed could have gone either way had the ball bounced differently at crucial times in the last furious five minutes. As club coach Macqueen at least had the consolation of seeing victory go to the second and third grade sides, his contribution there duly praised in the rugby columns of the *Sydney Morning Herald*: 'A man of integrity, Macqueen was determined not to let his players down. Although far from fully fit he made certain he was at the game and had a strong involvement in the final build-up. The grand final makes Macqueen a loser on the surface. But deep down he is a winner. Nothing more can be expected of a club coach than guiding all 10 sides—from first grade to fourth grade colts—into the semi-finals as Warringah did this season.'

Following this disappointing defeat he was ordered to remain at home for a strictly supervised convalescence. Dr Graeme MacDougall, not surprisingly, became the Macqueens' new family GP, and the following year would also take over as club doctor for Warringah.

In the weeks following the grand final loss Macqueen, for the first time in his life, went on long walks and together with Liz made regular visits to the peace and quiet of his Aunt June's farm at Wollombi. Here he also enjoyed endless hours sketching and painting. As his health returned so too did his competitiveness. Junie just happened to mention that a recent visitor, who was in training, had run up to the top of the mountain in thirteen minutes. Macqueen could not help himself. The challenge was on and exactly eleven minutes, seven seconds later he was waving from the same rocky point on the mountain top. After such a performance it was probably fair to say his recovery was complete. There was something else. Liz noticed a distinct change in his emotional outlook. 'There was no doubt that his attitude was different. He had become a much calmer person when dealing with difficult issues. His hard line approach to many everyday problems appeared to soften. His favourite song from then on became the Louis Armstrong classic, "What a Wonderful World".'

It was at the farm that I was finally able to reveal to Liz the impact of my experience when lying in the Intensive Care Unit of Mona Vale Hospital.

I realised that I had become so focused that I had lost all sense of reality and was neglecting many of the important things in life. This was another lesson I would never forget.

Consulting specialists

Rod Macqueen's third year as Warringah Club coach promised to be the most successful. His preparation was even more detailed and full of new initiatives. The now widely copied coaching manual was expanded to fifteen pages and included individual messages from the various expert advisers. The first grade side would also have the services of a sports psychologist. Macqueen had spoken to a local psychologist, George Shirling, who had been attending matches as a friend of club president, Ron Curry.

I believed that George would be able to help in the mental preparation of the team. I'm a great believer in bringing in specialist people whenever needed. George Shirling was a sports psychologist who understood the inner workings of a rugby side. I was able to use him as a sounding board to confirm my own thoughts and also to help come up with new ideas.

This also helped in the organisation and communication of the club, not just the psychological requirements of the players and teams. By operating in this fashion I could implement the necessary changes keeping an overall view of the big picture. I sometimes found it difficult when specialist advisors communicated directly with the team, not appreciating the ramifications it could have on the big picture.

Open lines, open minds

Celebrating its twenty-fifth anniversary the club was on an emotional high following the successes of the previous year. After winning the Club Championship the previous season, the new goal for the club, printed in capital letters on the front of the manual, was an obvious one—WIN FIRST GRADE. Although he didn't know it at the time this was to be Macqueen's last opportunity to do just that. But it was almost as though he had a premonition when he distributed a discussion paper to coaches at the beginning of the season in which he stressed the need to build an even greater club spirit and enthusiasm throughout all grades, and to establish strong foundations for the club's growth. He also highlighted the importance of communication between players, coaches and administrators. One of his greatest concerns was a return to the days of disunity and antagonism between officials and players. In the paper he outlined his views: 'A player who is not happy about something and feels uncomfortable about expressing his views to his coach or other officials will sow the seeds of discontent amongst fellow players in his attempt to rally support for his view. I suggest that all coaches clearly convey the message to their players that they are free to discuss any problem with senior officials, knowing it will be treated in strict confidence.'

My position on communicating problems was quite clear to everyone. They knew if they had a problem, I wanted them to let me know immediately and there would be no recriminations. Similarly if I had a problem with somebody, I would call them aside and honestly discuss the issue with them. At the same time, it was important that these players received support and encouragement.

Good communication in any team or group is essential for success—especially if there are constant changes in personnel, which so often happens in football. It's no secret that harmony leads to happiness and that breeds success.

Simply Randwick

By any measure it was another successful year for Warringah. Nine out of ten teams progressed to the semi-finals. Six teams battled for grand final victory. Three teams won premierships. But not the first grade. Once again Macqueen was denied the ultimate prize by his old foes, Randwick. Although some media reports were critical of controversial referee decisions, Macqueen rationalised the loss by praising the ability of his opponents.

I had to question my own game plan. With the coaching experience I have now, there may have been ways we could have beaten Randwick. I was still working on keeping the ball in hand and playing to an established pattern, when perhaps we should have imposed ourselves on them a bit more and forced them to change their style of game. But they were a very good team. In all the big matches, Randwick made sure they carried out the important parts of the game better than their opponents. While people talked about the brilliance of the side, I think it also had a lot to do with the ability of the players to do the simple things well. In the big games they placed their greatest effort on performing well in the most important aspects of play. The majority of their players were Wallabies accustomed to performing at the highest level.

Macqueen knew that he was still learning and would try to defy all odds to put that new knowledge into practice.

Back behind the goalposts

Even for the ever-industrious Rod Macqueen 1989 was a busy year. At thirty-nine, and a family man with two children, he was still first grade and club coach of the Warringah Rugby Club, was rowing surfboats competitively in one of the Collaroy A crews, and regularly travelling overseas as managing director of Exhibition Displays. In late July he was in South Africa as consultant for one of his major clients. During his stay he was introduced to Ian McIntosh, the coach of provincial rugby side, Natal.

I met 'Mac' through an old Warringah friend, Dave Pearse, who I was staying with at the time. Dave invited me to one of their team coaching sessions.

South Africa had been out of world rugby for some time due to their apartheid policies, and consequently they were falling way behind. Mac had been successful with his Natal team, but was having trouble in progressing with the style and vision he had for the game. When we met I was impressed and fascinated by his approach and I realised we had a great deal in common. That first meeting would later produce a lifelong friendship as we pursued similar paths in the world of rugby.

Much later, returning from an exciting tour of a private game park, Macqueen suffered yet another mysterious illness and retired to his hotel room in Johannesburg. He was up all night with symptoms a local doctor later diagnosed as a case of food poisoning. Macqueen returned to Australia on the first available flight, taking a variety of medications, which seemed to ease the symptoms. The following day after a leisurely brunch with the family he decided to relax with a quiet game of golf with his son Scott, now aged thirteen. Situated across the road from his home, the golf course forms part of Long Reef Headland, one of Macqueen's favorite places.

Golf was a sport Macqueen and Scott had only recently taken up and neither was very proficient, however walking a golf course together was invariably a rewarding, sharing experience between father and son. But even a quiet game of golf can have its moments. After striking a reasonable drive on the third hole Macqueen bent to retrieve his tee and felt a sickening thud to the back of his head. The enthusiastic young Scott had played a wild practice swing which knocked his father unconscious for several seconds. The blow inflicted a gaping wound, which required a trip to hospital and ten stitches. Quite accustomed to his father suffering a wide range of football and boating injuries, Scott was apologetic but reasonably laid back about the accident. Returning home from the hospital, he casually observed, 'Gee Dad, lucky it was a wood and not an iron or it could have been a lot worse'.

Macqueen decided it was probably time to stay indoors for a few days and recuperate from the food poisoning, the long flight from South Africa and a persistent headache, courtesy of Scott's wayward golf swing. After two days the headache worsened and the symptoms of food poisoning began to reappear. A concerned Liz phoned Dr

Graeme MacDougall. He believed the symptoms were probably a result of concussion but warned them to be careful if things worsened.

The following day Liz knew something was seriously wrong. 'When Rod got out of bed he complained that everything was blurry and his headache was intense,' she says. 'I followed him and immediately noticed that both eyes seemed to be moving around unnaturally. By the time I got him back to bed he could see nothing but shadows so I telephoned Graeme again to get his advice.'

There was no time to lose. MacDougall immediately arranged for an ambulance and a CAT scan at the local medical centre. Within an hour Liz was in the centre's reception area waiting for the results. But events kept moving quickly. Before any official report was prepared she was told her husband was being loaded back into the ambulance for the trip home. She had no alternative but to find her car and follow.

Back home they were soon joined in the bedroom by MacDougall who quietly explained what the scans had revealed. The problem was not related to the golfing accident in any way. The recent bout of sickness with a variety of unusual symptoms, was the result of something much more serious.

Graeme explained to me that I had a tumour close to my brain. It was haemorrhaging and required an immediate operation. He had already contacted one of Sydney's leading neurosurgeons who would be waiting for us at Sydney's Royal North Shore Hospital. He also confided that there was a possibility of permanent blindness.

I had been hallucinating for three days not knowing what was wrong with me. Finally when the facts were revealed it was surprising how totally clear my mind became. I went back over my life and realised how lucky I had been, with a happy, healthy family and no major financial problems. Life had been good.

It was a totally clear choice. I knew I could live with being blind. I wouldn't be helpless and I could still contribute and enjoy life. The other option was really clear also. If I had brain damage I would be a burden to other people. I couldn't imagine the prospect of being in this situation.

His voice was calm but insistent as he made a desperate plea to Liz: 'If I've got any sort of brain damage I want you to talk to the doctors or somehow, someway, make sure I don't survive. I want an absolute promise you will do that.'

Liz struggled to comprehend what he was asking, then promised she would do what he had asked. Later she rationalised to herself the pledge she had made. 'My main concern was that he went into the operation as calm as possible and with a positive attitude.'

A second ambulance was already on its way to their house. Always calm in a crisis, Liz felt remarkably in control despite everything as she climbed into the rear of the ambulance and held her husband's hand. To her relief the medical attendant was another friend from the Collaroy Surf Club—one of the benefits of living in a small close-knit community. He chatted with them throughout the trip, helping to ease the tension. On arrival late in the afternoon they were met by Dr Bill Sears, a surgeon with a quiet and reassuring manner, who confirmed immediate action was required. He told them it might not be a brain tumour as such. The growth appeared to be attached to the pituitary gland near the centre of the skull and was pressing against the optic nerve behind the eyes. It required a dangerous operation but one in which he was quite experienced. The normal procedure for this type of operation is through the nasal passages, however, as this was an emergency operation, it needed to be performed by cutting open the skull to avoid the potential risk of infection due to recurring sinusitis. But, there was a more serious complication. Because of the proximity to the optic nerve there was a strong likelihood Macqueen would be blind following the operation even if damage to the brain were avoided. He only confirmed what MacDougall had already suggested, but Liz felt a sudden chill. There was nothing she could do. She knew only that she must hold her composure to confront whatever lay ahead.

The fight

The delicate operation took more than four hours. Sears and his assisting surgeon removed a large tumour that was indeed attached to the pituitary gland, and bleeding into the brain. For Liz there were many anxious hours in the waiting room. 'Rod's sister Katy, Hitchie and his wife Marg sat with me during the entire operation. It was amazing what we talked about and laughed about. I think it allowed me to cope better by distancing myself from the immediate situation until the time came to face reality and deal with what the doctor had to say.'

As Macqueen was moved into the intensive care unit, Dr Sears told Liz he believed they had successfully removed most of the tumour but they would not know if the eyesight was affected until the anaesthetic wore off and the protective bandages removed. Preparing her for the worst, he cautioned there was still a strong chance her husband would be blind.

I remember coming out of the anaesthetic. I had a bit of a headache but I felt quite awake straight away and glad to be alive. When I first woke up I had a bandage over my eyes but I had the sensation of being able to see light and when the bandage came off everything was blurry but I could distinguish shapes. From the minute that happened I basically knew I would be able to see well enough to get through. I thought it was a miracle.

As I experienced an enormous sensation of relief I realised I was not alone. Liz was there next to me which was fantastic. I couldn't believe I was talking to her normally, almost as if nothing had happened. My next thoughts went to how much damage had been done and what would be my prospects in day-to-day life.

Liz was also surprised at how alert he was and how he was desperately trying to test his vision. 'He said everything was blurry and when he looked out the window he told me he could see a group of people standing there, which in fact was the shadow of a tree under lights in the courtyard.' It was now one o'clock in the morning and Liz stayed with him until four a.m. supervising two quick visits by other members of the family, before heading home for a much needed sleep. When she returned the next day Rod's condition had changed dramatically. He was sleeping for only short periods. Senior nurses told her he was suffering the normal effects of such invasive surgery, which caused confusion and hallucinations. They assured her the heavy medication combined with sedatives would eventually settle him down. Liz stayed by his side throughout the day and left late that night, along with Hitchie and Marg, when Rod appeared more calm.

I remember the hallucinations vividly. Everything was about corporate takeovers as I thought my company was under threat. It was a very stressful period for my business and when I looked at the curtains around me I thought I could see an audio-visual presentation by an American company which was making a takeover bid. I also thought I was being personally attacked and that people were trying to hold me down.

While these bizarre thoughts were running through Macqueen's tormented mind it wasn't all fantasy. In reality male nurses were in fact trying to hold him down and inject him with a hefty dose of sedatives because the intravenous medication wasn't having the desired effect. But, unfortunately for them, they were confronted by Macqueen's automatic defence mechanism. Whenever they moved in he fought them off. After several attempts the nurses retreated and when their difficult patient demanded a telephone they carefully passed one to him.

Liz remembers receiving a call at about three that morning, and was surprised to hear her husband on the other end of the line. 'He wanted me to contact Hitchie and for both of us to join him at the hospital as soon as possible. Once we arrived it took some time to quieten him down and convince him he was in no physical danger. He insisted Hitchie check all medication before it was administered, and wouldn't allow any nurses to approach without permission. For almost twelve hours he had nightmares where he believed he was standing on the outside ledge of a tall building and he kept yelling for Hitchie to wrap an arm across his chest to stop him falling. Together we stayed with Rod until the immediate crisis passed. From then on it was a matter of keeping a constant vigil.'

Over several days the nightmares and hallucinations eventually disappeared. However, not overly impressed with some of the nursing staff, Liz spent many long nights curled up in the chair next to him. Macqueen recovered quickly and soon displayed his unique determination and independence.

Whatever it takes

'Because of the invasive nature of the surgery you will have to avoid the possibility of any further knocks to the head.'

One of the specialists involved in Macqueen's operation was standing alongside his bed in the recovery ward delivering advice which was becoming more and more unpalatable.

'I would advise that in future you avoid any form of contact sport. In fact, because of the extreme risk, I recommend you don't play any sport at all.'

For someone who had spent his whole life engaged in a wide variety of physical activities, most of them dangerous to some degree, this was devastating news. But, lying in a hospital bed still recovering from an illness which had almost taken his life, Macqueen reluctantly accepted this prognosis even though it would mean a dramatic change in lifestyle.

The words hit hard, but once they had sunk in there was a quiet resignation. It was an absolute revelation to me that I could be able to start to putting together my life without sport, but already it was looking pretty good. In fact very good. Over the next two days I started to sort out my life and was feeling comfortable with the prospects. Having been involved in sport since the age of ten, it was amazing just how easy it was to turn away from something I had loved all my life.

However when the neurosurgeon, Bill Sears, called in a week later Macqueen couldn't help asking whether the risks were so great that he should give up such an important part of his life. Sears was thoughtful. He slowly thumbed through the many pages of test results, meticulously inspected the various scans and graphs and then folded his arms and looked at his patient. With his usual quiet, measured delivery he announced, 'I don't see any reason why you can't carry on your normal way of life.'

For the fanatical sportsman, head still swathed in bandages, there was a tremendous wave of relief. Then Sears revealed some extraordinary, but logical, information: the tumour had been in place and slowly growing for a great length of time, all the while putting pressure on the pituitary gland and restricting its release of the body's vital, natural chemicals. The resultant imbalance had dramatically reduced the effectiveness of his immune system rendering it incapable of coping with stress. At last Macqueen's sudden bouts of illness before major sporting events or under pressure at work were explained. For much of his life he had been fighting an unknown enemy within. The nightmare was over. He had won, but only just.

The next item of news wasn't so well received. Sears explained that not all the tumour had been successfully removed. Some of the growth remained and would have to be destroyed by radiation therapy, which would be dangerous because of its proximity to the optic nerve. Fortunately a decision on when and how this would be done wasn't required straight away. There was an opportunity for recuperation, relaxation and a good deal of contemplation. Macqueen took full advantage of this precious window, spending more time with all members of his family. All noticed a transformation. His sister Katy found she had a very different brother. 'In our younger days I was very much in awe of Rod. He was a very cool older brother, who sometimes let me clean his shoes. He was friendly but distant, probably because of our age difference. But after the tumour operation he became a totally different person. Far more caring and considerate, not afraid to say, "I love you", and show his feelings. He became one of my best friends, someone I could always rely on. I always suspected that deep down he was a sentimental person, but it wasn't until after the operation that I really saw that side of him. His whole outlook on life had changed.'

Then there was a two-week family holiday to Fiji, followed by several quiet trips with Liz to Junie's farm and then some very special time with his father. With both having a background in commercial art they decided to dabble in oils. Over several months they headed off on regular painting excursions, to the farm and surrounding bush and often to their favourite coastal haunts. Together they created and captured the images that meant so much over many happy years— sweeping vistas of surf on sand, rocky foreshores and, of course, the imposing presence of Long Reef Headland, the towering, colourful rock face which had witnessed their early morning swims, fishing exploits from onshore and at sea, and their lingering walks. It was like an old friend. They enjoyed the relaxed creativity of brush on canvas but most of all each other's company.

It was a rare opportunity for me. Dad was getting on in years and we had both been too busy to spend as much time together as we should. It was an opportunity to enjoy quality moments with someone who meant so much to me. While enjoying that time together I really got to understand him more as a person, not just as a father.

When Dad passed away in 1992 I reflected on these times and thought just how lucky I was that we had been able to share them.

The crossroads of business

Meanwhile, Exhibition Displays had reached a stage where some serious decisions had to be made. In recent years, partners Paul Booth and Ed Ifould had left the company to pursue other business interests, leaving Macqueen and Ogilvie as joint partners. Prior to his illness Macqueen had been having discussions with Ogilvie, in relation to their company's direction. Their talks confirmed what each suspected. They had different thoughts on where they should be heading.

It was obvious to both of us that if the existing business was to continue one of us had to go in our own direction. Following meetings between the two of us, together with a facilitator, a decision was made. John would buy me out and Exhibition Displays would continue with the manufacturing side of the business and I would pursue a different course.

These situations are never easy but in the end we both achieved what we were looking for. Our careers continued but in slightly different directions.

Time for homework

Finally the time came to face up to the radiation treatment. Macqueen duly visited the oncologist he was referred to at Royal North Shore Hospital.

The doctor was brief and to the point saying that although there were some dangers involved, the treatment was relatively straightforward and could be started the next week. I was quite astounded that he wasn't interested in my comments and that he became quite indignant when I asked any questions. I wanted to know the size of the area to be treated, exactly where it was, what strength radiation would be used, and how many similar treatments the doctor had performed. For a person in his position, I found it an amazing attitude.

Once we both had calmed down a few facts emerged which I found disturbing. I was told a reasonably heavy dosage of radiation would be used, and, yes, there was a danger my sight would be affected. The chance of me going blind as a consequence of the treatment was about five per cent. The procedure was not all that common and the doctor had performed only six in the previous twelve months. I decided to investigate further. A check of other hospitals around Australia returned a varying range of statistics, none of which I felt comfortable with.

Macqueen was concerned at the high risk to his eyesight so he and Liz went even further. They spent weeks researching how similar treatment was done in leading hospitals all around the world. They ended up speaking with Dr Bill Wara at the University of California, San Francisco.

After studying my records he was only too happy to discuss the matter over the phone. His attitude, his manner, and most importantly his statistics, were a revelation. Dr Wara said his hospital had a new machine with improved accuracy, that he treated about one thousand pituitary tumours each year, that he would be using about half the amount of radiation first recommended, and the chance of blindness was far less than one per cent. With such encouraging information the decision was quickly made.

I have always been a great believer in asking questions. The answers invariably throw up many different options. In this case, it was obviously important considering both my sight and my life could depend on the decision we made.

Once the decision had been made, the family support team quietly mobilised once again. Marj and Ian Macqueen, Liz's parents Herman and Jane, and other close family members and friends had been there through both of Rod's life-threatening illnesses, caring for the children, looking after the house and the numerous other everyday chores. With Liz spending so much time with her husband, all help had been greatly appreciated. It would be again. By the time they were ready for departure, the necessary rosters had been drawn upon and all was under control.

I must admit that I was so preoccupied with getting myself through this period that I wasn't fully aware of all the efforts that had gone in by so many people. It wasn't until I was able to spend some quiet time after I returned from the States that I was really able to appreciate all the support I had.

Macqueen and Liz arrived in San Francisco in April 1990 prepared for a stay of about seven weeks. They were amazed at the friendliness and efficiency of the American medical system. The treatment was administered every morning each week day for a consecutive six weeks. Accommodation was provided near the hospital and a shuttle bus transported them back and forth, making what could have been an extremely stressful experience as easy as possible. Their appointment was at 9 a.m. each day and they were immediately ushered in for a preliminary talk with the specialist in charge. Liz was allowed to remain with her husband throughout, even watching the radiation treatment through a glass screen.

Doctors warned the radiation therapy would make Macqueen tired and temperamental which, he openly confessed, proved to be the case. As usual a very patient and supportive Liz helped him through, organising short weekend trips to local tourist destinations to break the hospital routine. Throughout the treatment Rod maintained his regular fitness regime, performing basic exercises and running for thirty to forty minutes each day. Toward the end of the six-week treatment period the doctors called them in for a progress report. All was going well and they expected the remains of the tumour would be completely eradicated without any lasting effects.

A new life beckons

For the first time in more than six months Rod and Liz looked at each other and realised they had a future to plan. They were looking at a blank page. Financially secure following the sale of their business and with their two children reaching independence, anything was possible. However there was an important new factor in the equation. After helping each other through a frightening, life-threatening episode, their day-to-day relationship had changed. Since the operation they had been tackling all their problems together. Now, more than ever, they were a team.

It all came together on a sunny afternoon in San Francisco Park. After spending a couple of lazy hours in a paddleboat on the nearby lake they sat together on a bench looking out over the water. Macqueen remembers discussing the different options. There was the possibility of moving to France where he'd been invited to coach a local rugby side. During their stay in San Francisco he'd also been approached to coach different rugby sides in California and to start up a new business similar to the one he had just sold. Alternatively he could start up a completely different type of business altogether, anywhere in the world. His extensive rugby contacts were offering numerous opportunities, particularly in South Africa. But several basic points kept emerging. They loved their lifestyle at home in Australia, especially in the beachside environment where they had spent all their lives. All they needed was a new challenge.

Few people have the opportunity during their lifetime to sit back and say, 'Where do we go from here? What direction do we want to take? Do we start with a clean slate?'

There were few options that weren't open to us. We were able to make a decision which took us in the direction we wanted to go.

The first decision was easy—they would start up a new business, but one small enough to allow him time to do other things. Macqueen was a little hesitant with the second decision but eventually the suggestion tumbled out.

I thought I'd like to apply for the position of coach of New South Wales Rugby Union. Queensland Rugby had been a lot smarter than us over the years and to beat them would be a real challenge. I felt I had something to offer. I believed I could put together a group of people that would mould a team capable of beating our main rivals.

It was the world of rugby yet again but surely it could be arranged so they were both involved. Now would have been the time for Liz's long awaited 'chat' but there was no longer any need. Having been through the last six months together, they both wanted to share whatever challenges were ahead. Liz agreed with his coaching plans, saying she'd be happy supporting him where she could. They'd be working side by side on the one project, but taking time out together. Macqueen recognised it as a significant change.

As the Qantas jumbo lifted off from San Francisco heading for Sydney, Macqueen was a man on a mission. On his lap was a foolscap writing pad supported by a briefcase. Before the seatbelt warning sign was switched off he was mapping out a proposal he believed would win him the position of coach and the chance to rejuvenate the struggling New South Wales rugby side.

Chapter 10

Teamwork

When Rod Macqueen entered the offices of the NSW Rugby Union in late 1990 he was entering a world which exemplified the procedures and traditions commonly labelled as old school tie. The last time he was in that office in Crane Place, in the heart of Sydney, he had been standing before a judiciary, waiting for judgement to be handed down. Charged with fighting, Macqueen had pleaded leniency on the grounds of extreme provocation. His pleas fell on deaf ears and he was suspended for two weeks.

After more than fifteen years not much seemed to have changed. Inside the small, old-fashioned building, the boardroom walls remained panelled in teak and covered with historic memorabilia. The occasional visitor was invariably dressed in the uniform of grey slacks and navy blazer. Macqueen wondered whether he would receive a more sympathetic hearing despite the overbearing atmosphere of conservatism.

Upside-down structure

Gary Pearse, the chief executive officer and former Wallaby, welcomed Macqueen into his office. The proposal Macqueen placed on the table between them suggested a radical departure from the traditional selection and management of a representative rugby team. In effect, it argued that control of the team needed to be wrested from the officials and placed in the hands of the coaching staff, who at the end of the day were the ones who had to live or die by their performance.

I believe that the administration and paid personnel should be there to support and work with the team management in achieving their common goals. It seems to be unique to many amateur sports, where you have a huge administration in place but where the team can be neglected and even be seen as somewhat of a nuisance. In reality the main goal of the administration should be for the team to be successful. The structure should be set up as a support network. But surprisingly what can happen is that the team becomes a low priority. In the case of NSW rugby, it seemed to me at the time, that the team was little more than an appendage to an organisation preoccupied with the day-to-day management issues.

Pearse, a successful coach himself, was on the same wavelength as Macqueen and totally supported the concept.

A decent proposal

In detail the proposal was an extended and refined version of the philosophy Macqueen had introduced at Warringah. In the accepted format of a business plan, it began with a three-page personal profile then established the rationale of what was to follow. Macqueen firstly stated his main reason for wanting the position.

> My interest in coaching NSW is strongly motivated by the fact that Queensland has been successful in recent years. I believe that with the right approach and attitude NSW can be the premier provincial side. Coaching aside, the 'off the field' problems, both political and financial, have made it extremely difficult to put the best NSW XV on the paddock. Players have suffered from fragmented coaching systems along with the perception, rightly or wrongly, that there are selection inconsistencies. As a consequence the NSW team is not getting the full support of club rugby, particularly in Sydney.

His solution was to set out a blueprint, which to many rugby followers would seem quite straightforward, but in reality needed a detailed backup strategy if it were to succeed at the representative level. He stressed four main objectives:

To make NSW the premier provincial side.

To regain respect for the code in NSW.

To set the foundation for the future.

To establish NSW players as the core of Australian rugby.

Then he argued five key points; if implemented they would mean a dramatic change in the existing organisation of NSW rugby. First was a reduction of representative games, which he believed would allow more time to prepare the side. Then he argued for a logical selection process, to put in place well-defined, clear and consistent selections right through from club to all representative levels. Thirdly, his ideas about a united coaching system argued for free and open discussion on the strengths and weaknesses of the current NSW team, and for all coaches to be consulted on the form of players, and to be part of the selection of the NSW squad.

Fourthly, he nominated effective communication as a vital ingredient for success, to promote harmony and a united positive outlook: strict policy would be not to publicly criticise players, and to offer a strong team approach. Finally, his ideas on 'a professional coaching approach' promoted the formation of an expert team of ten positions, ranging from assistant coach through to gear steward and video operator.

The proposal's conclusion was guaranteed to gain the attention of NSW officials who were being constantly criticised for their inability to match the success of their rivals in the northern state: 'At present Queensland claims supremacy of Australian rugby. I have produced a proposal that contains the necessary elements to bring that supremacy back to NSW, and also retain it for the future.'

The administrators of NSW rugby had sought submissions for a new coach. Amongst the applications Macqueen's was something akin to a mailed gauntlet, hitting the boardroom table with a resounding thud, daring to be picked up.

The selection process for the 1991 Waratah coach finally came down to a choice between Macqueen and several rivals promising the accepted, traditional methods. At the close of a disappointing 1990 season, the NSW executive opted for Macqueen's radical new approach.

In the ensuing media interviews he stressed that his prime objective was to make NSW the top provincial side, restoring greater pride in the sky blue jersey. He made no secret of the fact he was planning big changes but at the same time he said there would be no hidden agenda.

With his own selection only hours old, the shake-up had started.

Selecting the right team

At a time when all positions were still voluntary, Macqueen followed the precedent he had set at Warringah. He sought out a management team of people he believed had the necessary skills and dedication to work together and who were mostly successfully self-employed and able to devote a large amount of time to rugby. Many of the faces were familiar. The fitness trainer was Brendan Mockford; the players' manager was Bill James; former Wallaby halfback Peter Carson whom he had known only briefly through the rugby circle, but believed had the right approach and qualifications to be successful was assistant coach; the well-liked and experienced duo of Greg Craig and Ian Collier stayed on as physios; while George Shirling, the professional sports psychologist, again volunteered to make himself available whenever necessary. Macqueen believed psychology played an important part in the day to day workings of any team or company, and Shirling's advice on sports psychology in particular gave him a good grounding for decision-making. The important position of team doctor was taken up by orthopedic specialist Dr Myles Coolican. He was later joined by Macqueen's family GP Graeme MacDougall. The team manager, Gary Reneker, widely respected for his experience and professional approach, was readily accepted into the new-look management squad. In these amateur days with coaches and assistants giving their time free of charge, on a part-time basis Macqueen was proposing a totally professional approach.

I was lucky I was able to call on people who were in a position to provide time and commitment.

These people all had special attributes. Brendan Mockford and his larrikin style of training encouraged a new level of fitness. Peter Carson, a proud ex-Wallaby, got on well with all the players and contributed greatly to the backline moves and helped instil team ethos. Bill James worked tirelessly behind the scenes and was a great mentor for me. The different skills of the entire management team blended well together and would prove a great formula for the team's success.

Inclusive input

Many of the players were understandably apprehensive. Macqueen immediately met with the captain, Nick Farr-Jones, and influential senior player, Peter FitzSimons, to outline his plans and expectations. To Farr-Jones and FitzSimons Macqueen was an unknown quantity, noted only for his playing and coaching achievements with Warringah.

Macqueen was also aware the two men had earlier suggested that the players themselves could coach the side, and had already had some discussions with officials to that end. However it was obvious the trio had a common goal in improving team performance on and off the field and a mutual respect and understanding of how to achieve that end was soon established.

They seemed surprised that I was seeking their advice and that in future they would be encouraged to have input. It was quite an interesting reaction, however, whether in sport or business I've always enjoyed working as a team. I believe that by including people in the decision-making process you are much more likely to get a result that is supported and works. Additionally, those who are involved in the decision-making are able to see when things go wrong and therefore are able to help solve the problem. It is then very difficult for anyone to justify any criticism if they have been part of that process.

Self-discipline

Any doubts the NSW players may have had about a change in attitude and commitment by the new management team were soon dispelled when they arrived for the first training session at North Sydney Oval. Waratah and Wallaby flanker, Simon Poidevin, sums up the reaction of the players: 'It was totally different to what we were used to. We were introduced to a whole team of people ranging from the team doctor and physical trainer to a sport psychologist. We were given t-shirts, training jerseys, tackling bags, and everything was organised and run to a plan.'

The training session also provided a shock both for the players and the new coach. The starting time was 6.30 p.m. The players straggled in, up to twenty minutes later, which seemed to be the accepted practice. Macqueen waited quietly, watching. Not a word was said, and no activity was ordered. Finally, when the last player had arrived and was dressed and ready, they trained—and hard! Afterwards, Macqueen sat the players down and informed them every session would take exactly ninety minutes and that training would officially begin when the last person had arrived. He suggested they talk amongst themselves to decide on a time they could all adhere to. After a hurried meeting the team soon decided on a mutual time and the first standard of discipline was established.

I really felt this was an important part of the team developing more responsibility for themselves. In insisting that the team take control of the training time it made the situation their problem. Instead of me telling them they had to be there at six thirty it was their decision as to when they started and up to the team discipline to ensure they were then on time. It was simply a matter of starting when the last player had arrived. It was their problem and their call.

A clear start

Perhaps harder to accept was Macqueen's decision to train not twice, but three or four times a week. However, his determination to mould a team capable of sweeping all before it quickly generated a new enthusiasm. All came to appreciate the improvement in condition and fitness which slowly emerged under Mockford's new training regime.

Simon Poidevin remembers that although it was hard, it was innovative and good-humoured. 'It was very constructive, and when you came out of there you were exhausted, but felt very good about life. It provided a tremendous platform for the players to go into that 1991 year.'

On initially meeting Macqueen, Poidevin, like the other players, found him to be a hard taskmaster. Off the training field they discovered they were mixing with someone who displayed an affable and reserved disposition. But lurking just below the surface was Macqueen's quirky sense of humour, characterised by his quiet infectious chuckle.

Nick Farr-Jones was another to be won over by the new professionalism. In his regular newspaper column he pointed out that training four times a week was indeed hard. 'Being a solicitor, a father and a footballer at the same time isn't easy. Nevertheless, the point is that such time commitment goes with the territory of being a representative player.' He admitted he initially had doubts about the tough new techniques employed by Macqueen and his 'entourage of helpers'. Those doubts disappeared once he saw the results. 'It may sound a trifle trite to say it but Macqueen and Co. have done a fine job so far, particularly emphasising the need to develop team harmony and spirit.'

I believe that the decisions made at the beginning of any relationship with personnel, whether in business or sport, are crucial. Setting clear guidelines and standards from the start lays the foundations for the future.

Three in union

In the semi-darkness at the extremity of the training lights, four figures walked slowly along the picket boundary fence of North Sydney Oval. They were deep in conversation. Macqueen was impressed by the performance of the front row trio of Tony Daly, Ewen McKenzie and hooker Phil Kearns. During this quiet discussion on the secret business of front row play he delivered a considered observation. He pointed out that while they were a good front row, they didn't realise their potential to be the best. He told them he believed they could develop into the best front row in the world. All three were just beginning their representative careers in international rugby and all took his assessment differently. Daly laughed out loud, McKenzie went quiet and gave it some serious thought, while Kearns didn't know which way to react. The response prompted Macqueen to give their all-important relationship some help. To generate confidence and bonding between them he organised a series of boxing sessions under the guidance of Johnny Lewis, the trainer of Australia's world champion boxer Jeff Fenech. Although Lewis had no idea who Macqueen was he was intrigued by the thought of training three well-known rugby union players and readily agreed. The three players quickly came to enjoy the unique sessions with Lewis, achieving something special, alone together in a different culture.

From the beginning, it occurred to me that these three had a wonderful opportunity to be the best. All three had quite different personalities and I wanted to encourage them to become more united in their thinking. I decided to try something different that I hoped would develop a special camaraderie and confidence. It was only for a short period of time but I believed there was definitely a benefit. They could hold their hands up in the ring and their heads up on the field.

At the end of the year Daly, McKenzie and Kearns were the Australian front row combination which led Australia's charge to victory in the World Cup.

Beating bribes

With 1991 being a World Cup year Macqueen's original proposal to the NSW administration had included a three-match tour of Argentina with a single game in New Zealand on the return trip. The four-game tour turned out to be very successful and several important issues emerged.

Before leaving Macqueen knew the renowned parochialism of the referees would be a major problem. In all three matches against the Argentine provincial sides, Rosario, Tucuman, and Mendoza, this proved to be the case. On one occasion the Waratahs were penalised 32–8. After the match Nick Farr-Jones concluded that they were being penalised for simply tackling the opposition. 'It seemed to me the referee didn't like the fact we were stopping them from running.' Macqueen decided to solve the problem quietly and diplomatically.

At one stage I attempted to win favour with local officials before a match by greeting them with an armful of souvenir hats and t-shirts. This was obviously seen as a blatant attempt to change the South American interpretation of fair play. The team was punished accordingly. The adverse refereeing decisions brought out a special quality within the team, and Nick Farr-Jones showed great leadership. With so many penalties going against the team he was able to keep a level head and stop the players from being distracted. Additionally it made the team more determined to overcome the disruption of the poor decisions and to keep playing positive football.

The key to focus

The match against Tucuman provided a second invaluable learning experience for the side. The Australians were confronted by an atmosphere resembling a bullring. The crowd represented a psychological force opposing the fledgling Waratah side. As they ran onto the field the crowd spat and threw rubbish at them, then cheered on the local players as they tore in with aggressive and illegal play, unchecked by the referee. At half-time the score was locked at 3-all with the Waratahs struggling to hold their own. But they fought back scoring two tries to secure a draw. Simon Poidevin, who played a significant role in a game he remembers as one of the toughest he has ever played, gives credit to the instructions of the new coach: 'In our training, Macqueen had delegated authority to different players throughout the team, not just the captain and vice captain. When we had to change the game plan, in the middle of a noisy, extremely combative atmosphere, there was no concern over whether we had the authority to do so. "Macca" had provided that confidence, and if you like, put a fail-safe system in place.'

Macqueen was equally generous in his praise of the team.

It was a particularly inspirational performance by the side. They were able to make the decisions to change the game plan and adapt to the torrid conditions. If things are going wrong in a game, players in certain positions were given several options to draw on. This gave them the confidence to rescue any situation by changing their style of play or point of attack. Not having a 'Plan B' creates unnecessary panic and confusion. Additionally in this game there was an inner resolve that emerged which brought a new confidence to the side.

From that day Tucuman became a key part of the team's psyche. In all future games the catch cry 'Tucuman' was used to lift players to greater effort.

In most of the teams I've coached I've used keywords to trigger focus. In this case 'Tucuman' conjured many emotions within the players and in particular the memories of looking at the options and lifting their performance under adverse conditions. Therefore whenever we were confronted with a similar situation the players would automatically shout the name of the small village in Argentina—'Tucuman'.

Seize the opportunity

Following their success in Argentina the Waratahs returned to Australia via New Zealand to play the highly regarded provincial side of North Harbour, captained by former All Black skipper, Wayne

'Buck' Shelford. This match delivered another key point and played a significant part in the careers of three players.

Macqueen believed that individual positions required certain skills and if any player had those skills he could easily adapt. So he had no hesitation in moving quality players from one position to another rather than elevating other specialist players of a lesser standard.

The night before the game more than half the side was struck by a stomach bug. One winger was particularly ill. Macqueen selected another player as the replacement, even though wing was not his normal position. But this player declined, saying the only position he could accept would be outside centre or five-eighth. The selectors reassessed the situation and chose Rob Egerton, a fast attacking fullback who was instantly thrilled at the opportunity and had a great game that day.

Marty Roebuck was another player who was in outstanding form that match. The highlight of the game occurred when local hero, Shelford broke from a maul and was heading for the line with only the fullback to beat. Roebuck hit him head on and, not only stopped him, but picked him up and drove him back several metres. The roar of the New Zealand crowd turned to stunned silence. The Waratahs went on to win 19–12, thanks to Roebuck's match-saving tackle. The record books now show that both Egerton and Roebuck capped off the fairy-tale by playing for the all-conquering Wallaby team which secured the 1991 World Cup for Australia. But the player who'd declined the repositioning did not make the Australian squad and his representative career was effectively finished.

Sometimes stubbornness and tunnel vision can obscure the real issues. In this situation the game was changing and I have no doubt the player who refused to play in the position underestimated his ability to adapt. Alternatively, the other players made the most of an opportunity that was given to them. These chances only come around every once in a while. Recognising them and taking advantage of them is the key.

Team-builders

The simple act of Roebuck's tackle was a significant event in the building of the team's character and a new confidence began to grow.

Over the four games in an exciting new environment the team also developed its own camaraderie and ethos. The various characteristics within the team resulted in a harmonious mix.

Along with the tremendous leadership of Farr-Jones I was equally pleased that off the field there were a number of unofficial mentors already in place. These were senior players who set an example on behaviour and promoted rugby ethos and tradition. As well as Farr-Jones, outstanding team members included Poidevin, McKenzie, Tim Gavin, Marty Roebuck and Tim Kava. Peter FitzSimons also played an important role. An intelligent, quick-witted prankster, he was always doing something to keep everyone on their toes. At the same time he understood and revelled in the passion of representative rugby. I was slightly concerned by the quiet and reserved nature of our Tongan-born backrower, Willie Ofahengaue, particularly when I discovered that he hadn't brought with him a copy of all the intricate backrow moves handed out at the start of the tour. Late one afternoon I confronted him and questioned his knowledge. I was astonished, and more than a little embarrassed, to hear that Willie not only knew all the intricate moves in detail but also was able to suggest numerous ways in which they could be modified and improved. I never underestimated Willie again. It proved to me that each personality, each person had a place. As they began to communicate more and more the team began to gel as a cohesive unit.

Getting to know you

While Macqueen was getting to know his players they were also getting to know something about him. Unlike the teams he had coached at Warringah, these players knew very little about him. They were unaware of his dynamic drive for perfection and the respect he had earned on the local playing fields. But, as the new state coach, he soon earned the same respect by his behaviour and the way he treated those under his charge. Macqueen's character was quickly noted by the 'prankster', Peter FitzSimons, who would later become a respected rugby journalist and commentator. 'One of the reasons for Rod's success in controlling players was that he had a quiet air of authority. Almost a hint of menace which gave the impression, "Don't mess with me." I have seen him angry but I have never seen him go ballistic. He has the ability to remain in control. And although off the field he was a great bloke to have a drink with and enjoy time with, he was not one of the players, not really one of the boys. There was always a touch of reserve.'

As a commentator in later years FitzSimons would recognise the changes Macqueen was making to the style of rugby coaching, not just in Australia but all around the world. But in the amateur days of 1991, it was all new and sometimes a bit too hard. Especially for some notoriously reluctant trainers who thought rugby was a game that could be enjoyed by playing with passion and commitment but not with a great deal of homework. 'He certainly wasn't my kind of rugby coach. I just liked to go running around, bashing into people and having fun, making it up as I went along. Rod was the first coach I encountered who not only talked about a game plan, but insisted it be followed. From my understanding he was the first one to introduce sequence plays which are now commonly used by the Wallabies and most other teams but which he introduced to the Waratahs in 1991. Sequence plays are when the ball carrier is tackled and there is usually a breakdown of support. Rod trained players to go into formation immediately and perform practised moves that normally would have only been used from the set plays such as tap penalties. I think Rod was the first person to introduce that organised notion to Australian rugby and he later successfully imposed that system on the Wallabies.'

FitzSimons, like many other players, also discovered there was another softer side to the coach who demanded so much from the people under his control. 'He was always a strong advocate of putting family first. I had firsthand experience of this when my father died in 1992 and we were touring with the Waratahs. When Rod heard the news there was no to-ing and fro-ing, he just told me, "Your position on the team is safe, just go home to your family." I have never forgotten that. He would often talk about his own father and I think that was the basis for his personal concern.'

A detached overview

After his first overseas coaching tour Macqueen returned undefeated after four matches. But there was something else, a difference in the way they played. Despite the limited media coverage many commentators were picking up on this. The backs and the forwards were becoming more integrated, running off each other in close formation. Macqueen experimented with tap-kicks rather than seeking distance with kicks to the line which meant holding possession for long periods—a ploy which of course depended greatly on the defensive strength of the opposition. Moves involving the three backrowers became an integral part of the Waratahs' game. Interplay between the flankers and the halfback became a regular method of gaining easy metres and setting up first phase play. Using large hard-running flankers feeding off the backs during general play also created confusion in opposing teams. The Waratahs continued to gain in confidence and continued winning.

If things were going badly during the beginning of a match, Macqueen would use the half-time break to settle the team down and quietly issue new instructions. His calm and deliberately slow delivery quickly earned him the nickname 'Cones', with the players laughingly accusing him of smoking several 'cones' of marijuana beforehand. However, Macqueen was emulating the approach of the Mosman rowing coach, Terry O'Hanlon.

I had not forgotten that almost mystical experience on the waters of Middle Harbour where calm, quiet concentration had engendered strength, skill and focus. While the team was having a joke at my expense I had the advantage of a detached overview. In most cases a team doesn't need to be told if they are playing badly. When time is at a premium and things are against you, it is better to calmly assess and outline the situation and bring in simple but positive steps to rectify the problem. However, sometimes when players are pumped up during a match, and desperate to win at all costs, there can be confusion and a lack of direction. Sometimes an emotional outburst is needed but I'd only use this when teams are oblivious to their lack of urgency and commitment.

Putting goals in perspective

The moment of truth for the all-conquering Waratahs was now at hand. It was time for Queensland, unbeaten by the Blues in three years. The subsequent game provided everything that was expected and more—dashing backline play, uncompromising defence and rugged forward exchanges. But most importantly for the Waratahs it produced a well-deserved victory of 24–18. Unfortunately the win was marred by a raging controversy over scrum collapses. Members of the dominant NSW pack claimed the opposition had deliberately pulled the scrum down on at least ten occasions. The usually reserved Macqueen launched a scathing attack on both Queensland and the referee, pointing out that there was a concerted campaign being led by Australia to stamp out the practice worldwide. His main concern was the risk of serious injury to players. He told the *Sydney Morning Herald*, 'I hope that never happens again. You only have to go into a hospital spinal ward to see what I'm talking about. It was shocking.'

It was a rare and passionate outburst from Macqueen, prompted by a disturbing experience involving a close personal friend, that very few people were aware of at that time. Three months earlier there had been a terrible accident involving a close friend who was still in the spinal unit at Sydney's Royal North Shore Hospital.

I was having a quiet Sunday afternoon at home when the phone call came. It was Marg Hitchcock, the wife of my close friend and former Warringah teammate Kevin, calling to tell us he had broken his neck in a diving accident. The doctors were saying he would be a quadriplegic for life. Liz and I jumped in the car and went straight to hospital. I had this terrible image because it was exactly eighteen months before when I'd been in the same intensive care unit. Now our roles were reversed. I told the nurses I was his brother and walked in really not knowing what to say.

During the first few days there was not much anyone could do but offer words of support until the true medical situation became clearer. However Macqueen gave reassurance and advice to Marg who, like Liz had in a similar situation, was showing an inner strength and determination.

I remember saying to Marg she should look at the positives. That Hitchie was still the same person and he was still alive, that he could still think, his mind appeared to be clear and everything from there on would be a bonus. It was the first thing that came to me because it was the way I'd felt in my own situation.

The following three months were an extremely busy and emotional time for Macqueen. Apart from coaching the Waratahs, he was still rowing surfboats and running his own business. After each training session with the boat crew, then the Waratahs, he would go directly to the hospital and meet with Liz, who was spending most days there keeping Marg company. They would change places so she could return to look after their own family.

We joined other friends and members of the family doing massage and special exercises with Hitchie to try and encourage movement in his limbs. Hitchie and I shared the same sense of humour and despite the seriousness of the situation it was great to see his determination to get better. It was a long and extremely difficult time for all of us, but after three months when some movement returned followed by some short hesitant steps it was an incredible reward for all those involved. I also realised that the life-threatening accident brought a great emotional change. We now both shared a new perspective on life. The friendship we started as team-mates almost twenty years earlier was never more important.

The money game

To Macqueen being a team player was a crucial part of success. After seven games in 1991, the Waratahs were still undefeated and the next Queensland match was looming as the ultimate test for his new style of professional management. Justifiably proud of his close-knit squad of players Macqueen was hit with an unexpected request, to include established Wallaby winger, David Campese in the Waratah team. Australian coach, Bob Dwyer, was keen to have his form assessed for the imminent World Cup. Campese had just returned from a playing stint in Italy and had made himself available, although he had only played a couple of club games in Australia during the year.

Because it was an important part of Macqueen's philosophy that Australian rugby be supported by the provincial sides he consequently agreed, although it meant dropping the existing and extremely promising young winger, Alastair Murdoch. David Campese's individual brilliance and unpredictable style of play had won numerous games for Australia and thrilled rugby followers all around the world; he could virtually win a match single-handedly by an inspired act of rugby 'magic'. Macqueen was happy to have such a touch of genius added to his already winning formula, but was concerned that the strong feeling of camaraderie in the existing side could be disrupted.

Campese's involvement raised a number of unexpected issues. Some days prior to his first return match Macqueen noticed that Campese was wearing football boots bearing the logo of a rival sponsor. The team had a good relationship with their sponsors and had been careful to honour their commitments. During the amateur days, sponsorships were vital for the team to be able to obtain the necessary gear. Days prior to the game, Campese was advised by team management to put black tape over the offending logo. Once on the field, he ripped the black tape from his boots just prior to kickoff to expose the logo of his personal sponsor. To say Macqueen was unimpressed would be an understatement.

It was a real eye-opener for me to realise just how far commercialism had crept into rugby, even at that supposedly amateur stage of the game. There was an issue developing over what benefits money was bringing to individuals and whether this was threatening to take priority over the ethos of the team. It was the shape of what was to come.

The events of that match set the tone for an uneasy future relationship between the coach and the crowd-pleasing winger. Although Macqueen was an open admirer of Campese's contribution to Australian rugby, he was concerned that he was a player who put himself above the team.

It takes all kinds

David Campese was probably the most talented footballer Australia has ever provided. His instinctive game and his elusive running constantly amazed spectators and confused the opposition. The interesting thing about Campo, though, was not only did the opposition not know what he was going to do but neither did his own teammates. This proved to be extremely successful in many ways because he would appear out of nowhere to receive the ball and make a break out of something that seemed impossible.

It's always a great asset to have someone who does something out of the square and it is important to encourage this creativity. However, if a team had several Campos I believe it would be a total disaster because the left hand would not know what the right hand was doing. All the successful Test matches that Campo played in required the discipline of hard-working players, constantly putting their bodies on the line to secure possession. There were also players in mid-field with clear vision and direction, making the right decisions to put a back line into motion and create space. Committed defensive players communicating as a group to restrict the opposition scoring were also an important ingredient of those teams. There is no doubt Campo benefited from all of this and although his defence and ball security were widely recognised as being poor, his skills and ability were a magical ingredient for any side. A good blend of talent creates a good team.

As it turned out the match was won with a polished team performance highlighted by an outstanding effort from the front row trio of Daly, Kearns and McKenzie. Following the media controversy over scrum collapses in their first encounter a more stringent refereeing display this time kept the two packs on their feet. This enabled the Waratahs to use their obvious advantage. They again dominated the Queenslanders, forcing them backward in crucial scrums, building a strong platform for another blockbusting performance by the backrow, which led the team to a rousing 21–12 victory.

While side issues tended to sour the moment of triumph, the overall result was a ringing endorsement of Macqueen's vision and meticulous planning. The series victory over their previously dominant interstate rivals silenced any remaining critics of the new style of rugby management. At last NSW had regained supremacy as the number one provincial side in Australia. The primary goal of the new Waratah coach had been achieved. Now only two sides stood in the way of an inspirational clean sweep—visiting teams from England and Wales, the traditional stalwarts of rugby and all it embodies. Could Macqueen's squad overcome the might of England, the recently crowned Five Nations champions, and defeat the always passionate Welsh?

Well-orchestrated crescendo

'Poms Happy After Loss' was one newspaper headline. 'Winning Waratahs in Awe of England', was another. Strange headlines indeed for a state team that had just defeated the visiting grand slam winners of the Five Nations series. What had happened was interesting.

The British side arrived in 1991 lacking in match fitness and preparation, some not having played a game for six weeks. But while the experts predicted a soft opening to their tour the men in white gave a strong performance, staging a rousing comeback in the second half after trailing 21–10 late in the match. NSW held on to win 21–19, and later praised the strength of the opposition pack. The English played better than expected, but many of the Waratahs, despite their victory, felt they played well below the standard they had established for themselves during the year. It was perhaps best summed up and put in perspective by one paragraph in the *Sydney Morning Herald*: 'The NSW forward pack was magnificent in setting up a victory over England which is by far the biggest jewel in the crown of a 9–0 season, with Wales to come on Sunday.' Yes indeed, that was the call. Bring on the Welsh for the last game of the season and see if Macqueen's men can remain undefeated.

And so on that Sunday, for the Waratahs defeat was not an option. Total demolition was. The rampaging Waratahs did everything right, holding possession for long periods, combining backs and forwards in a variety of innovative moves, and totally outclassing the opposition. After many months of developing a side that had total on-field communication, this was the defining moment, when all things finally come together, like some divine happening. It turned out to be the blackest day in Welsh rugby history with NSW running in thirteen tries, five to David Campese, as they swept to a record 71–8 victory. It was the worst ever defeat for the proud rugby nation, and easily eclipsed their previously biggest loss of 52–3 to New Zealand. For NSW it was their highest score against a visiting national team, and their biggest tally ever, even surpassing a 47–16 victory against Queensland way back in 1928.

Afterwards the shell-shocked Welsh manager, Clive Rowland, compared the Waratahs to the 1987 All Blacks who won the World Cup. Rowlands declared, 'That's as good a controlled rugby performance as I've seen anywhere in the world.'

For NSW the season was an unequivocal success. It was the first time the Waratahs had gone through undefeated since their legendary namesakes of 1927. While the results were impressive on the record books, the way the victories were achieved meant even more to those associated with the team. It was a campaign that was planned and run professionally, both on and off the paddock.

The game turned out to be a fitting reward for the efforts of the season. All the teamwork, skills and preparation came together on the day. It was as close to the most perfect and satisfying game of football I had been involved with. The different combinations in the team all excelled with forwards and backs having an understanding that allowed them to totally dictate the game, retaining possession and off-loading the ball continuously. The team was relentless, keeping Wales under pressure for the entire 80 minutes. More importantly, the team had come together at the ideal time with Australia about to begin its campaign for the upcoming World Cup.

Winning rewards and records

In his first year as Waratah coach Macqueen achieved all the goals he set at the beginning. The team went through undefeated, downed rival state Queensland on both occasions, and achieved a record number of representatives in the Australian World Cup squad. In fact ten Waratahs played in the victorious World Cup winning team. As a further tribute to his coaching style, many rugby experts and commentators attributed much of the Wallaby success to the fitness and discipline of the Waratah component.

Simon Poidevin is just one who believes it was an important factor: 'I think in many ways Australia would not have won the World Cup without Rod Macqueen influencing the Waratahs the way he did, because he provided a core of very fit players for the Australian side.'

He also believes the innovative moves using the backrowers, Willie Ofahengaue, Tim Gavin and himself were another key ingredient. 'A lot of our backrow moves were transplanted straight into the Wallaby play. Even when other backrowers came into the team they worked in with Nick Farr-Jones as halfback, calling those backrow moves.'

For Macqueen, the successful season was complete justification for his style of coaching which blended integrated, professional team management with a strong emphasis on team bonding and camaraderie. His position as Waratah coach was assured and many commentators were already touting his name as a future coach of the Wallabies.

Fighting disappointment with discipline and determination

Bushwacked! The old colloquial term for an ambush was the only word to describe the way Rod Macqueen felt when he looked at the Waratah itinerary for 1992. After less than a month's preparation his side was locked into an unusually short tour of New Zealand against daunting opposition. In exactly seven days they would meet three of the strongest and toughest provincial sides. Returning home, they would have one week to prepare for an international against Fiji. The following week would be the first clash against arch rivals Queensland, who were looking for revenge and who would have had a much easier five weeks' preparation.

Macqueen was furious. He hadn't been consulted, there had been no thought put into the preparation for this year. The value of his carefully programmed start to the previous year had been ignored.

There was something awfully wrong. I was surprised that so many decisions had already been made. I had expected to be included in discussions regarding the preparation, however, the administrators had left the team out of the decision-making process on the makeup of the rugby year. If you were to look at the goals and mission statements of the NSW Rugby Union the success of the Waratahs should have been high in their planning. But instead the team took the lowest priority.

It was important that if we were to continue to be successful, we needed to develop a professional program and a vision for the year ahead. It was a complete turnaround from the year before. In my mind this was a return to the bad old days and my immediate thought was to resign.

Feeling betrayed by upper management, Macqueen spoke to the other members of his management team. All had a similar view. After the time and effort they had put in as unpaid rugby officials to achieve such an unprecedented successful season, they felt this was a backward step. Their professional dedication had only received amateur recognition. It was only a personal approach by the NSWRU president, Phil Harry, which salvaged the situation. He had supported and privately guided Macqueen through some difficult moments during the season and now convinced him and the rest of the management group to stay on for at least another year.

And so Macqueen's second year as NSW coach started with mistrust and acrimony. The only change to the management team came following the retirement of Gary Reneker for business reasons. This gave the Waratahs an opportunity to bring in a new skill into the camp and Edwin Zemancheff, a partner in a large international law firm, was invited to join the team. According to Macqueen, Zemancheff was an extroverted lawyer who brought a keen sense of humour mixed with a new level of professionalism into the management team.

He was first approached by friend and assistant coach Peter Carson, who said they were looking for rugby men with a professional outlook. Zemancheff happily accepted the position, but soon spread the idea that he was sought out because he could supply free and ready access to boardrooms with sweeping harbour views, numerous telephones and faxes, and even secretaries with time to spend on rugby business! Zemancheff quickly established a good rapport with Macqueen which would develop into a strong friendship. His first impressions of NSW rugby's bureaucracy were unfavourable and confirmed as the season progressed.

'I soon regarded the officials as the paid enemy. While they seemed to be doing very little at all, we, the amateur staff and players, were doing all the work for nothing. In the early days they certainly had no idea of what Rod was trying to achieve. He would go into their boardroom and fight tooth and nail to have our doctor and fitness trainer join us on tour, but they regarded the suggestion as little more than a junket. They could only see fifteen players running onto a field and did not understand there was a second team off the field. Perhaps because they were amateurs themselves, they couldn't understand the professional approach Rod was taking and the culture he was trying to put in place. His paramount concern was the welfare of the players and everything he did was for their benefit. As time progressed he was accused of being sensitive to criticism and he had every reason to be: it was totally unwarranted and unjustified.'

The New Zealand tour began well enough with comfortable victories over Wellington and Canterbury but the Waratahs were not playing to the same standard as the previous season. Then they hit Auckland. After twelve matches undefeated as coach, for Macqueen, this game was unlucky number thirteen. The tough Auckland combination, studded with All Blacks, belted the Waratahs 35–10. It was a comprehensive defeat made worse by five injuries during the course of the match. The record-breaking run of victories was brought to a shuddering halt. Matters would have to be rectified if the side was going to be competitive in the all-important battles with Queensland.

These games were crucial in deciding which players would earn a prized Wallaby jumper. It was a great example of the ramifications of poor preparation. With the amount of inexperienced personnel we still would have been competitive if we had had the time to put everything together. Unfortunately the combination of a short preparation and inexperience resulted in a loss.

Setting the ground rules

Macqueen told his team they had two weeks to regain the toughness and composure that had exemplified their play the previous season. With assistant coach, Peter Carson, he worked on regaining the fluent integration of backs and forwards. The importance of continued possession while probing different points of attack was constantly emphasised. By now the trademark of Macqueen's coaching was well and truly accepted by the players—commitment, organisation and discipline. Know what you and those around you have to do during a match and do it. If the fundamentals of the game and the multitude of strategies are practised, often enough they will come as second nature on the field. At least that is the theory. Although it proved to be a winning philosophy during 1991, Macqueen's insistence on perfection at training was a constant mixture of annoyance and amusement for many of the players.

Second-rower, Peter FitzSimons, who at the time was writing a regular column for the *Sydney Morning Herald*, felt obliged to give an inside report on the Macqueen method, in his trademark humorous style: 'He is not a barge and bash 'em coach, but nor does he have a particular rugby philosophy. Words that spring to mind about him are: organisation, discipline, planning, intensity, secrecy, method, organisation, discipline, details, discipline, details.'

FitzSimons revealed that his coach was a fanatic on detail, checking and double checking every possible eventuality. Did the reserve players know all the secret calls? Have seats been arranged for the physios? What was the latest forecast from the weather bureau? He pointed out that this was all done while retaining the respect and affection of the players. But while every aspect of play was practised over and over before every game, individual creativity was not discouraged. 'This approach does not kill flair, Macqueen is at pains to point out, so much as to give it a framework on which to grow. Thus far his approach has worked.'

It certainly worked for the following match. A week after returning home, NSW played expansive free-flowing rugby to defeat Fiji 52–6. Everything was back on track for the first Queensland game the following weekend. Or was it?

On their home turf at Waratah Stadium the Blues put in a spirited performance matching the visitors in all departments but it wasn't enough: the game was lost 23–18. The players regrouped to win their next two games convincingly, but the triumph was later soured by a defeat at the hands of the visiting All Blacks. Even worse was another loss to Queensland in their return encounter. It was a disappointing end to a difficult season and the cue for Macqueen's departure. While several media commentators hinted at political problems, Macqueen refused to be drawn in saying he wanted to keep pride in the NSW jumper.

He praised the commitment and talent of the players and said his reasons for leaving were purely personal. His son, Scott, was facing important exams at school while Jacqui was starting a new career in childcare and he needed more time to develop his expanding personal business. Both he and Liz had spent a large part of two years working and travelling with the Waratahs in a strictly voluntary capacity. 'For NSW to be successful a great deal of time has to be devoted by the coach and his back-up staff. That is extremely difficult with my family and business commitments.'

Lost lessons

In leaving, Macqueen was just as organised as he had been on his arrival. He had already prepared the way for his successor. At the beginning of the year he had brought in as a selector Greg Smith, the successful coach of the Sydney Eastern Suburbs Club. As such Smith was included in most of the team planning and general discussion, giving him an insight and input into the structure and running of the NSW team. When the vote for a new Waratah coach was taken Smith went in against a strong field of contenders with Macqueen's full endorsement. He came out with the job. His first comments to the media created a great deal of interest. He said he would not be continuing with the 'stereotyped style of play developed by Macqueen'. He would encourage players to throw the ball about and make the most of their individual skills. Ironically, five years later, Macqueen would take over from Smith as Wallaby coach during a time when Australian rugby was in turmoil.

When Macqueen left the Waratahs, so too did the majority of his management team and the structures and philosophies he had put in place two years before.

With the benefit of hindsight it could be said that Macqueen had set the ground rules for professional rugby several years ahead of time. He had put in place a large team of experts to cover every aspect of team management.

These were people who, because of their own financial circumstances, were able to devote almost unlimited time to analyse, develop and fine-tune a team structure, helping and supporting individual players to ensure harmony and encourage camaraderie. Unlike myself and the players, these people received no public recognition or profile from what they did, and yet they worked so hard. Hopefully, the rewards came to them through the good times and the success we enjoyed along the way.

It was a full-time operation which could not be justified in amateur sport. But Macqueen had set a blueprint for the professional era still to come, where those in similar positions would command six-figure salaries.

Chapter 11

Advantage Line

As he had promised on that park bench in San Francisco, Rod Macqueen's development of the Waratahs was due to the involvement of Liz. At the same time they were both working on another venture, equally as ambitious—the establishment of their new company. Visits to local libraries in San Francisco had revealed that even in the United States, there was little information on the theories and philosophy of point of sale merchandising. He realised the majority of business books and educational courses had been written by marketing or advertising people, who did not seem to understand or appreciate the philosophy behind in-store displays. This was despite the fact that research showed 65 per cent of buying decisions were made by customers while they were actually shopping and exposed to products. Macqueen realised he was looking at a business opportunity which apparently no company had so far addressed. After returning from the United States in mid-1990 he and Liz started a small business from a makeshift office at the rear of their house. The plan was for him to work as a consultant to major companies in the creative field where he excelled. It was a chance to start afresh, unrestricted by the parameters involved in this type of business. Unlike Exhibition Displays, which needed to support a manufacturing division, this business was to have total freedom of direction. The company would pursue a niche market specialising in nothing but the strategy of merchandising.

After meeting with clients, Macqueen came up with designs and strategies and returned with hand-rendered presentations while the only other member of the company, Liz, handled the necessary bookwork, phone calls and public relations. It soon became apparent that big clients wanted much more. In fact they wanted someone who could totally manage the merchandising side of their business, including the design, manufacture and installation. The small, low-key, family-based operation the couple had planned was about to expand almost out of control in the specialist market identified by Macqueen.

With a growing list of clients who wanted more than they could provide, they needed more staff. An advertisement for a salesman brought an unexpected reply. Macqueen was approached by one of his former employees at EDs, Frank Minnici. Already a good friend, Minnici had proved himself to be more than capable in sales and finance. After a short discussion the position of salesman disappeared. Instead they agreed to be partners. After a much longer discussion over drinks they also agreed on the company name, Advantage Line. In business, advertising can be broken up into 'above the line' and 'below the line', above the line being media advertising and below the line being all peripheral advertising activities. In rugby for one team to go forward they must break another type of line, an imaginary one drawn between the two teams. This is called the advantage line. Macqueen was well aware that to succeed in either rugby or business it's essential to break into opposition territory.

Minnici's early recollections are of high ideals supported by a low budget. 'Rod and I would visit prospective clients and, if they were receptive, we would leave with a briefing to come up with a concept design. On some occasions Rod would generate instant concepts on his sketch pad and at the same time I would provide on-the-spot quotes.'

Michelle Barnsley, another former employee, joined the team and they took up premises in a small office in Dee Why. Liz continued in her role as assistant to both Rod and Frank but within twelve months the business had grown rapidly. More staff came on board, including former Warringah first grade captain Matt Foldi, who by now had many years of experience in the finance industry. Matt was a diligent and loyal person, who fitted in perfectly with the philosophies they were looking for to develop the company.

Personal partnership

The original idea of their business being a small, low-stress operation had now well and truly disappeared. This was confirmed when an old friend in the shape of former client Revlon gave them their account. The sheer size of this forced a general expansion and Liz took over as the Revlon account manager. It was the first time she had taken on such a responsibility but she did so in such a way that impressed everyone, especially her husband.

After all the years I'd been involved in business, with Liz supporting me from home, I never really considered the idea of her working in the front line. We discussed it and Liz was confident that she could handle the new role. She understood the requirements, handled the day-to-day business easily and overall did an excellent job. It made me realise the talents that Liz had. Until now she had been performing domestic duties and support-ing me as a wife and mother of our kids. I hadn't really appreciated all her capabilities. I admired and respected her for it.

Macqueen was fortunate to have such a capable partner because not only was the new business expanding more rapidly than expected, the rest of his life was equally hectic. At the age of forty-one he was running the business, coaching the Waratahs, still daily visiting his injured friend Hitchie in hospital, and competitively rowing surfboats. Despite the fact it was only eighteen months since the invasive surgery on a tumour which had threatened to end his sporting career, he and his crew finished the season by taking out the gold medal for the Australian Masters Over 35 years category, at the Australian Surf Lifesaving Titles. During his rowing training Macqueen would find solitude. It was always his personal solution to the stress generated by his hectic life.

I always found I was able to overcome stress by seeking out a relaxed environment, be it running, swimming or in this case rowing. It was great to get out of the office and think only about rowing. Being out in the boat, looking out over the ocean, watching the sun set, not worrying about anything else but placing my oar in the water and feeling the weight of the boat as I pulled it through. I was in another world, enjoying the unique combination of physical exertion and emotional peace.

Battle plans win business

Macqueen was now working with a number of major companies on their merchandising strategies and ideas which had begun to crystallise during his research in San Francisco. And the results were beginning to show. He realised the opportunities to expand and upgrade the pres-entation of products was almost limitless. But to be successful he had to tap into the thought-processes of the customer.

There is so much more to the art of merchandising than simply making display units or putting products on shelves. My feelings went much deeper than that to what makes a customer decide on a particular purchase.

Every time I walk into a retail environment I see it as a battlefield. My clients' products are on one side with the opposition on the other, both fighting to attract customer attention and sales. I really take it personally and try to see how can we outmanoeuvre the opposition to make a greater visual impact to gain territory. My goal is to work out ways to establish my client as a category leader in their respective markets. Whenever I am briefed on a job I see it as a challenge to have a strategy that out-thinks the opposition. Whenever our client is the winner, so are we.

After one casual visit to a shopping centre, Macqueen was so taken aback by the presentation of one major product that he decided for the first time to go hunting for their account. The giant Eveready Batteries company had spent millions of dollars on merchandising units which, in Macqueen's opinion, were a dismal failure. They did not stand out from their competition and in fact were often used by retailers to hold opposition products. They were getting no benefit for their huge investment because their displays had become little more than a generic promotion for all types of batteries.

In my mind no thought or philosophy had gone into the promotion. After speaking to the rest of the Adline team, we decided to spend a lot of time and effort putting together what we believed would be a compelling sales pitch and explain to Eveready the philosophy behind successful merchandising as we saw it. That is, to make their displays stand out from the crowd, to enable consumers to recognise instantly the Eveready brand and automatically self-select. We made an appointment with senior management and gave a lengthy presentation. But they were already committed to another display manufacturer who had been their supplier for some time and were reluctant to change. However, we believed in the concept and invested a lot of money and eventually we secured the contract. We produced a full range of display units and promotional material which proved an immediate success.

Sleep at night

One of the things the partners often talked about in the boardroom was something they called the 'sleep at night' philosophy. It had nothing to do with how business pressure and long working hours affected their sleeping habits. It was about doing the right thing by their clients so that they had a clear conscience; setting standards they were happy with and sticking to them.

In the early years we weren't turning over large amounts of money but it was interesting to note that while we kept to our standards of quality and performance our clientele steadily increased. Every year there were many opportunities to make easy money by compromising our standards, but we refused. Instead of investing thousands of dollars in producing designs and full-scale demonstration units, we often could have won a contract by using cheaper materials to reduce costs. But we preferred to maintain our standards and our professional integrity which we then referred to as being able to 'sleep at night'. Eventually it became the catalyst for our success.

In a short period of time Advantage Line had attracted a number of large international clients. One of the first was a large multi-million dollar contract with Fuji film. All types of retail outlets were involved from small counter dispensers in corner shops through to the complete fitting out of photo mini-labs using floor stands, wall units, rotating units and assimilated poster panels. Called the A-Z of merchandising and involving more than twenty configurations all in the distinctive bright green corporate colours, it was the biggest merchandising drive Fuji had ever undertaken in Australia. All their retail outlets were waiting for the new display concepts. With one week to go, Advantage Line staff were working twenty-four-hour shifts to ensure they could meet the deadline. During this hectic period Macqueen was suddenly confronted with a major dilemma.

Macqueen was driving home one night when he heard on the radio that someone had been severely injured in a shopping centre when display shelving had collapsed on top of them. After a restless night he phoned Frank Minnici and suggested they re-examine their concepts for Fuji displays from a safety point of view. They discovered that one of the major display units which was in the process of being manufac-

Major decisions for the future direction in life were made on this simple park bench in San Francisco, 1990.

The New South Wales
front row that went
on to become the best
in the world, 1991.

Ewen McKenzie, Phil
Kearns, Tony Daly.

Celebrations after the
Welsh triumph and a
record-breaking season
of 10 undefeated
matches, 1991.

Macqueen's first
involvement with the
Wallabies.

With fellow selectors
Paul McLean and Bob
Dwyer.

Sporting moments with two South African provincial coaches who would later take over as Springbok coaches.

Above: Whitewater rafting on the Zambezi river with Ian and Rona McIntosh in 1992.

Relaxing after a game of squash at the home of Harry Viljoen in the coastal town of Hermanus, 1994.

A new building and a new rugby milestone: Advantage Line premises at Cromer, 1998.

This revolutionary new design for Revlon led the way for cosmetics in Australia.

Left: Macqueen's original rough sketch showing his suggestions incorporating the snow and the rearing horse, and of course, the name Brumbies.

Right:. The final Brumbies' logo, produced by a local advertising agency in Canberra.

ACT RUGBY UNION
IPC TEAM NAME

Names associated with area/country :		General names :
Pioneers	Diplomats	Falcons
Settlers	Commonwealths	Eagles
Rangers	Civics	Jets
Bushmen	Campbells	Jesters
Bushrangers	Lanyons	Maulers
Highlanders	Consuls	Wasps
Stockmen	ACT Alpines	Stingers
Stockers	ACT Ambassadors	Arrows
✳ Brumbys		Wolves
Boundary Riders		Harlequins
Bounders		Cruisers
Steamers		Centaurs
Diggers		Crusaders
Griffens		Contacts
Outlaws		Kinetics
Dingos		Energy
Wattles		Motion
Cowboys		Chills
Capitals		Chargers
Mosquitos		Centurions
Shearers		Serpents
Colonials		Sabers
Cockatoos		Chiefs
Fillys		ACT Admirals
Colts		Chameleons
Brindabellas		Cyclones
Bogongs		Challengers
Koalas		Caveliers
Bluegums		Lightening
Cicadas		Storms
Yabbys		Thunder
Kurrajongs		
Governers		

Left: One of Macqueen's early sketches of the uniform. This was further developed with player input to arrive at the final design.

Right: The original sheet of names that was put forward at the first committee meeting to decide the name of the new ACT team. A simple asterisk determined the final decision.

Wives and partners take a trip to the top of Mt Kosciusko during the Brumbies' first camp in the Snowy Mountains. From the very beginning they were included in many of the team's activities.

Brumbies early training session showing the colourful training jumpers.

King of the kids award. Owen Finegan is finally presented with his well-deserved award at the end-of-season dinner in 1996.

Other deserving awards to space cadets Stephen Larkham, Adam Magro, Joe Roff and James Holebeck.

The seven Brumbies who achieved their goal of making the Wallaby squad after the team's first year.

McKenzie, Roff, Macqueen, Finegan, Howard, Larkham, Gregan and Caputo.

Celebrations in the Brumbies' dressing room after defeating NSW in 1997 by a record score.

In only their second year, the Brumbies played in the final of the Super 12 against Auckland at Eden Park, 1997.

tured could be knocked over if it wasn't fixed to a wall. Although these units were specifically designed to go against a wall there was a possibility that someone could use them in a freestanding position. Production had almost been completed, and to make these units stable would mean starting from scratch at huge expense.

There was no decision to be made—we simply had to fix it. I immediately made an appointment with our client. I told him I had some good news and some bad news. The good news was that we had discovered a possible problem before it had occurred. I told him about our concerns regarding the stability of their major stand and then informed him that we had made the decision to widen the base and remould the covers, to ensure the unit was safe. I assured him that we would absorb all the costs. The bad news was that we wouldn't have the units ready in time for the launch, as we were already working twenty-four-hour shifts.

Understandably he was extremely upset, to the extent that I realised that this could jeopardise our future relationship with the company. But, although we were late with our delivery and their launch was delayed, it was an extremely successful promotional campaign. So much so, that Fuji became a long-term client.

Most importantly, we were able to 'sleep at night'.

Repetitive procedures

When encouraging his staff to think differently and be more creative with their product designs, Macqueen often called on his experiences in sport to show how small improvements could bring big results in the long term. One of his favourite analogies was the difference made by an improvement in the rowing technique of his surfboat crew.

We were having some problems with our rowing technique and we weren't happy with our boat speed. By using video analysis we discovered the crew were a little slow in lifting their hands at the beginning of each stroke. By slightly changing our technique to be much quicker lifting our hands we were able to place our oars in the water immediately, which gave us a six-inch advantage on every stroke. It seemed like a simple thing to correct, but the result was quite astounding. We worked out that in the average race there were approximately 150 strokes. So multiplying that by six inches it meant the oars were pulling the boat through an extra

75 feet of space in the water. For the same amount of expended energy, we were travelling much further through the water.

In applying this principle to business, it just meant being a bit more creative and clever about our designs and seeing whatever we could incorporate into our designs to make things easier and cheaper in the manufacturing stage. Coming up with improvements to repetitive procedures in both sport and business can mean big savings in time or money.

Advantage Line was responsible for developing the image of many major companies, one of which was the world's biggest toy manufacturers, Hasbro, the distributors of Star Wars, Action Man and Monopoly. For some of their most popular creations, they came up with the concept of 'Action Alley'. This consisted of aisles linked by suspended bridges depicting action characters. In shops like K-mart children were confronted by life-size replicas of their favourite characters such as Darth Vader, Action Man and Mr Potato Head.

Lady Jayne Hair Accessories was another company to benefit from Advantage Line who created for them a new presentation system highlighting the goods more as a fashion product. The system dominated the retail environment and was an immediate success. The subsequent Lady Jayne re-launch helped secure their position in the market place, increasing sales by almost 35 per cent.

Revlon, who still entrusted the company with their complete merchandising strategy, steadily expanded until it boasted display shelving estimated to cover a total of seven kilometres of retail space in Australia. Their harmonious relationship with Advantage Line continues to grow.

Humour and communication generate creativity

According to Frank Minnici a good sense of humour was an essential balance to their serious approach to business. 'Whenever the mood became too solemn at the office, Macqueen would always have something up his sleeve. On one occasion he put lipstick on the earpieces of some of the phones. He would then call the extension of the staff members one by one and invite them into his office. Macqueen would then demand an explanation as to why they were walking around the office with their ears coloured by the latest hue in the Revlon range.'

Some of the fun and games between employees did more than just create amusement and enjoyment for the staff. Macqueen began a rugby tipping competition; it soon expanded to include major clients and numerous high-profile rugby identities. Over a two- or three-year period, it seemed to develop a life of its own. Competition and sledging between participants became so intense, a weekly newsletter was circulated to spread the latest gossip and test players with trivia questions. Competition winners in a variety of categories were announced each year in a large hospitality tent on grand final day of the Sydney rugby competition. It cleverly promoted friendship and good-humoured rivalry between Advantage Line staff, their clients, current international players and former Wallabies, and cemented business relationships. It generated great interest in both business and rugby circles throughout the year, and has been carried on by other companies.

The same work ethic which was such an integral part of the success of Exhibition Displays also continued. If deadlines had to be met, it was still 'one in all in' with staff willing to work whatever hours necessary to get the job done. Similarly, the open and relaxed type of management that Macqueen had instigated and developed continued at Advantage Line. The friendly relationship between all staff combined with the complementary talents of the two partners saw Advantage Line expand and flourish.

Their approach to business was noted over many years by Denis Bond, the vice president, Asia Pacific, for Hasbro Australia. 'To me it seemed quite innovative at the time. The most obvious thing was the completely open atmosphere. I was surprised at the way people took criticism. If someone wasn't doing things the way they were supposed to, they were told straight out, and they accepted it. It was a refreshing laidback style of management so different to the traditional rigid line of authority. The relaxed open interchange of ideas really drew something extra out of the staff and I've adopted that technique myself.'

I always felt the office was working at its best when there were lots of good interaction between our staff. I've always encouraged people to talk about their jobs and what was happening, even if it was to employees that probably didn't need to know. The more we talked about it the more everyone knew the direction we were going in and therefore felt that they could contribute. The worst results came about when we became too departmentalised and lost our communication.

The person perhaps most proud of the company's expansion and success was Macqueen's best friend and mentor, his father Ian. Unfortunately during this period, at the age of seventy-six, Ian Macqueen collapsed while playing bowls. It was a short but emotional moment as his son saw him in hospital before he passed away.

Along with the rest of the family I had the opportunity to see him before he went in for an emergency heart operation. Half an hour later I was informed that Dad had passed away. It was a day I knew would come, but one which I had secretly dreaded. I loved Dad so intensely I was scared of how I would cope without him.

Thinking back, I know he went the way he would have wanted—playing his favourite sport, surrounded by his best friends. All the tears and grief were not going to bring him back. Rather than feeling sorry for myself, I knew Dad would have wanted me to concentrate on looking after Mum. They'd had a wonderful life together and now she was on her own. I knew that he would have wanted me to take care of her. I now realise just how lucky I was to have spent those many special days with him, after my operation. But I had lost my best mate, and the person who had set the standards I would follow throughout my life.

By now, Advantage Line was a thriving business with a multi-million dollar turnover and a finely tuned operation that ensured virtually trouble-free daily operations. This was fortunate because other circumstances were looming that would launch Macqueen back into the hectic world of rugby coaching. It was a situation that would necessitate important changes to the structure of the company.

Chapter 12

Towards Professionalism

Late in 1993 fate played a hand in the development of Rod Macqueen as a rugby coach. During the year the ARU had decided that state coaches would no longer be used as selectors for the Australian team. At the time Macqueen was having a rare break from rugby: strangely enough, competitive rowing in surfboats and building his own company was enough to keep him occupied. But he received a phone call regarding selection from the chairman of the Australian selection panel, Paul McLean, a former champion five-eighth who had played thirty Tests for the Wallabies. The pair had met during Macqueen's successful coaching period with the Waratahs. McLean, along with other selectors, believed Macqueen would be an ideal person to help determine which players should have the honour of representing their country.

Good news, bad news

At the time Macqueen saw it merely as a way of keeping in touch with the game he loved; however, the experience and knowledge gained would be invaluable much later when he won probably the most important coaching appointment of his life. And while he enjoyed travelling and watching the many games required to assess individual performances, the other advantages and perks of being an Australian selector did not sit comfortably.

The various social aspects of the position just didn't appeal to me. Although I enjoyed the company of some of the people, the constant series of dinners and meetings held little attraction. And of course the role of a selector can be most unrewarding. Everyone has opinions and unfortunately the selectors are the ones they feel they have to give it to. I spent many hours listening to people who mostly had self-interest at heart. I found not having a direct input into the performance of a team to be strangely unrewarding. From the outset we sat down with the current

Australian coach, Bob Dwyer, who I had a lot of respect for, and outlined a policy. That was always to be available to communicate with the players over where they stood as far as the selectors were concerned. We would have regular meetings and agree on player performance and standings within the team. Additionally we resolved that no player would hear about their selection or dismissal through the media. They would be contacted first by the selectors. Paul and I took it on ourselves to do this job and it turned out to be harder than first anticipated. Towards the end of our tenure we were tossing a coin to see who had the unenviable task of informing those players who weren't in the team, as opposed to the rewarding task of congratulating players who had made it. One of the observations I made from this was the different reactions of the rejected players. There were two distinct responses. One was disappointment but an eagerness to understand why, and more importantly, the question, 'What do I have to do to make the side?' The other was disappointment and resentment and non-acceptance that they weren't good enough. Invariably they would compare themselves to the player who had been selected ahead of them and begin to denigrate his qualities. To me this showed one type of player who had his own standards he was building on. The other player was unlikely to improve his own standards as his comparisons were always against someone else and he was refusing to accept the fact he needed to improve. We found that by far the greater majority of the former type of player ended up being successful.

Australia first

Macqueen's contribution to the social side may have been minimal but according to Paul McLean his input on the selection of players was quite exceptional. 'He viewed games differently to anyone I have ever come across. He could watch a game and see how it was unfolding and determine why it was unfolding in that way. He could point out all the factors as to why a particular team was not penetrating, even though they may have had all the players necessary to do so. He was able to assess that attack was being focused on a particular part of the field, that perhaps they were going out wide too quickly or they didn't perceive that there were gaps around the breakdown area. He was also able to identify a side's weaknesses far more definitively than other people.'

Towards Professionalism   **145**

They became good friends, each learning from the other. Macqueen also found an ally in McLean, who agreed with his views on the existing rugby hierarchy and how it was stifling the game.

What struck me most was Paul's ability to see the 'big picture'. This was a rarity in the closed-shop mentality of rugby hierarchy at the time. Although a staunch Queenslander, he always thought 'Australia first' and we would talk for many hours about what could be if we were not locked so firmly into the traditional structures and concepts of the game. In future years his insight would become invaluable to me. It allowed me to see things more objectively and take politics out of the equation when deciding on a course of action. Whenever I became disillusioned, he was the person I would ring for advice to help put things in their proper perspective.

Exchange students

Since leaving the Waratahs Macqueen had not been completely divorced from rugby. During his final months with the team in 1992 he and Liz played host to the Natal coach, Ian McIntosh, and his wife Rona. The Macqueens welcomed the visiting couple into their home when McIntosh arrived on a fact-finding tour of Australian coaching methods. Included in his itinerary was a visit to a Waratah training session where Macqueen showed him his latest innovations in training drills. In 1992 McIntosh asked Macqueen to do a presentation at the Natal Rugby Club's coaching conference. The invitation to visit South Africa was extended to the Macqueen family and included numerous tourist adventures including several trips to game parks and white-water rafting in neighbouring Zimbabwe.

Here Macqueen also gave a coaching clinic, this time to a local school side of teenage black children. While the skills and enthusiasm were pleasing, he was horrified to note that the players were so poor that each team, no matter what age group, shared just the one set of football boots. The insides were stuffed with newspaper to compensate for the size of the feet wearing them at any particular time. During their three-week stay, Macqueen and McIntosh spent many long hours together exchanging ideas on the development of the game.

It was also during this trip that Macqueen was re-united with another local coach, Harry Viljoen, who he first met in Australia in 1991. Viljoen was now assistant coach to McIntosh at Natal. It was another typical rugby-based friendship which developed midway through the following year when Harry and his wife, Magda, also stayed at the Macqueens' home during a visit to Australia. Like McIntosh before him, Viljoen attended a number of local rugby coaching clinics to compare the different methods and approach of the two countries. It was part of the regular interchange of ideas during the time and with all three coaches in charge of domestic teams, not competing against each other on a national level, there was no concern over the free exchange of information. This would all change dramatically in the years to come when all three men progressed to coaching Super 12 sides. And, in a remarkable twist of fate, eventually all would coach their national teams. In the meantime there would be positives and negatives for each of them. The first to benefit from their early relationship would be Macqueen.

Confusion and confidentiality

Paul McLean and Macqueen were in South Africa in 1995 as part of the Wallabies World Cup campaign when international rugby was thrown into turmoil. With the World Cup still underway, media magnate Rupert Murdoch had begun negotiations with the rugby establishment to inject a huge amount of money in return for television rights, and turn the entire game professional. His concept would have a staggering budget of $US500 million over ten years. Part of the proposal was to expand the existing and highly successful Super 10 competition, which was set up and run by an organisation representing South Africa, New Zealand, and Australian Rugby or SANZAR. Two more teams would be added to make it a Super 12 competition. It determined there should be three sides from Australia, four sides from South Africa, and five sides from New Zealand. At the time Australia had only two established provincial sides, New South Wales and Queensland; the third side would represent the Australian Capital Territory using the existing player base and resources of the local Canberra rugby side. But officials from New Zealand and South Africa were putting up fierce opposition. They believed Australia was incapable of supporting a third team and insisted it would have to prove itself viable in the first season.

It wasn't long before Macqueen received a message from ACT officials asking whether he'd be interested in applying for position as coach. At the time Macqueen was already being courted by NSW to return as their coach. But he saw the establishment of a new side as a far more challenging role. McLean, who was in Cape Town, with Rod and Liz when the proposal first came through, remembers his reaction. 'Rod was excited at the prospect of starting a new team from the grassroots and being able to do everything his way right from the start. He saw it as an opportunity to establish not only a management structure but virtually a complete club along the lines he wanted.'

However the transition to professionalism was thrown into confusion when officials learned of another proposal being hatched in secret. Australian entrepreneur Ross Turnbull was privately making plans to establish a renegade competition, completely independent of the establishment, bankrolled by Australian media mogul Kerry Packer and to be called the World Rugby Corporation. Initially few officials regarded it as a serious threat. Meanwhile, during this uncertainty for world rugby on the sidelines, there was disappointment for Australia on the field. The Wallabies were eliminated by England during the 1995 World Cup quarter-finals.

During this period of upheaval and disappointment Macqueen and Liz were spending some time socially with Harry and Magda Viljoen. During one visit Macqueen revealed details of his new coaching opportunity only to receive disturbing news in return.

I mentioned to Harry that I had been approached by the ACT and was seriously considering taking up the position. He reacted immediately, telling me to wait. Then he revealed that he had detailed information on the Turnbull-Packer plan to set up a totally new world rugby competition. It was the first time I had even heard of the alternative group. Harry told me he had been personally involved in some of the negotiations and that the Corporation's proposal was far more advanced than most people realised. Key players from the most important rugby nations were being offered huge incentives and many had already signed contracts and confidentiality agreements behind closed doors. At that stage he believed the rebel group had the upper hand. After a great deal of thought I told Harry I felt it my duty to pass on his information to the senior officials of the ARU and asked if I could break the confidence of our discussion. To his credit he agreed. After talking it through with Paul McLean I subse-

*quently relayed the news to the relevant Australian officials. They were
certainly surprised by the information but whether it had any effect on the
eventual outcome I never found out. But there was one thing I did know.
There were obviously many Australian officials and players involved in the
renegade proposal whom I regarded as friends yet who hadn't confided
in me. Perhaps they were blinded by the personal rewards involved. It
was only my relatively new acquaintance, Harry, a key person in the South
African camp, who had the honesty and integrity to see beyond the
money and warn me of the implications not only for myself but the game.
It's something I'll never forget.*

Money a consequence

Rugby entered a period of turmoil as the battle raged to see who would
control the new professional game. It was a time of rumours, secret
meetings, multi-million dollar proposals, competing contracts for top
players, and general upheaval. After months of political infighting, the
leading players were eventually persuaded to remain within the official
ranks and the Murdoch proposal won the day. It was time for the
establishment of a totally new international rugby competition. It
would be fully professional with players on contract receiving substantial payments virtually on par with rugby league. For perhaps the first
time in the game's history individual players were seen by administrators as the most important element of rugby. But what were they
worth?

In the middle of it all, McLean and Macqueen were asked to help
devise a scale of salaries for Australian players based on their ability,
past performance and future potential. It was a surreal exercise—
individuals who'd been playing rugby as unpaid amateurs were now
confronted by something previously only dreamed of. With two interested parties bidding for their services, players were being offered
salaries ranging from $40,000 to $300,000 a year. While many had
been receiving some income through unofficial endorsements in cash
or kind, this was commercialism on a grand scale. For Macqueen this
process crystallised the excitement and adventure the professional era
would bring. It also revealed a darker side.

*One of the interesting things for me over that whole period was to see
how some players and management I'd known all my life, trusted, and*

knew as good people, changed when money and professionalism came into it. I really didn't realise how much until years later, in some cases. In the aftermath when all the details came out, I came to understand how much it had affected so many friendships throughout rugby, and possibly still does so today. The simple truth is that when money was added to the equation it changed the core values of the individuals. Instead of provincial and Australian teams playing the game for the honour and pride of representing their country, money became their motivation. It was this that made me determined to ensure we retained our ethos and pride in the jumper. And to achieve a position where 'money must be a consequence, not a motivation'.

After so much disruption in the game of rugby worldwide the time was right for someone with a new approach. When the issue of professionalism was finally resolved Macqueen still had two opportunities: either to rejoin the established NSW side, or take on the challenge of establishing a new team in the ACT.

He knew Australia's third provincial side would only have one season to prove itself.

Chapter 13

A Whole New Team

Rod Macqueen had an important decision to make. Would he create a new football side in Australia's political capital, or return as the coach of the NSW Waratahs? He felt obliged, at least, to hear the proposal from Ian Ferrier, chairman of NSW Rugby who had been helpful and supportive over many years. A decision had to be made quickly before the beginning of the 1996 season.

As it turned out, it was an easy decision to make. It soon became clear the NSW management was still hamstrung by a lot of the traditions and old school-tie structures that would not work in the new professional era. There would still be a group of people from the board making judgement on the coach over matters about which the majority knew nothing. Not only that, the coach would still be answerable to the board and have to rely on them to supply everything for the team, rather than have input and a say on what was done. It was clear to me this was unworkable. Instead I had the chance to start afresh.

Starting with a clean slate

During final discussions in Canberra, one of the main concerns for ACT officials was shared by the other Super 12 nations: where would the players come from? Apart from several experienced members of the existing Canberra team, the only players available were those not already under contract to NSW and Queensland. Effectively these were regarded as the rejects and discards. But Macqueen had an important advantage. During two years as a national selector he had seen all these players perform. He had detailed knowledge on the abilities of the young players coming through the ranks and a number of former Wallabies who were considered to be past their prime. What the ACT officials didn't know during their discussions was that Macqueen had already contacted many of these players to find out their availability and willingness to try their luck with the new side.

Bringing players together

After two weeks of discussions Macqueen presented a business plan for the establishment of an ACT side. In the months to come many rugby observers would declare the operation of the new provincial side to be a new and inspired way of preparing and managing a football team. Yes, it was inspired but it wasn't totally new. Macqueen had been quietly working ahead of his time for almost a decade. His latest vision, or blueprint for success, was a more detailed and polished version of the same philosophy he had presented years earlier, first at Warringah and then with the Waratahs.

Macqueen's proposal outlined five main objectives. The first was to unite the existing Canberra club sides and ACT representative team to a common cause. This would make it possible to achieve his second objective of making ACT the premier provincial side—an ambitious aim even for Macqueen. He also stressed the importance of gaining the support of NSW and Queensland, which seemed an unusual objective given the historic animosity between those two sides and their reluctance to have competition from a new local team. But typically, Macqueen was already looking at the big picture, his vision transcending the rivalry of traditional state sides and focusing on the future of Australian rugby; all three teams should communicate and work together for the good of the national team. He also saw it as a crucial step towards his fourth objective for the ACT: to see as many players as possible wearing the Wallaby jersey. His fifth objective was as much a business approach as it was rugby, and this was 'To set the foundations for the future'.

The finer details of Macqueen's business plan included many initiatives that would be new to the ACT. A forum would be established for local coaches to be briefed to follow a similar training program; players from all levels of club rugby through to representative sides would have the same playing style and skills training; consequently there would be consistent selection criteria and a clear indication to every player that Wallaby selection was possible; all senior players would be tested on both fitness and skills and the information analysed and recorded on a computer program so that comparisons could then be made from year to year, not only on performance but also on injuries and the duration of recovery times. In his conclusion Macqueen made no secret of the fact there could be problems in bringing together players from vastly different playing cultures—the ACT, NSW, Queensland and overseas. Here he made a bold promise which no doubt caught the attention of those charged with making the final decision: he would create an atmosphere that would allow individuals to come together, put aside their differences and unite as a team. He even guaranteed that this would be achieved by the time the final side was selected for the start of competition in less than six months' time.

By any standards the plan was an impressive document. It had a definitive final paragraph: 'As discussed this would be for a period of two years after which time a new coach and system would be in place for the future.'

This statement proved to be strangely prophetic. But whether or not Macqueen wished to remain as coach after two seasons turned out to be irrelevant for at the end of his second year he would be offered the position as coach of the Australian team.

Two days after presenting my proposal to the board I was contacted and offered the coaching position. My first priority was to finalise the recruitment of players.

In putting together the side it was important for me to find individuals with leadership ability. Having these leaders in the key areas of the team would make it a lot easier from a tactical and on-field perspective. This proved to be an even more important ingredient than I thought at the time. It was also important that each player should have the right attitude and the necessary commitment to the team.

Some of the first recruits included Brett Robinson, a promising young Queensland forward who had just missed out on a contract, and Pat Howard, a Wallaby centre who was out of favour with selectors. They would later play a key role in the development of the Brumbies and make contributions not only on the field but also in team meetings, at training and in the dressing room. Such player contributions would have been unusual, if not unheard of, before the professional era. Robinson and Howard would join several outstanding players already representing the ACT, including Wallaby winger Joe Roff, and scrum half George Gregan.

One important player didn't need to be approached. Former Wallaby prop Ewen McKenzie was negotiating with NSW when he heard Macqueen had won the ACT appointment. He remembered Macqueen's professional style of coaching with the Waratahs three years earlier. 'I knew he had a good eye for people and the ability to get them heading in the right direction. NSW had always had good teams on paper but no one had been able to get the best out of the players. He managed to do that. It certainly wasn't a financial decision. Living in Sydney with my family meant there were all sorts of logistical problems that would make it difficult moving to Canberra. But it was an opportunity to get involved in a new environment where everything would be professionally organised. I knew he'd do it the right way and get things in place. So I just rang Macca and said I wanted to be involved.'

Macqueen was also sounding out the other essential members for his new venture, the management team.

I was impressed by the professionalism shown by the Canberra people and knew several would be ideal for the structure that needed to be put in place. I was also keen to bring in some people I had already worked with such as players' manager Bill James and sports psychologist George Shirling, who I would use on a part-time basis. The most important aspect would be to unite these people from different backgrounds to a common cause. While I had done this successfully in the past, this time it was going to be completely different: for the first time it would be a fully professional management team working with a fully professional rugby side. In fact it was the first time for such an arrangement anywhere. One thing I did know was that a key ingredient would be the input from the players.

In the name of the Brumbies

When Rod and Liz Macqueen walked down the aircraft steps and onto the tarmac of Canberra airport, they were confronted by a mass of television cameras and reporters. Believing their flight was carrying an important political dignitary, they tried to walk around the waiting media to collect their baggage. Only when they were surrounded and bombarded with questions, did they realise that the arrival of the coach for the new ACT rugby side was a major news event for the nation's capital. Along with Queensland and NSW, the ACT now had a provincial rugby side to compete on the world stage. But what were they called, what would they look like? How would they play? Deciding on a name was one of the first items on the agenda.

We were starting with a side that was brand new with no history or tradition. We had the opportunity to develop our own image and the name was going to be an important part of that. It occurred to me that we could pick up some of the traditions and heritage that came from the famous Snowy Mountains area. With this in mind, it wasn't long before we were thinking of stockmen and horses and flicking through the poetry books. After many long hours of discussion with family and friends the name came from an unexpected source. I received a call that night from my secretary Helen. Her son had put forward a name that struck an appropriate chord—'The Brumbies'.

Grey decisions

It was an inspirational suggestion. The name given to the wild bush horses was immortalised in one of the country's most popular pieces of classic literature, *The Man from Snowy River*, by Banjo Patterson. It was truly Australian and invoked the great traditions synonymous with the mountain region of the local area.

When the sixteen members of the administrative committee, which included player representatives, sat down in a conference room they were prepared to debate and select a name from a list of seventy-two suggestions. The choices ranged from Australian names such as Dingoes and Kookaburras, to established international names like Chargers and Cannons.

I believed that the name 'Brumbies' would be ideal, but there was a problem. The decision had to be made by a committee and in business I have often found that committees have trouble making bold or creative decisions.

In my experience, a committee of more than six or seven members will not come up with a dynamic or innovative decision. Whenever I had to suggest a colour to our clients I always had a problem: if I was talking about a corporate logo or colour I would always get the same result, the only colour the committee would agree on being grey. It was always the compromise, the safe and neutral option. So whenever I wanted an innovative decision I would always choose a small group to decide. I've always referred to this as the 'grey decision'.

Macqueen set about achieving a democratic decision but overcoming the committee mentality. His strategy was simple but effective. As chairman he produced a list of seventy-two names.

I then put forward the name Brumbies as my preference and explained why. When doing so I placed an asterisk next to the name and asked for the paper to be photocopied and handed around the table, suggesting that everyone put a circle around their five favourite names.

Because everyone's copy had an asterisk alongside just one of the names, it was reasonably predictable that it would attract their attention.

Sure enough when all the lists came back, Macqueen was able to announce that Brumbies would be the name of the ACT rugby team. It was the only name that had been selected by everyone at the table.

Selecting the design and colours of the football jersey was more involved. In this Macqueen thought it crucial to get input from all the players. Macqueen did several sketches and put the various options to the team who then added their thoughts. The final design of plain white with a dark blue saddle across the shoulders and with a squared off 'V' outlined in a deep yellow on the front, was widely acclaimed and accepted by everyone including the administration.

Macqueen saw the decision on a Brumbies logo as another critical part of establishing widespread recognition of the team tradition and culture. Travelling between Canberra and Sydney he had been sketching different versions of a logo featuring a wild horse rearing proudly with a background of snow-capped mountains. His ideas and sketches were passed on to a design company in Canberra and the final result was strikingly close to his original concept.

Foundations for the future

The team's first training camp was held in crisp spring sunshine at a homestead-style resort complex at the village of Jindabyne, a popular snow skiing resort during winter. What better place to hold the first official run for the ACT Brumbies than at the foot of Mt Kosciuszko in the Snowy Mountains!

The training camp had an important underlying purpose. Macqueen was concerned that since he had begun bringing his team together, they had heard information and direction only from him. He decided on a corporate solution and appointed a professional facilitator to promote his ideas and programs, generate discussion and input, and come up with solutions, but still leaving him to be in charge overall. He chose John Arthur, a business facilitator with rugby experience. Arthur organised a conference room, later called the 'Team Room', which was set up in a businesslike atmosphere with whiteboards, overhead projectors and video equipment. From this time on rugby team rooms would never be the same.

For enthusiastic rugby players expecting to start a four-day camp by running around an oval passing a football, it all came as something of a shock. On arrival they were ushered into the room where Macqueen and Arthur presented a vision of what the Brumbies could be all about. Macqueen played a videotape of the 1991 match between NSW and Wales, where the proud men in scarlet were demolished by 71–8. This was the basis for the style of game he wanted them to play, with backs and forwards linking together offering continuous support, the quick recycling of possession creating numerous opportunities for the backs. The session lasted more than half a day and Macqueen was impressed by the way players responded. Some were reticent at first, but as time went on all began to participate and soon volunteered their own ideas. By the end of the very first day, players not only had an input but came away with goals, team guidelines and an overall sense of purpose.

Much of this was contained in Macqueen's obligatory documentation, the ACT rugby manual which stretched to a comprehensive twenty-five pages. The cover left no doubt as to the level of commitment that would be required: 'ACT Rugby, Taking on the World'. The title was a suggestion from the new media liaison officer, David Pembroke. Macqueen first met 'Pemby' at Warringah Rugby Club and now heard that he was working in Canberra as a journalist for the ABC. Macqueen believed he had a lot to offer. He knew Pembroke was a very keen rugby man with a marketing background. Not long after a lengthy discussion between the two, Pembroke came on board.

While many team manuals in this era simply gave a game calendar, player contacts and a president's note, Macqueen again produced the detailed format which had already proved successful. As with Warringah and the Waratahs, its main points were to increase the essence of the running game by improving on the basic skills, the close linking between forwards and backs, developing a new style of attack, and establishing strong defensive patterns. Along with the guidelines and goals came a detailed skills and training itinerary. The year was broken into camps with each week set aside for specific drills. They aimed to improve players in areas such as endurance and power, recovery, reaction, and agility.

Under siege

Macqueen also took the opportunity to impress on his squad the fact that they had been brought together not because they were 'rejects' but because they were good enough to combine and develop into the best team in the Super 12.

To achieve this the team needed their own identity. One of the most important points I wanted to get across was that we could not afford to develop a siege mentality. A lot of the players had been rejected or ignored by other established sides and had every reason to believe they were outcasts with a point to prove. I felt the approach of 'everyone else is wrong and we are right' would be destructive for the new side. It had been used in the past by the local Canberra team to rev them up because they only played one major representative game a year against NSW. One of the downsides of having a 'siege mentality' is that when you have your head set firmly in your own territory, when new ideas and methods are being developed, you don't pick up on them, and when you don't pick up on progression, you very quickly get left behind. Here we were in a competition with twelve teams where we had to develop as a team with skills across the board. We said the Brumbies were going to be around for a long time, and weren't going to be one-year wonders. We would work at being smarter, making sure we did our preparation and our homework. Our team goal was not only to win as a team, but for as many of our players as possible to gain selection for Australia. For that to happen the team would need to play well and to develop the necessary standards. We could not feed off a siege mentality which is basically a short term fix. It was all right for the press and public to believe we were outcasts and rejects, but it was important that we didn't believe it.

Feeding competitiveness

For those players who had never been involved with the Macqueen style of coaching, there was another surprise in store. Everything was organised. Ewen McKenzie couldn't help smiling as he watched the 'new boys' directed to the training field where all the necessary equipment was in place with training staff ready to start. For them it was a new and refreshing experience. Also different was the style of training. Macqueen organised a variety of different drills which were basically designed to increase the skill level of players arriving at the breakdown. Included were games to improve co-ordination and reaction times. The rugby players found themselves organised into smaller teams, sometimes playing soccer, an hour later Aussie Rules and later in the day a game of softball. It was fun, it was competitive and they enjoyed it.

One of the first things I noticed when playing alternative types of ball games, was that the players became far more competitive and their work rate was greater than when they were doing normal training. I decided to increase the number of games so we could assess different players performing in a wide range of situations. The more competitive the games, the more the players pushed themselves.

Exploring other worlds

There was also a new approach to defence, with an expert advisor seconded from rugby league. Macqueen invited to the camp one of his neighbours, Des Hasler, a former ARL representative known for his aggressive tackling. He talked to them about communication in the defensive line and how to improve their tackling technique. An even more unexpected advisor was a local wrestling coach and his two sons, all of whom had represented Australia in the Commonwealth Games. Working with small groups they taught a variety of wrestling throws and judo moves aimed at dropping opponents to the ground as quickly as possible and rolling them over so the ball could be stolen.

One of the features of the camp was the amount of time backs and forwards were run together rather than training as separate units. Through all the different games and exercises they worked in groups, forwards and backs mixed together, with nominated captains.

The aim was to develop a culture of interactive multi-skilled players. I've always believed that there's much to learn from other fields. You can sometimes become so insular and blinkered in one area that you fail to see all the opportunities. There are always other ways of doing things. By getting specialists from other areas you get the best possible advice from different perspectives. This often opens up innovative ideas and develops new skills. It's also a lot more interesting than doing the same repetitive work week in week out.

Indepth concepts

One of the aims of multi-skilling the players was to maintain possession. For the uninitiated, the first phase of play is always a set piece such as a scrum or a lineout. If the side in possession takes the ball into a ruck or maul that becomes the second phase, the next ruck the third phase and so on until they lose possession. The longer a side retains possession and the more phases they can string together the greater opportunity they have to stretch the defence and make a breakthrough in attack. The ability to retain possession for long periods and patiently work through a variety of phases would become a winning feature of the Brumbies' play—the strategy instilled from this first training camp.

Macqueen also came up with a concept to divide the field into a grid so players could be directed in defence and attack using a simple code. It was a system that would be improved and developed during his time with the Brumbies and later introduced into the Wallabies with enormous success.

When I was looking into the preparation of the Brumbies it became obvious to me that we needed some sort of communication system to allow the players and coaching staff to quickly identify different positions on the field. Although the principle was not new and had been used in other areas, I came up with a system that divided the field vertically into eight channels which we subsequently numbered. To provide a grid reference each half of the field was divided laterally into two, giving us four zones which we nominated a, b, c and d. In this way virtually every position on the field could be identified by a number and letter. This turned out to be invaluable in developing our game strategies.

Rugby defence was becoming well organised and difficult to break right across the field. We spent hours upon hours practising with the channel system code, calling in players to help retain possession after a tackle. We performed these drills so often that it started to become second nature to the players, enabling them to hold onto the ball through many phases of play. In attack, it got to the stage that when a player spotted a weakness in the opposition he was able to call out the grid reference and the side would automatically move the ball to that area and launch an attack in numbers.

Alternatively, we had the ability to attack indepth down the channel. This skill became particularly important as the lateral defences of the opposing teams developed. We were able to attack vertically at a lateral defence.

Plan your work, work your plan

Each day at the training camp began with a meeting in the team room. It wasn't a lecture session, rather, an interactive format that continued back in Canberra and became a key part of their preparation throughout the season, and the following year. The topic could be anything from new attacking and defensive moves to future travel or accommodation arrangements. As coach Macqueen would sometimes lead discussion, and at other times he would give the floor to senior players. Regardless of the subject, comments, criticism and suggestions were encouraged from everybody in the room.

Most people in the squad were by now well aware of Macqueen's reputation for having a businesslike approach but were still surprised by the professional structure he was putting in place. Even team manager Phil Thompson was caught out. A former representative player for the ACT and manager of the local under-21s side, he believed himself familiar with all forms of rugby management.

'In the early days Rod's meticulous approach to every detail really was a culture shock. It was no longer the amateur football approach where players would turn up for training on a Tuesday and Thursday night and just get into it. We went from part-time club training to being professional, which was a big jump forward.'

I hadn't realised it but as we had so much more time available, it was all starting to look and run much more like a business, which when you look at it was exactly what it was! It was having this approach that enabled us

*to adjust so quickly to the ever-demanding changes of playing profes-
sional, modern rugby.*

Send out the clowns

Before full-scale training had even started, one of the forwards suffered
a serious injury, which ruled him out for rest of the season. At the
suggestion of the Canberra rugby management, Macqueen brought in
a young second-rower with the nickname of 'Googie'. He was a tall,
strapping country kid who already knew the majority of those at the
camp. Arriving at his first training session, looking very much the
worse for wear from the night before, he quickly joined in with a large
grin on his face. Macqueen soon discovered the big goofy smile came
with an attitude to match.

*Within minutes of starting the training session I was questioning the
decision to bring him into the side. As we began our series of ball retention drills he started stumbling, falling over and dropping the ball. The
more the players laughed at him, the more he played the fool, purposely
tripping over and throwing the ball at their feet. I waited until the session
was finished before I called him over. He had only been with the side for
about an hour and he was about to be the shortest-lived Brumby ever. I
suggested that if we had wanted a clown we would have paid for a clown
and asked him whether he was really serious about playing football. I think
he was shocked by my direct approach and to his credit, he looked me in
the eye and said 'It won't happen again.' It didn't.*

Young 'Googie' kept his word and would later play a crucial role in one
of the most important matches of Macqueen's coaching career.

Life includes everyone

While the players were getting to know each other as a team, their
wives and girlfriends were also getting to know each other for the first
time. In an unusual move, they too had been invited to the first official
camp. They spent most of their time together, and walked to the top
of the snow-capped summit of Mt Kosciuszko where they sipped on
champagne and developed new friendships. They had the opportunity
not only to make each other's acquaintance but to see first-hand what

changes professional rugby was about to make to all their lives.

I was now a confirmed believer in balance as a key ingredient to happiness and ultimately success. It was important to include and encourage the wives and partners in this new venture. Fortunately, Liz was the catalyst for this. While she knew the importance of rugby, her values and understanding of the partners' needs became an integral part of the development. If there were any concerns Liz would sort them out through the management, or come to me and we would suggest ways we could give people the best possible support.

By getting the balance right and understanding that life comprises many goals and challenges, of which sport is merely a part, I found that I was generally able to put both my business and sport into their right perspective. I realised that there are always sacrifices to be made, but the important thing was to recognise those who made them.

The name game

It was nearing the end of the official training camp and most players had collected the inevitable nicknames. The quiet, almost invisible, Steve Larkham was laughingly dubbed 'Bernie' after the central character of the hit movie *Weekend at Bernie's*. Appropriately enough Bernie in the movie is the corpse of a murdered gangster. Two young visitors to his weekend retreat must carry him with them at all times pretending he is still alive for their own safety. In the minds of his teammates, Larkham apparently had all the presence and personality of Bernie the corpse. Macqueen thought the name was extremely clever, as it was appropriate. He also thought it was appropriate when he was suddenly and then constantly, referred to as 'Long Shanks', the unofficial title given by the Scots to the English king, Edward I, in the movie *Braveheart*.

Not having seen the movie I was pleased with my new title, believing that the players had a high regard for my wisdom and authority. Not long after I made a point of seeing the movie and was amused to discover that 'Long Shanks' was recorded in history as being one of the cruelest most oppressive leaders of all time.

I couldn't help but reflect that maybe my discipline at the camp had been harsher than I realised.

Leaders and losers

The time had come to select a team captain.

After consultation with other members of the management team our manager Phil Thompson and I believed three players stood out, including Brett Robinson. Now that everyone had spent time together and become familiar with each other we decided on a different approach. Rather than having an open vote, which can sometimes cause embarrassment or divisiveness, we quietly mentioned the possible names to each player individually. The overwhelming support was for Robinson. When the decision was announced it turned out to be a popular one and later still, a very effective one. Firstly Robinson had all the necessary leadership attributes. His football ability ensured he was an automatic choice in the side. He was respected by his colleagues. He was intelligent and had an open vision of the game. He was prepared to make hard decisions and support them. He was able to put team above self. And lastly he passionately believed in the concept of the Brumbies and was prepared to put in one hundred per cent.

Strangely enough this wasn't the first discussion on the captaincy. The subject had arisen earlier during contract negotiations with another player. The meeting had left Macqueen dumbfounded.

A local Canberra player had insisted that one of his conditions for signing up was that he would be named captain. At the time we told him that decisions wouldn't be made that way at the Brumbies. We assured him that the captaincy would be selected in a democratic way and that everybody in the team would be eligible. He stood firm and so did we. He decided not to sign and crossed over to play rugby league. The stand we took was extremely important. If we had agreed to that demand the whole fabric of the team would have been doomed from the very beginning.

Brumbies in tune

Knowing the importance of team camaraderie, Macqueen also encouraged the players to develop a team song. Fortunately two of the forwards, Peter Besseling and Geoff Didier, had a musical background and they created some inspirational lyrics to the tune of the popular Australian song, 'Click Go the Shears'.

As we were a new side, we had the opportunity to develop our own song that both the team and supporters could identify with and sing with pride. I was pleased to see that the players had inserted a line that stressed the importance of playing for our country—'Proud to be Australian with a Brumby on our chest'. They used those words deliberately because they felt that other provinces tended to be very parochial, sometimes to the detriment of their country. We wanted to put Australia first.

As he had done at Warringah eight years before, Macqueen personally had the song professionally recorded and presented to the ACT administration. When the song was played at a team meeting it was accepted enthusiastically.

Opening minds is the key to unique decisions

Team players were also given a say in the range of clothing they would wear, both casually and at official functions. On this occasion Macqueen didn't get his own way. One person with definite views when given the opportunity was Ewen McKenzie. Like most front-rowers he had the hulking size and shape that would give any tailor nightmares. He declared that in all his years of representative football he had never had a comfortable, correctly fitting outfit. He was promptly nominated the 'team tailor' and instructed to join a group searching for a suitable ensemble that would hopefully make everyone happy. Again it was Macqueen's way of giving individuals a feeling of involvement in the team spirit, even when the results weren't always to his liking. Being in favour of a traditional rugby blazer, he was surprised when the players responsible walked into his office wearing dark charcoal suits. Taken aback at first he then admitted the idea was original and looked distinctive. But when he asked them what sort of badge they were going to have on the pocket they just laughed. They didn't want a badge or logo at all. That started a lengthy debate during which they tried to convince their 'old-fashioned' coach they would feel more comfortable wearing something they were happy with. In the end he agreed. Macqueen admits it was the fear of being tagged 'old-fashioned' that eventually swung the argument.

One of the sponsors was a local menswear fashion house who supplied a fashionable shirt and produced a distinctive tie that was different to anything else done in rugby before. The coach was happy—at least he was until the players turned up with the tracksuits and training jerseys of their choice. Macqueen was horrified when confronted with designs in hot pink and black. He was the one who had asked for player input and now he had it. For the rest of that year the 'conservative' coach watched his players happily training in jerseys featuring pink and black stripes.

To outsiders, these decisions may have seemed unimportant or even insignificant. But in reality before they had even played a game of rugby, the Brumbies were establishing themselves as a unique and innovative team. It was a sentiment summed up by Ewen McKenzie. 'Rod trusted us to be involved in all areas of decision-making both on and off the field. I certainly enjoyed that level of trust and think I developed personally as a result. We didn't always agree on everything but when you have people giving input you have to expect different opinions and that's what it's all about. Otherwise there's not much point in doing it.'

As the Brumbies began taking an increasing amount of his time, Macqueen realised he could no longer properly fulfil the role of managing director of Advantage Line. He and Frank Minnici discussed how management of the company could be restructured so it could still run smoothly during his long periods of absence.

We recognised that while I could still be involved with the projects and the directors' meetings, there was a need for a full-time managing director. After several days' discussion, we agreed that Frank should take over that role and I would revert to being non-executive chairman, which basically freed me up from the day-to-day running of the company but still allowed me to be involved in the big picture. With this decided, we brought in an account director to take over Frank's existing duties, allowing him to concentrate on his new position.

Melrose Place

With almost half the new Brumbies' squad coming from interstate, accommodation had to be found that would be suitable for both single and married players for more than three months. This was another chance to do something different and bring players closer together. Rather than have team members scattered in hotel-style accommodation, management decided to look for a block of apartments or town houses. After much investigation, ACT general manager, Mark Sinderbury, with the help of Liz Macqueen, eventually found the Pinnacle Apartments in the suburb of Kingston. It was an ideal location close to sporting facilities, shops and transport. The local media was taken by the concept, and after a period of time dubbed the complex 'Melrose Place', after the popular American TV program.

I was very pleased with the positive emotion already building in the side. Everything we were doing was breaking new ground. This was because we were going through a revolutionary process. Most businesses and sports have an evolutionary process where changes take place naturally but we were in a situation where existing structures were unable to cope. We had to start from the beginning and think laterally to solve the problems as they arose. It was fortunate for us that we were starting a brand new side. We didn't have the baggage that a lot of the traditional sides were carrying coming into the new professional era.

With every last detail attended to, full-time training commenced, and Macqueen was able occasionally to return to Sydney to keep in touch with his business and family affairs.

Missing friends

1996 was also a year marked by some sad moments. During a working session with his team at Advantage Line Macqueen received the news that his close friend and former business partner Ed Ifould had passed away. Ed had a massive heart attack while enjoying one of his sporting passions, working as a crewman during a yacht race. It was a total surprise to everyone because he was a fitness fanatic in his late forties. Ed's death upset Macqueen for a number of reasons.

We had been close friends for many years having played rugby together and worked with each other as partners at Exhibition Displays. At a time when the company was doing extremely well, Ed had surprised us all by announcing he wanted to leave his job. Although he was very good at what he did and was financially secure, he told us he wasn't enjoying himself and wanted to make a change in his life. Ed told me he was envious of the man who ran his own business driving a truck collecting industrial waste from factories in our area. He decided to buy the business, work shorter hours with less stress, and enjoy more time with his family leading a more relaxed lifestyle. At the time, Ed's decision reminded me of the lesson I had learnt many years before from Dr Rowley Richards, that if you weren't enjoying your work, then it was time to make a change in your life. It was a strange coincidence because this was the exact message I had stressed to players with the Waratahs and was currently repeating to the Brumbies. Telling them to work hard, to achieve success but to make sure they enjoyed life along the way. It was sad when Ed left our company but we all supported him knowing he had made the right decision. He and his wife Jenny turned the waste collection business into an extremely successful one and had never been happier. That made his unexpected death so much more difficult to understand and accept. I found it hard delivering the eulogy at his funeral, but all those present were happy in the knowledge that he left us living life to the fullest and enjoying himself. Ed was a great family man who left a wonderful legacy to his family.

Not long afterwards the team at Advantage Line experienced another emotional episode involving a friend and long-term employee. The senior member of their installation team, Derek Saunders, developed terminal cancer. Apart from his time with Advantage Line, Derek had been one of the original employees at Exhibition Displays, and his association with Rod Macqueen went back more than twenty years. Frank Minnici was the first to learn of Derek's cancer. Greatly distressed by the news, he immediately called Macqueen to discuss what they could do to help their old friend and employee. 'Derek was an integral member of the company. He was truly one of the team and we decided he should be looked after as much as possible, both emotionally and financially. We quietly advised him to come to work only when he felt he was able, but we kept him on the payroll as he struggled with the illness. When he was unable to come to work, Rod and I visited him at home with his family on a regular basis, until the end came after a very difficult six months.'

For Macqueen it was another difficult eulogy and an insight into the balance between sport, work and everyday life.

Looking back now, they are the things that have meant most to me in my business career. Understanding that business is such an important part of life and the people you work with are part of your own life. They are not just there to help run the company and generate income. I believe we all had as much fulfilment from Derek during those difficult times as we did during all the years he worked with us prior to his illness.

on the lineouts *by confusing the opposition with some*
for the first time we showed a new brand of aggressive
it showed we had a very strong bonding within the side
develop further.

edients

very first game people in the rugby world were shown the
ditions and style of play that would become synonymous
mbies.

watching that game from the Brumbies' private box was
osition than most to appreciate exactly what had been
president of the ACT Rugby Union, David Lewis had
preparation at close hand. He had been involved in rugby
twenty-six years and more recently had been the manager
ralian under 21s and the emerging Wallabies. Lewis knew
more than just winning a game of football. He was
Macqueen had three months to get them ready. NSW and
had months, years, but he had three months and he did
that's rarely been publicised, exactly what he did in that
th period. He had the vision to be able to identify what the
were. He identified what the goals were. He identified the
that he needed to achieve it, and he just went about it.'

bers of our management team had not worked together before
de for an exciting start. As time went on I began to appreciate
hat everyone brought with them. Apart from Bill James who had
ith me in the past, there was Phil Thomson, a policeman with an
friendly demeanour who brought respect to the team and
overcame everyday problems without fuss or difficulty. Stuart
n was one of the most professional fitness trainers I had ever
ross and added something extra with his impromptu guitar-
sessions. Our hard-working physio Gavin Malouf was another
member of the team, as was Doc Hughes, the ultimate profes-
ith a great sense of humour and a liking for the odd beer. Jake
, a former Wallaby and the father of our centre, Pat Howard, also
a prominent part during these first two years and developed a
pport with the players. I learned a lot from Jake and appreciated

Chapter 14
Style of Play

Before the Brumbies' first scheduled Super 12 match, Macqueen organised a short tour of Japan. The trip to one of the weaker rugby nations was a deliberate choice designed to deflect attention from Australian and international media over the fledgling team's performance. Macqueen wanted the team to experiment and get to know each other outside the glare of publicity, which their formation had already attracted.

Our four-match tour of Japan was critical to our preparation for the Super 12. While we had been training for two months, our matches in Japan would give us the opportunity to test our playing patterns against reasonable opposition. The tour would also build unit skills and develop the forwards and backs into a harmonious and competitive outfit.

But Macqueen was anxious for the Brumbies to develop their own culture as much as their own playing style. They were still constantly branded by the media as the team of rejects and no-names from other states.

We needed to establish our own identity. As it turned out, the playing style of the Japanese themselves was very beneficial for us. They were basically trying to keep the scores against them to a minimum and so played very negatively. At every breakdown they threw eight players onto the ground to kill the ball. It was very frustrating at times because to be successful we had to be innovative to overcome their negative play while still developing our own skills. Although it wasn't planned that way, it certainly helped us to develop our style. We had to find ways to stop them killing the ball because our whole style of play was based on retaining possession and mounting attacks from different phases of play.

Judging standards

The Japanese tour proved a success for the two purposes Macqueen had sought. They had developed a distinct pattern of play and just as importantly, bonded together and created their own team culture. A great deal of the latter could be attributed to the rules and regulations players had set for their own behaviour. Before embarking on the trip Macqueen had suggested they come up with their own set of standards, which was put together by a small group headed by Brett Robinson and Pat Howard. The night before they left all members of the squad were given a typed booklet detailing what was expected, ranging from the various modes of dress for different occasions to rules of behaviour. At any one time all members of the party would be wearing the same uniform. When travelling by aircraft and at all official functions, they were to wear suit and tie. At any other time in public they were to wear the team shorts or long pants with appropriate belt, shoes, socks and team shirt. Even at breakfast the minimum dress was team shorts and shirt with collar. The penalty for any offender was levied by a 'Court Judge', usually Brett Robinson or Owen Finegan. It was a system used several years before with the Wallabies and one which worked well, with players going to great lengths to catch each other out. The rules applied to everyone including Macqueen, who was notoriously vague and absentminded. He claims he was inevitably preoccupied with ensuring that every last detail had been double checked and was therefore easy prey. At the end of the tour he was the first one to admit he was the greatest and most punished offender, to the delight of team members.

The fines levied depended on the seriousness of the offence and the person who committed them. They were usually announced during the traditional team 'happy hour' following a match or at the end of a normal day. The usual minimum penalty was to skol, or drink in one gulp, at least one large beer. For non-drinkers the consequences were worse: they were ordered to eat something they were known to dislike. Unfortunately, Macqueen often found himself confronted with a row of full glasses. After spending so much of his life as a player and then a coach he accepted it in good humour. Joining in the happy hour was one of the few times he could relax and genuinely enjoy the company of the players. Other members of the management team consistently say Macqueen was able to walk the fine line between being 'one of the boys' and maintaining

his position of authority. An[...] and arguing with his players [...] that can make or break a play[...] instinctively how far he could [...]

After returning from Japan[...] that could compete with the es[...] They had only two weeks to pr[...] tition draw could not have been[...] home turf at the Bruce Stadium[...] the ACT Brumbies would be on [...] African side from Transvaal. With[...] team was known for their uncom[...]

Answering the questions

As the Brumbies ran on the field t[...] a deafening roar of support from [...] A turn-up like this of rugby uni[...] Canberra, but something that was [...] games to follow. The support was u[...] eeing decisions in favour of the Bru[...] decision in favour of the visitors loud[...] could do no wrong and as the game[...] home team became even greater.

The game itself was hard and tightly[...] sive defence negated the Transvaal [...] backline moves, although not always s[...] the visitors. Perhaps most significantly w[...] created in the lineouts by constantly m[...] positions in the line at the last moment. [...] ually complained to the referee that the [...] tricks, but they simply couldn't understan[...] and they worked, frustrating not only the [...] providing a wealth of possession.

The final result was a 13–9 victory for t[...]

It was a great relief to have won that first g[...] been learnt and solidarity strengthened. It wa[...] building of our team. We proved to ourselves th[...]

*the many inspirational quotes he sent to the team before each game. And
then, of course, there was Quinza, and older, passionate rugby man who
put a lot of hard work into the needs of the team. He was a great compan-
ion and a good sounding board during the early days.*

*The majority of these people were a relatively unknown quantity to me
at the beginning; however, with the special qualities each possessed, they
quickly helped the team progress into the new professional era.*

Success builds confidence

The next visitors to face the Brumbies and their vocal supporters were
the Wellington Hurricanes, one of the leading New Zealand provincial
sides. The Brumbies attacked with their new style of rugby and again
they achieved victory. In a very tight match, they missed scoring
opportunities through simple handling errors but clinched victory
with a runaway try in the last minute, 35–28.

In the third successive home match they faced the daunting might
of the premier New Zealand provincial side, Auckland. Firm favourites
to win the competition, the team was loaded with experienced All
Black representatives. The rugby writer from the *Canberra Times*
predicted a record crowd of 15,000. He was wrong. In excess of
17,000 people turned out to support their new heroes. They had
plenty to cheer about. After a slow start by the Brumbies the supporters were soon in uproar when their team clawed back from 3–17 to
eventually beat Auckland 40–34. In a great display of fast-flowing
rugby, both teams scored five tries with the local side thrilling the
crowd with their attacking flair. The local and overseas 'experts' who
had predicted the Brumbies would be the competition easy beats were
struggling for explanations. The ACT players and management now
knew they had a winning formula, and were determined to keep up
the momentum. But it wasn't to be.

Forgotten foundations

The players were quiet, staring at the floor. The Brumbies were in an
unfamiliar dressing room, pondering an unfamiliar result. They had
just been thoroughly outplayed on the home ground of a rampaging
NSW team. The committed opposition side had played well, the
Brumbies had played poorly, and they knew it. The NSW side had also

gone into the game undefeated and confident, and they were the ones who carried it through. But although his players were downcast, Macqueen looked for a positive side.

It was our first defeat, however it was also a great start to building the foundations for the future. We had fallen into the trap of believing that we were much better than in fact we were. We had forgotten many of the reasons for our success in the earlier games, our scrums, lineouts and ball retention. Somewhere between leaving the dressing room and running onto the field we had lost our direction. This served as a watershed for us and became a reference point to revisit when needed.

The inner strength of the Brumbies showed through in their following home match where they completely reversed their form to defeat the strong South African side from Natal, coached by his old friend Ian McIntosh.

By now, different sections of the media were commenting on the fact that the Brumbies did not seem to panic when behind on the scoreboard. They fought to maintain possession and continued their unique style of play until they invariably combined effectively to engineer the necessary scoring opportunities. This approach was probably best explained in a speech given to the team before the Natal game by imported Argentine prop Patricio Noriega. Although he usually only spoke at any length with the help of an interpreter, Noriega insisted he give the usual pre-game talk and in a passionate address he told them they had not yet completed the foundations of their new side and should not lose focus: 'We can talk about this as much as we like but unless we get out there on the field and do it we won't be building. We'll still just be talking.'

During their second half comeback, the Brumbies scored five tries with dashing backline play. But most talk after the game from club officials and the media was about the display of 'composure and resolve' that was often mentioned by Macqueen and his players. Fittingly the Brumbies' man-of-the-match was Patricio Noriega.

Involving everyone

During their initial matches on home soil the Brumbies were kept extremely busy. There was much more to professional rugby than training and playing football. There were public appearances and other commitments. There was also Macqueen's desire to encourage local community support by making players contribute in various ways. During the week the players were rostered to visit schools and clubs where they would demonstrate a number of training drills and invite the schoolboys or club players to join in. This exercise had two purposes. It created a feeling of belonging for the Brumbies, especially those from interstate, and it was a way to fast track some of their innovative ideas into school and club rugby. David Lewis saw it as an example of how Macqueen's promotion of a unique Brumbies' culture had also helped the players develop personally. 'Rod placed a very strong emphasis on the way people conduct themselves on and off the field. It became part of the Brumbies image. He has this wonderful knack of being able to identify the talent and qualities of an individual and knows what he has to do to bring it out in them.'

SWOTting Reds

The Brumbies' first match on foreign soil proved to be disappointing for several reasons. Losing to the New Zealand provincial side Waikato was bad enough but a serious injury to captain Brett Robinson made it worse. Regarded as their most inspirational and consistent player, Robinson suffered a depressed fracture of the cheekbone and was sidelined for at least six weeks. He became the seventh Brumby to suffer a broken bone since the beginning of the season, and it placed enormous pressure on their limited resource of players.

There was one match that Macqueen looked forward to with both anticipation and unease, the contest against his old nemesis, the Queensland Reds—even though it was at Bruce Stadium where they remained undefeated. Macqueen couldn't help but remember the passion in both victory and defeat when playing against Queensland as coach of the Waratahs. Once again it was a matter of courage and composure under pressure. Despite this they scored twice late in the match to hold a nail-biting lead of 21–20. Queensland had the opportunity to grab victory in the last thirty seconds when awarded a penalty only thirty metres out and to one side of the posts. The result appeared a forgone conclusion as the Reds' second rower and Wallaby captain John Eales lined up the kick.

It wasn't a difficult shot for someone who had been kicking almost faultlessly throughout the competition, but as he moved in to strike there was a deafening outburst of booing from the local crowd. When Eales missed the goal there was thunderous applause from the Brumbies' supporters. It was a memorable moment for Eales, who would later lead Australia to World Cup victory. 'I couldn't believe the crowd was so one-sided. It was the first and only time I can recall being booed on Australian soil.'

The Brumbies' different style of play wasn't the only reason they were causing problems for opponents on the field. By the time they ran onto the paddock, they knew everything there was to know about the strengths and weaknesses of the team they were about to play. Early in the season Macqueen involved all his players in research on the upcoming opposition, using the recognised business tactic of SWOT analysis. Separated into groups, the players would examine videotape of their opponents' three previous games to determine Strengths, Weaknesses, Opportunities and Threats.

Using the established business practices of SWOT analysis gave us a clearer way to string together our thought processes. It was especially appropriate to rugby because of the many intricacies that come into the game. It was an easy method of sorting out the critical issues and establishing the things that had to be done. It also had some other notable benefits. At the end of each week we would look at the SWOT analysis on the opposition and use it as a checklist to see if we had done enough work on combating their strengths and taking advantage of their weaknesses during our practice sessions.

One player would get up and tick off the various items one by one so that at the end of the day everyone in the team would be prepared for the game and wouldn't have a million 'what ifs' going through their minds. I could also rest easy the morning before a game knowing that we had done our homework and effectively put it into action in our preparation. Not only that, but the players themselves were conscious of that preparation. This is when we began using a key word just before going into a game. The word was 'knowing'. During the game if we 'knew' the opposition well enough we would 'know' what to do if they changed their game plan. The players on the field would 'know' how to change their own game accordingly.

As an observer at some of the meetings, David Lewis could see confidence building within the side. 'It was something Macqueen did very well. He involved his senior players in the decision-making to a degree which I hadn't seen before. But not only that, everyone had a say—even the reserve players were making a significant contribution. If someone was making a contribution and Rod felt there was more in the player's argument, he acted as a moderator and would help draw more out of him. That's part of his strength—he knows when to consult, when to seek advice, and how to foster togetherness. The whole thing was done collectively. It gave the players a feeling that they were part of the process, and that does wonders for confidence.'

The relevance of risk

One of Macqueen's constant problems was the reluctance of people to change, both on and off the field. Rugby union had been played for over a hundred years and although the type of player and fitness had changed the new structures that had to come into place to cater for professional rugby were constantly being questioned by long-serving rugby officials. Players, too, were often reluctant to adjust or experiment. As usual Macqueen was ignoring convention and looking at every possible option in his drive to progress and gain an advantage.

During an early brainstorming session with the players, Macqueen repeated his thoughts on the importance of catching the opposition by surprise, of doing the regular parts of the game in a totally different way.

One example I often refer to is the way a restart of play from the 22-metre line would inevitably follow traditional practice. Because the player kicking the ball was right-footed he would kick to the left-hand side of the field about ten metres out from the line. I pointed out that the opposition would have placed in that area their tallest player. He would have spent the past ten years practising to catch such a kick. Around him would be a number of players who similarly had spent years practising ways of supporting him and blocking the rush of forwards following the ball. I produced statistics that showed in the 1995 World Cup the opposing team won possession almost 80 per cent of the time.

Together we then discussed various options and 'what happens next' to overcome this obvious way of losing possession. They came up with numerous variations that were put into practice from the very next game. The results, and the reactions, were fascinating. The Brumbies started by kicking the ball to the shortest opposition player no matter were he was standing and invariably regained possession. Opposition teams soon countered by standing their taller players next to shorter members of the team. We then stood our whole team of players along the line and passed the ball from one to the other until it reached someone who was unmarked. He then tapped the ball a short distance across the line and regained possession himself. This tactic worked extremely well until opposing teams again countered by ensuring that every Brumby was individually marked. Anticipating this, we had already planned and practised another counter move, which was simply to kick the ball over the top into open space, again allowing our players to rush through and seize possession. We used similar tactics for the restart of play from the centre of the field.

All this unfolded in front of fascinated and disbelieving crowds. To them it was exciting and adventurous football being played on a spur-of-the-moment basis. They had no idea how much thought and practice had been spent on the different variations.

To most people watching, it was extremely dangerous to kick the ball at random not knowing what the result would be. The most interesting point about all of this was the perception that although this was very exciting and innovative, it was extremely risky. In fact the greatest risk was to go back to the traditional way of kicking the ball out ten metres to where the tallest opposition man was standing. The risk of not regaining possession was always there but our statistics showed that instead of losing the ball 80 per cent of the time it was reduced to 50 per cent or less. But even now when I'm watching any game and see a team feeling themselves threatened under pressure I notice they invariably resort to the traditional 22-metre kick. Why? Because they still can't shake the old belief that anything else is a risk.

The same happens in business. People tend to use traditional methods because they feel it is safer. But I believe if we are more innovative, and open up our minds, the risks of failure are far less and the chance of success more certain.

The Brumbies were heading into every game far better prepared than many of their more experienced opponents realised. At the time they were being roundly praised for playing with enthusiasm and passion when perhaps more suitable words would have been preparation and innovation.

Stakeholders get their share

In the modern professional era of rugby there was much uncharted territory. One aspect crucial to success was the importance of sponsorship. With this in mind the Brumbies' management organised a sponsors' lunch or dinner before every match. Here executives and senior staff from various companies could mingle with officials and players. Macqueen took this a step further. He made a conscious effort to make sponsors feel as though they were part of the club culture by taking them into his confidence and sharing information before the game.

Before each match, after I had spoken to the team in the dressing room, I would join the sponsors at their pre-match function. Usually it was about half an hour before the game started. I'd let them know which players were taking the field, which substitutes would be used and I would also tell them the tactics we planned to use. This proved enormously popular and ensured we always had a great roll-up of the people who were so important to the support of the team. Many were surprised that I was reasonably relaxed before a game and able to talk openly about what we were going to do, but I found it quite a natural thing to do because all my work and preparation had been done. By that stage it was up to the captain and the players to prepare themselves mentally before running onto the field. It was almost like allowing a client into the company boardroom to be part of a group decision-making process. They weren't just outsiders offering financial support and then watching from the sidelines. By confiding to them our all important team tactics they felt themselves to be part of what was going to be a successful venture.

Missing the point

South Africa is a beautiful and attractive destination for tourists. For touring rugby sides it is a traditional graveyard. The Brumbies suffered a heartbreaking loss to Western Province and were defeated 23–10 by Northern Transvaal in a game dominated by farcical refereeing. It was a game they desperately needed to win if they were to have any hope of remaining in the competition. The Brumbies returned home filled with a mix of elation and despair. They needed Natal to lose their final two matches to stand a chance of making the semi-finals. In preparing for their own final match against New Zealand's Otago, they vowed to produce a game their supporters would remember. They did. In a devastating mix of driving forward play and sweeping backline movements they were able to inflict one of Otago's biggest defeats. Elated with the scoreline of 70–26 the players couldn't help but feel cheated when they missed out on the ultimate fairytale of playing on for the Super 12 crown in their first year: they failed to make the semi-finals by just one point, even though they won more games than the team that took the final place in the semi-finals. The reason for this was the new system of bonus points awarded to teams that scored more than four tries in a match or were defeated by less than seven points. But the Brumbies had defied all odds and predictions by successfully combining to play entertaining and creative rugby, achieving greater results than even their supporters dared to hope.

No excuses

The Brumbies' season was best summed up by the *Sydney Morning Herald*'s Greg Growden, who referred to their mixture of discarded and unwanted players as rugby's 'bubble and squeak', in other words the leftovers of Australian rugby. 'A diligent ACT team management, revolving around their excellent coach, Rod Macqueen, were able to construct a solid team base and extraordinary morale. It was no easy task mixing together diverse performers from Canberra, Sydney and Brisbane. But Macqueen succeeded in his endeavour to show the other two states the importance of a strong third province in Australia, along the way giving his team the ideal platform to play some invigorating, breathtaking football.'

Growden's comments echoed those of other rugby commentators but he also seized on another important point which was to become a hallmark of Macqueen's public persona: not complaining about the many factors which worked against the Brumbies preventing them from achieving them even more. 'Macqueen could have whinged about contentious refereeing decisions but he refused to. Instead he constructively called for neutral referees. Similarly, Macqueen could have publicly despaired long and hard about the crucial players he lost through injury. But he didn't. Instead he had to repeatedly mix and match his line-up, which to the surprise of all except ACT players and management, kept performing against the strongest opponents.'

Excusing a loss by complaining about outside factors once the event is over doesn't change the result. It's a fact in any sport, and a lesson I had learnt the hard way over many years, especially during my time rowing in surfboats. One of the unique yet exciting things about surfboat rowing is the amount of luck that comes into the sport, due to many different elements including rips and currents, the variations in wave patterns and the constant danger of equipment damage or failure. The result is a sport where there is always an 'excuse for losing'.

There were many excuses when the carnival was over, always a sad story. 'We were in front when a wave broke over the boat and filled us up.' 'Our bailing pump broke.' 'The winners caught a wave from behind while we were caught in still water.' I was guilty of these great excuses on many occasions and Liz knew every one of them.

Yet despite all these variables, in general the great crews were still able to overcome the odds and win consistently. They had to be good enough to make their own luck. They had to be that much better mentally and physically so that they could come from behind, make up ground, and win. They didn't let the many variables and the elements overcome them, or use them as an excuse. It is this level of thinking that makes champions: 'What happens next—don't leave anything to chance'.

In any endeavour, once you start justifying performance with excuses you will never reach the standards required to be successful and ultimately the best.

Seventh heaven

The end-of-season function was a celebration not just for the players. The jubilation extended to families, officials, club management and even the corporate sponsors. It transformed from a dinner into a party that raged throughout the night. There were two major highlights. Firstly the presentation of individual player awards. For the first time the sense of fun and camaraderie which had buoyed the players throughout the season was shared. Individuals were awarded silly prizes to match their personal faults, habits or idiosyncrasies. Coach

'Long Shanks' Macqueen was officially awarded kingship with a glittering crown. Owen Finegan, the perennial joker affectionately known as 'The Big Kid', was fitted out in a baby bonnet and bib. The burly Noriega, renowned for his dancing exploits, was forced to step into a bright pink dancing dress. Four players who were often regarded as being so vague as to be on another planet were crowned with homemade silver helmets and dubbed 'The Space Cadets'. It was an insight into the spirit that had bonded a group of strangers into an inventive and exciting team that was capturing the imagination of rugby enthusiasts around the world.

The performance of the team had received the recognition it deserved, but would the performance of individuals receive equal recognition? The answer from the Australian selectors was a resounding yes. When team manager Phil Thomson read out the Wallaby selections for 1996 the gathering was stunned, then elated. The names of no fewer than seven Brumbies were listed in the Australian side.

For me it was an incredibly proud moment. A very special part of my life occurred that night. When seven Brumbies made the 21-man squad the emotion that ran through the crowd and players was quite surreal. Six months before we had set ourselves a goal and now seven of our players had reached it. These were players who without the opportunity of playing for the ACT would not have been in contention. Would not have even been considered by the selectors because they would have been out of sight and out of mind. The Wallaby selection was a vindication of the decision to establish a third provincial side. More importantly, for me, it was an endorsement of the way we had set out in a businesslike fashion to establish a fully professional structure with clear goals and a multi-layered support system.

The deaf valleys

Having achieved so much it was hard to believe the Brumbies then needed to compose themselves for one more encore performance to finish the season. They were scheduled to meet the visiting Welsh test side in a warm-up match for the visitors. The extraordinary irony of this final contest was not lost on Macqueen. The last time he had been personally involved with the men in scarlet was five years back when as coach of NSW he orchestrated the 71–8 humiliation of a proud rugby nation. It was the videotape of that same match he had used at the first Brumbies' official camp at Jindabyne to demonstrate what a team playing an innovative, fast-moving style of game could do to a side playing traditional safety-first rugby.

For the Welsh it was a nightmare revisited. In front of their adoring home crowd the Brumbies swept in for ten tries winning the match 69–30. The Welsh officials later admitted it had been a lesson they needed to learn. They had not been prepared for the speed or the sheer physical nature of the Brumbies' style of play. For Macqueen it was also a lesson of sorts.

I must admit I was quite surprised. It appeared Wales hadn't learnt much from the time we last played them in 1991. After five years they were still playing old-fashioned rugby in an era that demanded creativity and a professional approach.

The initial Super 12 series was the first test for fully professional rugby. Among rugby followers and commentators there was no argument as to who had come top of the class. Macqueen was universally voted best coach of the series and the performance of the newborn Brumbies the most outstanding. Seven wins from eleven games was testament to Macqueen's meticulous preparation. For the first time rugby was a truly serious business led by a man expert at blending the principles of business and sport. Macqueen's final comment to the media at the end of the series should not have raised eyebrows. When asked if he was pleased they had finished the season on a high note by defeating Wales he replied in the affirmative, but added that planning was already well underway for next year. It was a timely warning for any future opponents wise enough to listen. While most teams around the world were struggling to copy the style of play developed by the Brumbies in 1996, he was already several steps ahead, devising the tactics others would have to confront, control or copy the following year.

Chapter 15

The Rugby Revolution

The Brumbies' motto in their second year was called 'One Step Ahead'. It was a fitting title. Macqueen was well aware the opposition would be tougher after their success the previous season. There was a general feeling that other sides who had underestimated the 'new boys' of the competition would now be prepared. The main goal for the season was once again to achieve Wallaby selection for as many players as possible. Macqueen was also determined to ensure that this time they would make the semi-finals. He wanted the players to be aware they should always be one step ahead of the opposition. He consulted sports psychologist, George Shirling, for his opinion. Shirling agreed it would be the perfect thought to put in the minds of the players, to convince them that by doing their homework and match preparation in great detail, they would have a virtual secret weapon when confronting the opposition.

The challenge of change

In putting together their plan for the season Macqueen and other members of the management team discussed how much the game of rugby had changed in just one year, and how widely recognised the Brumbies were as the innovators. As Macqueen had predicted, the very nature and culture of the game was transforming and the responsibility of individual players had already changed dramatically.

I recalled how former Wallaby prop Chris Handy often referred to the game as a musical recital with the forwards being the piano lifters and the backs the piano players. I pointed out that concept no longer applied.

There was now little difference between the role of each player outside of the set plays of scrums and lineouts. Now each player lifted the piano off the truck, carried it inside, wrote the music, played the piano and sang the song. It was interesting to me to see that in business and in football traditions tend to stifle progress.

It truly was a revolution. Rugby players were now training full-time and everything they did from weights in the gymnasium to their consumption of food was being supervised. During the game there were fewer interruptions and stoppages, giving them less time to rest. The amount of continuous game time had risen by up to thirty per cent. This meant they needed a different type of fitness. Because both forwards and backs were continually running from one phase to another they needed to be not only multi-skilled but also more physically mobile. This had to be catered for in training.

Changes in coaching were no less dramatic, and so rapid, the systems in place couldn't cope. The new breed of coach needed to have managerial skills so he could see the big picture. He wasn't there just to do the on-field work but to be a facilitator as well. He had a staff to manage, a medical team to supervise, player recruitment, media commitments and responsibilities to sponsors. There was also next season to plan for and the ongoing strategy of the 'game plan'. Additionally, there was the onerous task of studying videos. In the new age of rugby, rivals had the opportunity to study each other's performance week by week. It wasn't unusual to introduce a creative backline movement one week and have the same move used against you the next. Some sides were surging ahead, others were struggling.

Because of the different nature of the game brought on by professionalism, a number of sides were unable to adjust or cope. From our point of view we needed to think outside the square to stay in front. I believe we were lucky because we didn't have a lot of the restrictions that were holding back some of the established clubs. We were able to make our own decisions and cut across the normal traditions and barriers. From the beginning we were able to develop our own structures to cope with the demands of modern rugby. This worked very much in our favour during that time.

Statistically speaking

Statistics, analysis and more statistics. If one thing typified the professional approach to the modern game it was the need to know everything possible about your opponents. To this end videotape became both a blessing and a curse. Over the previous season Macqueen had put in place a system to cope with the stream of videos coming in from every game played in the Super 12. Every week, three people employed outside the management team studied each tape and compiled the various statistics of play. Management would then examine the videos individually and arrange editing of scrums, lineouts and other aspects of the game. The finished edited tapes would then be presented to the team along with a breakdown of the important data. In this way the Brumbies were able to examine special team moves and general tactics. They were also able to pinpoint the strengths and weaknesses of individual players. It was expensive, time consuming and at times tedious. But it was essential. Macqueen was aware that other teams were going through a similar process and knew those that weren't were suffering on the field. New Zealand teams were especially fast to adopt any new technology. Soon the importance of analysing every pass, tackle and kick was brought home to everyone involved. An independent computer company in New Zealand developed software that simplified and quickened the process. It advertised on the internet that basic statistics on every match in the Super 12 competition were available at short notice—to anyone willing to pay the price.

With the enormous amount of money involved, rugby was changing almost on a weekly basis. By using the latest technology and unlimited human resources the innovation of one side was soon in the game plan of their opponent. To remain competitive we were forced to keep thinking and to keep evolving.

During the first get-together with his management team Macqueen was adamant they should be openminded on every single aspect of the game; the element of surprise would be crucial in winning. It was a tactic continually stressed throughout the new players' manual, entitled 'Brumbies' Business Plan 1997'. This program included a detailed breakdown of the team's strengths and weaknesses and how they could be improved, and even included suggestions to help players organise their personal lives to minimise distractions during the playing season. One section was devoted to ways of catching the opposition by surprise during any restart of play; these suggestions would later be debated at team meetings where they would bring a rush of ideas from players, ideas which developed into some of the team's most adventurous and successful tactics.

Making decisions easy

Macqueen's creative approach to the game was by now infectious. Even before the first training session several players approached him with their own new ideas. To capitalise on this enthusiasm, the first gathering of Brumbies in 1997 was not a traditional training run but a think tank. Once again the location was in *The Man from Snowy River* country, this time at the Thredbo Ski Resort, a different venue at higher altitude with rugged scenery and excellent facilities.

There was an air of excitement as suggestions and creative ideas bounced around the room. Brett Robinson and David Giffin proposed various options which Macqueen then helped develop and refine. These moves later became hallmarks of Brumby play. One in particular was to prove an ongoing headache for all opposing teams: it was a totally new way of structuring the rugby lineout. They suggested splitting the lineout in two, leaving a large gap in the middle. There would be at least one player jumping for the ball in each group with the usual support. Opposing teams would soon discover that the Brumbies' halfback could receive the ball and run straight through the large space in the middle of the line. He would then be followed by the other forwards, who, if not able to make a clean break, could immediately form a ruck or maul well over the advantage line. The position of halfback could also be taken by a large mobile forward or, alternatively, a speedy winger. The variations were many. Of course once these options were seen in action, opposing teams would go to great lengths to defend the weakness in the centre of the line. This then opened the way for the Brumbies to switch the attack to the back or front of the lineout. If these areas were covered, decoy runners could charge through the lineout while the ball was passed quickly out wide. The sheer number of new possibilities it opened up for attack made it difficult to play against and extremely confusing. Teams who eventually encountered this strategy for the first time found their normal defensive pattern in total disarray.

The process for devising such tactics with player input could have been a long and difficult one. Macqueen found that an established boardroom tactic simplified matters.

It was a similar situation to the selection process of the Brumbies' name. It was important for me not to be involved in long arguments in a committee situation. For example, whenever we had all the forwards together we could never agree on new ideas in the lineout because everyone had their own opinion. I arranged for the four main people involved to make a decision on each new tactic. I found when they presented it to the rest of the team everyone agreed. It was a simple but effective principle. While the process had to be simplified it was essential the players were all involved at some stage in the decision-making process.

Changing team psyche

Finding new ways to win a match wasn't the only consideration. Making sure they earned maximum bonus points whether they won or lost was equally important. Macqueen reminded his players how in the previous year, it was a team which had won fewer games who had made the semi-finals ahead of them.

We established that it was important to concentrate on the bonus points rather than simply the win or loss. The interesting sidelight to this was the effect it had on the team psyche. By concentrating on the bonus points, the team became very positive, focusing more on the way we were playing rather than worrying as much about the outcome. The result was that they became very composed and analytical which was a great help in the tight games.

In the new era of professional rugby union, innovative attack was not the only change. Macqueen knew defence was becoming all important in shutting down attacking moves mounted from long periods of possession. Macqueen sought advice in this area from rugby league, which was definitely superior in the art of aggressive and punishing defence. Coincidentally, the Thredbo Resort was also being used as a pre-season training venue by the North Sydney Rugby League Club. There was a regular exchange of ideas between the two sides. Macqueen was particularly impressed by the North's defence coach John Muggleton, a former Australian representative, and sought his assistance on a permanent basis. With the approval of North Sydney the man regarded in rugby league circles as one of the best defensive experts in the game was soon travelling to Canberra from Sydney once a week to pass on his knowledge to the Brumbies. Muggleton did more than just pass on the league way of doing things. He took the time to analyse and understand the different style of play in rugby and made suggestions which immediately proved effective. It was to be the start of a long-term relationship which would change the type of defence carried out not only by the Brumbies and later the Wallabies, but by rugby teams all around the world.

Building added value

While the Brumbies' team tactics were evolving and the pre-season training camp was changing location, so too was Macqueen's company Advantage Line. During his frequent trips back to Sydney, he was supervising a move into new premises. His business partner, Frank Minnici, had suggested that it was time to acquire their own building, and after some discussions they agreed to make the move. The small business which had started in the back room of Macqueen's house, then moved to a two-room office, had now progressed to double storey premises with a nearby warehouse. They felt it was time to establish everything under one roof and bought a block of land which already had plans approved for a basic two-storey development. However, as usual Macqueen wanted 'something special', and although they probably couldn't afford it, and although the area didn't really warrant it, the two partners redesigned the whole building. Following their usual approach to business and keeping in mind their lifestyle, they increased the recreation areas and included a huge outdoor entertainment area, a concrete slab which was added to the top of the garage section. New curved roof lines and full glass walls added a 'touch of class' to the building, and when finished it became something of a landmark in the area. Another feature of the building was two flagpoles on either side of the company logo. One carried the national flag, the other displayed the flag of the Australian Rugby Union. As usual, Macqueen's business and rugby commitments were heavily intertwined.

Advanced warning

The second season for the Brumbies wasn't going to have an easy beginning. Their first match was against Macqueen's old rival, Queensland.

The fanatical Queensland crowd roared in anticipation as the game began in the confined and intimidating arena of Ballymore. They and the fired-up Queensland players were determined to see a victory over the team of upstarts from Canberra who had beaten them the previous year. They were to be disappointed. In a hard-fought contest the Brumbies turned back the renowned attacking strength of the Reds' backline and confused their forwards with numerous variations of the new split lineout strategy. It was a good start to the season, and one which warned all other Super 12 sides the Brumbies were back—and playing an even more advanced style of rugby. This simple start was to change the formation of the lineouts forever.

Nothing's a secret

The following two games were in South Africa against Transvaal and Natal. The Brumbies played well but lost both matches by a small margin. The most important aspect was that, true to their initial planning, they scored four tries in each match, therefore picking up two valuable bonus points. If they were disappointed at losing they were flattered to see their own tactics being used against them, and not only by their provincial opponents. While they were training before the Natal match, a local school side was practising on the adjoining oval.

When the coach approached me he asked if I would like to see the schoolboys run through their paces. I was more than happy to but in only a few minutes I was in a minor state of shock. I suddenly realised I was watching a mini-Brumbies team in action. They were playing all our moves including complicated forward and backline manoeuvres and even the latest variations of our split lineout. It was an absolute eye-opener to see the influence we were having on rugby. It reinforced what we already knew. To keep winning we virtually had to reinvent ourselves every week.

There was also an amusing side to the Natal match when Macqueen confronted a South African spy. Ian McIntosh, Natal coach and Macqueen's good friend, liked opposing teams to train on a ground below the local Kings Park Stadium. McIntosh had a vantage point from the top of the stadium which allowed him to study the tactics of the opposition. Knowing this, Macqueen organised a training session on the other side of town but halfway through their session he noticed a figure lurking behind a nearby fence.

Upset that someone had been sent to spy on his team, Macqueen managed to circle the area and catch the intruder by surprise. He was shocked to find the crouching figure was none other than McIntosh himself. Initial embarrassment quickly turned to laughter and Macqueen had an amusing story to tell other senior people in the Super 12 competition. He was pleased that even in the new professional era of big money and intense rivalry it was still possible to have the same friendly relationships that had been such a treasured part of the amateur game.

I found that throughout that whole era there was still a camaraderie with the opposition and the ability to enjoy ourselves. It was also a critical part of the team environment. Even during the trying times with long airline journeys, moving in and out of hotels, and the constant round of training sessions and meetings, there was always time for fun. The structures that we had in place such as relaxing golf days, novelty tours and of course the 'happy hours' when added to the many different personalities combined to create a great atmosphere. Because the team enjoyed themselves they trained harder and worked harder.

Being too far ahead

Constant innovation resulted in resounding victory when they played their next game against the New Zealand side, Canterbury, before a home crowd at Bruce Stadium. A feature of the game was a number of moves which involved interplay between backs and forwards. During the flight home from South Africa, Macqueen had scribbled out some diagrams and thoughts which he passed on to George Gregan and Brett Robinson. They came up with a series of clever moves revolving around the scrum base. One of the moves used against Canterbury was so confusing the Brumbies immediately scored a try. Unfortunately it also confused the referee to such an extent he disallowed the try and penalised the Brumbies. Perhaps he could be forgiven: a scrum was put down near the Canterbury tryline and the open side flanker, Owen Finegan, lingered behind play then bent down to tie his bootlaces. As planned, the blind side winger immediately moved in and took

Finegan's position on the side of the scrum. When the Brumbies won the scrum the giant Finegan stood up and sprinted. Taking a short pass from the halfback, he ran straight over the top of the opposition flyhalf to score a try.

My elation soon turned to despair and frustration. The referee noticed that Finegan was a flanker and assumed there hadn't been the required eight players in our scrum. He disallowed the try and awarded a penalty against us. At that stage we learnt that if we were going to do something totally new or radical the referee had to know in advance what we were planning. We now had halfbacks standing in the lineouts, forwards in the halfback position—nothing was sacred. It introduced yet another complication to an already complicated type of game. In the past it was not unusual to check with referees for their interpretation of particular rules. Now it seemed we would have to give them virtually our full game plan as well.

Balance on the run

The early morning mist was still clinging to the surface of Canberra's Lake Burley Griffin as the lone jogger threaded his way along the path and into the local park. The runner left the established track and weaved between trees beginning to shed their autumn leaves. With so many important decisions to be made Macqueen would regularly seek peace of mind by literally hitting the road. With feet thumping on a well-worn track and mind turning over problems of the moment, the answers would eventually come.

These running excursions became a ritual over the years no matter which part of the world I happened to be in at the time. In Canberra my favourite run was around Lake Burley Griffin and through the park. It was invariably peaceful, disturbed only by the screeching of local bird life, parrots, rosellas and currawongs. The scenery here contrasted sharply with the place where my first regular runs began. These took in the beach, the cliff tops and ocean views provided by the track across Long Reef headland close to our family home. Jogging began more as an enjoyable way of keeping fit, but it also soon became my personal escape and a way to clear the mind. In those days I could resolve business dilemmas by a solid hour run across the headland, but then with my involvement with the

Waratahs and later the Super 12, different problems arose, and I sought different escape routes. Another of my favourite runs is in Brisbane where a cycle track takes me along the riverbank behind office blocks and boutique restaurants until it reaches tropical gardens and a stretch of mangrove trees. Off the path is a timber walkway, which takes you through the mangroves. It's a world away from the bustling life of the city and all it represents. I would always make a point to detour along this walkway as a constant reminder to take time out to smell the roses and put everything into perspective. In all my runs I managed to find a spot that would be my 'life's reminder', a place that would automatically put my mind at ease. Everyone needs to find an escape that suits them and their lifestyle.

Self-interested parties

After two more home town victories the Brumbies felt the excitement of leading the Super 12 competition despite the dire predictions of all the 'experts'. Part of the excitement was due to the fact the Brumbies were playing the way they wanted to play. The constant input from everyone involved created an invigorating and harmonious atmosphere within the side. Macqueen called regular self-management sessions, which became known as SM; these allowed players to decide not only on tactics but also issues of management. If a full training session was scheduled for a Thursday and the players believed they had done enough homework and didn't need it, representatives would approach Macqueen and he would agree to cancel the training run. However, after a while Macqueen realised that a lot of the SM sessions were going only one way—that of the players. At the next meeting he declared the sessions should be called SI, explaining that it meant Self Interest. He told the Brumbies a problem was developing because they were beginning to make decisions to suit themselves rather than putting the team first. After a lengthy discussion they eventually agreed and a self-satisfied Macqueen thought that it was the end of the matter. About two weeks later he discovered it wasn't.

One of the players stood up and addressed the rest of the team, saying we were having a problem with RSI. When I inquired what RSI meant, he declared it stood for Rod's Self Interest, to the amusement of everyone in the room. Many believed that I was pushing everything the way that I wanted it and not listening enough to the players. Someone cited one instance where I had postponed a team session so I could play golf with another coach. I realised they had me. I had to agree that perhaps I too was abusing our system of self-management. At the time it was dealt with in a humorous manner but it showed just how relaxed and open the communication was between us. In a way it was the ultimate test of how effective the system was. As the overall manager who put it in place, I had been caught out and corrected without any disruption or acrimony.

Playing in harmony

The players were now well aware of the importance of getting it right. Macqueen's meticulous attention to detail and constant badgering of individuals to get everything working perfectly was bringing results. Media commentators and opponents, however, were still looking for reasons for the Brumbies' strong performance. They were no longer saying that opposition teams were underestimating their strength. But no-one seemed to understand it was a matter of the Brumbies doing their homework, carrying out the endless preparation and combining it with their constant stream of new ideas. The South African sides in particular were finding it hard to comprehend the speed of the new game and consequently were lagging in the competition.

The Brumbies were on top of the world. They were playing fast and furious in a manner which confused all opposing teams and no-one could stop them. It was like different sections of an orchestra blending effortlessly together to produce a stirring masterpiece. Macqueen could have been forgiven if he had dragged out his old videotape of 'Bolero' and enjoyed the magic of it and the sweet enjoyment of the combined result. Fortunately he didn't.

The great benefits of failure

The next New Zealand game was against competition favourites Auckland. It was the game everyone in the competition had been waiting for—the established champions playing the lively combination of 'misfits and rejects'.

The Brumbies were comprehensively defeated. It was a bitter blow and one which prompted a general consensus amongst their rivals that the Brumbies weren't the great team they believed themselves to be. Macqueen took a positive message from the defeat. They were playing brilliant and creative rugby but at crucial times everything hinged on holding possession at all costs. In some rehearsed moves all players converged on one section of the field to force a breakthrough by sheer weight of numbers. If the ball was lost there was no-one in position to stop the opposition from scoring. It was exciting, adventurous play but any mistakes were punished. Some adjustments needed to be made.

It was a tribute to Macqueen's insight and the team's professionalism that the situation was turned around in the very next match, still in New Zealand, against Otago. It was a game played in atrocious conditions of rain and slush. In contrast to all their previous matches the Brumbies did not attempt stylish, scintillating backline play. They retained possession at all costs and came away with a valuable win on foreign soil. The media later branded it a boring and tedious spectacle, not the type of rugby now expected of the Super 12. But in the dressing room Macqueen paid tribute to his players who all knew they had played in a special way to achieve a specific goal. It may have been boring to watch but it took courage and commitment to play in a style completely out of character to win the day.

The Auckland match was a turning point for us. They played very well and they punished us every time we turned over possession. Auckland were extremely well coached and when we did lose possession they took advantage by spinning the ball wide and catching us out of position. At the time our philosophy was always to be on attack because we had faith that we would not lose the ball. So in a game when we lost the ball we got what we deserved. It was very much a business or management-related problem, a situation to be treated as a setback and not a disaster. It was a time to reassess and modify our approach. This we did and it was a tribute to everyone concerned that we were so quickly able to turn a negative result into a positive. We now had the skills to be able to change our game plan. This gave the team another dimension.

The fine line between arrogance and confidence

'The ACT has turned the Waratahs into the funniest stand-up comics on the Super 12 circuit', blasted one newspaper report.

If the Brumbies could reinvent themselves and change from playing fast attacking football one week to grinding trench warfare the next, could they reverse their style yet again only one week later? The answer, as a hapless NSW outfit discovered, was yes. The Waratahs ventured to Bruce Stadium hoping to repeat the thrashing they handed out to the ACT 'new boys' the previous year. Although coach Matt Williams and other officials were quoted in the media as having enormous respect for the Brumbies, it was widely accepted that the Wallaby-packed NSW team would outclass their opposition. Instead the result was an embarrassment for the men in pale blue and a triumph for the Brumbies, led by man of the match, Brett Robinson. In front of a record home crowd of almost 19,000 fans, the Brumbies demolished the visitors 56–9, with eight unanswered tries. It was the biggest ever defeat for NSW at a provincial level, and their greatest loss since a drubbing by the All Blacks way back in 1924. For the Brumbies the win gave them a perfect ten out of ten home record. In two years of the Super 12 they had never lost a game on home soil.

Everything went so perfectly to plan that even Macqueen was shaking his head in disbelief. Not only did the original battle plan work perfectly, a second range of options planned and practised in detail was not even required. To make matters even more embarrassing for the NSW team their board of directors was in the Brumbies' sponsors' room when Macqueen gave his usual pre-game address where he outlined a strategy that the Waratahs were expected to counter. Amazingly, they didn't.

There was another side to the match which made the victory for the Brumbies even sweeter. In the dressing room before the game they could hear the Waratah coaching staff psyching up the players. There was much ranting and raving about aggressive tactics. The Brumbies players listened to it all with quiet amusement. This was so alien to their own style of preparation. They had done their homework, knew how they were going to play, knew the strengths and weaknesses of their opposition and were merely waiting to put their plans into action.

After the match, in contrast, the Waratah dressing room was deathly silent. It may have been a lesson for NSW but it was also a lesson for the Brumbies. The situation reinforced one of the basic tenets constantly espoused by Macqueen.

One of the things we prided ourselves on was to know and respect the opposition. There is a fine line between confidence and arrogance but a huge difference. A lot of people believe you must be arrogant to be successful in a team environment. I don't believe this is the case. In any environment I think it's imperative to respect the opposition and understand the difference between confidence and arrogance. The confident person who respects the opposition is able to go out knowing what to do while at the same time learning from the opposition. An arrogant person with no respect doesn't know their opposition and learns nothing. Although they may be very talented one day they will be found out and they will fail.

In the age of professional rugby it was not only the style of play that had changed. The role of spectators was also changing. In some cases even more dramatically than the vociferous chanting and singing of the parochial Brumbies' home crowd. Running out to play New Zealand's Wellington Hurricanes on their home turf the Brumbies were greeted by a deafening roar from a record crowd of 42,000. Looking at the sea of faces was an almost surreal experience because many of them were identical. They were surrounded by the snarling, bald-headed image of Hurricane's prop, Bull Allen. The majority of the spectators were wearing masks of the aggressive and charismatic player. It was an imaginative and intimidating promotion which made for an even more threatening welcome for the visitors. As the game got under way the snarl on the masks didn't change but the faces underneath did. The Brumbies finished the 1997 season in the same style in which they started. Already assured of a place in the semi-finals they needed to win this last match of the year to play the all important semi-final on their home ground. They scored early and kept on scoring, finishing the match with five tries and the all important bonus points which assured them of the home ground advantage the following week. George Gregan was acclaimed Man of the Match and also won the title of Best Player in the Super 12 competition. It was all they had hoped for. Only two matches stood between them and the title 'Super 12 Champions.' Ironically the semi-final match, although being played on their home ground at Bruce Stadium, would be against the same opponents, the Wellington Hurricanes.

Smelling the roses

In keeping with his philosophy of recognising important milestones, Macqueen thought it was time for a personal message to his players.

So often during the year he had talked to them of the importance of taking time out 'to smell the roses', to pause and enjoy the moment. He sought Liz's ideas about making an unusual but telling gesture, and so as each Brumby arrived for their first training session before the semi-final, Macqueen presented him with a single rose. For any other group of hardened rugby players the situation would have been laughable, the message incomprehensible. But for the Brumbies it was a meaningful insight into the personal priorities of their coach. For Macqueen it was an important statement about his views on keeping a balance between winning and enjoying the game.

It's a time I will always remember. How important it was to sit back and reflect, to savour the achievement. Even though we had not finished the season we had attained an important goal. It was important to appreciate the special moments in the journey.

While Macqueen and his men were smiling and quietly joking as they waved the roses symbolic of smelling sweet success, there was a problem. Others in the vicinity didn't quite understand. To Macqueen's horror several newspaper photographers arrived and began snapping shots of this most unusual scene. Fortunately he was able to impress on them that it was a very private moment, not one to be shared with the general public. Who knows what connotations would have been attached? Regardless of any sort of explanation there is little doubt that the image of Rod Macqueen and the Brumbies would have been changed forever.

Helping Rod with these unusual projects was not the only contribution Liz made to the team. Apart from liaising with wives, partners and other family members, she also advised Rod on many team activities and provided constant personal support.

For someone who hadn't been involved in a lot of my sporting life, Liz was now playing a major role. We were working side by side as a team and she was contributing greatly to keeping harmony within the side. The special thing was that Liz could do this without being intrusive, by working behind the scenes and quietly making sure everything was just right. She also helped keep me on track and stopped me from becoming totally preoccupied with rugby. Liz was very quick to remind me when I was straying from my ideals. She would often write little messages to me, sometimes in the form of poems, that would bring me back to earth. One of the most pertinent was:

Remember that little rose bush that you took the time to smell?
Well let me tell you now that it's not doing very well,
It's wilting, and it's dying because of its neglect.
How easy it is to want in life, how easy to forget.

Liz ensured we spent some time away from rugby during our extended stays in Canberra which again helped me keep everything in perspective. One of my lasting memories was the chance to see a visiting exhibition at the National Art Gallery. It was a rare opportunity to view the best works of English impressionist, Joseph Turner. I found this sort of balance gave me a much better perspective when I had to make the hard decisions.

These outings would have surprised the many Brumbies who looked on their coach as a hard taskmaster with little time or inclination for anything beyond rugby, but of course few in the rugby world were aware of Macqueen's background in creative drawing and his ongoing love of sketching and painting as a form of relaxation, even as a refuge from the relentless pressures of business and professional sport.

For the individual Brumbies the establishment of a comfortable home base turned out to be a master stroke. Their apartment complex may have been dubbed 'Melrose Place' as a joke, but its importance in the success of the team could not be underestimated. During the three-month period of the Super 12 competition at least fifteen members of the squad were away from their home states and 'Melrose Place' provided the perfect solution. When the players were in residence there was a constant stream of arrivals and departures—wives, children and girlfriends—and working quietly in the background, making sure everything ran smoothly, was Liz Macqueen. David Lewis recognised the importance of her support role over the two seasons. 'When all these different people came from out of town, Liz went out of her way to make them feel welcome. That was absolutely crucial and Liz was the one who made sure there was harmony and family support. She wasn't asked to do it and she wasn't paid to do it. I think she contributed so much because she believed in what Rod was doing and she wanted to help.'

This concept of a permanent team base proved so successful it would be later used to unite the all-conquering Wallabies.

There were other unexpected pressures on the players. The success of the Super 12 competition generated enormous interest from the media and members of the general public. As well as their regular coaching clinics in schools and rugby clubs they were constantly scheduled to attend functions ranging from private dinners with sponsors, to appearances in shopping malls. In the words of team manager Phil Thomson, who was the all-important link between the players and management, they were in effect celebrities. 'It has been an evolving and educational process for the players both in their approach to football and in their general lifestyle. Now they are public figures with large amounts of money invested in them, they have had to learn to handle the additional pressures. It's a whole new way of doing things and while most of them are coping extremely well, some are still coming to grips with it.'

Business as usual—or is it?

At the start of the previous season 8000 supporters had turned out to cheer on the Brumbies. In this last home match of the second season 24,000 fans filled the ground. The outcome was never really in doubt with the Brumbies securing a 33–20 victory over the Wellington Hurricanes. The following week they would be off to Auckland to play the competition favourites for the Super 12 trophy.

During the season the Brumbies had certainly attracted enormous support and almost fanatical publicity in the local media. In the week leading up to the final even this was surpassed. Congratulations and messages of support came from every quarter including the prime minister and the ACT chief minister. The side had truly captured the imagination of Australia's national capital.

There were no illusions about the fact that in the final they would be taking on an exceptional team. But players and management believed they knew what tactics would be used against them and early on decided not to treat the game differently to any other. The catch cry was 'business as usual'. Macqueen thought it essential to keep his players as relaxed as possible in the lead-up to the big game. Everything went smoothly until the morning of the match. When they peered out the hotel windows they saw that the clear skies had disappeared and torrential rain was falling. It was perfect weather for Auckland's bruising style of forward game and certainly not conducive to the quick passing game plan of the Brumbies. It was not too late to change tactics, but Macqueen decided to keep faith in the skill of his players and not try to out-muscle the Blues upfront.

In the meeting room before the game the team went through their normal procedure but Macqueen could see that nervousness was starting to take hold. It was the first time the team had been in such a match. He thought it would be a good idea to lighten things up for a short period. When it was time for the last pre-game instructions he spoke to every player individually using not their name but instead their nickname, giving them special humorous advice. His unusual approach had the desired effect. As he went to each player in turn the laughter and joking increased and he felt the tension in the room slowly disappear. If only the partisan crowd waiting at the ground could have seen what was happening back at the hotel. Dressed in Auckland colours, many covered in blue war paint, they were already baying for blood. What they would have thought of the Brumbies sitting in the room laughing and joking at such a critical time is hard to imagine.

When the Brumbies took the field they were relaxed, ready to play and carried out their game plan to perfection. Sadly they were to be denied victory. The heavy rain made the conditions slippery and the execution of their plan to throw the ball wide difficult and dangerous. Several key passes which could have resulted in tries went to ground at the last moment and one was intercepted to provide a gift five–pointer to the Blues. Auckland played exactly the way they were expected to, and the counter measures the team devised almost succeeded. But they didn't. After a hard-fought contest in difficult conditions, Auckland clinched the Super 12 crown 23–7. Macqueen shared his players' disappointment but was later philosophical about the loss.

Perhaps with the rain we should have changed our tactics because the extra pressure on our mid-field did bring uncharacteristic mistakes that turned the tide in Auckland's favour. If anything it could be seen as a matter of me misreading how we would react under that extra pressure even though we believed we could sustain their pressure, we should have had another plan in place. However, there's no doubt that Auckland were definitely the better team on the day.

A team established

Macqueen's disappointment was tempered by two separate experiences. When calling his players forward to receive their runners-up medal, captain Brett Robinson called out the nicknames Macqueen had used in the dressing room. It brought a smile to their muddied faces and revealed just how strong was the bond the team had developed during the season.

And then, later, they had to wonder, did Auckland really win the final? When the Brumbies returned to Canberra airport their initial impression was that local people mistakenly believed they had won. They were greeted by a cheering crowd and supportive local media, all of whom congratulated them for the success they had achieved. The treatment of a losing team was almost unprecedented. At Macqueen's suggestion, club officials readily agreed to send players and their partners on a three-day holiday to the Queensland resort of Coolum. On their return they were treated to a civic reception and presented with the keys to the city. The Brumbies may have failed to secure the Super 12 crown but they had won the hearts and minds of their supporters.

The congratulations and praise flowed freely, but for Macqueen some messages were more important than others.

As a coach, some of the nice things you get from time to time are personal responses from the players. After the 1997 final, I received a number of letters from individual players. This may have seemed a small thing, but to me it meant far more than many of the other accolades I had received up until then in my coaching career.

For Macqueen it was to be the end of his two-year reign as Long Shanks, king of the Brumbies. Among many of the newspaper articles which subsequently appeared praising Macqueen's achievement, one from Brett Robinson stood out.

'Rod ran the Brumbies like a business. But in saying that, it was a business where every employee has an input. He's not a coach who stands over his team. He's not a raver. He ran ideas past us and we'd think, "Jeez, that's radical, but we'll give it a go". Rod certainly has tremendous man management skills as well as an outstanding rugby mind.'

Robinson, like other players, also recognised the other business aspects that Macqueen had introduced. The team was not a single entity with one person in charge. It was divided into different departments or sections, each with its own leader capable of making quick decisions to capitalise on changing circumstances. This approach would be developed and improved in later years when Macqueen took charge of the Wallabies until it became a crucial part of their success.

In assessing Macqueen's contribution, David Lewis says he did much more than simply establish a football team. 'The ACT Rugby Union owes Rod Macqueen an enormous debt of thanks for what he did through his vision, and what's more important to me, for even taking on this great challenge. But that's the measure of this man. He made all the people sit up and take note of what he'd achieved, and Australia's task in winning the World Cup would have been much harder had the Brumbies not been established. They made a significant contribution to Australian rugby both on and off the field.'

More to life than rugby

Around this time Macqueen made a rare public statement about his personal thoughts on the importance of rugby and the role it played in the lives of everyone involved. He seemed to be the only one aware that professionalism could destroy the future of many talented people. He revealed his thoughts to the *Sydney Morning Herald*. 'Some real problems have arisen in rugby that will have to be addressed, problems that go to the very nature of the game and what it means. When I look at our team, we are very fortunate that we've got intelligent players here, players who have gone to university, who have careers outside football. We have to be very, very careful not to lose this. We are now entering an era of full-time rugby players and that's a concern. We need to address, urgently, how to keep the education and careers of players going. We have to take a step back and look at how we can keep these values alive.'

Macqueen then repeated a statement he had made several times before. It came from Rod Macqueen the successful businessman and family man, and was a statement which many find hard to accept: 'I've got to say coaching has never been my life. Rugby has never been my life. I make no pretence about that.'

It was a classic pronouncement. But those who knew him well, knew he was much more than a one-dimensional rugby man.

For the forward-thinking Macqueen the team's outstanding success also inspired a moment of reflection and introspection.

While I believed my management style was efficient I also realised it drove a lot of people mad. My insistence on leaving no stone unturned to give the players and management the best possible preparation meant I was constantly checking and rechecking what we had done. In retrospect I could see that sometimes I would go over the top and I was often accused of having meetings to prepare for meetings. While I believe I was right in some instances, in others I could see that I needed to relax a little. In both sport and business I have always tried to encourage free and open communication so people can make positive suggestions or air any grievances they have about issues or other people. And that includes me. There is no doubt that sometimes I became too dictatorial and things would start to go wrong before I was able to realise it. I have often found myself in that position throughout my career and when able to recognise the situation, or at least be alerted to it, I have tried to make the necessary changes to move forward.

After two enjoyable years with the Brumbies, Macqueen was forced to make a momentous decision. Would he consider a third season? He had only planned to stay two years and had stressed that in his original proposal when accepting the position. But given the team's unprecedented success, including the impressive fact that after two seasons the Brumbies were undefeated on their home ground, ACT officials were pressuring him to break his original commitment.

And he was tempted. If he accepted it would also mean disrupting the plans he had made to have a successor groomed and ready to take over. During his term Macqueen had worked with a number of assistant coaches who could have filled the position; however he favoured bringing in someone totally new—Eddie Jones, who at the time was coaching in Japan. Jones was a former player with the Randwick club and had coached their second grade. During the past season he had invited Jones out to their training camps and had also sent him videotapes of their games. Macqueen felt that more than anyone Jones understood the style of coaching and how the game of rugby was changing.

While Macqueen was agonising over his future with the Brumbies, members of the Australian media already had him labelled as the next coach of Australia. There was growing criticism of the incumbent coach Greg Smith, and every time the Wallabies lost a match, the phone calls to Macqueen increased.

At that time I honestly had no intention of applying for the position of Wallaby coach. Despite what everyone had been saying during my years with the Waratahs and then the Brumbies, it was never one of my goals. Our company was extremely busy and taking a lot of my time and both Liz and I found our arrangement with the Brumbies fitted in perfectly. While based in Canberra it was easy for us to commute to Sydney for business and family matters, and we genuinely enjoyed the company and support of all the local people involved. A full-time job coaching the national team was not a consideration.

Macqueen set about planning his third year with the Brumbies.

Chapter 16

The First Test

Plans, however, can rapidly come undone. Soon after deciding to seek a third term with the Brumbies, Macqueen did find himself applying for the position of Wallaby coach. However, such was the vexed nature of the process, that he also found himself stepping away just as quickly.

Finding common ground

The chain of events which led to Macqueen's application began with the resignation of current Wallaby coach, Greg Smith. Smith was at long odds to remain as coach after heavy losses to New Zealand and South Africa during the just completed Tri Nations series. Australia had been defeated by the New Zealand All Blacks in their last seven encounters, five of them under Smith. As media commentators had pointed out there was no chance of winning the World Cup in two years' time if Australia had no hope of beating the All Blacks. The trigger for Smith's departure was a devastating 61–22 loss to South Africa in Pretoria.

Along with three other candidates, Macqueen was approached to apply for the position. He was up against strong opposition, including his long-term adversary, Queensland coach, John Connolly. Before formally applying, Macqueen had a preliminary discussion with John O'Neill and found they shared common ground. Both had a successful background in business and understood the need for an honest, no-nonsense relationship between the coach and senior administration. A qualified solicitor and a former Young Executive of the Year, O'Neill also mixed sport with business, playing and coaching rugby in the Sydney club competition. He took control of the ARU after the 1995 World Cup when the organisation was a shambles with crippling financial problems. Under the old amateur system of rugby administration it had a staggering twenty-five separate committees. O'Neill reduced these to a handful and set about attracting high-profile sponsors and the much-needed cash flow they represented. Many thought he was ruthless and heavyhanded, but he streamlined the organisation, preparing it for the professional era.

Both Macqueen and O'Neill had strong personalities and there was a wide feeling that they wouldn't get on, however Macqueen believed they had much in common.

I felt we had an affinity from our very first meeting. I had the impression that I knew where I stood with John, whether it was good or bad, that there were no hidden agendas. I made it clear I wanted a say in the selection of the people who would work around me and he seemed receptive to that. I was impressed because he asked me for my opinion on what needed to be done. He wanted to know what changes I would make and how I would see the whole system working. I was extremely comfortable with that upfront business approach.

John O'Neill recalls a meeting that revealed problems from the past: 'Rod was very wary and innately suspicious of rugby officialdom. It was almost certainly a hangover from his days at NSW where things didn't always go very well. I was very upfront with him and I was pleased that he was the same with me. I made the point that the success of Australian rugby and the Wallabies depended on the two people who would end up sitting in my office, mainly myself and the eventual coach. The nature of the relationship had to be built on trust and once that trust had been developed we could do some very good things.'

O'Neill made it clear that if Macqueen eventually won the position he would be given every support but would have to reciprocate. 'I wanted him to give me the benefit of the doubt and give me the chance to prove I'd be supportive, but at the same time I'd be challenging and not just signing the cheques. As we were both businessmen I'd be asking that things would be justified and substantiated.'

Macqueen decided it was time to prepare a battle plan, not only to secure the coaching position for himself, but to restructure the management system which looked after the team. Needing solitude and time to think, he retired with Liz to the sanctuary he had used so often, Junie's farm. It was here in a quiet corner of the Australian bush that a blueprint for the future of Australian rugby was formulated.

Seven-point plan

For Macqueen the presentation of his proposals at ARU headquarters was a comfortable and familiar experience. Just as in business, he was delivering a presentation to potential clients, many of whom were successful businessmen in their own fields. In a session that lasted forty-five minutes he expressed his ideas and answered questions about his proposals on a wide range of topics. What was the biggest problem confronting Australian rugby? Were players more motivated by money than the love of the game? How long would it take to revitalise the team?

He set the tone on the first page of his proposal which featured a seven-point plan. The opening summary was less than complimentary about the state of the game for which they were responsible. It was more akin to a company managing director admonishing his senior executives than a man submitting what was, in effect, a job application. Although Macqueen may have felt he had an affinity with O'Neill, he would now find out if he had a similar relationship with the other board members. He pointed out what to many should have been obvious, that the standard of rugby had improved dramatically over the past two years since the advent of the Super 12 competition, largely due to a combination of a truly professional approach, stronger competition, changes in law and extensive use of video analysis. He believed New Zealand had fully embraced the new style of play, using a more organised coaching and management structure. And South Africa was beginning to follow. Macqueen's assessment of the current Australian administration was highly critical. 'Australia has failed to adjust to the modern game and basically has ignored the progress made at Super 12 level. As a consequence Australia has not progressed, either on the field or off the field, and unless we take immediate steps to address this situation we will be left further behind.'

The corporate analogy continued in the specific proposals of his seven-point plan. His first point was to establish what he termed a 'Rugby Business Unit' with an independent budget enabling it to run all rugby-related activities within the ARU. He saw it as crucial in building the foundations for the future.

His second concern was to ensure all three provincial teams had a common goal in contributing to the national side. From his coaching experience, he already knew they were highly competitive against each other but did not always have the interest of the Australian team at heart. He suggested a restructuring of coaching roles to encourage input and interaction at all levels.

Macqueen's third point was to instigate an innovative plan and structure which would take Australia through to the 1999 World Cup. Fourth on the list was a proposal to have access to the relevant personnel and research to ensure up-to-date expertise and information was always available. This would include some unorthodox coaching methods using boxing, judo and sports psychology.

Macqueen also wanted to instil the same team spirit which had proved so instrumental in his association with the Waratahs and Brumbies, to develop camaraderie and a positive attitude while using player input to establish firm guidelines and principles. He wanted players to share in the 'ownership' of the Wallabies. He felt it important that players believed the administrators were working 'with' them, rather than the players working 'for' the administration.

The very public denigration and demolition of his predecessor could well have prompted his sixth point: to establish a controlled communication system to ensure positive responses from all media. This would require a meeting of all players, administration and support staff to establish clear direction for contact with the media. He suggested there be two totally separate streams of information: one which related to internal strategies and objectives would be strictly confidential: a second would be relayed to the media and would include only the messages they wanted the general public and opposition teams to hear.

His final point was aimed at establishing a strong foundation for Australian rugby in the future. Once guidelines and strategies had been developed for the national team, a program would be developed to spread these guidelines to all levels of rugby throughout the country.

John Connolly had given his own presentation immediately before Macqueen and by sheer chance they passed each other outside the building in front of the media. It could have been an awkward moment but the pair laughed, shook hands, and wished each other well.

The ins and outs of coaching

On 8 September 1997, Macqueen put down the phone in the living room of his Collaroy home and called out to Liz, 'I've just withdrawn my nomination for the Australian coaching job.'

After weeks of talks, both public and private, Macqueen felt disappointed but at the same time almost relieved it was over. The trigger for his withdrawal was the phone call he had just received from the Australian Rugby Union. The board of directors was about to make a decision between the two final applicants seeking the position of Wallaby coach. During the call a board member gave him a message he didn't like.

I had pointed out in my proposal that for me to be able to implement it successfully, I needed to be involved in the appointment of the coaching team and that I would have to be confident that we could all work together. I made it quite clear that I was not intending to nominate only those I wanted, but merely needed to be part of the selection process to ensure our management had the necessary skills. In the past, coaches were selected for their on-field experience, not necessarily taking into account their off-field qualifications.

Macqueen's stand went against the traditional operation of the ARU but he remained firm. The success he had achieved with the Waratahs and the Brumbies was only possible because of the mixed skills and the relaxed, friendly environment of the management structure. With his extensive experience in business and coaching he was well aware that one disruptive member could destroy the performance of the team.

During the phone call I was told that they were getting very close to a decision but in this case they didn't feel it appropriate that I had a say on who my assistant coaches would be. I didn't have to think twice about it. I basically said that under those circumstances, I was no longer a candidate for the job. When I told Liz the details of the conversation she agreed with my decision. We had been under a fair amount of stress there was almost a sense of relief.

We actually had a little laugh about it together and said, 'Oh well, let's get on with our life.' As far as we were concerned it was all over and we started to plan our next season with the Brumbies.

Their strange mixture of disappointment and relief was short-lived. Only minutes later they received another phone call saying his conditions would be accepted and asking if he would reconsider his nomination. Macqueen agreed. The waiting, the pressure and the uncertainty returned. It was several hours before the phone rang again. This time it was the chief executive officer of the ARU, John O'Neill, calling to inform Macqueen that he'd been officially appointed Australian coach. O'Neill offered his congratulations and added that due to all the controversy and speculation they would be announcing his appointment the next morning.

He later confided to Macqueen that the decision had been a close one, with his appointment clinched by the vision of his seven-point plan. 'To be fair, Connolly interviewed well but Rod gave a professional presentation. It was very impressive.'

Macqueen and Liz's first response was to celebrate with an embrace, a kiss and a bottle of wine. The second reaction revealed Macqueen's experience with the media during his term with the Brumbies. He called David Pembroke, the Canberra journalist who had helped him in the past with public relations. Macqueen thought he might need some advice because he expected intense media interest the next day. Just how intense he would soon find out.

Playing the media game

Macqueen ducked and weaved as he answered question after question about the future of Australian rugby. They were annoying, repetitive, and came in rapid succession. They came not from a room full of journalists but from his media advisor. It was the morning of the press conference scheduled to announce Macqueen's appointment. He and David Pembroke were driving around and around Sydney streets practising for what he knew would be an intense grilling. Macqueen wasn't happy with the line of questioning because it centred around whether he thought the previous coach Greg Smith had performed badly, and whether he, in turn, was capable of building a team able to defeat the All Blacks. However, he also found the interrogation enlightening as to the different ways the journalists would go about getting their stories. Macqueen worked on the techniques of getting around specific questions and slowly mastered the art of answering with what is known in cricket terms as a 'straight bat'. This meant not being controversial, not making bold predictions, just delivering a general, positive message.

An hour later he walked into a noisy room bathed in the glare of television lights and punctuated by camera flashes. When the questioning began, the assembled reporters were obviously after a juicy headline. Macqueen was thankful for his tedious drive around Sydney streets. What do you think of Greg Smith as a coach? Did you think Smith disrupted the team with constant selection changes and putting players out of position? Is our team capable of beating the All Blacks? What are you going to do to make sure we can beat the All Blacks?

Subsequent media reports stated Macqueen had been positive but generally non-committal on most subjects. One newspaper article even said the new coach had gone out of his way to answer questions with a 'straight bat'. Macqueen had survived his baptism of fire. He felt a glow of relief and satisfaction, and gratitude to Pembroke! He'd have to take back all the complaints he'd made about the repetitive questioning. No doubt it would cost him a few beers.

However, he and Liz were not prepared for what followed: a constant stream of flowers, champagne, and letters of congratulation. Both had believed, perhaps naively, they would now have some breathing space to organise their new lives, but they were wrong. In their home at the time were two telephones, a fax machine and two mobile phones. For the next week all rang constantly virtually twenty-four hours a day. Macqueen was surprised that one of the first congratulatory calls came from his supposed arch-enemy, the coach of the New Zealand All Blacks, John Hart. It was a warm and genuine welcome into the ranks of international coaching and sowed the seed for a friendship that would grow in the years to come. Media organisations both Australian and from other rugby nations all around the world tried to make contact, each chasing their own exclusive story. Macqueen was stunned.

I just couldn't believe how much our lives changed in one week. We are people who enjoy our privacy and quiet times, and we felt totally overwhelmed. It was running out of control and by the end of that week I was so mentally drained I began to wonder if we had made a big mistake. At one stage Liz and I actually sat down and discussed whether we would be able to continue. In the end we agreed we had made the decision together and that somehow we would just have to adapt to these changes and get on with it.

Only now did he fully understand what it meant to be the person many believed was in control of a nation's rugby destiny. It seemed that the expectations of a proud sporting nation were now his sole responsibility. Everyone wanted to know if he could restore the Wallabies to their former glory. How soon? And how? But answering media enquiries was all very well. Meantime Macqueen had a few other, minor things to do. He had only three weeks to prepare the Wallabies for a tour of Argentina, England and Scotland.

As usual, whenever I had to get my mind around something I took time out to go for a run. I took one of my favourite runs along the headland at Long Reef. As I took in the view overlooking the peninsula I became quite emotional as I began to realise the significance of having been given the Wallaby coaching job.

What an honour it was to be chosen to prepare our national players to compete against the best in the world. I vowed to myself that I would do everything I could to make the Wallabies the best-prepared side ever.

Lateral rugby

The first positive step was a four-day camp at Wollongong, south of Sydney. With such limited lead-up time, Macqueen made no changes to the existing Wallaby squad who were captained by John Eales. Instead he hoped to improve their performance by introducing some alternative methods of training and encouraging players to think differently about every aspect of the game. The conflict over the personnel in his management team, which nearly cost him the coaching position, was now forgotten, and Macqueen was extremely pleased with the team that had been mutually selected. His assistant coach was Jeff Miller, a former Wallaby flanker with twenty-six test caps and a member of the Australian World Cup winning side in 1991. His only coaching experience was with the Australian seven-a-side team but Macqueen was impressed by his business-like approach and people skills.

Jeff Miller was a senior executive with a large Australian company and had tremendous business and organisational skills. Because he hadn't coached a major rugby side there was a lot of criticism initially from within the Queensland rugby ranks from people who believed he wasn't experienced enough. But I believed he had exactly the right qualifica-

tions for the role we needed him to play. Jeff proved to be a tireless and committed worker who worked closely with me and, as his role developed, he became an excellent conduit when it came to negotiating with the players. From very early on I had no doubt that Jeff had the potential to become a future Australian coach if he wanted to choose that path.

Jeff perfectly complemented Tim Lane, who was to be our backline coach. Tim was another former Wallaby, and was extremely laid-back. He enjoyed the on-field training with the players, often joining them in the many competitive games we introduced to improve individual skills.

Miller and Lane readily embraced the Macqueen style of coaching; in fact, it was one of the main reasons Miller signed on. 'I was really impressed with the Brumbies and their style of play, and it was extremely exciting to get involved and do this with the Wallabies; to do it as a coach, having previously been involved as an Australian player. The professionalism and the precision was something that knocked me back immediately. Rod was taking the game from an amateur era to being completely professional. He had absolute belief in the programs he was putting together, in his goals, how he was going to get there and the structures he needed to put in place.'

Our management team quickly came together, bringing many different and special attributes. Already on board from last season was team manager, John McKay. At first I had reservations regarding our working relationship and his loyalty because he had been a good friend of Greg Smith; however any concerns I had were quickly dispelled. John turned out to be an exceptionally hard worker who also had great organisational skills and his relaxed approach and dry sense of humour often defused any serious problems within the team. As well as attending to all the team's medical needs, Dr John Best had a strong religious commitment and he and his wife Megan played a valuable supporting role in the day-to-day problems confronting players and their wives.

Macqueen would later add his favourite expert on aggressive defence and a conditioner who would raise Wallaby fitness to a standard unheard of in professional rugby.

Players were allocated into groups and given separate tasks, and a communications system was developed for the different group leaders.

Even with such a limited time in camp they introduced the channels system which had proved so successful with the Brumbies. Squad members from other states quickly adapted to the strategy of running and supporting each other in depth. Although much of the training was totally new, Macqueen was pleased to note that everyone was more than willing to try the different techniques. The front row had already experienced Macqueen's forward thinking and attention to detail. Even before the camp they had spent three days together in Sydney studying videos of their Argentine opposition and practising scrum-maging techniques under a specialist coach.

But for some members of the squad Macqueen may have gone too far too quickly when he decided to show videotapes to encourage lateral thinking. In corporate circles the work of creative thinker Edward de Bono is readily accepted as a tool for success. Macqueen watched the faces of his Wallaby squad as they listened to one of de Bono's more recognised scenarios. It concerned a city in Italy that wanted to restrict car parking easily and without expense. Dé Bono's solution was to enforce a new law requiring anyone parking in the city to leave their headlights on, a simple idea that instantly resolved a seemingly impossible problem.

I was trying to get the players to think outside the square and change the mindsets of playing the game in the traditional way. It was interesting to see the reaction of the players. Some just couldn't grasp the connection of de Bono's lateral thinking philosophy to a new approach to rugby, but a number of the players could and I noticed a greater enthusiasm and willingness to come up with new ideas over the ensuing weeks.

The Brumbies had already proved the value of attacking traditional ways of thinking. Perhaps their best example was the way they trained and played with multiple skills. Instead of training the traditional way, with backs and forwards, the majority of their sessions involved dividing into groups of odds or evens depending on the number on the back of their jerseys, mixing the team so that every player learned to work with each and every teammate practising all facets of the game. Macqueen referred to this type of training as 'forax'—combining forwards and backs.

Now Macqueen was encouraging this way of thinking within his new contingent.

To many members of the squad the training was radically different. To keep things in balance, Macqueen stressed they were not setting any major goals other than to improve their standard of play. At the beginning of the camp he made clear to all players that winning the two Test matches against Argentina was not their main objective. They were to practise and improve the style of play they would use later in the tour against England and Scotland. Playing in a manner to counteract the tough, forward-dominated game of Argentina might help them win but it would not help develop the standards required to defeat the more established rugby nations on the way to their ultimate goal—the World Cup.

Measuring the standards

The tour of Argentina gave Macqueen the information he wanted about the Wallabies' on-field performance. But it was the information about the players' attitude which was perhaps even more important. The result of his first match as Australian coach could not have been better. The team played the new structured style of rugby for which they had been training and ran in twelve tries to win 76–15 against Macqueen's old foes at Tucuman. The next game against Rosario was a close victory, with the Wallabies unable to produce the same form while under pressure. The first Test, although another win again, didn't produce the style or standard of play they were all seeking. But it was not so much the game as the players' reaction following the second Test which told him there was much to be done.

Macqueen was shocked as he looked out across the field at the Ferro Carril Oeste Stadium in Buenos Aires where the opposition celebrated victory. It wasn't the loss that concerned him, it was the behaviour of his own players in defeat. Some were straggling towards the sideline with their heads down. Others were sitting or lying on the field staring at the sky in despair.

Only then did I realise just how far our standards had slipped. I was stunned and embarrassed to see our players lying on the ground after a Test match instead of standing on their feet as people who had just represented their country. There were two ways of looking at it. If we had won the Test we would have said everything was OK and continued, but by losing we learnt a valuable lesson. Their attitude in defeat was a catalyst to make us sit back and say everything had to change. We still have a videotape of those images and have used it countless times as a motiva-tional tool. It wasn't just the way they played, it was the breakdown in the fabric of the team, and the lack of belief in themselves. Standards are an integral part of any team or business. Not only having those standards but knowing how to rate them, how to keep them at a high level and constantly striving to reach an even higher level. The best person to be the keeper of the standards is yourself.

The message on how far those standards had slipped was reinforced the same evening during the after-match function. Two of the senior players representing the team approached Macqueen and John O'Neill saying they'd had a get-together and needed to discuss a serious matter. Macqueen immediately brightened, believing the players had realised they needed to improve team spirit before their next Test match against England. Unfortunately the message he received wasn't exactly what he was hoping to hear. After studying the itinerary the players had realised they would be staying in a hotel at Windsor outside London during preparation for the Test. They'd all decided it would be more appropriate if they could stay in a city hotel where there would be more nightlife. The usually affable Macqueen was shocked for the second time in the same day.

These players had just lost a Test match and were reacting in a way that I couldn't comprehend. Here they were only hours later showing more concern about the sort of nightlife they could enjoy in London than how they were going to solve their on-field problems. I was furious. It was a real wake-up call for me. Fortunately, John O'Neill saw the same situation and was equally unimpressed.

When the team arrived in England, they stayed at Windsor.

Obstructive criticism

Only halfway through his first overseas tour as Wallaby coach, Rod Macqueen was feeling the pressure. To make it worse, the Australian media was as harsh as the English weather. There were rumours about rifts in the Wallaby camp. Press conferences were peppered with ques-tions asking whether the Brumbies in the squad had too much influence in the day-to-day preparation of the team and were getting preferential treatment. Macqueen found this alarming. As far as he and other members of management were concerned, there was no open hostility between the players and no-one had made any official complaints. He recognised there was a difference in attitude between the players from the three different provinces. The Brumbies' players were more accustomed to having input during team meetings, but this was taken into account. He was going to great lengths to make sure everyone had an input into the game plan and agreed with the final decision. But the Australian newspapers still reported that many players were disgruntled and the Brumbies were running the show.

The media attacks continued following the English Test. Although the Wallabies improved on their performance in Argentina they were not playing at their best and the match finished with a draw. Macqueen's previously good relationship with the media was becoming strained. He was beginning to wonder what type of miracles were being expected from a coach who had been in charge for less than two months. As he had explained to the players, he was not trying to win every Test by a large margin at any cost. Rather, he was trying to develop a new style and method of play that would bring the success demanded against the major rugby nations of New Zealand and South Africa. This point was either misunderstood or overlooked by the media.

The rugby journalists may have been doing their job but their attacks almost caused the resignation of the coach who would soon be seen as the most successful in Australian history. Macqueen was unaccustomed to such relentless scrutiny and personal criticism. As coach of the Waratahs and the Brumbies he had achieved great success and although there were some negatives along the way, the media had been generally kind. He was also working on business principles where decisions made in the boardroom on personnel and strategy were kept private. But as coach of the national side he was under a much harsher spotlight. The rugby specialists believed they, and members of the Australian public, had the right to know everything both on and off the field. In England it all became too much and he decided he wanted out. Aware of the situation, O'Neill made a special visit to Macqueen during a training session. Unlike the reporters, he and Macqueen were privy to the underlying factors within the squad that had been exposed in Argentina. Changing the coach wasn't like waving a magic wand.

There was a deeper problem within the team, a lack of discipline and a lack of structure. The pair went for a long walk in the darkness on the edge of the field.

John and I discussed the attacks of the media and he basically reminded me that that goes with the territory. He knew the situation was extremely fragile and urged me to see the tour through. The criticism itself was not the issue—there is absolutely nothing wrong with criticism as long as it's constructive. But a lot of what was coming out was very personal and was attacking my professional integrity. I didn't feel that I should have to expose myself and my family to this.

I also spoke to my friend and rugby confidant, Paul McLean, who was becoming a good sounding board for me when the going got rough. He was always able to provide calm and steadying advice. On this occasion he had a similar message to John. Both convinced me to ride it out and put myself above the personal attacks.

Insights and highlights

An interesting sidelight to the England tour was a visit to the home side dressing room at Twickenham. After one training session Macqueen asked if he could walk through and look at all the facilities. Purely out of interest he attempted to enter the empty English change-rooms. A stern-faced official told him it was off-limits. Intrigued by the refusal, he later returned and found an obliging cleaner who unlocked the doors.

To my surprise I found the English rooms to be almost twice the size of the visitors' changerooms and included a separate room large enough for players to practise. I found this an interesting way of giving the home side a distinct advantage, especially the ability for a proper warm-up in the notoriously bitter English weather. What intrigued me most was that this obvious hometown bias would have required the collusion of the design-ers, architects, and builders right through to the RFU officials. I found that type of thinking hard to comprehend.

The tour was rescued by a good team performance which brought a victory over Scotland. The free-flowing interchange between forwards and backs began to work and there was a notable improvement in the control of the ball. It was the first sign that Macqueen's perseverance with holding possession and attacking in depth was paying dividends. Gone at last were the mistakes and handling errors in midfield which had prevented the ball reaching the talented outside backs. One of the highlights was the performance of Steve Larkham at fullback, with most commentators remarking on his speed and elusiveness. 'Stephen Larkham revealed the instinct of the great games player with two startling tries against Scotland. They came out of the blue, dumbfounded the Scots and partly saved the tour. The Wallabies were inspired by the gangly, shy and astonishingly talented Stephen Larkham at fullback.'

Macqueen noticed something else. Whenever Larkham was under pressure in a tight defensive situation surrounded by opposing players, he always managed to find space and his reactions were deceptively quick. His play reminded Macqueen of an experienced flyhalf, and he made a mental note for the future.

The game was also the first time Rod Macqueen was introduced to royalty and at the same time it gave him a taste of his captain's sense of humour. Two months before, John Eales was present when another coach referred to Macqueen as 'Roddy'. As they walked away Macqueen muttered under his breath, 'I hate it when he calls me Roddy, he's the only one who can do that.' Now in the centre of a packed Murrayfield stadium, John Eales introduced each player in turn to a politely smiling Princess Anne. When he reached the end of the line he grinned broadly, looked straight at Macqueen and said, 'Ma'am, I'd like you to meet the coach, Roddy Macqueen.'

It was a memorable private joke that Eales had saved up for two months. Macqueen winced and silently vowed to come up with a suitable payback. No, make that a few more paybacks.

Test matches against Argentina, England and Scotland had produced disappointment on the field but the Wallabies had learned a great deal. Preparation for the following season in 1998 would show whether it was enough.

Chapter 17

Establishing a Base

'We have to solve some major problems or we're not going to make it through to the World Cup.'

This was the opinion Rod Macqueen expressed to John O'Neill on their return to Australia. Now in early December most people in the rugby world were relaxing and preparing to enjoy a well-deserved break over the Christmas holiday period. However, the two men guiding Australian rugby decided action had to be taken immediately and convened what they called a rugby summit, inviting the coaches, administrators and senior players from each of the three Australian provinces. It was an all-out discussion with everything on the table to decide what had to be done about the lack of harmony between the three provincial teams. Macqueen was astounded by the attitude of the Queensland coach, John Connolly. It became obvious during the open discussion at the meeting that while other coaches were prepared to work towards a common goal of preparing players for the Wallabies, Connolly wanted his players trained and prepared to play for their state during the Super 12—only then would they be made available to the Wallaby program.

According to John O'Neill the rugby summit didn't produce the answers but it revealed the divisions which were preventing the development of a national program and created an environment for change. 'It was a matter of do we want to set ourselves a goal of winning the World Cup or do we chuck it in? It was a real turning point. Connolly was exposed at that conference because everyone else was so agreeable. He kept baulking at giving any commitment.'

Connolly's obstructionist attitude confirmed Macqueen's worst fears. Many of the players were being indoctrinated to put the state team first.

Healthy rivalry between the states was something to be encouraged but for the national team to be successful there needed to be a consensus on the

*vision for the modern game and the type of skills and fitness required. I
actually got on well with John Connolly and had a great respect for him as
a coach. There's no doubt that he has a very successful formula for winning
games. Unfortunately, part of his approach was to isolate the team and be
very insular. Obviously this made it extremely difficult when we were trying
to get cooperation and direction for Australian rugby. Both South Africa and
New Zealand already had coordinated programs between their provinces.
Australia desperately needed to adopt a similar approach but this could
only be done with the full cooperation of all the state coaches and players.*

Macqueen now fully understood the source of the undercurrent of
friction which had quietly disrupted the recently completed tour. He
knew the necessary changes would take more than just the verbal
assurances from those at the meeting. When it was time to bring the
Wallaby squad together the following year he would need to have in
place a structure and environment able to create and nurture a new
distinctive culture for the Australian team. Macqueen had already
made a detailed analysis of what he believed were the basic requirements needed to start the process.

Past development

Rebuilding just the Wallaby squad would only be a short-term
solution. Replacement players coming through the system for years to
come needed to be schooled along the same lines. To assess the
thinking process currently in place, he arranged a meeting with
Australian development officers, the men responsible for creating
training programs and policies for clubs throughout the country.
Macqueen was surprised to find they believed they were up-to-date
with all developments and at the cutting edge of rugby. He didn't think
so, especially when he heard they thought the type of football being
played depended on who happened to be the Australian coach at the
time; it was an idea totally opposite to his philosophy of establishing a
long-term, unified approach.

*I explained the game was changing rapidly and we needed the ability to
react quickly. To demonstrate the point I suggested the game could*

suddenly change to the extent it was played with a round ball with two basketball hoops on either side of the pitch. They thought for a while and then told me if the game changed in that way then they would start making adjustments when it happened. That basically answered my question. There was no vision for the future. The development officers were doing an exceptionally good job, however they were still developing skills designed for a game that had changed dramatically. We needed to identify where the game would be two years from now, or even further down the track, and develop programs to introduce the appropriate skills to carry us through these changing times.

For the Wallabies to be ahead of everyone else Macqueen needed the full understanding and support of his own management team. An early brainstorming session with his two key members, assistant coaches Tim Lane and Jeff Miller, confirmed he had the right people at his side. Both quickly grasped the concept that forwards and backs should be virtually interchangeable and the game could indeed be played in a totally different way.

Forwards needed to have the running and passing skills of the backs, while the backs would have to learn the techniques of rucking and mauling. The principle was that if we developed these new skills, no matter how the game changed, we could go in any direction we wanted. Tim and Jeff were both supportive of this way of thinking; and with this vision we put forward ideas and expanded on them. They were exciting times.

We talked about the problem of confronting the strong defensive lines that were now spread right across the field preventing the traditional attack of backline play. The ultimate game plan would be where we had the ability as a team to seek out opposition weaknesses and attack them as the opportunity arose, rather than run onto the field as a programmed unit. Once we had developed these skills we could do anything with our game.

While we agreed on these principles and wrote them down as a vision for the future, we also decided they would not be set in concrete and would be reviewed on a regular basis.

We also started to think, not only about our current players, but also about Wallabies of the future. Our vision had wide-ranging ramifications for selections. We would need players who were good enough and smart

enough to understand our new approach and be able to make decisions
on the field. We also wanted players to understand Wallaby traditions and
work standards which we referred to as the Wallaby ethos.

Flying de Bono Bros

It was time for direct action. Together with his management team
Macqueen decided on a radical course of action to instil the new way
of thinking into Australian rugby. Armed with their vision, they visited
every club side in NSW and Queensland, and held seminars in
Victoria, South Australia and Perth. Macqueen and each member of
his team would give a presentation on the different aspects of management and game play that should be urgently addressed. The fact that
the Australian coach and his senior advisors thought it important
enough to spread the word personally, was a message in itself. It was
the first time that such an ambitious project had ever been attempted
and those who attended were both impressed and receptive. To most,
the professional approach to every aspect of the game, and the unexpected addition of lateral thinking, was all new. The whistlestop tour
to change the mindset of so many people deserved an appropriate title,
and one quickly appeared thanks to the dry humour of team manager
John McKay: the name, 'The Flying de Bono Brothers' may have been
a joke but the results certainly weren't.

We needed to change the mindsets of everyone and fast-track the neces-
sary skills to take us forward with modern rugby. To do this we had to take
our vision directly to the source rather than via the traditional methods.
Within one year, we could see evidence of these skills coming through. It
proved to me there is always a better way of doing things. Sometimes you
have to break out of the normal process totally to get a point across. In
just a few months we had introduced the Wallaby training program
throughout the country by going to the grassroots of rugby.

The student teacher

Macqueen was not only a travelling teacher but a travelling student. To
find out how the game would develop in the professional era and how
relationships would change dealing with full-time professional players,
he also sought new ideas from experts with many years' experience in

their own field. He went to different states and spent time with the coaches of successful teams in other codes: rugby league coaches, Chris Anderson from the Melbourne Storm and Wayne Bennett from the Brisbane Broncos; the Australian Rules coach of Perth's West Coast Eagles, Mick Malthouse, and senior AFL administrator, David Parkin. Much of the information he gathered proved to be invaluable, including an AFL system of collating statistics which was redesigned to meet the specific needs of rugby union. It became a long-term project for Jeff Miller and one which was to give them a decided advantage in the final build-up to the World Cup.

The rugby league concentration on hard-hitting defence prompted another important decision. Macqueen again approached the former advisor to the Brumbies, John Muggleton, who was soon employed full-time to develop a new system of defence for the Wallabies. At the time the typical rugby league pattern was for the defender to stand outside his opposite number so he could move in, knock the player to the ground and hold him there. The new faster style of rugby union needed a different defence but with the same speed and aggression. Muggleton developed a pattern where players moved up quickly, sliding across the field but with the intention of hitting the opposition hard and driving them back behind the advantage line. Wherever possible, as in league, the ball carrier would be hit by more than one defender.

'Muggo' had now been working in rugby union for some time and he was adapting many specific rugby league techniques to suit our game. His ability to understand rugby made his contribution especially effective, and our emphasis on defence became much greater than in the past. He also introduced many different types of tackles for different situations.

We practised his different techniques repeatedly, so much so that the team became extremely proud of their improvement. In fact they actually enjoyed working on their defence which was something quite foreign to the rugby culture of the past.

But Muggo brought much more to the team than his defensive and technical expertise. His larrikinism and strict adherence to standards helped develop the team culture.

Rugby purists would have been horrified if they had known what was happening behind the scenes with the importation of techniques from a much-denigrated alternative game. But for Macqueen rugby league had even more to offer—a new type of fitness. He could see that his players were already struggling to keep up with the speed and the extra body contact of the new game, and these demands were about to increase. In 1997 the premiership-winning rugby league side was the Brisbane Broncos. The fitness expert responsible for their peak condition was a trainer called Steve Nance, the same Steve Nance, who had rowed surfboats alongside Macqueen with Collaroy. In 1998 Nance was again on the team, lured away by Macqueen with promises of an exciting, lucrative, globe-trotting lifestyle and the chance of World Cup glory.

There were no existing fitness programs in any sport that met the requirements of the new professional rugby union player. It would be up to Steve Nance to find out just how far the human body could be pushed over eighty minutes of rugby union.

A united front for a common cause

Physical fitness was one thing, but far more important was commitment and attitude. The rugby summit had exposed the underlying conflict between the cultures of the three Australian provinces. The Brumbies were accustomed to speaking their minds and helping develop their own style of play; some members of the Waratahs were able to make suggestions, but most were reluctant to get involved in decision-making; while the Queensland contingent were accustomed to being given instructions and following them to the letter. With Macqueen as national coach, many of the Brumbies believed their game plan was the one that would be simply adopted by the Wallabies. In fact, their game plan was just part of a multitude of factors designed for success. Now the same type of structure needed to be set up but, with input from the Wallaby squad and management team, it would produce a different outcome which all could be happy with and call their own.

The Brumbies' pattern of play had developed over the last two years so it was difficult—firstly for the Brumbies to see it should change, and secondly for Queensland and NSW to accept the Brumbies' game plan as their own. Ironically, if we had just imported this game plan into the Wallabies it would have been completely against all the principles the Brumbies had put in place in the beginning. The answer was to have input from all concerned. Although the vision basically remained the same, the way of achieving it varied depending on the various skills and characteristics of the individual players. By doing this, once again everyone felt they had an ownership of the plan, and accepted the style that was being developed.

A home away from home

Caloundra is a large but friendly holiday town on Queensland's Sunshine Coast. Boasting several good surfing beaches, a number of small shopping villages, and numerous restaurants and cafés it could easily be described as the perfect vacation spot. At the beginning of 1998 it was known only to locals and a limited number of holiday makers who appreciated a quiet retreat. But within months it would be known throughout Australia as the home of the Wallabies.

The Wallabies' full season's itinerary had already been planned and all accommodation booked in advance when Macqueen raised the possibility of operating from a base camp, just as he had with the Brumbies. He discussed with his new management team the advantages, even though it meant changing plans and bookings that had been painstakingly put together. A camp would provide the environment he believed necessary to bond, strengthen and develop the team. Over the previous four years all Australian teams playing in Test matches would travel a week in advance to the city where the game was to be played and live in a five-star hotel. But the usual hotel accommodation had numerous disadvantages: endless bus trips to and from training grounds, problems finding suitable gymnasiums, meetings in corridors and waiting for lifts, as well as the neverending round of meals in restaurants and cafeterias. A permanent base camp would mean everyone could come and go as they pleased and not be living out of a suitcase. It would be a first for any national sporting team. To Macqueen's relief the management team agreed with his suggestion. Full support from John O'Neill also ensured approval from the ARU. 'It was a bold move going anywhere because in many cases it would be far away. It was a question of access to the team from a marketing point of view because the team wouldn't be in the city of a test match until a few days before. But we had to weigh up the most important thing, and that was the preparation of the team.'

The search was on for a home away from home.

A number of venues were investigated but the quiet and friendly environment of Caloundra was the unanimous choice. Key factors for choosing Caloundra included its close proximity to the commercial airport of Maroochydore, a mild year-round climate and a number of large holiday complexes with single-storey, village-style accommodation. One in particular stood out. The Oasis resort featured everything they were looking for, including comfortable three-star apartments, some self-contained, others with shared kitchen and laundry facilities.

Caloundra offered the environment we were looking for where players could create a lifestyle similar to the one they were familiar with at home. As a management group we had already set standards we wanted to follow and we knew that big changes would have to be made. One of the things we thought really important was to have a balanced life and that's when we started to question some of the old traditions. With the increasing strain and workload that we knew was coming we decided that having a base camp would be the best option.

When it came to cooperation from local authorities it seemed nothing was too much trouble. Being a small country town the nearby oval, Lighthouse Park, was poorly grassed. But on Macqueen's second inspection the greenkeeper from the local Pelican Waters golf course arrived and ceremoniously laid a section of lush green turf at Macqueen's feet. Impressed by this display, he smiled in approval and agreed it would make a great playing surface. Work on re-turfing the entire oval began the very next day.

The local swimming pool, adjacent to the oval, was ideal, but the nearby gymnasium was poorly equipped. Local authorities were only too happy to give their high-profile guests virtually unlimited access to both facilities. In a gesture which reciprocated the improvement of Lighthouse Park the Wallabies' management packed the gym with the latest in high-tech body building equipment, which was then made available to everyone.

Nothing was finalised, however, until the right people had given their opinions.

It was important that John Eales, as captain of the team, was included in the final decision of the base camp. Macqueen invited him to inspect the complex and general environment that would be their home during the test season. Fortunately, Eales agreed with the Caloundra concept.

With the establishment of Caloundra about to receive official approval there was only one more thing to do. Macqueen sought a final opinion from Liz.

Liz agreed the venue appeared to be perfect and so we decided to celebrate with a quiet dinner at La Promenade, the local waterfront café. But our plans for an intimate evening didn't take into account the impact the Wallaby plans were having on everyone in the local area.

Within a short time the owner came and introduced himself and confessed he was a keen Wallaby fan. He told us how excited everyone was about the Wallabies moving in and how important it would be for the town. Within an hour another fifteen locals had joined our table and our quiet evening turned into a full scale party. It was characteristic of the town and the friendliness of the people. We knew we had made the right choice.

Chapter 18

The Goal

THE BEST WAY TO MAKE YOUR DREAMS
COME TRUE IS TO WAKE UP

This quotation by the French philosopher and poet, Paul Valéry, was the first message printed on a players' manual which had now evolved into something extremely sophisticated. It implied a message Macqueen wanted the players to understand. The attitudes and practices of the past needed to be forgotten. They had to open their minds to the new approach required to succeed in international rugby. Under the new regime they would discover many changes including a personal diary that would map out every detail in a busy itinerary right up until the World Cup. The quotation exhorting them to 'wake up' introduced the first of three stages in a vision proposed by Macqueen: 'The Beginning', 'The Journey', and 'The Destiny'. These three stages detailed the steps needed over a two-year period to achieve World Cup success. 'The Beginning' described the initial training, sacrifices and direction needed to bring the Wallaby team to a standard high enough to take on the rest of the world, and contained their goals during the 1998 season.

The Beginning, the Journey and the Destiny

'It is through this period of time that we need to firmly ensure our direction, putting together a team that is working together to achieve a common goal. We want to create a team in which selflessness is the primary driving force and we have thirteen Test matches to achieve this.

'Any journey must have a beginning and a destination. To be successful we must choose the right direction in the beginning to commence our journey. That's why we have a clear plan in place for the way we want to play football, the type of players required to play the game, and the type of fitness and skills needed to be successful.'

Details on 'The Journey' would be added as the team achieved its goals throughout the season. 'The Destiny' was self-evident, being victory in the World Cup. Final information and inspiration to achieve this goal would be provided in the lead-up to the tournament. But for the vision and the two-year plan to be successful 'The Beginning' had to provide the platform and the diary would become one of the key elements here. The book itself was an organisational masterstroke, prepared months in advance by Macqueen and his management team.

I was working out of a diary myself at the time and it seemed a good way to map out the players' preparation. I thought it was important to have a businesslike attitude right from the beginning. The beginning is all about changing the mindset of the players. To be successful we realised we had to change and the first step was typified by that quotation.

John McKay, Jeff Miller and the rest of the management team endorsed the concept and rigorously set about putting all the necessary plans in place.

It was supported by a mission statement, in which Macqueen made it clear what was expected of the Wallabies:

- Set ourselves the highest possible standards, never resting in our pursuit of excellence, both on and off the field.
- At all times be positive in our approach, whilst constantly seeking new ideas and innovations.
- Keep ahead of the game, making use of the best technologies and resources available to us.
- Study and respect our opposition.

Self-management

The diary, which was in the form of a hefty ring binder, took Macqueen's concept of a team manual to a new level. It contained much more than the usual information on management personnel, fitness advice, diet information and a basic playing style. The diary started with inspirational quotations and poems designed to outline a philosophy for a steady build-up concentrating on World Cup victory. The day-by-day section was filled with information giving no player any excuse for not knowing where he should be at any time or what he should be doing and wearing. Some of the detail included: times for team meetings and training sessions; meal times and locations; travel arrangements including flight numbers and times; medical examinations, press conferences and individual and team promotional appearances; and all Test match details including the kickoff time and each referee's name.

The rear of the diary comprised individual sections with details on the management structure, information on base camp accommodation and finances, procedures for team meetings, standard player contracts, and judiciary procedures in different countries. It also included information on drug awareness, the Wallaby sponsors, obtaining match tickets and submitting medical claims.

In the past Macqueen had been accused of being overly meticulous and too pedantic in his preparation. This took it to a new level. But the benefits were obvious even to his harshest critics. The days of international players being informed of what was happening the next day by having a sheet of paper slipped under their hotel door during the night were now gone. Not only would the Wallabies know where they were going and what was required of them in the finest detail, they would know how and why. And in reversing the onus of responsibility from the management to the players there would be no more excuses for lack of preparation. With the everyday minutiae set down twelve months in advance the players could concentrate on what they were there for— winning rugby matches for their country.

Not all parts of the diary suited everyone. Some players appreciated the many quotes and inspirational messages while others thought they were unnecessary. A few thought the diary program too regimented because they believed they were already capable of organising themselves on a daily basis. However, taken across the whole group of players, coming as they did from different backgrounds with different values and intellectual capabilities, the result was a message for everyone. It brought them together by filling the gaps in the character of individuals and creating a common language and a common bond.

John O'Neill saw it as a crucial factor in creating the unity that had been lacking: 'I think the introduction of the diary sent a message. What we were into here was a major change in the management program which also required significant cultural change. Messages like these can be done in different ways and one of the best is the introduction of something like a diary which carries a big message about discipline.'

People for positions not positions for people

The team management provided further guidelines when they spelled out the type of game needed to win the ultimate prize. A one-page summary called 'The Vision' stressed that the entire game would be built on performing the basics correctly and consistently, underpinned by desire and passion.

To turn the vision into reality Macqueen needed the right players. As the management structure and facilities were being finalised the crucial process of selecting the squad was just getting underway. In this task Macqueen wasn't hamstrung by a selection panel: apart from himself there were only two other voting members, assistant coaches Tim Lane and Jeff Miller. They had a united purpose, to pick not only players that were in form but players ideal for each position. When the Super 12 competition began, they selected a side each week which they believed would be the best combination to play for Australia at that particular time. Regular communication with the players and their individual coaches let them know how their performances were regarded. An interesting example was Steve Larkham, who was playing fullback for the Brumbies. After the first few matches Larkham was regularly selected, but as flyhalf, not as fullback. Eddie Jones, the Brumbies coach, agreed to bring Larkham in closer for different moves from phase play, giving him greater experience playing closer to heavy defence. Macqueen organised videotapes of Henry Honiball and Andrew Mehrtens, the respective flyhalves for South Africa and New Zealand, to be sent to Larkham so that he could study their style of play. When he was eventually named in the Australian side as flyhalf, journalists commented that it was a risky selection but worthwhile because he deserved to be somewhere in the team without displacing the incumbent fullback Matthew Burke. They were unaware the selectors had virtually had him in place since the previous year, for a very good reason.

It was a matter of people for positions, not positions for people. It is a great example for both business and sport of selecting someone for the position involved. If we had put him in place and he didn't have the skills required it would have affected everyone around him, just as it does in a business. As it turned out Larkham did have the right skills and the whole team benefited from that.

Selecting the right players in the first instance was crucial, so the management team had devised a process which they hoped would minimise mistakes. Macqueen believed that immeasurable disruption would be caused if several wrong selections went unnoticed for any length of time.

We put together a rigid system in the following order. It was a model I thought could also be used in selecting potential employees for a company.

1.   *Vision on the game—to understand the type of game we would need to play to be successful over the following two years.*
2.   *Skills—the type of skills that would be required by the players to achieve that vision.*
3.   *Select players for positions not positions for players.*
4.   *Succession planning—mixing experience with potential to have a balanced team at all times.*
5.   *Combinations—establish good working combinations in key areas such as halfback and flyhalf.*
6.   *Consistency and balance—consistency in selections being important to maintain confidence and stability.*
7.   *Leadership qualities—seek out leaders for the various key groups within the team.*
8.   *Team ethos and work ethic—the ability to work well as a team and put the team first: 'We not me'.*

The process we put in place to do this required a viewing program for every Super 12 game, which would involve:

1.   *Three voting selectors and one outside person from other areas of rugby such as under 19s and 21s.*
2.   *Allocating specific domestic games to each of the above personnel. The aim was that in groups of two to four we would attend the games from each province and discuss the perform-ance of the various players.*
3.   *Selecting a Test team after every round, not necessarily the form team for the week but the team that we believed would be the strongest should we be playing a Test that week.*
4.   *Video viewing with the use of upgraded technology and also arranging one-on-one videos on individual players.*

5. *Looking at statistics across all games by position and comparing our players to equivalent player statistics from other countries.*

Camp Wallaby

In the last week in May 1998 the Oasis resort in Caloundra became Camp Wallaby. The full squad of players arrived and began investigating the place that would be their home for the next two-and-a-half months. They arrived with many unusual items under their arms, everything from surfboards, fishing rods, water skis and golf clubs, to tropical fishtanks and personal microwave ovens. They were about to prove the effectiveness of the first ever base camp for an international rugby team. There were mixed emotions. Some were looking forward to the relaxed holiday atmosphere, while others were openly unhappy about being based so far from home for such a lengthy period of time. John Eales summed up the different feelings of all those involved. 'I think there was a bit of anxiety from both players and officials. Players especially tend to loathe a change of environment and there was also concern that Rod was just trying to do with Australia what he'd done with the Brumbies. It was like anything in life—some of your biggest fears are of the unknown and once you face the reality it's not a fear anymore. After we actually moved in everyone was very positive, it was set up extremely well and we could all feel the benefits of what was happening.'

Messenger or master

As captain of the Wallabies John Eales was the most important player in the side; he was the team leader who would also become a vital intermediary between players and coaching staff. At two metres tall and weighing 115 kilograms Eales also had extraordinary athletic abilities and all-round football skills. By the end of the World Cup campaign he would be regarded as one of the best second rowers or locks ever to have played the game, and his goal kicking prowess would make him Australia's highest ever point-scoring forward.

Having played in the World Cup tournaments in 1991 and 1995, Eales' experience was obviously invaluable, but his definite ideas of how the game should be played also caused some initial conflict with the new national coach. However, the immediate success of the Caloundra concept and Macqueen's no-nonsense professional approach soon cemented a strong friendship. The pair developed an early understanding that any contentious issues would be thrashed out in private and the final decision strictly adhered to: in front of other members of the squad the two never showed disagreement. This special relationship between captain and coach added a unique and additional strength to the Wallaby campaign.

We felt that John's role was more of a players' representative role, a messenger, not one that had enough input into the day-to-day operations of the team. Whenever players had an issue John would seemingly pass the message on rather than address it. So one of the first things that needed to be sorted out was a leadership issue. I spoke at length to John O'Neill about the situation and at separate times we both broached the subject with Ealsie. Jeff Miller and I also had a meeting to determine what the job description should be for the leader of the Wallabies. This job description included the necessity to be involved in the decisions that were in the best interest of the team and once consensus was reached, to support those decisions regardless of the reaction of any of the players. To John's credit he asked many questions, including an assurance that he would be heavily involved in the decision-making process. Once this job description was agreed upon, John, with his usual commitment and enthusiasm, set about fulfilling this role.

The real world

Initially it was the small things that made a big impression on the players at Camp Wallaby. For example, making their own breakfast rather than getting dressed to go to a hotel restaurant then returning to change and prepare for training. Or the fact that they didn't need to be transported to and from training at the oval, pool and gymnasium. They also realised how enjoyable it would be to have families come to stay and share the experience. Eales noted a positive change in atmosphere. 'The guys already got on with each other extremely well but it made everyone feel a lot more comfortable in the sense that we were part of a more natural environment. I've got to say it was a very big move by Rod. It was a bit out of the way, particularly for the Sydney and Canberra players, and it also incorporated a whole new philosophy because it involved the families with the team. The management structure and whole camp setup was totally new. It's easy to look back now and say it seems like a logical thing to have done, but at the time it was a sensation, and in many ways one of the best things that happened in professional rugby. It was a great innovation.'

Being self-sufficient meant doing a lot of minor domestic chores which for many players was a new experience. There was the inevitable catalogue of misadventures and humorous incidents, such as the time when Steve Larkham and winger Joe Roff were discovered sitting in the laundry room wondering why their clothes were taking so long to wash. The whole camp soon knew they had been caught watching their laundry tumble around mixing with detergent powder—inside a clothes dryer. They weren't the only ones having difficulty coming to grips with some of the more mundane aspects of everyday life. Rod Macqueen later openly confessed he could never master the mystery of the laundry process and when Liz wasn't present he paid the resident laundry woman to take care of all his washing needs.

Under new arrangements for the Wallaby preparation Macqueen could have few excuses for not keeping up with daily affairs. Liz was also based permanently in the camp working as his personal assistant, looking after his needs, keeping on top of all the secretarial work and, as usual, constantly liaising with the players' partners.

We not me

The serious business of becoming the best rugby union team in the world began the first morning after they arrived at Caloundra. A team meeting was scheduled for 8.30 and everyone was there well before starting time. There was no excuse for not knowing where and when as the meeting was the first item of business printed in the players' diary.

The team room was to become a very special place, an inner sanctum restricted to players and team management only. It was a place where the various working groups could gather in private at any time to study opposition strengths and weaknesses and where individuals could spend time doing research on opposing players. Here also the different committees could gather to discuss the many issues involved in the day-to-day team activities—the disciplinary committee, which handled any problems concerning players and issued warnings or fines, the social committee which met twice a week to plan entertainment and fun activities for the players, and of course the various football committees that set the weekly programs and ensured everything went to plan.

The team room walls were bare, except for a number of messages strategically placed by Macqueen. Inspirational quotations intended to make his players think of the commitment required for the campaign ahead, they included:

> *The harder you work, the luckier you get.*
> Gary Player, golfer

> *A winner says, 'I'm good, but not as good as I ought to be.'*
> *A loser says, 'I'm not as bad as a lot of other people.'*
> Anonymous

> *If you want something badly enough, and I mean badly enough, chances are*
> *that you'll wind up getting it.*
> Johnny Unitas

Macqueen wanted an environment where there would be a free and honest exchange of ideas. The main priority for the whole management team was to eradicate forever the lack of pride and self-belief that had shown itself so graphically in Argentina and still lingered after the games in England and Scotland. They wanted to establish a new Wallaby pride and culture, where the players and management worked together as one. He needed a free flow of suggestions and ideas from all three provincial groups so they could develop their own innovative moves in attack and defence. They needed to produce a style that suited their own individual talents, to produce a fast, imaginative game similar to that pioneered by the Brumbies, but one that would be theirs alone. To encourage this, Macqueen referred players to a page in the diary where he had composed a special message he hoped would provide the inspiration required: 'Rugby is a sport that involves a number of talented athletes coming together and thinking and moving as one. To do that successfully we need to trust each other on a deep level and know instinctively how our teammates will respond in pressure situations. We have no time or consideration for people who are not prepared to put the team first.'

To emphasise his insistence on a 'we' not 'me' syndrome Macqueen had included one of his favourite poems, a classic piece, originally from Rudyard Kipling's *The Jungle Book*. More recently, it had become a lesson taken from the book *Sacred Hoops*, by Phil Jackson, the legendary coach of the famous Chicago Bulls basketball team.

Now this is the law of the jungle
As old and as true as the sky
For the wolf that shall keep it may prosper
But the wolf that shall break it must die
As the creeper that girdles the tree trunk
The law runneth forward and back
For the strength of the pack is the wolf
And the strength of the wolf is the pack.

Robyn Poidevin, the wife of ex-Wallaby Simon Poidevin, had given me a copy of Sacred Hoops. *She was of the opinion that I would enjoy reading the book.*

At the time, I believed there was something missing from the team psyche. Phil Jackson's philosophies summed it up perfectly. He had a number of high-profile, top players in his side and yet for him to be successful they needed to have the 'we not me' attitude. It is a simple phrase but something we would go on to use in all our decisions. I found the book very interesting.

Serious games

The move to a full-time camp at Caloundra proved successful when from day one a new culture and discipline in the side began to emerge. The more relaxed accommodation and low-key country atmosphere combined with the detailed management structure promoted the changes so desperately needed. A free interchange of ideas between players in the special team room became an important aspect, the introduction of the business diary another.

The relaxed atmosphere was very conducive to coming up with new ideas and helping people think differently about the game. There was more time to spend one-on-one with the players where we could explain how we wanted them to adjust to the modern game.

Three Wallaby forwards were bent over double at the end of the football field dry-retching with exhaustion. It was the end of the Wallabies first serious training run under conditioner Steve Nance and all the players were suffering. The largest forwards, the tight five, had been found out. Jeff Miller was shocked to see that some of the players were so overweight they were actually waddling onto the training field.

When Steve Nance came on board he had photos of the Brisbane Broncos League team, before and after he began their training. By the time he had finished with them they were lean and mean and looked like professional footballers. In comparison our guys looked unfit and soft.'

Steve Nance set about the task for which he was employed, to make the Wallabies the fittest rugby side in the world. He used a combination of running, swimming, weights, boxing, and tackling bags, and although the basic methods weren't new, the techniques and competitive games made training different and at times enjoyable. One of the key ingredients was pitting players against each other so they pushed themselves to the limit. It was intense, hard, exhausting, but it was rewarding. The results began to show and Macqueen was pleased with the progress being made by Steve Nance, even though he was frustrated because so much had to be done in preparation for the first Test match against England.

His squad had just finished playing for their individual provinces in the Super 12 competition. Before the first round had begun both Macqueen and Nance had spoken with all the other coaches and detailed the type of fitness training they believed was now required, but, in some cases these instructions were not being followed. Unfortunately, many of the players were still not fit enough.

The game was becoming faster and faster. There was more body contact so the players needed to be leaner and more powerful. The wingers needed to have the strength to take up the ball and crash through tackles, while large forwards standing wide in the defensive line would be called on to tackle speedy outside backs. This was virtually unheard of before in rugby union. The game was now being played continuously for long periods of time and therefore we needed to be aerobically fit.

Sacrifices for the ultimate goal

To reach the World Cup the Wallabies first of all had to qualify by playing the smaller Pacific nations of Tonga, Fiji and Samoa. Therefore this was their main goal for 1998. However, they were also committed to play home Test matches against England and Scotland, in addition to the Tri Nations series against South Africa and New Zealand. To complete the season they had a short European tour including Tests against France and a return match against England. This meant a demanding thirteen Tests in six months, with some of the toughest games only four days apart. To achieve all this, the Wallabies had to attain and maintain an optimum level of fitness. Macqueen also knew his players would have to be fit to avoid injury. The sooner they reached peak fitness the better, but it meant his squad would be tired and jaded leading into the earlier games. The first Test against England was only ten days away. It was not the ideal preparation. But it was unavoidable if they were to maintain the commitment to complete their journey and to realise their destiny.

The essence of the team

Macqueen soon understood there was much more to the Wallabies than he had first realised, something deeply ingrained in the character of the national side.

I had now been with the Wallabies for a number of months and I was beginning to see the real nature or soul of the team. I believe it related back to the personalities of the more recent coaches. The team still had the larrikinism which was so evident in the lovable character of Bob Templeton. He was an old friend of Slaggy Miller and had always been very supportive of me throughout my early playing and coaching career. Bob Templeton was a passionate Australian who demanded players give their absolute best for their country. At the same time he enjoyed his rugby and the revelry and social activities that came with the Wallabies.

Then there was Alan Jones. With his intelligence he set about putting into place the structures and disciplines required in a winning side. Jones was merciless in his vision. He insisted the players understand the histories and traditions of the Wallabies. He even organised a professional choirmaster to ensure they not only knew the national anthem, but could sing it bloody well.

Bob Dwyer was another devoted rugby man who passionately believed in the vision he had for a running game based on positive play. Bob had a great knack of being able to recognise and recruit players with particular skills, from any level of football.

I believe all the special qualities of these coaches were still inherent in the Wallabies. I saw it as a very important part of my job to retain this and try to build on it. We spent a long time in the preparation of the team ensuring that all these legacies played a major role in everything we did. There might be other words for it but I always call it soul. It's the essence of the team. The point of difference.

Life at Caloundra was not all hard work. Where time allowed, team competitions were organised to ease the pressure of repetitive training. There was also quality time to enjoy the beach and to relax while regular outings helped make the Wallabies part of the local community and maintain a balanced perspective. Macqueen's first initiative was to organise a visit to the children's ward of the Caloundra hospital. During the visit John Eales and a number of senior players handed out Wallaby caps and badges to a large group of surprisingly happy and healthy looking children. To the delight of journalists and photographers present they stayed for some time, chatting and signing autographs. As they eventually left the players were interested to see some of the children changing their clothes and also preparing to leave the hospital. Did their visit have miraculous healing powers? The visit certainly captured the imagination of the media, with photos of the Wallabies gesture splashed across the front pages of local newspapers. It was a public relations coup with the players enjoying the opportunity to visit some young supporters, but by the end of the same day some interesting information had filtered through. The true situation was that Caloundra hospital had no patients in the children's ward. Embarrassed officials anxious to cooperate with the generous offer of a Wallaby visit had brought in a number of children from the local school especially for the occasion. It proved that while the Wallabies were prepared to do everything possible to promote good relations with the local community, the community in turn was desperate to reciprocate.

An unusual part of the national team's preparation would be regular contact with children of all ages. After training sessions at Lighthouse Park, local school children would gather in large numbers, waiting for autographs which the players readily and cheerfully gave. During school holidays the players' own families would join the camp and the Oasis resort's main street, by now officially renamed Wallaby Avenue, would be called Sesame Street. On any day during free time players would mix with the children playing ball games and riding bikes up and down the thoroughfare.

The introduction of push bikes for players was another unique innovation. When they first arrived all squad members were given the opportunity to buy a discount package including a bike, helmet and security lock. It was the encouraged and soon preferred mode of transport of getting to all training venues and nearby social activities. It was also a great social leveller. The new flashy cars of the now well-paid players were left parked in garages, and, apart from their obvious size and bulk, the players were soon indistinguishable from others moving about the holiday region.

On one occasion the cycling players also provided the children with the chance to launch a surprise attack. Organised by Steve Nance, they prepared an ambush armed with water balloons. As it happened, the first person to return from that morning's training session was the coach. He was immediately and mercilessly bombarded. Macqueen then at least had the satisfaction of sitting back and watching the players ride in unsuspectingly to be thoroughly drenched by the screaming, laughing crowd of youngsters. After changing, the players regrouped and launched a counterattack which led to a night of general fun and games that set the tone for future family visits. If management had been looking to establish a relaxed and family-orientated lifestyle for the players, they couldn't have been more successful.

But would this success be mirrored on the football field? Could the dispirited, disjointed and disappointing team of 1997 be reinvented after just ten days together at a small tourist village in Queensland? The questions would soon be answered at Suncorp Stadium in Brisbane against the touring English side.

Chapter 19
The Beginning

A classic initiative

On the morning of the first Test in 1998 against England, one of the Wallabies taking part in the team meeting hadn't played for sixteen years. Greg Cornelsen was part of Macqueen's new initiative to foster tradition within the Australian team. Before every Test match a former Australian representative under the title 'Classic Wallaby' would address the team on the importance and meaning of playing for their country. Cornelsen, had played twenty-five Tests as a flanker for his country and was renowned for his passion and commitment on the field. On this occasion the same emotions were displayed in his address to the new breed of Wallabies. Honoured by the invitation, he had spent the previous two months preparing his words. It was an impressive and moving moment for everyone in the room and one which would set the tone for the future. His short speech had a profound effect on those present, as did the procedure that Macqueen had decided should follow. Cornelsen then presented John Eales with his jersey for the match. Eales in turn presented each forward with their jersey before calling on the vice captain to do likewise with the backs. It was a quiet, symbolic ritual which would be repeated before every subsequent Test match with a different Classic Wallaby from the ranks of former players. They would include the greatest names from Australia's proud rugby past, many of whom would unashamedly shed tears as they expressed their feelings of representing their country. The Classic Wallaby would then travel to the match on the team bus, seated beside Macqueen.

I came up with the idea for a number of reasons. I felt there was alienation between former Wallabies and the breed of players in the new era. It seemed to me many of the old representatives thought the professional players were in it for the money, not for the honour of playing for their country. My intention was to bring them together. Speaking to the Classic Wallabies on the bus, I was gratified to find that without exception they felt honoured to be back in the fold and were quite emotional about it. On the other hand, the team members showed enormous respect for the former players and talked about what they had said for days afterwards, recalling little messages that had been passed on. Some of the more memorable speeches came from some of our older Wallabies. I remember Des Connor who played twelve Tests as halfback in the late 1950s. He talked of how the team colours represented the green of the Australian gum leaves and the gold of the wattle, the national flower. Many of those messages remain with the team today and continue to help nurture the team culture. Invariably the Classic Wallaby would travel alongside me on the team bus to the Test. For me personally, it was a wonderful experience to be able to share that time with so many of our great players of the past.

Putting theory to the Test

'Walloped!' The newspaper headline said it all. The Wallabies had given the English side a rugby lesson they would never forget—a record score of 76–0 including eleven tries. It was the worst loss in 127 years of English Test rugby. The new look Australian side played the game Macqueen had been training them to play, with the speed and urgency he wanted. The win was set up by the forwards who dominated possession in all phases of play giving the backline a wealth of opportunities. Playing his first game at flyhalf, Steve Larkham was in scintillating form, continually beating the opposition with superbly timed passes and finishing the game with three tries. He was named man of the match in a game where all members of the team were able to showcase their skills.

The only thing that soured the match was the fact the win came against a team which had already been labelled the worst to leave the shores of England. A dispute between the English administration and the private millionaires who owned the various clubs had meant the majority of experienced players were left at home. Even before the match the ARU had blasted their English counterparts for sending such a poorly prepared side on tour. Afterwards Macqueen confessed the game was more like a training run than a Test match. His fit, well-drilled side was up against a weak opposition who hadn't done their homework and became more tackle shy as the game progressed. But there were many positives. The Wallabies now knew what they were capable of, but also knew that to win the World Cup they would have to repeat this type of performance against a far more committed defence. Spectators who enjoyed such a crushing victory would have been surprised at Macqueen's talk in the dressing room afterwards.

Even though we were ecstatic with the win we didn't get carried away with it. We talked about our standards, what went right and what went wrong. Despite the winning margin we had a lot of dropped balls, missed tackles and lineouts that hadn't gone our way. In leading the discussion I wasn't being critical of the team, I was encouraging the players to be critical of themselves to see what could have been done better.

Proof the team could repeat the performance against a better side came in front of an appreciative Sydney crowd the very next week. The touring Scottish team played tough and creative football and held the Wallabies to 13–3 at half time. But after the break the Australian combination finally clicked and swept to another record victory of 45–3. Perhaps more important than the score line itself was the way in which it was reached. Scottish coach Jim Telfer admitted they were unable to counter the tactics of Australia's powerful backrow: 'We're not used to the physical impact of guys like Toutai Kefu and Willie Ofahengaue coming through at us all the time.'

For the unfortunate Scots a similar brand of powerful rugby was unleashed seven days later in Brisbane. The Scottish forwards were ferocious in the rucks and mauls and the score line was closer but the control and composure of the Wallabies ensured victory in the style they'd been training to perfect.

Macqueen was particularly pleased with the results because he believed the team was physically tired due to Steve Nance's relentless training program. It wasn't publicly known that they were not preparing specifically for each match. But everyone in the squad was well aware that the overall goal was to acquire the necessary power and fitness to play the type of game needed to win the World Cup.

Looking from the grandstand

For new assistant coach Jeff Miller, the early games highlighted one of the attributes which set Macqueen apart from other coaches in any sport.

'The biggest lesson Rod's taught me was how to take a step back and not be emotionally involved. There's a time when you need to be emotionally involved and a time when you need to be removed and it's finding that balance that's important. It was difficult for me because if I didn't become excited to some extent, and I didn't have the adrenalin flowing, I couldn't think fast enough to make the decisions. We could be 30 points in front and there wouldn't be a smile amongst us. It allowed you to have that focus and concentration to analyse what was happening in the game.'

Chiefs among the Indians

In the past the Wallabies would have a day off on the Monday to recover, following a Test. They would also have a rest day immediately before a Test match. Under Steve Nance this was turned around and Mondays became what was known as 'a day at the office'. Regardless of the players feeling battered and sore he discovered that the best results were achieved by making this the toughest training day of the week.

Before each Test match the team would have a two-day rest and a light training run on the eve of the game. This session, which would last as long as it took to get everything right, was directed by the players themselves as if they were on the field and under match conditions. It became known as the 'Captain's Run'. Rather than spending the day before a Test worrying about how they would perform, the players had the opportunity to work out any concerns or individual issues so they were relaxed and in the right frame of mind for the game. Although the captain was in overall charge different players were nominated as group leaders, each having responsibility for a different area of play. David Giffin was in charge of calling the defensive lineouts, John Eales for attacking lineouts, David Wilson for calling the kickoffs, George Gregan for backrow moves and defensive patterns while Tim Horan made decisions for backline attack. Each spent countless hours studying videotapes and discussing different options with teammates to come up with new ideas for each of these phases of play. By involving both the forwards and backs in the decision-making they could react immediately to any weaknesses in defence and attack and were able to direct players to specific points in their grid of channels and zones. This meant players would arrive in numbers and they were able to defend or attack with support coming from behind and in depth.

A number of different decision-makers within the team took the pressure off the captain and vice captain and if either was forced from the field there would be no real disruption to how the team functioned. The players were also able to react when things changed on the field during a game because they understood exactly what they were doing. They were able to make the necessary adaptation if the game wasn't going the way we expected without any argument or panic. The players were responsible for their own action and therefore able to believe in what they were doing on the field. I believe this was one of the key factors that was to make the team so successful.

A test of characters

After a short overseas tour, a number of home Test matches and countless weeks of training and team discussions, the unique abilities and personalities of individual players began to emerge. Members of the public only saw the Wallabies on the field as a team, united with a common purpose. Off the field, Macqueen was coming to know them like members of his own family. He knew their strengths and weaknesses, all their foibles and infuriating idiosyncrasies.

Every team has its own characters. Owen Finegan was one of our hardest-running forwards and invaluable coming off the bench as an impact player. He was also the team joker. Owen soon found numerous ways of getting to me. One of his favourite tricks during training was to yell out, 'Heads', meaning there was a ball in the air and we should take evasive action. Because I was invariably facing the team with no-one behind me I was usually the only one with no view of what was happening elsewhere on the field. As he'd call out his warning, I'd instinctively duck and cover my head, much to the amusement of everyone else who knew there was no ball in sight. This was the same player who, whenever boarding or leaving the team bus, would religiously toot the horn, knowing it distracted and annoyed me. During team discussions, players were free to make suggestions as I mapped out game plans on a whiteboard. Owen quickly noticed my poor spelling and would call out suggestions which involved long and obscure words, which left me stumped. Although these were annoying little traits, they also brought a lot of laughs which added to the team morale.

Tim Horan was another joker, always ready to lighten the atmosphere with a one-liner or funny story. At the same time, as one of the most senior players, he took our performances very seriously. If things weren't going well on the training field, he'd be the first to call a stop and say, 'Listen guys, this just isn't good enough. We have to do better.' And because he was so highly regarded the others would quickly stop and listen.

I found George Gregan almost a contradiction. In the public eye he was the talkative livewire on the field, often flashing a huge smile either to taunt the opposition or respond to a reaction from the crowd. Yet off the field he was very serious and set very high standards for himself. More than anyone else, he worked hard to make sure he was always at the peak of physical fitness for every match. He did everything possible at all times to improve every aspect of his game and when playing he led by example. I thought George would have to be one of the best footballers in the world, but in his early playing days George had several detractors and was continually being compared and judged by the standards of the past. The fact is he was a product of the future, the ideal model for the modern footballer.

A keen golfer, George was forever challenging me to a game which included the inevitable bet on the side. My limited ability was well known, but it was only after numerous losses that I discovered he always sought me out when needing some easy cash. George amused the team by dubbing me his 'personal ATM'.

One of our key players who deservedly attracted a lot of attention was Stephen Larkham. On the field he was a wonderfully expressive player and invariably the centre of attention. His running style was naturally deceptive. While at times he appeared to be moving in slow motion, in reality he was quick and extremely elusive, creating time and space for the players around him. He has the uncanny ability to move through traffic. Some people call it vision, others call it natural ability. Whatever it is, you certainly can't train people for it. When not displaying his talents on the field, he was quiet and reserved, hence the nickname 'Bernie'. He tended to keep to himself and was fascinated by all the latest video games. Before one Test match I noticed him in the team room where, instead of reviewing the game strategy, he was totally absorbed playing with his video control unit. I didn't say anything, thinking it was probably his way of relaxing before a big game. However, I noticed he ran onto the field without his usual headgear. When I queried this with our medical team they reluctantly informed me he'd also arrived without his usual protective strapping, his distinctive headgear and, not only that, without his boots! I wasn't impressed and figured out the reason why. I had a quiet talk and suggested that in future he ignored the temptation of video games and concentrate on preparing himself for a match. He was typically sheepish about the whole thing and to his credit it certainly didn't affect his game, then or since.

Reversing SWOT to get on top

Knowing the opposition was a key to the team's planning process. The now established method of SWOT analysis (studying the opposition's Strengths, Weaknesses, Opportunities and Threats) played an important role. But Macqueen discovered it was becoming boring and monotonous and was not always producing the appropriate results, so he reversed the process. Before each game the Wallabies would also do a SWOT analysis on themselves from the opposition's point of view.

It invariably turned up interesting points and provided me with an insight into how the players regarded their own abilities. Taking a business approach we worked in group tasks. To avoid the 'grey decisions' I always made sure that I would pick small groups rather than the team as a whole. This way I knew I would get the most adventurous and creative ideas. The various leaders would go away and look at the different aspects of the game and come back and make a presentation to the team. We'd spend many hours studying the results both on the opposition and ourselves. We didn't make too much noise about it because we didn't want the opposition to know how much we knew about them.

The art of war

Without knowing it, Macqueen had for many years been applying techniques similar to those of Sun Tzu, an ancient Chinese warrior and philosopher. His book, *The Art of War*, compiled more than two thousand years ago, is regarded by many to be one of the foremost books on strategy ever written. Macqueen was discussing his own strategies for an upcoming match during a game of golf with close friend and former assistant coach Peter Carson. Another member of their playing foursome remarked that his plans and philosophies sounded familiar to the tactics espoused in a book he'd been reading on ancient battle techniques, a book which was now gaining recognition in the corporate arena. A few days later a copy of *The Art of War* arrived at Macqueen's home.

I found the book fascinating. A great deal of its content was very similar to the strategies and philosophies we were using both at Advantage Line and in rugby.

One technique in particular we often used in our game plans. To launch an attack at the opposition's strongest point then, using a second force, strike in numbers at a point of weakness. But probably the most telling philosophy that would be repeated continually concerned the value of knowledge according to Sun Tzu:

> *Know yourself and know your enemy and*
> *in a thousand battles you'll never be in peril.*
> *Know yourself but know not your enemy,*
> *and your chances of success and failure will be equal.*
> *Know not yourself or your enemy,*
> *and in every battle you'll be in peril.*

This passage took Macqueen back to the victory over NSW where the Brumbies comprehensively demolished their opposition by a record score. At the time he knew their own preparation had been crucial and the size of the win had also been due to arrogance on the part of the other side. It was a perfect example of entering a conflict totally unprepared.

The art of strategy

During this period, the team was continually developing new attacking strategies. Many of the moves which would later help carry them through to World Cup victory came from a combination of individual creativity, reverse SWOT analysis and a touch of inspiration from ancient Chinese battlefields.

In accordance with our vision, we believed the hardest team to play against would be one that constantly sought out, and attacked, opposition weaknesses. Sun Tzu called it 'attacking like water through valleys'. Using sequence plays we would sometimes plan to run a move four to five phases after our initial set play. We always made a point of having several options so that we could change at the last moment, depending on the reaction of the opposition.

In developing our attack we would also take into account what we would do if the roles were reversed and the opposition played a game similar to our own. It would be a difficult strategy to counter but one option was to aggressively impose ourselves, offering no obvious weaknesses and forcing them into a pattern that brought about mistakes. Another was to set traps: show an apparent weakness and lure the opposition into taking a particular course of action. We could then close the trap knowing what options they then had available to them.

In addition we continued to develop special plays where we would change the running lines of our players to confuse the opposition's defence. Some of these plays came from rugby league and involved decoy runners. I found it interesting that our use of decoys was constantly criticised by many officials and coaches from other countries. Ironically, this style of play had been used for decades in both the northern and southern hemispheres. It was only that we started using them continuously and at pace that it was seen as something different.

At the same time we continually tried to improve on the basic but crucial aspect of the game: securing possession from scrums, lineouts and kickoffs. We spent countless hours studying the opposition and exerted as much pressure as possible to steal possession at every opportunity. Performance in these areas became an important indicator on the winning or losing of games.

In everything we did the key element of our approach was to be unpredictable at all times.

The innovative and sometimes apparently opportunistic movements on the field were inevitably the result of many hours planning in the team room and practice on the training paddock. At all times the Macqueen strategy was to be structured but flexible, with a game plan suited to take advantage of any weaknesses in the opposition side. After so much preparation there was understandably great satisfaction for all involved whenever the Wallaby attack swept through the opposition like 'water through valleys'.

From war dance to showtime

The Wallabies changed their training program. After four weeks of intense fitness work they began to ease off in preparation for what many critics were touting as their first real test under the leadership of Rod Macqueen. It was the first of three matches against the All Blacks. These games would decide whether the Wallabies were capable of wresting back the coveted Bledisloe Cup from the Kiwis. The game was scheduled for the Melbourne Cricket Ground, which at the time had the largest capacity of any Australian sporting venue. They had a three-week break to perfect their tactics for the match and Macqueen was already confident their analysis had revealed the Kiwis were vulnerable. In addition Macqueen had already put in place a seemingly innocuous procedure which was designed to defuse the All Blacks' psychological weapon, the haka.

It was an issue that I thought about back in 1997 when I first got the job of Wallaby coach. It absolutely amazed me when I sat down and thought about the haka, that over such a long period of time no-one had come up with a counter measure. It's a Maori war dance designed to intimidate and frighten the enemy. For over 100 years it has been a problem for opposing teams around the world. What do you do about it? Stand still and stare them in the eye? Jog around and ignore them? Turn your back, which would be insulting? My whole aim was to remove it as a problem for us. While it's an important tradition which should be honoured, it put us in a bad position right from the start. Yet we had always accepted this as being appropriate.

Apart from the psychological factor there were other concerns. Opposition teams spend at least twenty minutes warming up their bodies for a game only to go out onto the field where they sing national anthems and then stand and watch the haka. The entire proceedings can take up to twelve minutes or more, which means the opposition inevitably cools down.

Macqueen decided Australia should have its own tradition and came up with the idea of a pre-game routine that involved the Wallabies remaining in their tracksuits until just before kick-off. They then formed a tight circle where each of the various team leaders went through the game plan. Only then did they strip off and get ready to play. This followed the usual pre-game activity and in the case of New Zealand would follow the haka. Coincidentally the routine lasted about one-and-a-quarter minutes, the same time taken to perform the haka. Although developed specifically to counter the impact of the emotional Maori war dance, it would have been a controversial move to introduce it in a match against the All Blacks. Therefore the routine was first performed during the first Test match of the year against

England, and was subsequently repeated against Scotland. At these matches it raised little comment.

In the most anticipated match of the year more than 75,000 people packed the Melbourne Cricket Ground to see if the Wallabies could defeat the All Blacks after seven successive losses. The pre-match build-up had been almost unprecedented and the pressure on the players and management team was intense. But Macqueen knew the players were confident in the strategies and game plan they had devised and practised. He also believed they were about to defuse the psychological factor of the haka. It wasn't until the Wallabies lined up in centre field that the ingenuity and real purpose of their pre-kickoff routine became apparent. They waited patiently as their Kiwi opponents screamed out the aggressive war chant ending in the traditional leap and threatening glare. Then, fired up and ready to play, it was the Kiwis' turn to wait while the Australians formed their pre-match routine huddle with their arms around each other and calmly discussed tactics. Once mentally prepared, they shed the warmth of their tracksuits and took up position, ready for the game to begin.

By not going straight into the game after the haka it allowed us to start when we were ready. The haka then became part of the pre-game entertainment and not part of the actual game itself. It is a great tradition and should be respected but should not be used as a weapon against another side, giving the All Blacks a psychological edge before the game has even begun.

Measuring up

The game produced spectacular football from two sides who at first appeared evenly matched. When the All Blacks surged to an 8–0 lead many expected the Wallabies to fold. But they held their composure and continued with their game plan with backs and forwards continually attacking straight down the field. Every move the Wallabies played in their previous games now had a subtle variation to it, changing the direction of attack. It was a tactic the All Blacks later conceded negated the many hours of research they had spent on the Wallaby pattern of play.

They successfully used their pattern, integrating the backs and forwards. One of these involved fullback Matthew Burke and worked to perfection. It finished with him driving through the middle of a ruck to score a try. At the final whistle Australia ran out victors 24–16 and the crowd—including fans from both sides—rose to applaud the spectacle which had exceeded everyone's expectations. In a record-breaking performance Matt Burke scored all of Australia's points, including two tries, and was named Man of the Match. It was their fourth Test of the year and their fourth victory. But there was another significant factor. Macqueen had been able to select exactly the same run-on side for all four matches. In the past there had been much criticism about the chopping and changing of the Wallaby lineup.

It wasn't a perfect performance but one which showed team cohesion was improving. It was still early days but the constant practising of skills was evident in our pattern of play. The players were able to understand each other and communicate on the field and were interacting instinctively and with more confidence. The most pleasing thing was that in the dressing room after the game, the players were analysing what we had not done well, rather than dwelling on the significance of the win. There is no doubt that by constantly changing the members of the team it becomes disruptive and the confidence necessary to play to your full potential can't be generated.

Only well after the match could Macqueen fully appreciate what beating the All Blacks truly meant. Before the match he had arranged an address to the players by former Wallaby coach and media personality, Alan Jones. As one who had coached the Wallabies to a previous Bledisloe Cup win, Jones stressed what the competition between the neighbouring countries meant, what excitement it generated not only amongst spectators at the game but also among the general public. Macqueen regards Jones as the greatest motivational speaker he has heard, and his words certainly stirred everyone in the room that day, but Macqueen was too preoccupied to realise the importance of winning such a high-profile match. Jones had warned them it would be a tough and close contest and advised them to play the game 'minute by minute'. It was a phrase that fitted in with Macqueen's philosophy of playing the game to plan without being preoccupied with the outcome, and he repeated the words at half-time to keep the players focused. With victory achieved, Macqueen celebrated with the players but was still oblivious to the euphoria the result had produced.

It was still early days and this was our first chance to get a measure on how far we had progressed. I've always tried to remain emotionally removed from a game so I can make clear decisions during the match, and I can honestly say I wasn't awake to the occasion. It wasn't until later when we walked through the streets of Melbourne and heard people singing 'Waltzing Matilda' and saw them waving the Australian flag that I realised the significance of what we had achieved.

This significance was brought home even further the following day when newspapers across the country trumpeted the Wallabies' victory over their traditional foes from across the Tasman. They all gleefully embraced the news that at last Australia had a team that could match and beat the might of New Zealand, a feat that had not been achieved for almost four years. Several reports quoted former Wallaby fullback Glen Ella, who compared the difference of the new to the old: 'The team is now settled and they are going to fight and die for each other. That wasn't the case with Australian teams the previous couple of seasons. The enthusiasm of the young guys is contagious and this is bound to come through and help Australia in the World Cup.'

Lessons from losing . . .

But to win the World Cup they would also need to be capable of defeating the existing cup holders, South Africa. A week later in a mistake-riddled match in Perth, the Wallabies went down by just one point, 14–13. Trying to play their expansive game in wet conditions, they failed but both captain and coach refused to blame the weather.

There is no doubt that I was extremely disappointed but at the same time, I knew that we had learnt some valuable lessons. Once in front early in the game we tried to shut everything down too soon. That was probably one of our biggest learning experiences and a particular milestone for us. I've always found that the best way to learn is from your mistakes, providing you don't make them twice. You can learn much more from mistakes than you can from success. After watching video replays of the game, we realised how more and more negative we became as the game progressed. The players saw how important it was for their style of play

always to remain positive and to keep attacking. Even at the time I knew
we had let ourselves down and admitted as much to the media.

. . . And from winning

In Christchurch two weeks later the headlines told a different story
when the Wallabies defeated the All Blacks for a second time to
clinch the Bledisloe Cup. Once again the Wallabies played to their
full potential to secure a momentous 27–23 victory on a ground
where no Australian side had won a match in the past forty years.
The win included some inspiring performances including a magnificent game by lock Tom Bowman. His mobility around the field and
crushing defence showed Australia had at last found a formidable
second-row partner for the incomparable John Eales. For dedicated
rugby enthusiasts the highlight was no doubt a try scored by Matt
Burke two minutes before half-time. The Wallabies retained possession and recycled the ball for six phases of play, then ten, twelve,
fourteen and onwards until Burke dived over the line after possession
was held for an unbelievable eighteen phases. It was controlled rugby
at its best.

The Wallabies had now been working for a number of months on the
skills required to play continuous rugby and this was the game that saw
it all come together. Maintaining possession through eighteen phases,
which was unheard of at that time, showed they were playing the type
of rugby they had all been talking about at the start of the season.

When a beaming John Eales lifted the silver trophy head high to the
delight of Australian spectators only then did the despairing Kiwi
supporters, shocked by their team's defeat, realise the giant silver cup
was about to leave their shores for the first time in four years.

While the Wallabies were rightfully ecstatic in victory, they were
equally respectful towards the vanquished. In his first taste of Bledisloe glory, Macqueen had vivid memories of the demeanor of the All
Blacks at the after-match function.

I was incredibly impressed with the humility shown by their coach, John
Hart, and indeed all the players. Although they obviously knew local
commentators would be looking for excuses and scapegoats, they took
the defeat extremely well. From our point of view, the amount of time

and effort spent practising our skills was now starting to show on the field.

Sharing the trophy

If Macqueen was slow to realise the significance of the win in Melbourne it was a different scenario this time round. He was over-whelmed with emotional congratulations from the time the Wallabies left the field in triumph until well after he arrived back to his Collaroy home. There were many unusual and amusing incidents along the way.

Celebrations at the team hotel soon involved the many Australian supporters staying there as well as several Kiwi supporters. The cup was the guest of honour. Filled with beer, it was constantly passed around so everyone could share the moment. The New Zealand weather was unseasonably cold and snow was forecast for that evening. Despite the fact it was August, Macqueen and Eales privately agreed it was a festive occasion that deserved a special gesture. Before the match, they made a pact to celebrate victory in a special way. They agreed to stand arm-in-arm in the snow at midnight singing Christmas carols. When the promised snowflakes failed to materialise, they sang carols regardless, but in the hotel bar where they were soon joined by everyone else. This began a ritual that would be observed for years to come. The pair would contrive to celebrate together in a different and unusual way after every major Test victory. The next morning when Macqueen woke alongside Liz in their hotel room in Christchurch, he was momentarily surprised to see the trophy at the foot of the bed. The reality was still sinking in.

Passengers on the Qantas jumbo about to take off from Christchurch were startled to see the Bledisloe Cup sitting in its own reserved seat in business class. The Australian pilot, revelling in the precious cargo he was about to transport, invited Macqueen onto the flight deck as the plane taxied onto the runway. In seeking permission for take-off he couldn't resist a parting shot at those in the control tower. 'I must remind you this Qantas flight to Sydney is seeking priority clearance. The Bledisloe Cup is leaving New Zealand shores forever.'

The reply from the control tower was prompt and to the point. 'Permission for take-off is refused.'

The ensuing silence alarmed Macqueen, but the conversation soon resumed and after several joking remarks between control tower and aircraft, permission was eventually granted. When the Australian coach made his way back to his seat the importance of the win was reinforced yet again. His appearance brought a round of loud cheering and applause from all the passengers, most of whom were Australian rugby supporters returning home.

I didn't realise how much it meant to so many people. And to see the attention the Wallabies were receiving was just incredible. This and the whole experience in Christchurch made me realise just how important it is for the public to feel part of the occasion—after all, without their support winning isn't nearly as exciting.

The celebrations continued when we arrived in Sydney. There was a huge crowd waiting for us when we came out of customs, cheering and waving banners. Once again it was a tremendous showing.

There was more to come. With the offices of the ARU closed the Macqueens had no option but to take the trophy home in a chauffeur-driven hire car which had been booked for the occasion. They sat in the back while the famous trophy, secured by a seatbelt of course, travelled in the front next to the driver. Halfway home they were overtaken by a police highway patrol car which ordered them to pull over. At first they were concerned then confused until the two policemen asked permission to have a closer look at the cup. There was no traffic infringement—the policemen had recognised the gleaming silver trophy and, being rugby fans, couldn't resist the opportunity to have a personal share in Australia's moment of glory.

That night the cup was again the centre of attention at a victory party. This time in the Macqueens' lounge room surrounded by neighbours, family and friends. For a rugby icon normally secured in a display cabinet, the famous Bledisloe Cup was rapidly becoming a party animal.

The office with no fixed address

With a three-week break before the next Test match against South Africa, most people would assume there was an opportunity for the Wallaby coach to take an extended break. Unfortunately that rarely seemed to be the case. The nerve centre for the Wallaby campaign is not Caloundra or ARU headquarters, but wherever Macqueen happens to be. Similarly, as company chief, his headquarters was not necessarily at Exhibition Displays or more recently Advantage Line. At all times of the day and night, Macqueen is in constant touch with those who matter, ensuring everything possible is being done for the next challenge, or the new project. Friends who have called into the family home for a quiet drink and a chat often do so in between a constant round of phone calls; for example, a call from the team doctor to advise on the progress of an injured player. This prompts an immediate call to one of the assistant coaches to discuss the options of a reserve player just in case. A call to team manager John McKay to ensure that reserve would be ready to travel if necessary. An incoming inquiry from a journalist looking for an interview on the upcoming match. A call to partner Frank Minnici to check on the progress of a particular design or to question the outcome of a presentation to a new client. And so it goes on. The calls and decisions are made quickly and quietly, with a tone of authority that demands, and gets, immediate action.

Family and friends understand how he manages to cope and take it all in his stride. They know him as a complex character who thrives on challenges and achieving goals; a highly competitive person who insists on doing everything perfectly and expects the same from those around him. Liz and others working with him are quite accustomed to being asked to drop whatever they are doing so that a crucial problem can be solved or that a last minute chore can be completed on time with every 'i' dotted and every 't' crossed. His ability to envisage and quickly solve complex problems often leaves others floundering in his wake, asking for more information in an effort to keep up with his train of thought.

Over many years Macqueen has been accused of being 'out of action' or 'not in the office'. He may be out on the golf course, swimming laps in the family pool or off on one of his favourite jogging trails. These occasions are a break from the constant phone calls and other interruptions to his daily life, but they are rarely an escape. Far from it. On his own, in a relaxing environment, is where he's able to think clearly. Some of the biggest, most important decisions and creative ideas come while he is 'out of action'.

Making a negative a positive

The Wallabies journeyed to South Africa confident of victory. With a solid four days of preparation near Johannesburg and a well-researched game plan they ran onto the pitch at Ellis Park unconcerned by the deafening roar of support from the crowd of more than 70,000. But as the match progressed they were overcome by a number of factors. The Wallabies didn't play to their full potential, the Springboks were ruthless and methodical. Although it didn't have any direct bearing on the outcome of the match the behaviour of the crowd and game organisers ensured it was an unpleasantly memorable experience for the Australians. With twenty minutes to go the Springboks had an unassailable lead and the crowd smelt victory. Australian players near the sideline were pelted with oranges and other rubbish and loudly abused. At the same time the song 'We are the Champions' began blaring out over the public address system. At the final whistle the South African players raised their arms in triumph, winning the Tri Nations trophy with a 29–15 victory.

The players were still despondent when they arrived back in Australia. The Wallabies felt they had done everything right but had still been defeated by a side which on the day played a better game. Now they had only four days to prepare for the third and final match against the All Blacks at the Sydney Football Stadium. Having already secured the Bledisloe Cup with their two earlier victories, the Wallabies could have been forgiven for easing off. Instead it was the opposite—the South African experience had wounded their pride and stirred them into action. Even Macqueen was taken aback by the attitude of his players.

The loss to South Africa triggered a positive response from the players. We'd already won the Bledisloe trophy but from day one the players were absolutely committed to winning the last game. It was a real test of character given the toughness of the previous match and the amount of travel involved. We actually eased off on our training but worked hard on our game plan and when the time came they were ready to play and really wanted to win.

Unfortunately once on the field not everything went to plan. In a close and spirited first half marred by numerous penalties against both sides, the All Blacks surged ahead and went to the break leading 11–0. Against the mighty All Blacks such a position traditionally meant certain defeat. The score line would have been closer except that Wallaby fullback Matt Burke had missed three comparatively simple shots at goal.

In the Australian dressing room there was no sign of panic as players and officials went through their now established routine. First there was a medical inspection of all players with a report quickly given to Macqueen. Then John Eales stood and gave his thoughts on what was happening and how their strategy should be changed. He was followed by vice captain, George Gregan, and then any other player who felt they had something positive to offer. As in every half-time assessment the emphasis was on advice being delivered in a cool and calm manner. There was no criticism, only suggestions to remedy any problems and thoughts on possible changes in tactics. As usual, the coaching staff of Miller, Lane and Macqueen had conferred just before half-time and decided on a strategy.

On this occasion Macqueen had a serious problem that needed to be turned around: Matt Burke was kicking badly. Even worse, the more he kicked the more his overall confidence seemed to drop. Macqueen first went to Eales, his second string kicker, and established he was content to take over the goal-kicking duties. Then he approached Burke, but rather than telling the champion fullback his goal-kicking was below standard, he suggested he had a more important role for him.

For us to win the game, we needed Matt to become more involved by joining in as many attacking moves as possible. I suggested that it would be better to relieve him of the goal-kicking responsibilities so he could concentrate more on this part of his game. This was an extremely difficult situation to turn around. We had to ensure that Matt and the rest of the team saw the change as a positive step, not a negative reaction to a situation that was threatening to lose us the game. By putting it this way we were able to turn a negative into a positive and everyone was comfortable with the option taken.

The strategy brought results almost immediately and Burke responded with a great second half. Soon after the resumption of play, Eales kicked two penalty goals to bring Australia back into contention. A further exchange of penalty kicks left the score at 14–9

New Zealand's way with only ten minutes left to play. What followed was a piece of play that made Macqueen's quiet half-time talk seem inspired. Halfback George Gregan made a dashing run down the sideline deep in New Zealand's territory then at the last moment passed inside to a charging Matt Burke who crashed over the try line under the weight of three defenders. John Eales calmly converted the try from wide out to give Australia the lead for the first time. A further penalty just before the final whistle saw Australia win an absorbing contest 19–14.

Unfortunately, Burke's outstanding try came at a price. The multiple tackle which buried him across the try line badly dislocated his left shoulder; the injury would later require a full reconstruction, keeping him on the sideline for almost six months.

The series had delivered one of the greatest Australian rugby wins of all time. It was the first 3–0 whitewash of the All Blacks since 1929. Media reports for the following week were detailed and effusive: Macqueen was Australia's 'saviour', 'the magician', and 'master coach'. In a quiet moment amid the adulation and celebration, Macqueen thought back to the days before his first Test match against England only nine months earlier when media probing and innuendo had almost forced him to walk away from the job. Only the talks with John O'Neill and Paul McLean had convinced him to stay. Those discussions included the advice that intense media attention and public expectation was all part of the job. He had now experienced that attention at both ends of the spectrum. The quiet, almost reclusive Macqueen was uneasy with both. A more pleasant thought flickered into life. At his first press conference as Australian coach more than twelve months before, the barrage of questions had a central theme: 'Can you build a team capable of beating the All Blacks?' The people who were asking that question were now writing the answer.

It was ironical that although we had achieved success, we hadn't set ourselves any specific goals other than winning the World Cup. Winning the Bledisloe Cup had, in fact, been a result of the standards we were now setting ourselves. Earlier feelings were that our standards weren't high enough because of the poor performances against the South African teams. It was at that stage that Jeff, Tim and I decided that this was the end of The Beginning and the start of The Journey.

The journey is the reward

> *'This is not the beginning, this is not the end,*
> *this is the end of the beginning.'*
>
> Winston Churchill

This quote had been presented to the team by Phil Kearns at one of their previous Test matches—another initiative to encourage greater involvement by the players before each game. Macqueen believed this was the appropriate quote to start the next part of the diary, 'The Journey'.

On the front page of the diary he stressed that:

> The object of our 'beginning' was to ensure our direction and create a team in which selflessness was the primary driving force. We have achieved this—earlier than expected. At the same time, we have created some memorable outcomes including record wins against England and Scotland, bringing home the Bledisloe Cup and beating the All Blacks 3–0, a feat achieved only once before.
>
> It is now time to look towards our Journey, which will lead us to our Destination—the finals of the World Cup.
>
> Victory in the World Cup will be our ultimate prize but it is the journey along the way that is the reward—enjoy it.
>
> Now we have our direction, we need to go forward and take another step up. We need to continually set ourselves higher standards and be totally committed to reaching the ultimate performance.
>
> Today's preparation determines tomorrow's achievement.

A new quote was also added to the team room. 'The Journey is the reward.'

The matches against Fiji and Tonga brought record scores but the team from lowly-rated Western Samoa played a physical style of football that had the now seasoned Wallaby combination struggling. The ferocious tackling, much of it very close to the legal limit destroyed any chance of the Australians carrying out the fast flowing game plan which had proved so successful against the other two Pacific nations. However, they held their ground, changed their tactics and managed a reasonably comfortable win. It showed Macqueen that the side was capable of adapting to a totally different type of opponent. It also proved that the many months of training with a system of group leaders, able to coordinate changes of tactics on the field, would be invaluable in the countdown to the World Cup.

Sacrifice and victory on foreign fields

The twenty-six members of the Wallaby squad stopped in the middle of their training session in Sydney before leaving for a short tour of Europe. They all stood to attention and bowed their heads to observe one minute's silence. It was 11 a.m. on the eleventh day of the eleventh month 1998—Remembrance Day, the day Australians commemorate the signing of Armistice documents to end World War One.

The following day was overcast and drizzling rain when the team bus eased to a halt. Most of the players were sleeping after their long flight to Paris. They were now on their way to the provincial capital of Lille to play a French XV before a single Test against France. This was a special stopover at the village of Villers-Bretonneux, the site of a memorable Australian battle during the Great War where against overwhelming odds a major German advance was repulsed. It became a turning point in the invasion of France. It was also the site of a large and neatly tended war cemetery and a memorial to those who gave their lives.

The players and officials moved slowly amongst the rows of headstones, reading the brief inscriptions. It was a solemn moment. The team was later treated to a reception at the local town hall where the mayor of Villers-Bretonneux gave a moving speech praising the heroics of the young Australians who had saved his village from German occupation eighty years before. Behind him a large painting of the village was dominated by a skyline featuring clouds in the shape of Australia. It demonstrated to the players how high the Australian sacrifice was regarded in a small village so far from home. On behalf of the Wallabies, John Eales gave an emotional reply comparing the hardships and sacrifices of the two groups. Both, he said, represented their country with pride and honour, one playing a sport, the other prepared to make the ultimate sacrifice.

The event left an even greater impression on everyone than Rod Macqueen expected. He himself was patriotic to the extent he had a flagpole in his front yard in order to raise the Australian flag on days such as this.

It was a moving moment, reading the names and the ages of the Australians who had fought and died on foreign soil. Many were in their late teens and were younger than those in our touring party. We had arranged the visit with a special purpose in mind. We wanted to raise even further in the minds of the players the honour of playing for their country. I could almost see the thoughts running through the minds of our young squad who realised they were following in the footsteps of others. I think it left an indelible mark which was to surface later in the determination and courage of the team.

The match in Lille was against a typically tenacious French team but the Wallabies secured a win and received valuable preparation for the Test just five days away. It was the first rugby match to be held at the magnificent Stade de France and the passionate French were keen to emulate the heroics of their national soccer team in the World Cup final the previous year. The Wallabies were up against a side which had won the two previous Five Nations tournaments and were undefeated in their last ten Test matches. Urged on by the crowd of 70,000 the French played with their usual passion and flair, but it was not enough. Their hopes of an historic victory were dashed by an unusually aggressive but strongly disciplined display by the Australians.

As well as the concern about the upcoming Scottish and English tests, another issue arose with media accusations of performance-enhancing substances being used by the Australian team. The players appeared to be fitter, faster and stronger than their opponents and the media were quick to assume that the Wallabies were secretly using illegal drugs.

BHW: the secret supplement

During an interview with trainer Steve Nance, one of the French journalists questioned him on the accusations. Nance admitted that yes, the players were being given liberal doses of BHW. The surprised journalist began to write excitedly at the prospect of a major revelation until Nance explained that BHW actually meant 'bloody hard work'.

Twickenham in late November would be the last match of the season for the battle weary Australians. The English side was vastly different from the young and inexperienced touring party they had demolished 76–0 at the beginning of the year. The Wallabies faced a confident and hardened outfit determined to avenge the previous humiliating defeat. In dreary conditions a dreary game of football slowly ground to an end with Australia facing a loss in the final minutes. It came down to a matter of numbers. With only five minutes left to run, the Poms in front 11–9 and the penalty count running against them 19–8, the referee noticed a rare English indiscretion forty-three metres from the posts. This gave the Australians a chance. John Eales stepped forward and for the fourth time in the match calmly thumped a towering kick which again bisected the English posts and sank the hearts and hopes of the opposition players and supporters. The successful penalty delivered a 12–11 victory.

The Test match was neither pretty nor inspirational, but it was the end of a long hard year and worthy of celebration. Cigars were handed round in the dressing room afterwards but such was the disappointment in their performance there was more coughing and introspection than outward celebration. It was left to the ever-present wit of John McKay to put the situation in perspective. 'Eleven out of thirteen, that'll do me for Christmas.'

He was right. In a season which included an unprecedented thirteen Test matches they had lost only two, both to South Africa. One of them by a heartbreaking single point which cost them the Tri Nations victory. By any measure it was a long and difficult campaign which had established a structure and culture in readiness for their tilt at the World Cup the following year. 'The Beginning' had turned out to be exactly that: a successful preparation for the journey that would lead to their ultimate destination. What began with early training runs in the sticky heat of a Queensland summer had ended in the numbing cold of an English winter. Much had been learnt and everything put in place. 'The Journey' was well underway.

As the rest of the squad headed home, Macqueen made a short journey of his own to Ireland. This was no private holiday. He was looking for a suitable base camp from which to stage the Wallaby World Cup campaign the following year. He booked into a recently completed resort at Portmarnoch, a village outside Dublin. The complex was built alongside a golf course next to the Irish sea. After several days he knew he had found what he was looking for.

Chapter 20

The Journey Continues

At the beginning of 1999 everything was in place. Macqueen was happy that all the necessary preparation was on track in readiness for the Australian assault on the World Cup. Then the phone rang. The voice of John Eales gave him information he didn't want to hear. The Wallaby captain had suffered a freakish injury; in a normal weights session during training for the Super 12 season he had seriously damaged the AC joint in his shoulder. The team's leader and most inspirational player would be unable to play football for at least three months, perhaps longer. Hopefully he would be available just in time to play in the lead-up games for the World Cup tournament. With fullback Matt Burke still recovering from his shoulder reconstruction this meant two key players were out of action. But the old saying about bad luck coming in threes would soon prove correct. Macqueen was at Bruce Stadium several weeks later watching his new flyhalf Steve Larkham weaving some magic against New Zealand provincial side Canterbury. His enjoyment was soon extinguished when Larkham twisted awkwardly in a tackle and immediately clutched his leg. Macqueen feared the worst. Unfortunately he had every reason to do so: a medical report confirmed his main play-maker would also be out of action for at least three months. The inspirational Journey that Macqueen had spent so much time putting together was already becoming an ordeal. He desperately needed some good news, and it came from the dedicated and hardworking Jeff Miller.

The edge

In their quest to constantly seek out new ideas and technology, the Australian Rugby Union created the High Performance Division, which Miller headed. Throughout the Super 12 competition he experimented with the use of detailed video statistics on a computer CD ROM rather than videocassettes. Macqueen first became aware of the system when he was a guest in the coaches' box at an AFL match and saw the possibilities of adapting and expanding the technology. In consultation with Macqueen and Miller, the package was developed further by Australian software company, Fair Play. With perseverance, Miller finally came up with a system perfectly tailored to suit the demands of rugby. Each disk held the detail of a full game broken up into every aspect of play. Ironically, rugby statistics and analysis previously came from a company in New Zealand.

With this new system, for example, by clicking the mouse on the name of the team required, a menu would appear giving a full list of its players together with options ranging from tackles, passes and kicks to individual skills. Then by clicking on the name of a player and the word 'tackle' the program would automatically provide statistics and back them up by displaying every tackle that person had completed during that game, one after another in sequence. Similarly the process could be repeated for passes, kicks, runs, and so on. In this way the individual skills or weaknesses of any player could be analysed in minutes. The speed of a pass, the effectiveness of a sidestep, the length of a kick and the power of a tackle, but also a weaker passing action, an inability to sidestep off one particular foot or both, a favoured kicking boot, or a reluctance to defend. All the set plays could also be quickly and minutely examined. Any passing sequences repeated during a match could soon be flagged as planned moves and filed for reference.

This breakthrough in technology was also a revelation for the players. Armed with a computer and a fistful of CDs, every Wallaby would be able to study the performance of his opposite number examining statistics which had been collated over the previous two years. After several hours of tapping computer keys George Gregan would know the playing style and ability of All Black halfback Justin Marshall as well as Marshall knew himself—the average time it took for him to scoop up the ball and pass it, the speed of the pass, the length, accuracy and any special trick moves he might have. The same applied to every other aspect of Marshall's game, all shown in isolation and at normal speed, or slow motion or in freeze frame. How did he adapt to different opponents or weather conditions? Just select a CD from a different Test match and George would know in a couple of minutes. So would any other member of the Wallaby squad if they wanted to target one of the key members of the All Black side. 'Big Brother' was finally here and watching, at least on the field of rugby.

The CD ROM, however, was a two-edged sword. The players knew their opposition couldn't hide, but neither could they. Gone were the days when a forward could loiter at the back of a maul, or a winger could stay out of the action. Of course players had been under scrutiny through videotape for many years but always as part of the team. In this situation 'Big Brother' was the coach. Nothing was secret, nowhere was safe. Even a relaxing flight to the next match venue could be rudely interrupted by either Macqueen or Muggleton suddenly taking the seat alongside you, armed with a laptop computer. Remember the two tackles you missed during the last game? Well here they are in slow motion and let's see what went wrong. The pages and pages of statistics were no longer just numbers and names, they could be instantly translated into real life vision.

Learning the art of war was being simplified. When Sun Tzu stressed the importance of knowing yourself and your enemy, he didn't have the advantage of CDs and laptop computers. After two thousand years, opposing sides would now have no excuse for ignoring his words of wisdom. The eventual consequence would not be known immediately, but when sides became more evenly matched there would need to be changes in the rules of engagement.

Inner standards

When the Wallaby squad assembled at Caloundra for the first meeting of the season everyone received a new diary with the year's itinerary and goals listed in the usual meticulous detail. A new title page bore the heading, 'The Journey Continues'. The book listed their previous achievements, but even that was not the benchmark for the new season:

> Last year we built the foundations on which to continue our journey . . . our success now lies in our ability to continue to improve and set ourselves higher standards.

This theme was repeated at the first team meeting where Macqueen prompted discussion on the initial adjustments that would have to be made to allow for the loss of three crucial players. Regardless, performance had to be raised.

We continued to talk about the importance of standards both on and off the field and how it had to come from within. It wasn't something that management could set, it was something that had to come from within the team itself. It would be up to the individual players to lift themselves and find something extra.

The prospect of playing in the World Cup generated an air of excitement which was reflected in attitude and performance. From the first training session Macqueen detected a new level of intensity. In the absence of John Eales experienced flanker David Wilson was a popular choice as captain.

Although George had been an excellent vice captain in the side, he hadn't yet had the experience of the captaincy role. Both positions are quite different. David Wilson, however, had already captained Queensland and Australia.

Wilson ably led the team in preparation for the campaign which began with two Test matches against the touring Irish side. Australia comfortably won both games with the results overshadowed by reports of 'rough house' and 'boots and all' play from Ireland. The legacy of the previous years' self-criticism continued. Happy with victory, after each match the players discussed what improvements could be made and assured each other they could play a lot better. This time Macqueen wasn't needed to prompt the discussion, the players themselves knew what would be required to win the World Cup and were intent on reaching the required level.

It was evident that the players were already starting to think about the 'destiny'. They had ideas and suggestions already formulated before we sat down at the first meeting. I felt that everything was coming along more naturally and that the players and management were communicating as a team.

Testing communication

Preparations were helped by innovations in the team room. Macqueen devised a way of testing on-field communication between players. He would ask them to imagine they were on the field at a crucial point in the match.

I would put a scenario to the players: 'We're five points behind with five minutes on the clock. We have a scrum-feed on the left side of the field in our own 22-metre area, what action should we take? The subsequent responses from the various team leaders would give a clear picture as to how our communication system was working.

For example, the inside-centre would indicate the move he thought appropriate and tell the halfback. The halfback would then relay a coded number to the hooker, who was scrum captain. He would be responsible for directing the ball so it would emerge from the appropriate side of the scrum. The backrow captain would yell a coded message to the other forwards so they knew where the play was going. Of course, the point of all this was not only to test our on-field communication but to see whether we were making the right decision for the circumstances.

Nominating a range of scenarios like this would help the team to think and communicate as one. I often used a similar practice in business to check on the communication between departments. By suggesting differ-ent problems or scenarios I could then watch the process they used to come up with a solution.

While such innovations continued to give the Wallabies an edge over their opponents, other changes brought mixed results. Macqueen recalls one session later in the season that left him angered but knowing it was time for a change.

On one occasion I learnt a very valuable lesson. It was Owen Finegan's turn to go over the checklist of game tactics and to my annoyance, and a great deal of mirth from the players, he began sending me up. He went through every point mimicking my expressions as he went. 'We got that covered', 'We can't forget that', 'This can be something special', and so on. He had turned it into a comedy and I was quietly seething. After I thought about it I realised I was being given a timely wakeup call. It reminded me that I was becoming too repetitive, not looking for new ways to keep things interesting, yet still expecting the same results. Subse-quently we changed the approach to our whole system of SWOT analysis. We softened the approach by taking out some of the rigid discipline and made it more specific to rugby.

One hundred reasons to win

In 1899 at the Sydney Cricket Ground, Australia played its first rugby Test match against England and won 13–3. In the ensuing one hundred years Australia has held the imposing record of never losing to England on home soil. In 1999 that record was about to be defended in a high-profile, heavily promoted match called the Centenary Test. In an unprecedented move aimed at further enhancing the tradition of the event, both teams would play in their original colours. In Australia's case, this meant forsaking the familiar green and gold for sky blue. It was a sight which for one brief moment on game day would give Macqueen the strange sensation that he was once again coaching the NSW Waratahs. For the past eighteen months throughout training sessions and subsequent Test matches he had constantly reminded the Wallabies their main goal was to concentrate on perfecting a style of rugby capable of winning the World Cup. However on this occasion pressure from all quarters was immense. Unlike his first Bledisloe Cup match, the importance of the occasion wasn't lost. After all, as he told the team, it was an occasion that came around only once every hundred years. This team wouldn't be around to make amends if they failed. The English touring party was obviously of the same opinion. They arrived several weeks in advance and prepared for the match in a way surprisingly similar to the Wallabies—at a makeshift rugby camp based at a resort in Queensland.

The support team

For the historic clash at Stadium Australia Macqueen was working on a strategy to stir nationalist support. After the previous year's match against the All Blacks in Christchurch several players commented on the fact they had heard a small section of the crowd singing 'Waltzing Matilda'. They were uplifted by the popular bush ballad, regarded by many Australians as an unofficial anthem. The gravel-voiced country songwriter and musician John Williamson was in the crowd and was extremely impressed by what he saw. A keen rugby supporter, he approached the ARU offering to help promote the Wallaby cause in any way.

Macqueen now saw the perfect opportunity to take advantage of Williamson's offer and proposed that after singing the national anthem, he remained on the sideline to encourage a rendition of 'Waltzing Matilda' just prior to kickoff.

On match day the musical strategy began according to plan. After singing the national anthem the Wallabies formed their established pre-match routine. As the crowd of 83,000 people sat hushed, waiting for the whistle to signal play, Williamson stood up and burst into song, urging Aussie supporters around him to join in. But even Macqueen's meticulous planning could be brought undone. At almost the precise moment, unaware of the strategy, the ground announcer took over the public address system and began to reel off the list of sponsors supporting Australian rugby. Not even the booming voice of Williamson could compete and the opportunity was lost. At least for the moment.

Fortunately for the Wallabies, the game plan proved more successful. Although England stunned their critics and their opponents by playing attacking rugby and taking an early 7–0 lead, the Australians hit back. Two tries to speedy young winger Ben Tune only minutes apart turned the match just before half-time. The Wallaby tactics of support runners coming from depth and hitting the advantage line at pace continually splintered the defence. Veteran centre Tim Horan playing out of position at flyhalf led the comeback orchestrating the now established moves integrating forwards and backs. Whenever the Wallabies threatened the English line Williamson would encourage his impromptu choir to add their vocal support. Towards the end of the match the crowd needed no urging as 'Waltzing Matilda' erupted spontaneously around the ground. With a final score of 22–15, the momentuous victory kept Australia's record safe for another one hundred years. For Macqueen the match was a victory on two counts.

It was one of the few games leading into the World Cup where we spoke about the importance of the outcome; there was a sense of relief in the dressing room after the game. The other pleasing aspect was the development of the crowd support. There is no doubt that the players hear the crowd singing and supporting them and this can lift them immensely and can sometimes have a bearing on the result. It can also influence the referee's decision.

Following the game, media reports noted the unusual show of Australian nationalism. At last it seemed the Australian public had shaken off their conservatism. It was a trend that would grow and not only spur on the Wallabies but would spread to other national sports.

You've got to pull the oar

Before embarking on their World Cup quest the Wallabies had the small matter of contesting South Africa and New Zealand in the annual Tri Nations series. The first match, against South Africa, was at Brisbane's Suncorp Stadium. The Springboks displayed enormous power in the scrums to disrupt the Wallaby forwards but with several key backline players missing, were unable to take advantage. From Australia's point of view it was the opposite. The match featured a magnificent display from Matt Burke who returned from a ten months' absence to score 17 points, and a rampaging Tim Horan continually broke the defensive line to initiate try-scoring opportunities. Although in Macqueen's mind the team was still struggling to find a balance with the new players in the side, they showed enough cohesion to forge a decisive victory. The winning margin of 32–6 was the biggest against the Springboks in sixty-six years. Confidence was high for the following match against the All Blacks in Auckland.

From the time the Australians arrived on New Zealand soil, they were hit by a blackout. The nation was still in mourning over the previous year's loss of the Bledisloe Cup. The national answer to the embarrassing 3–0 whitewash was a predetermined and intimidating blackout. Wherever the Wallaby players looked they saw the colours of their opponents. Streamers at the airport, in shop windows, throughout the town, and on match day the ultimate gesture of parochial support: a crowd dressed in black, painted black, and waving black. Macqueen noticed another unusual feature of the crowd. The few Australian supporters were not grouped together in blocks of pre-booked seating. For some reason they were scattered in small pockets around the stadium, swamped in a hostile sea of black. It looked ominous. Still, Macqueen was confident his side was well prepared for anything planned by those wearing black on the field. He was wrong.

From the first whistle the All Blacks were ferocious. In attack and defence they were relentless, applying constant pressure in every facet of play. No team could have been fully prepared for the intensity of the men in black. After succumbing to the initial onslaught, the Wallabies regrouped and counter-attacked but when they eventually left the field the scoreboard recorded a 34–15 defeat. Macqueen took away some positives from an unexpectedly disappointing encounter.

It looked like they were going to build a very big score against us but it says something for the character of our side that they remained firm under pressure. On the day we were certainly beaten by a better team but some positives did come out of it. Sometimes when you have put such an emphasis on preparation, you assume it is just going to happen. I often referred to an analogy called 'pulling the oar' which came from my surfboat rowing days. We always made sure that our technique was perfect, our boat was as light as possible, that we had optimum strength and stamina, had worked on our timing and our race plan. We even studied the prevailing conditions in the surf. But when the starting gun was fired, none of that mattered if each of us didn't pull as hard as possible on our oar and didn't pull together as a team. There were times when you had done all the homework and preparation, that you became overconfident and virtually forgot to put in the maximum physical effort.

On the team bus back to their hotel the side was unusually silent. At first Macqueen believed it was disappointment but he later realised it was brought on more by surprise at how passionate and committed the All Blacks had been, particularly in the first twenty minutes. The deeply patriotic Macqueen was still struggling with the effectiveness of the New Zealand onslaught when he had an unexpected visit from John Williamson. The singer was in the middle of composing a song dedicated to the Wallabies called, 'Number On My Back'. It had a catchy melody and a rousing chorus:

> Could it be a dream
> My father's son that's me
> Humbled by the truth I am
> A golden Wallaby.

And I will seize the day
'cause it belongs to me.
I have a number on my back
I am a Wallaby.

That night Williamson joined the team and spent many hours just singing
songs and strumming on the guitar with a number of the disappointed
players. I think it gave him a good insight into the demeanor of the team.
After spending that time with the players he composed a new verse to the
song which I thought captured their mood and would become another
building block in the character of the side.

And if the ball won't roll my way
No matter how I try that day
I won't let my tempers fray
I'll fight on till the end.

And I will keep a solid chin
'cause champions don't always win
We'll keep on coming back again
And we will make amends.

Black humour

For Macqueen, there was more black to come. Following the defeat in Auckland, he took Liz to the Bay of Islands, a quiet, scenic region in the north of New Zealand. With the Wallabies enjoying a few days' break from their base camp, it was an opportunity for both Macqueen and Liz to spend some time together. They booked into a small guest house on Russell Island which was run by two New Zealand couples, and during dinner that first evening they shared stories and jokes with people from different parts of the world. It was a friendly evening which the Macqueens enjoyed immensely following the stress of the previous few days.

When they retired to their room they were confronted by a bed draped with black satin sheets. Resting on the pillows were the usual complimentary chocolates; however, the packaging bore the faces of 'various All Blacks'. It was a clever and good-natured shot at the visiting coach and one which was accepted with the good humour required to survive the intense rivalry of the two countries.

More is not always better

A one-point loss is not usually regarded as a disaster. But this one was. Playing at home, South Africa had put in a competent performance, but not a great one. In contrast, the Wallabies were a rabble. Privately Macqueen confessed he believed it to be the side's worst ever loss. Afterwards he was officially quoted as saying, 'We were technically inept.' For a perfectionist and a coach renowned for not publicly deriding the performance of his own team it was a painful utterance. His comments were brought on by some personal confusion. Everyone had been well-prepared, knew the game plan, was committed to the task at hand, but hadn't produced on the field. The performance was out of character for his team and Macqueen was taking it personally.

Where had we gone wrong? The result was a lot of soul searching by the management and by myself. No matter how well you plan there is always another way of doing things and perhaps we had taken some wrong options. Sometimes you can fall into the trap of continuing to add in an attempt to make sure you are well prepared. Perhaps in our obsession to get everything just right we had incorporated too much in our program and without realising it the players were becoming fatigued. Over the ensuing weeks we went back over everything and reorganised some of the preparation areas. We needed to freshen our approach if we were to continue to get the best from the players. Our new program included more rest time. It had become obvious to us that more was not better in this case.

Regardless of the reason for the loss, it brought home a statistic that was extremely painful for Macqueen: despite all his success as a coach he was yet to coach a team to victory on South African soil.

Time out at home

Fortunately for Macqueen there was a refuge. In the short period before his next commitment with Australian rugby he did what he usually did. He switched off and returned home to the normality which kept his life in perspective. A game of golf with Liz and close friends. Time to catch up with daughter Jacqui. A short fishing expedition with son Scott. A visit to the nearby Collaroy surf club for a casual row with old friends in one of the surfboats. There were always drinks and home-cooked meals with neighbours and friends who habitually dropped in to see how their 'old mate' was faring. Outside the high-pressure world of professional rugby to those close to him Macqueen was the same person he had always been. Relaxed, easy-going with an infectious laugh, happy to enjoy what are so commonly referred to as the simple things in life.

Some of the most important include time with his mother.

Since Dad passed away, Mum has become very much her own entity and is an inspiration to all around her. She still lives life to the fullest and continues to enjoy short trips around Australia with her good friend Gracie. Her busy day often includes a game of bridge with friends, but never a day passes without her doing something for someone else. It's either charity and canteen work for Mona Vale Hospital, visits to her sick and ailing friends or just caring for the younger generation of her ever-growing family. There's always one of us over at her beach house, simply because we like being there. Her great grandchildren, her grandchildren, daughters, sons and daughters-in-law, and of course me. Living over the road, Liz and I are fortunate to be able to share these times with her. We often get together for an evening brandy, where we share our thoughts— moments that invariably include her favourite toast which is 'tongue in cheek' and so totally contrary to her real beliefs— 'here's to us and bugger them all'.

Passion, patriotism, performance

John Williamson eased the microphone away from his mouth and stopped in mid-song. But the words to 'Waltzing Matilda' continued to reverberate around the towering stands at Stadium Australia in Sydney. The atmosphere was already charged with high emotion generated by the sheer presence of a world record crowd of 107,000 rugby supporters. They were drawn by the desire to see if Australia could avenge the devastating defeat by the All Blacks in Auckland. On this occasion it wasn't the ground announcer who stopped John Williamson from performing his prearranged rendition of the popular Australian song. He stopped because he realised the crowd had taken over. The All Blacks had completed the haka to cheers from Kiwi supporters. Now it was Australia's turn. As the players performed their pre-game routine they were inspired not only by the vocal support but by the vision of gold. Everywhere they looked in the massive stadium they saw a reflection of their colours. Gold banners, gold jerseys, gold scarves, caps and flags. It was Australia's answer to the Auckland blackout and the Wallaby supporters were doing their part. Now it was up to the team.

In the lead-up to the match Macqueen detected a different feeling within the squad. To retain the Bledisloe Cup, secured in such spectacular fashion the previous year, the Wallabies needed victory or a draw. But for their own reasons they needed to win, and they wanted to win.

From the first day of preparation, they were all actively involved in the game plan—none more so than Rod Kafer who had been called in to solve our flyhalf problem. We needed to impose ourselves on them, take them out of their comfort zone and put them off their game. We had a variety of specific tactics to turn them around. One was to deliberately give them the opportunity to run the ball from their own 22-metre line which wasn't part of their natural game, and with our defence ready to counterattack if they tried to kick out of trouble. We also wanted to attack the blind side of the ruck whenever possible because we knew they tended to have their weaker defenders tucked in that area.

Once again Alan Jones had been called on to present a motivational speech on the morning of the match. He emphasised the historical significance of the stadium, built on traditional Aboriginal land, and the honour of playing at a venue which would soon be seen around the world showcasing Australia as host of the Olympic Games.

Now inside the scene was set. On this occasion there were to be no disappointments. Despite the fact that John Eales and Stephen Larkham were watching from the grandstand, the Wallabies played with confidence and intensity. Rod Kafer, substituting for Larkham, played as he did for the Brumbies and contributed to the game plan. The Australian backrow made valuable ground around the rucks. Combined with tactical kicking, the All Blacks were kept pinned in their own half. This allowed Matt Burke, now fully recovered from his shoulder injury, to capitalise on a string of penalty opportunities. The final score of 28–7 was Australia's biggest ever winning margin over New Zealand.

The crowd loved it. Australians had once again proved their ability to show passion and their willingness to support their country spontaneously and openly. It was a phenomenon which would capture the imagination of the public at large and keep all areas of the media buzzing well into the following week. It was a fitting way to end the regular season and a perfect mental preparation just prior to the Wallabies' departure for the World Cup. This was reflected in the dressing room immediately after the game. The celebrations included personal congratulations from an excited Prime Minister John Howard, but for Macqueen the highlight was in the congratulations the players were bestowing on each other. He felt the team had once again found belief in itself.

Chapter 21

The Destiny

How do you tell a man who for many years has been one of your best players and most loyal personal supporters that he will miss out on his dream of playing in the World Cup competition? Macqueen was about to face this dilemma as the Australian squad gathered at Caloundra for their last week of preparation before heading to Europe.

A conscience decision

The final makeup of the squad had been decided except for a number of last-minute medical checks. There was also a question mark over Brumbies' captain Brett Robinson who had been struggling for some time with a shoulder injury. Leading up to the final camp Macqueen had been told the injury was responding well to treatment and he had given Robinson right up until the last day to pass the necessary tests. Although confident, Macqueen was dreading the final medical examination because of the close association he had built up with the player who had been instrumental in helping him create the unique and successful entity that was the Brumbies. When the phone call from the team doctor finally came the news wasn't good. After consultation, the doctor and both physios decided that the injury would take at least another two to four weeks to heal. As first replacement for open side flanker David Wilson taking an unfit Robinson on tour would be too much of a risk. He was out of the side.

It was the hardest decision I have ever had to make as a coach and one I knew I had to deliver personally. Brett was one of the most dedicated, selfless players I had ever been involved with. He had given everything and worked so hard over the last few years to be part of the World Cup squad. He deserved to be there. By the time I got to his room Brett was obviously distraught and holding back tears. As I spoke to him I began breaking down too. To think that we'd come so far together and he'd nearly reached his goal, but it was all over. I consoled him as best I could and told him if someone else was injured on the tour, there might be another opportunity to call on him. But at that stage I think we both knew it was all over. As much as I would have liked to turn a blind eye to his injury and take the chance, I knew there was only one decision to be made and that had to be in the best interest of the team. I was later disappointed to learn that Robbo had been told by someone that I had bowed to media pressure and had ruled him out so that we could take Tom Bowman, the more popular choice with the media, as his replacement. My decision was based on the reliable medical evidence of our team doctor and team physios and I had to accept their conclusion.

In the end, the only consolation from this emotional incident was that I knew in my own mind that I had made the ethical decision.

Our destiny is in our hands

Elsewhere, however, with only a week before departure, excitement in the squad was mounting. The majority of the squad had been together since 'The Beginning' and had successfully completed 'The Journey'. It was time for the final stage of the plan which had been laid out almost eighteen months before.

The final inserts for the diary contained a blueprint for the World Cup and began with a brief message from Macqueen.

We have made the long hard journey to our destination. Both players and management have made many sacrifices along the way. We have endured long hours in the gym under Steve, we have suffered the hardships through time away from home and absence from families. Through this time, we have learnt a great deal and we must use this knowledge to ensure we reach our ultimate goal.

We will use the lead-up and the early games to finalise our game plan, using a different strategy depending on the opposition. Our initial focus will be on Ireland but our preparation will take into account our expected finals' opponents. We will hold back some of our sure fire moves for the later championship games. Additionally, we will develop some along the way.

By the time we reach the final, we will confidently be able to adjust to any situation required on the day.

Now when the players entered the team room they were greeted by a forty-foot banner which read 'Our Destiny is in our Hands'. The banner would be taken with them throughout the tour and hung in every meeting room along the way—a simple but effective reminder that their final goal was within their grasp. Almost.

Different games for different reasons

The Wallaby squad arrived at their base camp in Portmarnoch and immediately prepared for their first game. The players unpacked at their hotel, changed clothes and walked out ready to play. But there wasn't a football in sight. Instead they selected a range of clubs and readied themselves for a game of golf. Most of the players were hackers, but a few were almost good enough to take it up as a second professional sport. Yet this wasn't a casual game, but part of a well thought-out plan by the medical staff. They wanted the players to relax after the long flight but also to stay awake as long as possible so their body clocks could adjust.

Following a request by Wallaby management, the resort had obligingly agreed to make a temporary oval nearby for the exclusive use of the Wallabies. It was the perfect location to get ready for their first three matches, scheduled for different grounds in Ireland. The quiet location also suited Macqueen's plan for a low-key build-up. He hoped the majority of media attention would be on New Zealand and South Africa, which turned out to be the case.

The golf tournament between the members of the squad produced some terrible play, numerous lost balls, damage to the course and great team spirit for the start of their tour. The feeling was enhanced the same evening at a welcoming function organised by Guinness, one of the main sponsors of the World Cup, an event which led to what could best be described as a 'relaxed mood', featuring a team singalong. The most popular song was already the John Williamson tune, 'Number On My Back', which was sung with great enthusiasm. To make matters interesting, Macqueen had a weary visitor at 2.00 a.m. It was Joe Roff asking the question, 'Just wanted to know if you wanted someone to talk to?' Just what Macqueen needed. The following day, also planned by the medical staff, was another rest day where players lounged around the hotel enjoying a few quiet drinks. By now a number of the Australian reporters following the team were becoming concerned. Was this the highly professional rugby team everyone had made so much fuss about? After two days a football still hadn't been sighted.

Some weeks before, the management team had sat back and talked about how crucial those first few days would be. How important it was for the team to be relaxed and mentally prepared for what was ahead. It was decided that we should take time out and relax for a couple of days before the heavy and demanding schedule began.

Policing the play

The following day, trainer Steve Nance began his strenuous fitness program and the unrelenting routine established at Caloundra was underway. Under Nance training was always very hard, but it was also fun. All the knowledge he brought with him had helped the players adapt to the new standards required to lift their personal performance. As the momentum increased, Macqueen changed his approach and began to upset not only the players but some members of the management team.

There is a fine line between knowing when to switch on and when to switch off. All sessions start in a lighthearted mood during the warm-up and stretching phases and that has to disappear when the serious training begins. If it didn't I stepped in and abused the players for not having the dedication and commitment and not knowing when to switch on and get it right. The typical Australian larrikinism in the team made it hard for me as a coach at times. The players constantly joked and niggled each other throughout training sessions, even those before important matches. It's a national trait and one that seems to work in our favour. It certainly baffles other national teams who often treat final training sessions as a serious military exercise. The problem for me is to make allowances for the joking and yahooing without it interfering in the preparation. It's often hard to be the ogre when in reality I would prefer to be part of it all.

Balancing people and perspective

Throughout the final World Cup preparation a fine balance was kept by the unique combination of experienced coaching members. They had co-opted the help of veteran coach Alex Evans who had been through the 1987 Grand Slam campaign with Alan Jones and had kept some association with the Wallabies for much of his life. A former rower, he got on extremely well with Macqueen who often used him as a sounding board. Together they had many late night discussions about how they were progressing and whether they were getting everything right. Evans was nominated at the World Cup to be the keeper of the standards and was a great motivator. He often didn't say much, but, according to Macqueen, when he did it always came from the heart. Coupled with the experience of former Wallabies Jeff Miller and Tim Lane, this provided a perfect mix which the players could relate to. Evans and Lane had a more laidback approach which was a nice contrast to the more intense attitude of Macqueen and Miller.

The Wallabies were also fortunate to have physiotherapist, Greg Craig in the squad. Craig had been with the team in all four World Cups and was well known for his ability to get injured players back onto the field weeks, and even months, earlier than expected. With the help of another well-respected physio, ex-Wallaby Cameron Lillicrap, they often achieved the impossible and were working overtime to keep the players on the field.

Away from the spotlight and constantly looking after the needs of the Wallaby team were two unsung members of management—Scott Harrison, their guru in video statistics and Ben Spindler, their gear steward. Both were dedicated and willing workers whose work behind the scenes was vital to the team's performance.

While to the players Macqueen may have seemed aggressive and irritable at times, he had another agenda. Before leaving for Ireland he had borrowed a videocassette from former Wallaby and his assistant coach with the Waratahs, Peter Carson. It showed not only game highlights of the Grand Slam tour but much of the off-field socialising. Macqueen was surprised at how much fun the team had along the way and could see how important it was in promoting harmony. He decided to encourage and if necessary organise social events to bolster team bonding. One such event was a visit to a traditional Irish pub not far from their hotel. By the end of the night John Eales and several other players jumped onto a small stage and gave an impromptu display of Irish dancing with the locals cheering them on. It was widely reported in the local press and generated a great deal of positive comment and enthusiastic support from the Irish rugby supporters. But once again some reporters began to question the commitment of the Australian side. Another lighthearted moment for the squad was a game of beach cricket organised after a particularly tough training session. During the match some of the players realised Macqueen had a questionable bowling action but instead of complaining, they belted his deliveries into the nearby Irish Sea. It was all good fun and no doubt a partial payback for the coach's new belligerent approach in training.

The strength of the wolf is the pack

Macqueen was pleased with the spirit building within the thirty-man squad but just how close they had become was demonstrated by an unprecedented move by the senior players. During a short private meeting, they agreed that all members of the squad would pool their payments received during the campaign so that everyone would receive an equal share. This selfless gesture was contrary to the usual practice where only the twenty-two selected players received the substantial Test match allocation while the others received expenses and a much lesser sum. It reflected an unusual strength of unity and purpose and confirmed the 'we not me' attitude that had developed within the side.

Unexpected motivation

If the Wallabies needed any further inspiration to win the World Cup it came from an unexpected quarter. Former Wallaby hero David Campese was reported in Australian newspapers saying that he believed the Wallaby play was boring and that the All Blacks were the team most likely to win the competition. Even more inflammatory were criticisms Campese made about their style of play and individual players. This incensed the Wallaby squad, who felt betrayed by one of their own. The feelings in the camp were summed up by Phil Kearns, Australia's most capped hooker, in his newspaper column: 'We don't mind if he thinks we can't win the World Cup. That's his opinion and he's entitled to it. But to say our performance to beat the All Blacks at Stadium Australia was "crap", and to bag centre Daniel Herbert and to say players get paid too much has really put him off-side. Normally we ignore his comments but there comes a point when you have to say enough is enough.'

The last thing you would expect was for one of your own countrymen to bag the team before the tournament had even begun. However, in the end I think it had a positive effect because I'm sure it made the players even more determined to succeed.

Winning every battle to win the war

Their first game against Romania in Belfast was all they expected. The opposition players were big and extremely physical and the Wallabies didn't have everything their own way. Macqueen was happy with the defence and some of the basic moves that were tried, and overall was reasonably pleased with the winning performance of 57–9. Both he and the players knew they still had a long way to go.

What many outsiders didn't know was they were following a specific training schedule aimed at having the team peak in the final matches. During the early games against weaker sides they knew they would be tired from intense fitness training and would make mistakes as they experimented with different tactics and players. Only those present during discussion in the team room knew they would be happy to win the early games regardless of the score line, so long as the game plans and standards they put in place were followed. In addition many of their best attacking moves would be held back.

Their second match against Ireland also went to plan but was marred by numerous ball-handling errors which spoilt many try-scoring opportunities. Macqueen had expected the Irish to repeat the 'boots and all', intimidating style of play they had tried in Australia earlier in the year. They did just that to the delight of the home crowd accustomed to such tough displays at the infamous Lansdowne Road Stadium. For the first half the Australians were unsettled and drawn into the brawling tactics. The most disruptive was Irish flanker Trevor Brennan who continually attacked some of the Wallabies behind play. The situation was turned around dramatically when he upset Wallaby powerhouse Toutai Kefu who broke the strict code of discipline and retaliated. Brennan received a quick and ferocious battering before the referee intervened and issued Kefu with a severe warning. He was fortunate not to be sent from the field but was later suspended for two matches, removing an important element from the Australian attack. Although media reports were critical of the Australian performance, Macqueen was satisfied with the 23–3 result and the fact that the team was on track and steadily improving.

There was a lot of speculation before the game about the Irish being capable of beating us and it was one game that had worried me for some time. In fact I mentioned to Liz beforehand that if we could win the game against Ireland I believed we would go on to win the World Cup. Although the performance wasn't up to expectations the players, as usual, knew exactly what had gone wrong and were confident in their own minds they could put it together when it mattered. We were careful not to let this come out to members of the media. We were happy to let people think we may have been struggling.

The rest of the tour began on a sour note following a medical report on hooker Phil Kearns which revealed that a badly damaged foot would rule him out of any further matches. Kearns was immensely popular with everyone on the squad and it was a sad moment when it was announced he would be sent home. Macqueen was also faced with the difficult decision of who would replace the suspended Kefu, in the all-important quarter-final game. He wasn't helped by the team's performance against the American Eagles in their last pool match. It was an opportunity to use many of the backup players in the squad and the new combination produced a disjointed display. Despite being a comfortable 59–19 victory it was not the sort of effort they were hoping for to lead into their first sudden death match in the tournament against the host nation, Wales.

Cultural exchanges

The Welsh had acquired former New Zealand coach Graham Henry, a man Macqueen respected greatly. He had guided Auckland to victory over the Brumbies in the Super 12 final in 1997. And since taking over the Welsh side he had guided them to ten straight Test victories in the past twelve months.

Henry made a point of repeatedly saying how remarkable it would be should they beat the Australians and how great our team was. It amused me that the coach of a northern hemisphere team was now praising the opposition. It was typical pre-match hype from a southern hemisphere coach and the opposite of those in the north who tend to talk themselves up. It's an accepted ploy to give the opposition a false sense of security and to take the pressure off your own side. In return, we of course praised them and talked about how well they'd been playing so far. Much of it was right because they were a very improved side. I know the constant praising of each other was a frustration for journalists at the regular press conferences. They were trying so hard to force us into saying something controversial about the opposition but we refused to take the bait.

Given his good relationship with the media Macqueen felt comfortable that things were progressing on his terms. But it wasn't to last. He brought himself undone with what he thought was a flippant but relevant comment about the magnificent new Millennium Stadium at Cardiff, built especially for the tournament. The structure boasted several outstanding features, including a roof that could be closed within twenty minutes. When at a press conference Macqueen was asked if he was worried how his side would perform in wet weather, he just laughed. He made what he thought was an obvious point, that weather was irrelevant because the stadium roof could be closed to preserve perfect playing conditions. The following day the Australians were labelled 'wimps' for being frightened to play in the wet. During three press conferences the next week, Macqueen was continually interrogated about this issue.

In the end I thought the questioning was becoming a bit of a joke and I finally said what I thought they wanted to hear. That the Wallabies were prepared to play in any conditions. I realised that there were irreconcilable differences between the philosophies of northern hemisphere rugby and Australian rugby. Here we were once again confronted with the reluctance to accept change. The advent of modern technology gave us the opportunity to play in perfect conditions, and the opportunity for spectactors to watch the best teams in the world display the best possible game of rugby. Looking back now I still think there is a funny side to it. I can't see the reason for having a roof on a stadium if you're not going to use it. To me the only reason you play rugby in the wet is because it is a necessary evil if you don't have a roof.

Passion and poise

What is passion in the context of rugby? According to the Welsh media it was an ingredient which could win them the game. Macqueen was interested by the amount of discussion it generated. There was plenty to talk about. The Welsh were hosts of the tournament, the team would be playing in their new home stadium for a place in the semi-finals, and they would be urged on by a predominantly parochial crowd singing the emotional songs for which they were renowned. This would stir passion in the men in scarlet. But was it relevant? Macqueen didn't think so.

I believe passion is often used as an excuse for those who haven't done their preparation. These teams often know they are lacking in some way but believe by trying harder and being aggressive they will somehow win the game. I see passion in quite a different way. Passion is something that needs to be built over a long period of time, it needs a foundation and needs to mature and to be nurtured. Sometimes it means losing games to help develop passion and it's something that is gained by players working hard together to form a team ethos. It was something I knew our team had developed, and something which was emerging more and more as we continued to play together.

While the Australian side was confident and prepared for an emotional encounter, among some of the senior players there was a feeling of unease, a faint feeling of déja vu. Something that could be felt but not said, a fear of failure. They had been in this situation before and the memories were unpleasant. Four years previously during the first World Cup quarter-final the Wallabies had been unexpectedly knocked out of the competition by England. The coaching staff noticed that the memory of defeat was preying on their minds.

The week leading up to the Welsh quarter-final was the most nervous I'd ever seen the team. They were more nervous than they would be before a final. And I'm talking about senior players like Tim Horan and Jason Little. They, like many others, were in the team that was knocked out in the previous World Cup in South Africa. They told us that when they were on their way back after losing, they arrived in Perth at the Qantas lounge to be met by all the Australian supporters heading out, expecting to watch them play in the final. The players still remembered their deep embarrassment and how they left in silence as quickly as possible.

It was a moment the senior players didn't want to relive, and one the new players had no wish to experience. They desperately needed to go at least one step further and reach the semi-final.

Fifteen minutes into the game, the rain came tumbling down through the open roof of the Millennium Stadium. With the ground already slippery underfoot from rain earlier in the day, the conditions now became treacherous. After a strong start the Wallaby game degenerated with many dropped balls and final passes going astray. It appeared the Welsh team had been coached to kill the ball to slow down play and disrupt the Wallabies' need for continuity. At half-time the Wallabies held a slender 10–9 lead but the players felt they were in control. In the dressing room they went through their usual routine, first with Eales giving his assessment followed by Gregan then any other player who had something pertinent to say. It was then the turn of Macqueen and his assistant coaches to add their thoughts with the benefit of viewing the game from a lofty vantage point. During the match they had been sending short simple messages down to the field to add to those already being made automatically by Eales, Gregan and the other leaders within the team. Now was the time to find out who could see what was going wrong and what changes needed to be made in the second half.

In all our many games leading up to the World Cup, I believed the system had been working well. But here I realised it reached a new level. The assessments and suggestions made by the players themselves aligned almost perfectly with those that we had to offer. In virtually every case we were able to say, 'Yes we agree, that's where we see the game is going, this is what we need to fix up the second half.' The years that we'd been talking about judging ourselves, setting our own standards and not looking at the scoreboard were paying off. The team was now self-regulating.

After resumption of play the Wallabies showed outstanding discipline in not conceding one penalty within range of the Welsh record-breaking goal kicker, Neil Jenkins. They were rewarded with two late tries to seal the match. But for Macqueen the most telling moment came with seven minutes to go during a torrid scrum when the Welsh captain Scott Quinnell called out, 'Where do you think you're going?' From the second row, John Eales called back in his usual controlled voice, 'To Twickenham son, to Twickenham!'

To Macqueen this highlighted the difference in passion. The Welsh passion manifested itself in aggression, while the Wallabies' passion showed in commitment and self-belief. While Macqueen was typically diplomatic about the match, centre Tim Horan couldn't resist a parting shot at the Welsh administration after another annoying question over the stadium roof. 'It was disappointing they didn't close the roof. It's a bit like having a Ferrari in your garage and then going out and catching a bus. If it's there you should use it, because the weather probably spoilt the party a little today.'

Changing tactics

The 24–9 win set up a semi-final showdown against South Africa at Twickenham. But to beat the Springboks the Wallabies would need a perfect game plan, and more. Macqueen and his assistant coaches discussed every conceivable option, possibility and eventuality.

Then came some disturbing news. Wallaby team statistician Scott Harrison, searching for any possible advantage, came up with a revelation. During the World Cup, teams in possession of the ball in their own half for more than two phases of play were being penalised, predominantly for ruck and maul infringements. The penalties were giving easy points to the opposition.

Although invaluable, this information presented us with a huge problem. We were a team who always felt our first option was to hang onto the ball and run it out from our own territory whenever possible. But this new information meant the referees would now be refereeing the attacking team, so we would have to change. We weren't being rewarded for continuity of play or having the skills to hang onto the ball. In fact teams doing that seemed to be the ones which were losing their games. We therefore decided that, instead of playing our natural game in our own half, we would change our tactics and kick down-field after one or two phases. That would pin down the opposition in their half so the statistics would then work in our favour.

Another problem had arisen during the World Cup and it was apparent to everyone. For reasons known only to themselves, tournament organisers had abandoned the system which proved so successful in the Super 12 competition, of awarding the yellow card and sin-binning players for deliberate or professional foul play. Effectively, this meant that when an opposing team looked certain to score a try it was apparent to spectators and commentators that defenders in sheer desperation were illegally holding onto the ball or deliberately infringing which then incurred a penalty.

It was a predetermined tactic which was very frustrating to the attacking team. All the coaches appreciated the situation and realised it was better to give away a penalty worth three points than risk a seven-point try. It was a matter of take your choice and the obvious answer was three points. This was made clear to the players which resulted in numerous deliberate fouls, fewer tries, and a lot of penalty kicks.

The basic thrust of our game plan was to attack the flyhalf area in strength and then to throw the ball wide. Other tactics we rehearsed from day one in Caloundra would now be used for the first time. They included standing George Gregan in the lineout with Larkham taking his place in the halfback position. It gave Larkham more opportunities to run close to the defensive line where he could feed support runners coming from different angles. We felt his elusive running would further confuse the defence.

Leave nothing to chance

The management team also prepared a contingency plan for every possible eventuality, another example of Macqueen's concern about 'What happens next'. At the beginning of the World Cup campaign they had compiled a checklist containing sixty-odd points which they examined the night before every Test. It included everything from weather conditions, spare studs for players, replacements for every position to the timing of bringing on the bench players. It also gave a course of action in the case of each player if they were injured, sent to the blood-bin, repeatedly incurred penalties or showed deficiencies in play. In other words, the checklist gave them an answer for every 'what if' that could arise during a game. On this occasion they took it even further, discussing the ramifications of the game ending in a draw and going into extra time. If it remained a draw the match would be awarded to the team scoring the most tries. If no tries were scored, victory would go to the team with the least number of players sent off during the tournament. (Incredibly, if this was also equal, then the winner of the game would be decided by the flip of a coin!) Australia had a clean record whilst South Africa had one player sent off in an earlier match. A draw would give the Wallabies victory. Following usual practice during a team meeting, the full squad went through all the options including the situation of the match extending into overtime.

Oddly enough it was a scenario that had been suggested in a message of support from the Australian cricket team, who had defeated South Africa to win the Cricket World Cup the previous year. Captain Steve Waugh concluded by saying, 'There is only one thing better than beating the Springboks; that is tying with them and beating them on a countback.' It was unlikely to happen but still something the Wallabies had prepared for just incase.

Mind over matter

On the team bus travelling to the game Macqueen was watching centre Tim Horan intently. The strong running back showed no change in his usual pre-match demeanor, sitting with his head up, chatting with fellow players. His behaviour belied the true story. The previous morning, Horan had contracted a severe stomach virus and had spent twenty-six hours in bed managing to keep down only three pieces of dry toast. The medical team had constantly monitored his condition and were extremely concerned, but at the last moment Horan insisted he would play. Because he was one of the fittest players in the squad and was recognised for his incredible determination, Macqueen made the final decision to keep him in the side.

During the trip to the ground Tim behaved as he always did. He talked to the other players about tactics and shared in the usual nervous jokes and ribbing of each other. No-one would have known there was anything wrong. It was amazing to see how he could control or ignore his physical problems, and it confirmed to me that psychologically he was the toughest player in the squad.

Extra time for composure

As expected the match was a close and absorbing contest. The game unfolded almost exactly how they had anticipated in team meetings throughout the week. The two sides were evenly matched but the Australian game featured Tim Horan's strong hard running which continually broke the defence, and the unstoppable charges of several forwards, notably Toutai Kefu, around the flyhalf area. Running into a strong and swirling headwind the Wallabies were calm when they entered the dressing room at half-time leading 12–6. The necessary tactical changes were being automatically made on the field when required, all according to their pre-match plan. As usual Macqueen was able to remain emotionally detached and was comfortable with the play.

As against Wales, the management and the players were thinking as one. There was a total calm in the room and a feeling that it was all going to happen. It was just a matter of making sure we held onto the ball for long periods of time, and played the game in their half.

The second half was almost a replay of the first with no tries being scored and only an exchange of penalty goals to keep the scoreboard moving. Several minutes into injury time Australia was leading by three points and seemed to have won, when a heart-stopping 40–metre penalty goal from Jannie de Beers brought the score line back to equal, 18–18. The game would go into extra time. As the final whistle was still sounding, John Eales, in an inspirational display of captaincy, ran from the field, leading the rest of the team. His actions showed there was no sense of despair or gloom, but rather an urgency to regroup and get on with the game. Macqueen was already waiting inside with the rest of the management team.

It was interesting to see the faces of the players when they came in. There was no sense of desperation but instead a quiet resolve. In their assessment both Eales and Gregan said it was disappointing we had to play another twenty minutes but we had discussed the possibility and it was now a matter of getting on with the job. I added very little except to remind everyone we still had plenty of time. We didn't need to panic or rush our play and we didn't need to score in the first five minutes. We needed to get into their territory early and wait for them to make the mistakes. I concluded by saying, 'No penalties'.

As the players filed out the door to the roar of the crowd, backs coach Tim Lane made a chance remark to Steve Larkham. During the match his opposite number Jannie de Beers had taken five shots at field goal with only one success. Lane mentioned to Larkham that if he found himself in the right position he should take the opportunity himself.

The Wallabies continued their game of patient tactics, kicking the ball down-field and keeping the ball in hand as much as possible and moving it wide to tire out the big Springbok pack. Each team had now kicked a penalty goal, taking the score to 21–21. Sure enough, the breakthrough eventually came, not with a clever backline move or a brilliant individual run, but with a freakish kick from Steve Larkham. He made a drop goal attempt from 45 metres out which wobbled and dipped tantalisingly before eventually limping over the crossbar. The faces of the Wallabies showed a mixture of joy and disbelief, none more so than Larkham himself: it was the first field goal he had ever kicked in a Test match. One more penalty goal by Matt Burke brought his final tally to eight. It was a faultless display in difficult conditions. The extraordinary spectacle ended with a final score of 27–21. The game and a place in the final belonged to Australia. The man of the match was a unanimous choice—an exhausted Tim Horan.

Once in the dressing room we sang the national anthem which had become part of our after-match procedure during the World Cup campaign. I did the usual press conferences and then a strange feeling hit me. I returned to the dressing room and sat in a back corner by myself for about twenty minutes. I was completely drained. For the first time, emotion had overwhelmed me and I couldn't speak to the players. When John O'Neill came into the room I just grabbed him and held on. I don't think he knew what hit him. After a few moments I regained my composure but it was a new and strange experience for me.

Media reports around the world described the Larkham field goal in great detail and trumpeted the fact he had single-handedly launched the Wallabies into the final. Within the team itself however the remarkable feat was viewed differently. As John Eales explained, such acts of individual brilliance were expected and shared by the team as a whole: 'The great thing about our team over the years is that we've got so many individuals, and you can't win without them being individuals. Whether it was Steve Larkham at a moment like that or Matthew Burke scoring a match-winning try against the All Blacks, or George Gregan making a try-saving tackle. So many different players have done brilliant things at certain times to lift the team, and together that makes the team.'

Coincidentally his words mirror the inspirational message of the Rudyard Kipling poem that Macqueen had included in the team diary twelve months earlier. The strength of the wolf being the strength of the pack.

At the time the momentous victory over South Africa also strengthened the bond between Eales and Macqueen. It allowed them to enjoy the pact they had made with each other before the game if they were to be successful—to drink champagne under the stars with their respective wives, Lara and Liz. They savoured the moment, again at the symbolic stroke of midnight, in the garden of the team's hotel.

Vive la France

The Wallaby players laughed and cheered as they watched the French team score try after try against the All Blacks. The whole squad was gathered in their hotel meeting room, watching the second semi-final live on television. Not one person in the room had any doubt the All Blacks would win the game and meet them in the final. For months they had studied every facet of the All Blacks' play and their game plan was already prepared. In fact after defeating South Africa, Macqueen had already started reviewing his video analysis of the New Zealand side. Now they were enjoying the luxury of sitting back and watching their old foes struggling to overcome a spirited and typically unpredictable French combination. During the first half Macqueen thought the All Blacks played quite well but were becoming frustrated by the French who were intent on destroying any continuity by lying all over the ball on the ground. At one stage the penalty count had reached a ridiculous 17–2 against the Tricolours who were also turning on the usual variety of illegal tactics. In the second half the structured play of the All Blacks, which the Wallabies knew so well had virtually disintegrated and the French were now scoring adventurous tries from all parts of the field. The score line suddenly ballooned in favour of the French side and the Wallabies were laughing, now almost in disbelief. Then the game ended. There was deathly silence.

I don't think any of us expected the All Blacks were actually going to be beaten. Now the realisation had started to sink in that we were about to

*embark into unusual territory. We had been so singleminded in our prepa-
ration that we had not even considered the fact the French could beat the
All Blacks and get through to the final. Our months of meticulous preparation had given us the feeling that we could overcome their more
predictable style of play. That comfortable feeling was now gone.*

While the players and management team were stunned, talking about
how they would need to counteract the unique play of the French,
John O'Neill believed the Wallabies already had the answer. 'It was an
extraordinary experience watching the All Blacks disintegrate when
playing the French. But I had every confidence that we wouldn't have
the same problem because of our defence. Even if the French produced
something totally unpredictable our ability to regroup under pressure
was second to none.'

Homework to be done

One member of the Wallaby squad was to suffer immediately. When
Rod Macqueen rose and walked over to their statistician and video
analyst, Scott Harrison knew what was coming. 'You want me to look
up all the current games of the French side and put them on CD ROM
overnight, don't you?'

   Macqueen nodded. By the next day the necessary information was
available. Every lineout, every scrum, every tackle, and every restart of
play had been sorted into their various areas so the Wallabies could
analyse what the French were doing. The team needed a game plan
different to any other.

*While other sides like New Zealand had a definite pattern of play which
was repeated, the French didn't. They were excellent at taking advantage
of any opportunity and counterattacked from all parts of the field. We
were suddenly faced with a team that wasn't programmed, but acted
instinctively.*

   *The strategy we decided on was very similar to one of Sun Tzu's
philosophies: 'Do the unexpected by attacking the opposition's
strengths.' We wanted to force them into playing a particular pattern.
We believed the French ability to counterattack came from the strength
and mobility of their backrow, so we planned to hold the ball for long
periods of time and continually attack around the flyhalf position,*

thereby forcing the backrow to continually tackle. In the second half we expected gaps would open in the middle of the field. During development of this team the use of our bench players was a critical part of our tactics. If we needed tighter defence in the middle we'd bring on a player suited to that purpose. If we could see the game opening up and opposition players tiring then we'd bring on our fresh ball runners. Once the advantage line was broken we could then throw the ball wide.

This play was practised all week with the reserves in the squad running in opposition. Again they also took into account their new statistics which showed the referees in the World Cup were penalising the attacking team trying to break out of their own half. Reluctantly they decided to kick extremely deep into the opposition half or if necessary kick the ball out. It was a difficult decision because it was negative play, opposite to the style of continuous phase play which they had been practising for the past two years.

During training the reserves also imitated the aggressive and illegal play of the French fifteen. These tactics had received wide media coverage after many All Blacks complained of quite serious injuries, especially to their eyes.

I had a long conversation with John Eales and we agreed that if it occurred we would make it obvious not only to the referee but to the spectators and to the huge television audience. If anyone needed treatment after eye-gouging or having their private parts grabbed, the medical staff would also be told to make it obvious why the treatment was being given. The referee would also be approached for an assurance illegal tactics would be closely watched. And we kept one ace up our sleeve. If the French persisted then Eales would threaten to walk the whole team from the field, which had only ever been done once before in rugby union.

Messages from mates

In the lead-up to the match the team was swamped with messages of support from all over the world in the form of letters, faxes and video clips. One videotape put together by the Australian host television broadcaster Network Seven included inspirational thoughts from numerous Australian sporting identities including Olympic swimming legend Dawn Fraser, current Olympic swimmers Ian Thorpe, Kieren Perkins and Samantha Riley, Australian cricket captain Mark Taylor, and former tennis great John Newcombe. The squad became quite emotional as they realised the weight of national pride they were now carrying.

The mood was lightened by the last interview on the tape. The image of a beaming Phil Kearns appeared, sitting in his lounge room without a shirt. He told the team how important it would be for him to watch them play and win the game. One of the things the team had spoken about many times during the campaign was keeping the opposition scoreless which was referred to as 'keeping them nude'. At the end of his emotional speech Kearns stood up and said, 'And above all, remember to keep them nude.' Everyone was amazed to realise he was standing in front of them totally naked. All those in the room burst out laughing as the Australian larrikin spirit once again proved its worth.

Chapter 22

Glory

We'd been two years in the preparation and the moment had finally come. It was the day of the World Cup final at the Millennium Stadium in Cardiff. The week had been fairly relaxed. There was a genuine feeling within the camp of 'knowing' that we'd done the work. At a personal level, I had the opportunity to spend the previous evening with Liz and friends who had been part of the whole campaign since we arrived in the UK. John and Del Nolan, my sister Katy and her husband Coleman, and our son Scott were also there. As usual, we sought out a Japanese restaurant: it had become a ritual and almost a good luck omen each pre-Test evening to dine on sushi. It wasn't always easy to find Japanese restaurants in some parts of the world, but somehow we managed.

The fateful day was very much like any other. We went through our normal preparations which began with a team walk. The players were all in their tracksuits and although quite jovial were definitely focused. Making our way out through the foyer of the Cardiff Bay Hotel, we encountered lots of Australians wishing everyone good luck, and the players handled it exceptionally well. We walked down alongside the river where we played the usual games put together by Steve Nance, which were always a relief and emotional outlet for everyone. We played tunnel ball and other games and as usual the larrikin element came out. The players took the opportunity to sledge each other and have a bit of fun on the way. I'm not sure how a lot of other coaches would react, but I was quite happy with this because I knew it was their way of relaxing and shaking off any last-minute nerves. It also revealed the closeness of the side. Even though some of the players were more nervous than others, no-one took offence at the typical personal insults which were flying around.

When we came back into the hotel I made the usual calls back home. First to Mum and our daughter Jacqui, then close friends and neighbours and, of course, Hitchie. It was another important part of my match day routine.

There was a knock on the door. It was time. I knew it would be John Eales, a minute early as he usually was. He came in and he was very excited although just stating the obvious—that he was really looking forward to the game. We agreed that we'd already said it all, but still what we had to do was get the best possible performance out of the players. So today, different to most other matches, we were really concentrating on pride—pride in the jumper, on getting up the type of enthusiasm that's needed for such a momentous occasion. We would play minute by minute and give it our best all the way through. We talked again about the importance of keeping the players focused, not being put off by the predicted rough house tactics of the French. We also decided that after the final, in our usual manner, we would have a special get-together. In this case we agreed to meet in the middle of Caloundra Oval, where it all started two years earlier, with our wives and a bottle of champagne. We'd toast the World Cup in the middle of the field. With that last agreement John left.

I sat back in my hotel room to think. I was just looking at how far we'd come and how focused the players were. Then I moved down to our team room to get ready for our meeting. I noticed that Jeff Miller, Alex Evans and the forwards were speaking in very serious hushed tones. The backs in their usual manner were a little bit more lighthearted, but Tim Lane was going through their moves piece by piece. We all came together inside the team meeting room where I met former Wallaby prop, now television commentator, Chris 'Buddha' Handy. He was to be our Classic Wallaby before the match. Chris is one of rugby's characters and he had been with us on almost every Test, commentating from the sideline and sharing in the friendships after the game. He knew the team well and in turn the players had a tremendous respect for him. Chris admitted later that this was the most nervous he had been other than his first Test, and that it was a moment that would never be matched again for him in his lifetime. Chris didn't let us down in his address to the players, speaking with great emotion and passion. He explained the immense pride and honour it had given him to be chosen on this occasion, to be representing all the Classic Wallabies of the past; how he was overwhelmed to see the huge number of Aussie supporters wearing their green and gold in the streets of Cardiff. He described the feelings he had when he played for the Wallabies; what it meant for him to link arms with his teammates and sing the national anthem; how he felt that the entire country was watching him and that he was there to represent them. Buddha then told the players that although they had earned this opportunity and deserved to be in the finals, it was an unwritten contract that they must 'leave no gas in the tank' at the end of the game. Before he handed John the captain's jersey, Buddha presented him with a special bottle of 1991 Australian vintage wine, a symbol of 'The Best of the Best', which the 1991 Wallabies were in winning the World Cup. He said it was now their turn to make 1999 a vintage year for Australian rugby and once again be 'the best of the best'.

To me what stood out was the genuine feelings the Classic Wallabies had brought to the side over the last two years every time they handed the captain his jumper. This was no different. After receiving the jumper John Eales got up and addressed the side, talking about how far we'd come and the fact that the game was ours for the taking.

He was equally emotional as he thanked Buddha for presenting him with the jersey and for the gesture of the vintage wine. He highlighted what a great opportunity it was to play in the World Cup final and that it was one that we had worked towards for a long time and couldn't waste.

Again the players displayed their larrikinism. As each one received his jersey all the nicknames were called out. Not just their usual ones, but others they had acquired through various indiscretions in the preceding weeks. It caused an unexpected break in the mounting tension; it was some lightheartedness in the face of battle for every player: Matthew Burke, Ben Tune, Daniel Herbert, Tim Horan, Joe Roff, Stephen Larkham, George Gregan, Toutai Kefu, David Wilson, Matt Cockbain, John Eales, David Giffin, Andrew Blades, Michael Foley, Richard Harry, Jason Little, Nathan Grey, Chris Whitaker, Mark Connors, Owen Finegan, Dan Crowley and Jeremy Paul. The team we'd selected to carry Australia's colours to the World Cup was almost ready.

As arranged, John McKay read out a fax we had received from the head of the Australian peacekeeping force in East Timor, Major-General Peter Cosgrove. His message of support was totally unexpected. The team listened in absolute silence.

Your campaign to bring home the Rugby World Cup started many months ago, and now you stand on the threshold of your greatest challenge and your greatest victory. In the last few months, we have watched you every step of the way from here in East Timor. We think we know of your sacrifice and dedication and the unrivalled teamwork you have achieved to get you to this point. As Australian Service Men and Women standing in this violent, desperate place we see in you our sporting champions, ready to do what must be done to win, just as we must do the same.

You have our heartfelt congratulations for what you have achieved to be on this threshold. You have our greatest confidence that as Aussies you will make us proud.

Play well and win—for us, among many if you like. Play well and win for Australia. But mostly, play well and win for the champion team and the team of champions that you have become.

Signed 'Yours in Rugby' Peter Cosgrove.

PJ. Cosgrove, AM MC
Major General

It was extremely emotional for us to realise that the soldiers who were risking their lives for our country were also following the day-to-day preparations of the Wallabies for this match.

Then it was my turn to speak. I reflected on the last two years and the amount of preparation we'd put in and mentioned that there is always a reward when so many sacrifices have been made. This, I said, was their day to receive that reward.

Macqueen then took the comparison of military sacrifice to another level. He produced a sheet of paper containing information that he had asked David Pembroke to research in the Australian war archives. Macqueen read to the team an extract from the diary of a young lieutenant in charge of a light machine gun company in March 1918, during World War I. The members of No.1 Section, 3rd Machine Gun Company, were confronted by overwhelming odds as they prepared to defend the small French village of Villers-Brettoneaux—the same village and battlefield the Wallabies had visited the previous year. In spare but chilling words Lieutenant Bethune stressed their position would be held whatever the consequences. He made six points:

1. This section will be held, and the section will remain here until relieved.
2. The enemy cannot be allowed to interfere with this programme.
3. If the section cannot remain here alive, it will remain here dead,

but in any case it will remain here.

4. Should any man, through shell shock or other cause, attempt to surrender, he will remain here dead.
5. Should all the guns be blown out, the section will use Mills grenades and other novelties.
6. Finally, the position, as stated, will be held.

Just twelve months before, the team had spent one of their most moving times walking past the graves in the French countryside around Villers-Brettoneaux thinking about those soldiers and their sacrifice. Now the Wallabies were about to face the ultimate battle in their own campaign—ironically against the French.

As I read the piece out to the players there was silence in the room. It was obvious it meant as much to the players as it did to me and the rest of the management team. It was then time for the quote of the day. In this case we'd singled out Jason Little. He was perhaps nearing the end of his career and was close to playing one of his last Test matches. He chose a quote from Herb Elliott, the great Australian Olympic runner, and it was extremely appropriate for the day:

There is the point of no return where you have laboured so long, sacrificed so much, that you can't go back. You must reach your goal and trample on anyone who tries to stop you!

As the players walked out of the hotel room I took the opportunity to shake a few hands, mainly the older players who had contributed so much to the final week's preparation. I noticed an obvious composure within the side. We went downstairs to the foyer and once again we walked through crowds of Australian supporters who wished us all the best. It was a privilege for me on this day, representing my country, being chosen as the coach to take these players to their ultimate destiny.

As the team bus tried to drive out we found we were blocked by two cars parked on the side of the road, stopping the bus from even starting its journey to the stadium. Our police escorts really didn't know what to do. With the help of Alex Evans and Buddha, the management and some of the players—dressed in their suits—picked up the back of the cars and moved them round to allow the bus to get through. For a moment I had a strange feeling that we might not even be able to get to the game.

Once at the stadium we walked into the dressing room, where some of the players sat around and read some of the programs, before starting to change and go through whatever routine they normally did before a game. The more aggressive positions, such as the flankers, tended to be a lot more nervous and edgy than the others. The backs were more relaxed. Some players have particular idiosyncrasies that never change. John Eales was the same as he was before any big game. He was excited, never nervous, and looking forward to the prospect of playing before such a huge crowd. I always found that unusual, because most players just wanted to get out and get it over with as quickly as possible.

Later, when we walked out onto the ground to check conditions, I was particularly interested in the atmosphere, realising how deafening it was for the players and how hard it would be for them to hear each other during the game. As usual we walked across the pitch where we were surprised to find that we were about to play a World Cup final on a ground that had very little grass on the field and was very wet from the roof being open. What we realised was that large areas of mud had been sprayed green for the cameras.

Back in the change room we spoke about our tactics again. We went through our normal warm-up routine and as usual Steve Nance did his job extremely well. We finally got the players together so I could have my last words before they went out. I reiterated that this was our destiny. I told them it was something they deserved. Finally, I again quoted to the team the last piece of Lieutenant Bethune's orders to his men at Villers-Bretoneaux:

'Finally, the position, as stated, will be held.'

And then I walked out of the room. It was now up to them.

As they had done two weeks before, the management team went up in the lift to take their places in the stand. All had coordinated their watches down to the last second, and checked their two-way radios. But this time, unlike the quarter-final, they would not have the comfort of a private box. The Wallaby management had done their usual homework during the week to assess where they would be sitting for the final game. They'd discovered that, for reasons best known to the managers of the multi-million-dollar tournament, the coaches' box had been sold off to corporate sponsors. The coaching staff from both teams would be sitting amongst the crowd. The Australian contingent was surrounded by spectators from South Africa and France who were bewildered to see the group of men in suits settling in with laptop computers and communications equipment.

The game itself went very much as predicted. We were always looking to secure possession and minimise mistakes. And attacking when we had the opportunity. We knew it was going to be hard early and the French didn't disappoint us. They also didn't surprise us in other areas. There was some phantom eye-gouging, and the word that we'd put in with the referee during the week paid off because he was trying to single out the offenders. Unfortunately he was unable to pick up exactly what was going on and it got to the stage where John Eales finally threatened to walk off. This was our pre-arranged tactic, and even though we didn't intend to follow through, it did put enough pressure on the referee and the French. The players finally realised they couldn't continue to do it, they had to play football.

The game plan the Wallabies had practised all week started working. They were continually running moves to tie up the mobile French backrow of Juillet, Magne and Lievremont, forcing them to tackle, making them tired. The more the Wallabies had the ball the more they ran at that area, and the more tired the French became. As the opposition legs started to drag the Australians started to see opportunities appearing late in the first half. By the end of the first half they were leading 12–6. That's when the team knew the chances would come in the second.

Just before half-time the game was reasonably close but we had that inner feeling that we were in control. We walked up to the lift with two minutes to go only to find we no longer had a security guard to accompany us. By this stage the players were walking into the dressing rooms below and we were joined by the French management who were equally as confused as we were. When a lift arrived we got in and they asked if they could come with us. It was quite a strange moment to have the management teams from both sides travelling down together in silence. Half-way down, the lift stopped and the doors opened. There was a raucous crowd outside. I moved forward and said, 'Coaching staff only, no, no', only to be told by a paramedic with a man in a wheelchair that he had an emergency, he must come in. Unfortunately the emergency was a drunk Frenchman who immediately proceeded to throw up all over the floor and our shoes. We all raced for the entrance to the dressing rooms, holding our hands over our faces. The players later told me it was the most distressed I had ever looked during a half-time talk.

By the time I actually reached them, the players were all ready to go through their routine. After the medical staff announced there were no injuries it was time for Eales to address the team. In his now familiar summary role, Eales got it right again. He said that the win was coming, that we could see them physically tiring, we only had to keep going and the opportunities would come. Gregan got up and basically agreed. No-one else had anything to contribute at that stage and none of the management team or myself had anything specific to add. We felt things were going exactly the way we'd discussed, and that opportunities were starting to come and we should make the most of them. To increase the pressure we decided to call moves which would involve our large wingers running at their small inside backs. Then we would bring on our fresh benchplayers as planned, and hopefully take advantage of the gaps we expected would open up.

As the players ran back onto the field the management team returned to their seats following a lift journey that was thankfully uneventful. With the game unfolding as expected, the crucial decision for Macqueen, like any general, would be when to commit his bench-players. These are not second string players, on standby in case a player is injured or tiring, as many people believe, but impact players who join the game with a specific purpose, and plenty of fresh energy to make the breaks and press home any advantage. Despite the tumult and the sheer enormity of the occasion, Macqueen still sat stonyfaced, watching intently. The scene was indeed reminiscent of a military field commander in centuries gone by, watching from a distant high vantage point as events unfolded on the battlefield below. Staff on either side making occasional observations. The general making decisions and quietly despatching messages to the field. On the millions of television sets around the world the image was calm, relaxed, impassive. Only Macqueen was aware of the anxiety within.

I was constantly conferring with Jeff Miller and Tim Lane, forcing myself, right throughout the game, to think of the big picture. Think of the game and what was unfolding, of anything we'd forgotten, of any additional strategy we could employ to ensure we were going to win. The timing for the benchplayers had to be right, especially for flanker, Owen Finegan, who was a key figure in our attack. We were doing quite well and staying ahead thanks to the exceptional goal-kicking of Matt Burke. Our first try exemplified what this team was all about. It came after a rush of phase play with backs and forwards feeding off each other and one of our backs taking the traditional role of a forward by securing the ball from the break-down: it was then fed to winger Ben Tune who crashed through the defence to score.

There was less than ten minutes to go. We were showing the usual composure and a call went for the ball to be thrown to the back of a lineout. Finegan had just run on from the bench and there was a call for him to be involved in the next move. Seconds later he brushed past several tired defenders and scored. It was a coach's dream come true. We had stuck with our game plan and everything had fallen into place.

That try clinched the game. There was a sudden release of emotion. Macqueen and those around him all realised at the same time they had achieved their goal.

We all sat there, knowing what it meant. There was no shaking of hands or physical display of emotion. But there was a quiet acknowledgement amongst us. We had fulfilled our destiny. Jeff Miller called over the two-way radio to run the rest of the benchplayers onto the field, those that hadn't yet had the opportunity to, so that they could share in the occasion.

As we played out the final minutes, my mind went back to how much time the management alongside me and all the players had put in and how richly they deserved the win. At the same time I started looking through the crowd for Liz—my partner, who'd spent so much time with me and had made so many of the sacrifices along with myself and the players—and for my friends.

At that stage Jeff Miller said we had to leave. With seconds to go the score was 35–12. We got up from the seat and moved towards the lift. At that moment I saw Liz, who'd come across from the stand with Scott. I just put my head on Liz's shoulder, gave her a hug and said, 'We've done it.' I also gave Scott a hug. There were tears all round. It was one of the most emotional experiences of my life, and despite the huge crowd, a private moment for all of us.

The rest of the management team was now urging me to get in the lift to go down to the players. I said goodbye to Liz, jumped in the lift and went down. We came out from the lift and went down through the tunnel to an amazing scene. To see the sheer exhilaration on the player's faces was a wonderful reward, one that is just too difficult to describe.

In the past I've been accused of being unemotional after matches. But I can never remember being more excited than this time. Every player I came up to one by one was on an absolute high and just couldn't control their delight. John McKay and the rest of the management team were amongst the players sharing in the jubilation.

We lined up on the side of the field to be presented to the Queen and to receive our medals. Although it was an honour, it was also an agonising time because we desperately wanted to run around and talk to each other.

It was truly great to stand there holding the World Cup with Jeff Miller and Tim Lane who'd worked so hard, as had the rest of the management team. It was a wonderful feeling of what teamwork can do. People have often asked me how I felt. I felt like I was in a boat crew. I felt like I was in a rugby team. I didn't feel like an individual.

A short time later as I again held the Cup I noticed John Eales had formed a circle with a number of players to sing the national anthem. Instinctively I walked into the middle of the circle and placed the Cup on the turf. I then stepped back, and with arms wrapped around one another, all forty-two of us sang 'Advance Australia Fair' like it had never been sung before.

Then everything started to hit me as we went around looking at the crowd. I'll always remember seeing the glistening tickertape and the crowd coming down to the fence as we walked along. As I walked, I stayed behind the players, watching them celebrate and taking it all in. It's impossible to describe how much pleasure there is in seeing others do what you can only contribute to. As we completed our lap of the field I looked up and as clear as anything could see Liz and all my friends waving their scarves. I looked up to them proudly, thinking, 'This is what it's all about.'

The dressing room soon afterwards was pandemonium. Everyone was hugging each other and it was a great feeling of relief. Then one of the players got up and filled the World Cup with beer and said, 'John Eales, world champion'. John Eales then took the Cup and handed it to George Gregan. Everyone in the room yelled out, 'George Gregan, world champion'. This then went round to every single person in the squad.

By then John O'Neill had come into the change room, as had a number of the other directors. I found it difficult to look John in the eye because

I was still so moved. The amount of support he'd given this team was enormous. John was called up with the rest of the staff to drink out of the Cup and the call went round, 'John O'Neill, world champion'. There was another special moment when John Eales produced the bottle of vintage red wine which had been presented to him earlier by Chris Handy, who had by now joined us in the dressing room. The symbolic gesture of sharing this with everyone did not go unnoticed by our Classic Wallaby, who didn't mind the expensive wine being shared around in about forty cheap, plastic cups.

After at least an hour the celebrations in the dressing room were beginning to die down. When one of the officials came to me and said, 'There's someone at the gate called Mac claiming to be a friend of yours.' I really didn't know who it was, so I went with him. There, standing at the entrance with a lot of autograph seekers, was my old friend Ian McIntosh, the Natal coach from South Africa. He'd been waiting outside for an hour. Mac said to me, 'Rod, congratulations, I just had to come and see you. Wonderful victory.' Seeing an old friend there after so much time meant so much to me. I said to him, 'Why didn't you come into the dressing room? Why didn't you let me know earlier?' He replied, 'No, no, I just wanted to wait until you were right and let you know.' It brought back many fond memories as well as sealing a friendship that was formed many years before.

Macqueen wasn't alone in embracing the win as much more than a personal victory. It is testament to the closeness of the squad that all were quick to acknowledge the contribution of others. As captain, John Eales is well aware of the input from those both on and off the field: 'For all of us on the field I'm sure it was a mixture of relief and elation. For two years we'd been heading towards the one goal and we'd just won the final. There was no tomorrow, that was the end of the day. The team management were just as important as the players. They were playing for Australia as much as we were, and there was a very real feeling in the side that reflected that. Every time we played a Test match they'd try and be as good as they possibly could be as if they were playing the match. Their contribution can never be overestimated.'

Assistant coach Jeff Miller attributed much of the success to the detailed preparation and planning: 'The whole two years just seemed to roll to plan the whole time, which was quite amazing. We were fortunate we had world-class players who had committed themselves wholeheartedly to the task. For me it was a relief that we actually achieved our goal and obviously there was a fair amount of satisfaction. I was very happy for the guys after all the work they'd put in and the sacrifices they'd made. It was great to see their dreams come true. For me the feeling could never be as good as being a player, but it comes bloody close.'

The CEO of Australian Rugby Union, John O'Neill, was far from being some distant administrator. He too was regarded as an integral member of the squad: 'Winning the Cup in 1999 was one of the highlights of Australian rugby. The way the team performed, the execution and the planning—it was a great victory for all concerned. I think composure was the key word. I often told the players what a privilege it was to watch them, to see them working under pressure because they always stayed in control. I consider myself lucky to have been in the dressing room afterwards to join them in singing the national anthem. It was a great privilege and one of the highlights of my life.'

At the closing dinner later that night at the Cardiff International Arena, Macqueen and Liz made a point of speaking to the coaches of other World Cup teams. In the new world of professional rugby those in charge of the national teams are not the bitter enemies they often were in days gone by; most are on friendly terms and mix comfortably together on a social level. Macqueen especially goes out of his way to establish close relationships, perhaps too close if the truth were known, to some of the more rabid supporters. Certainly some All Black fans would be horrified to learn that he and their coach John Hart often enjoyed a round of golf between Test matches. They often relaxed in each other's company like two businessmen with a common interest, but separating work from pleasure. They talked about many things, trying to ignore the topic of rugby. Although from time to time the obvious subject came up. No doubt both knew many loaded questions were asked and both knew more than a few lies were told in answer. But they had similar views and respected each other's opinions.

Macqueen had been shocked by the way the New Zealand media had turned on Hart after the All Blacks had failed to make the final.

One of the first things Liz and I did at the after-match function was seek out John Hart. He was very down but as always he was in control. I felt

Jacqui's 21st birthday. A proud dad gives the speeches.

Spritely mum, Marj age 83, showing Rod a few moves on the dance floor.

Rod's oil painting of Long Reef Headland depicting the place he loves and the area for many of his runs.

The vision that confronted the
Wallabies: page 1 of the diary, 1998.

The realisation that he was entrusted
with the honour of guiding his
country in rugby.

Different ideas like this surf carnival kept life interesting for the Wallabies.

Teams line up for surf race.

George Gregan and Daniel Herbert compete for the beach flags.

One of the many strange sights confronting Caloundra residents.

Wallaby hooker Phil Kearns riding his bike to training.

Sharing the celebrations. New Zealand and Australian supporters drinking out of the Bledisloe Cup at the hotel in Christchurch, 1998.

Mates on different missions. Rod and Hitchie compare their recent achievements.

The Bledisloe Cup returns to Australia after four years. Christchurch, 1998.

The golding of the Wallabies.
Crowds respond to calls to show colours at the Tests.

Waltzing with Williamson.

An Australian record crowd of 109,000 bursts into song at the encouragement of
Australian country and western singer John Williamson.

Villiers Bretteneux.

The gravesites of the World War I battlefields in France that had such a moving effect on the Wallabies.

Rod and Liz take time out in the Cotswolds.

The Japanese meals pre-Test became a ritual. Here Rod shares the night with family and friends on the eve of the World Cup final.

Liz, family and friends on the way to the final of the World Cup at Millennium Stadium in Wales.

The scoreboard says it all.

The final score in the World Cup between Australia and France, 1999.

The hard work was all worthwhile. Wallaby emotions overflow after winning the World Cup.

The coaching trio had worked together for the ultimate achievement.

Tim Lane, Rod Macqueen, Jeff Miller with the World Cup.

Alex Evans and Steve Nance with Rod and the World Cup.

Family celebrations after the Cup victory. Liz, Rod and son Scott share the moment.

Rod holds the World Cup during the tickertape parade in Sydney.

Australia takes the Wallabies to heart. Tickertape parade, Town Hall, Sydney.

Wallabies and the World Cup are guests of honour at a dinner hosted by the Prime Minister John Howard and his wife Janette at the Lodge.

Another goal achieved: Australia's first Tri Nations victory.

The end of an era. Four of Australia's stars of the World retire from the Wallabies.
Tim Horan, Jason Little, David Wilson, Richard Harry.

A chance for everyone to smell the roses.

John Eales, Chris Handy, Gordon Bray, David Clarke, Dilup Kumar join in celebrating after the Tri Nations victory in South Africa.

Rugby's CEO John O'Neill adds a Gallic flavour to the celebrations.
Ewen McKenzie, Tim Lane, John O'Neill.

A personal farewell between captain and coach after Macqueen announces his retirement during the second Lions Test in Melbourne.

A victorious farewell. Macqueen and Eales acknowledge the crowd after winning the Lions Series for the first time in history.

Celebrating the final chapter.

Macqueen and Hitchie reflecting on the historic Lions victory.

All in the family.

Bringing home the spoils after a four-year journey that involved every member of the family. Rod, Liz, Jacqui and Scott.

very sorry for John because of the vitriolic way he was being treated back home after the All Blacks' unexpected loss. He had done his best. In fact I thought he'd done a good job. Perhaps the players weren't ready for it, or perhaps they were too self-assured. But the way he was being crucified by his people back home astonished me, particularly someone who had been as loyal and good for New Zealand rugby as he had been. It made me sit back and think how I would react if it was me. I knew I'd be just as sad and disappointed.

I thought how terrible it would be to have the public so much against you, and how fickle the job could be. It's not a matter of life and death, but people can be so emotional and savage about their sport. I can see no reason for such singleminded and personal attacks when the person involved has sacrificed so much and is obviously doing their best. I've always believed that it's very important to keep things in perspective.

For all of the Australian squad the night was a long and memorable one, if not always for the right reasons. After the official dinner, we adjourned to a local nightclub where a separate room had supposedly been booked for a private party. It was to be a low-key event where players could spend time with family and friends and generally unwind. The security arrangements were quite simple. The only people to be allowed into the room would be those wearing green wristbands, which had been sent to us earlier. But unbelievably, the management had seized on the opportunity to make a financial killing and had widely promoted the event, selling tickets and wristbands. By the time we arrived we could hardly get in the front door. There were literally hundreds of people already packed inside wearing green wristbands and waiting for the Wallabies to arrive. In fact, when I fronted the doorman and showed him my wristband he didn't recognise me and said there was no more room and wouldn't allow me in. Eventually we managed to sneak in through a side door so we could find our poor touring party of relatives and friends who were there waiting for us. We quickly deserted the function organised for our 'quiet get-together' and returned to the Cardiff Bay Hotel. Once everyone was reunited we managed to get on with our well-deserved private party. The best part of the night for me probably came later when we headed back to our rooms at about five o'clock in the morning. I sat down on the floor in the corridor with my family and close friends and sang all the old songs we knew. I kept thinking back to where it all began and who had helped along the way. It was a moment of fulfilment. I felt completely at peace.

For probably the first time in his life, Macqueen had no mountain to climb, no vision to pursue. After achieving almost everything there was to achieve in surf lifesaving, and developing a thriving private business, he had now secured the ultimate prize in rugby. His principles throughout had remained the same. They had enabled him to take an out-of-form squad of players and in less than two years turn them into the best rugby team in the world. That night he rested knowing that for him the final whistle had brought an end to the experience of a lifetime.

But the incredible elation felt by Macqueen and the Wallabies was also shared by a much larger team. An entire country was celebrating its heroes, and the publicity-shy Macqueen was about to find out just how significant eighty minutes of football can be.

Chapter 23

The Best is Yet to Come

If Rod Macqueen had vivid memories of the tickertape drifting down at Cardiff's Millennium Stadium, these were soon overshadowed. Back in Australia the tickertape once again filled the air, this time during noisy street parades in four capital cities—Brisbane, Sydney, Melbourne and Canberra. As open-top cars carrying the Wallabies slowly wound their way through city streets, people called out their individual names, even those of the coaching staff, as they threw streamers and waved flags. In Sydney alone 200,000 people turned out to congratulate the world champions. Newspapers everywhere carried front-page colour photographs and provided special lift-out sections supplying every detail of the team and their journey to World Cup victory. On talkback radio stations around the country it also seemed to be the only topic people wanted to discuss.

One of the things that pleased me most was that people weren't just talking about our success but the manner in which it was done. It obviously wasn't just the achievement of winning the World Cup but the demeanour and attitude of the players. I think it was obvious to everyone how much the Wallabies cared about their country and how hard they had worked to reach their goal. And I think that more than anything appeared to touch the hearts of many Australians.

Partners in celebration

The final tickertape parade was in Canberra. Once a dedicated rugby league town, it was now rugby union crazy thanks to the performance of the Brumbies and now the Wallabies. A civic reception at the town hall included politicians from all political parties. But a special low-key event came later that night when the squad and their partners were invited to dinner at the official residence of Prime Minister John

Howard, who was noted more for his almost fanatical support of the Australian cricket team. He now revealed to Macqueen that he was also extremely supportive and knowledgeable about rugby.

It was very interesting to be able to share private thoughts with such a high-profile person as the Prime Minister. It was a fairly simple and quiet gathering which included his wife Janette and their sons. We chatted throughout the night and there were just a few informal speeches. There were also awards and birthdays to celebrate with the prize in each case being a drink from the World Cup. I was surprised and gratified when at one stage Debbie Lane, the wife of assistant coach Tim Lane, stood up and acknowledged all the work Liz had done during the campaign. She then ordered Liz to drink from the World Cup, which she did to loud applause. And as an Australian I was pleased to see both our Prime Minister and his wife quite naturally take their turn at drinking from the golden trophy. It was a wonderful night, which I don't think anyone wanted to end.

It was another select gathering some weeks later which undoubtedly put life into perspective for Rod Macqueen. During the course of one afternoon and evening he shared close moments with Liz, enjoyed numerous childhood memories, was heartily congratulated by business associates, and was roundly denigrated and laughed at by family and close friends. It was New Year's Eve 1999, and his fiftieth birthday.

Liz had organised a very special event. Starting from their family home at Collaroy basin, a luxury coach took guests on a mystery tour which delivered them to a grassy clearing on Long Reef Headland. The panoramic ocean views were complemented by chilled champagne and a string quartet in black tie which struck up the powerful melody of Louis Armstrong's 'What a Wonderful World'. As daylight slowly faded over the Pacific horizon, the moment was suddenly interrupted by the sizzling roar of a rocket set off from behind a nearby clump of bushes. Within moments a giant, colourful explosion lit up the darkening sky, celebrating the last sunset of the old millennium.

The romantic interlude on the headland, which symbolised so many happy moments in the couple's life, was soon followed by a more traditional party back at their home. Those present represented a cross-section of Macqueen's life: family, neighbours, childhood friends, rugby mates, boat rowers, and senior company executives, all mixing easily together. A video presentation brought birthday wishes from those who couldn't be present, including numerous business leaders, rugby coaches and friends from around the world. If Macqueen had any ideas that he would now be treated with greater deference by those in his close circle, they were soon dashed when the time came for speeches. Due credit was given to his achievement as the World Cup-winning coach, but any personal failings or unusual character traits were mercilessly tossed around. Typically, Macqueen laughed along with everybody else and then when given the opportunity reciprocated in kind.

If I could have picked a perfect fiftieth birthday when I was younger this would have been it. I went for an hour's run in the morning along the headland. Liz and the kids were healthy. All my immediate family were there to celebrate with me, the only disappointment was that Dad was not there. As for the party, Liz had thought of everything. She knew me so well, she knew my special friends, songs, and places. And of course it came at the end of a year where we had achieved so much success together.

Through the setbacks and achievements in his life all these people had treated him in the same fashion, helping him appreciate the value of down-to-earth friendship. Despite reaching extraordinary success, no-one wanted him to change. Neither did he. This was his life.

Management on the move

While the Wallabies had won so much on the field, they were about to lose a great deal elsewhere. As so often happens in any business, their success brought changes to key personnel who either retired, were promoted or were lured away by the competition and big dollars. Team doctor John Best, arguably the number one sports physician in the country, was promoted to medical director of the ARU. The management skills of assistant coach Jeff Miller were recognised by the ARU and he was appointed general manager of the High Performance Unit, where he would develop a support team for all areas of Australian rugby. Similarly, their computer expert Scott Harrison was promoted to concentrate on a new website for the Australian Rugby Union.

Other members of the successful management team received lucrative offers from overseas which they found hard to ignore. The coach of the Wallabies' backs Tim Lane and conditioner Steve Nance were lured to a provincial side in France. These positions were taken up towards the end of the Tri Nations series and Macqueen was extremely disappointed by their departure. Both had agreed to remain with him for another two years following the World Cup success. It was a joint commitment that had reinforced his own decision to sign up for another term. But Macqueen realised that changes were inevitable and didn't stand in their way.

All had prospered under the Macqueen regime and these changes represented a step-up for those concerned. In some cases, strong friendships had been forged; however it was now time to call on some new resources; people with similar skills. Brumbies' assistant coach, Ewen McKenzie, who had also played under Macqueen with the Waratahs and Brumbies, replaced Miller as the assistant coach. Macqueen had recognised the significance of his contribution to the Brumbies as well as his hard work and attention to detail. Glen Ella, one of the famous Ella brothers, took over from Lane as backs' coach, while Michael Jamieson replaced John Best and Peter McDonald came in for trainer Steve Nance; both Jamieson and McDonald were from league backgrounds. These changes to the management team sparked a new enthusiasm within the squad.

Immediate goals

With the World Cup safely stored in the trophy cabinet and back-to-back victories in the Bledisloe Cup entered in the record books, only one prize was still unclaimed: victory in the Tri Nations series. At the first meeting in ARU headquarters, this was nominated as the goal for the 2000 season.

From the time Macqueen entered senior coaching with the Waratahs he had always set new goals and a different agenda for each successive year.

During the previous two years the main aim had always been to win the World Cup, but along the way we had also been confronted by the Bledisloe Cup and Tri Nations series. At least on this occasion we had just a single, short-term goal: victory in the Tri Nations series.

In planning and developing their style of play for the upcoming Test matches and eventually the next World Cup, they knew that future try-scoring opportunities would not be foiled by deliberate acts of foul play. At an International Rugby Board conference held one month after the World Cup, IRB delegates were amazed to learn that various national coaches had ordered their sides to give away a penalty rather than concede a try. After digesting this information, the delegates acknowledged the value of showing players a yellow card and sending them to the sin-bin for ten minutes. During the conference Macqueen pointed out that if the sin-bin had been in operation during the 1999 tournament many more tries would have been scored and spectators would have been treated to a more enjoyable spectacle. Although the result of a combined admission by all coaches at the conference, the final decision justified the personal campaign Macqueen had waged from the very beginning of his term as national coach. The style of play which he had developed depended on quick recycling and movement of the ball. The fact he could not successfully use the same style of play in the World Cup had been a constant source of frustration. Perhaps now rugby fans would see the game reach its full potential.

Look back to go forward

In assessing the coming Tri Nations series, the new management team looked back. They were particularly interested to examine what had occurred after Australia won the World Cup in 1991 only to have their new squad eliminated early from the 1995 competition. With this in mind he knew it was imperative to find the best possible motivation and a motto to inspire the Wallabies.

I remembered their campaign statement for 1995, 'Mission Repeat'. From my own experience I knew the mission would have been doomed from the start. Repeating what had already been done was not a strategy for success. After our World Cup victory in 1999 I was well aware we still needed to improve in every area, to keep ahead of the opposition if there was to be any chance of continued success.

When the Wallaby squad gathered at their home-away-from-home at Caloundra they received the now essential diary. Once again,

Macqueen had provided a motto for the year ahead: 'The Best is Yet to Come'.

The phrase came from a poem, 'The Battle of Christchurch', written by the sports fanatic and writer, Rupert McCall. It was written after the Wallabies' epic victory in Christchurch in 1998. The many stanzas give a colourful and glowing tribute to the heroic contributions made by each player, and the poem finishes with a message that would become inspirational in the Wallabies' preparation. The final stanza of the piece reads:

> In the wake of what's behind you,
> let your rugby dreams remind you,
> that your future starts tomorrow,
> and your best is yet to come.

These words encapsulated exactly what Macqueen wanted to get across to his players, and the message was repeated constantly throughout their preparation.

Setbacks and comebacks

In two early Test matches against Argentina, the Wallabies won comfortably but were widely criticised for being lethargic in their play. In a strongly promoted match against South Africa for the inaugural Mandela Challenge Plate, they were again successful. The game earned the Wallabies another entry in the record books, being their tenth consecutive Test victory. It equalled the best performance of any Australian rugby side. The game was played in Melbourne's new Colonial Stadium with the moveable roof closed to keep out the elements. The score line was flattering but rugby commentators noted the Wallabies still appeared disjointed and lacklustre. Macqueen wasn't concerned. In fact he didn't expect anything else. The team was not carrying out specific Test preparation but was training especially hard to reach peak physical fitness for the first Bledisloe Cup match against New Zealand, a match which also counted as the first in the Tri Nations series.

The match at Sydney's Stadium Australia would be acclaimed by many as the greatest game of rugby ever played. A record crowd of 109,874 packed the stadium, expecting a monumental contest. They weren't disappointed. As usual the Wallaby preparation was meticulous and Macqueen was confident their tactics would give them an early advantage.

However, from the kickoff, the All Blacks held possession and immediately scored a converted try. One minute later they scored again . . . and kept on scoring. After only eight minutes the Wallabies were trailing by an unbelievable margin of 24–0. The Australian supporters were stunned, and Macqueen's new assistant coach Ewen McKenzie was close to panic. On the outside the Australian coach looked calm but on the inside his stomach was churning and his mind racing.

From the time the first try was scored we started sending messages to John Eales to stay calm, forget the scoreboard and establish our pattern of play. We kept sending out the message to get the ball and hold possession at all cost. During that short period the same message was probably sent out a dozen times. From the understanding that the team had developed, everyone knew that if we could get the ball we could make it happen.

At last, everything started going to plan. With control of the ball the Wallabies hit back and to the delight of the huge crowd the two sides left the field at half-time locked at 24–all. In a comeback unrivalled in contests between the two nations, it set the stage for a thrilling finale. With just three minutes to go and the Wallabies holding the lead 35–34, a rugby miracle still looked certain. Unfortunately at the end of the day it wasn't to be. The All Blacks' winger Jonah Lomu scored a try down the touchline, sealing victory in the last few minutes.

Although we hadn't won, this had been the ultimate test of the team's composure and they passed with flying colours. In fact they had taken another step up and proved that 'The Best was Yet to Come'. I honestly felt that despite the loss the team was now complete and capable of achieving anything. We had picked up two bonus points which meant we were still in charge of our own destiny.

Soon the team was back on track with a crushing win over South Africa. The crowd at Stadium Australia wasn't treated to a spectacular free-flowing game on this occasion because of rugged defence from the Springboks who were desperate to shut down the talented Australian backs. After taking the initiative in the first fifteen minutes with driving forward play, the South African side lost momentum and spent most of the game grimly defending its own line. The Wallabies held possession for long periods, launching wave after wave of attack trying a variety of backline moves against staunch defence. Their persistence was rewarded with just two tries, one to Stirling Mortlock who put in a Man of the Match performance. While far from glamorous, the victory received enthusiastic support from a vocal partisan crowd exceeding 77,000 which burst into a song at every opportunity. The final score of 26–6 reflected Australia's dominance and kept the side in contention for Tri Nations success. The stage was now set for another thrilling clash with the All Blacks to decide the Bledisloe Cup in the two-match series. With the contest to be held on New Zealand's home turf at Wellington, the pressure was well and truly on the Wallabies. With great respect for the new All Black coach, Wayne Smith, Macqueen sent his side into the match, as usual, with a specific game plan. However, there was one unusual tactic.

We had organised to play a number of different options on the moves we had played in previous weeks. We knew the All Blacks would have studied these and would be waiting for the moves to turn up in our attack. The only unusual thing we did was to make a last-minute change to the run-on side. We had named Matt Cockbain, our specialist jumper at the back of a lineout, in the run-on fifteen, knowing the opposition would stack the rear of their lineout to combat his ability. Instead we sent out a running backrower, Jim Williams, in his place.

Kicking goals

In an evenly contested match the strategy paid off. The Wallabies scored early in a move involving Williams that resulted in a backline break and saw Stirling Mortlock touch down under the posts. Late in the second half when the All Black lineout jumpers were replaced, Cockbain was brought on. He won several crucial opposition lineout throws that allowed the Wallabies to hold possession deep in All Black territory. Under constant attack, the home side lost their discipline and conceded a penalty close to full time. At this stage Australia was trailing by two points. The penalty was awarded right on the touch-line but Mortlock, the Wallabies' specialist kicker, was off the field, so John Eales took the kick that soared through the posts giving the Wallabies a last gasp one-point victory. For the first time in history Australia retained the treasured Blesdisloe Cup for the third time in succession.

The referee's whistle sounded as he awarded a penalty to Australia, close to the touchline and with only seconds remaining. The situation was virtually identical to that in New Zealand but this time the match was being played against South Africa in Durban. Again, Australia was trailing by two points and this time the Tri Nations trophy was the prize hanging in the balance. On this occasion, goalkicker Stirling Mortlock was on the field and captain John Eales, despite his own victory-winning kick against the All Blacks, had no hesitation in handing over the ball. Just one difficult kick at goal would decide the truth of that motivational phrase, 'The Best is Yet to Come' which had started their season. The ball travelled straight and true and for the second time in the season, the Wallabies won a momentous match in the dying moments. Although both the All Blacks and the Springboks no doubt felt cheated by losses in such extraordinary circumstances, Macqueen had a different view.

I felt victory came because of composure, the ability to stay competitive and in the game to the very last. I see composure as a belief in yourself, a confidence that you've done the work, planned and prepared for every different situation so that there are no surprises. This team had gained composure not only through preparation but by learning from their losses as well as their narrow escapes. The players knew each other's game very well and as a team worked well together. In the end that was the telling factor which allowed us to be in a position to win.

Sharing success

As usual Macqueen and Eales had their pact to celebrate victory. On this occasion it meant jumping into the hotel swimming pool. This time they were not alone. They'd been celebrating in a room with several other players and family and it was a large and rowdy group which hit the water together.

It was one of those very special nights and one of those spontaneous moments. After the pair had taken the plunge into the pool, they urged both the ARU chief John O'Neill and chairman David Clarke to join them in their swim. When they realised they had no choice, both agreed. After removing their shoes and particular items of clothing, folding them neatly in a pile, they jumped in too. However, they had forgotten about the ever-playful Macqueen, who quickly left the water. 'Gentlemen . . . you forgot these!' To their astonishment, they turned to see a grinning Macqueen tossing their shoes and their clothes in after them. What a unique sight it was—the captain, coach, chief executive and chairman of an international sporting side all frolicking together in a swimming pool, along with Australian journalists and other team members, like schoolboys celebrating their first major victory.

At this time everyone had good reason to celebrate. The Wallabies were now without doubt the most successful Australian team in history, and Macqueen the most successful coach. The trophy cabinet at ARU headquarters in Sydney was not only full but overflowing. In addition to the World Cup it now contained the Tri Nations Trophy (versus New Zealand, South Africa), The Bledisloe Cup (versus New Zealand), the Mandela Challenge Plate (versus South Africa), the Cook Cup (versus England), the Hopetoun Cup (versus Scotland), the Lansdowne Cup (versus Ireland) and the Puma Cup (versus Argentina).

At the end of the 2000 international competition, under Rod Macqueen, thirty-seven Tests were played with an outstanding success rate of 82 per cent, an extraordinary achievement given the all-important and consistent victories that mattered. There was not only the World Cup and the Tri Nations series, but the dominance over New Zealand, a country where to say rugby is the national obsession is a statement of fact.

The Macqueen success raised numerous questions: how could a country distracted by Aussie rules, rugby league and soccer continue to win with such a small support base? Soccer alone boasts junior membership greater than the combined totals of the three other codes. On the eastern seaboard rugby league generates enormous media coverage where it has long been recognised as the game for the masses. At the Melbourne Cricket Ground some club games in the Aussie rules competition draw up to 80,000 fans. In the rugby heartland of Sydney and Brisbane, club matches are lucky to attract a couple of thousand spectators. The undoubted successes of previous coaches were one thing but Macqueen's contribution was unique: a finely-tuned business management team and a personal vision which remained unmatched.

The future depends on early decisions

The year 2000 was a golden one for Australia. As well as its unprecedented rugby success, Sydney hosted the biggest sporting event of all, the Olympic Games. Hailed as 'The best Games ever,' they captured the imagination of the world and stirred Australian national pride even further. Unfortunately they also created an unexpected headache for Rod Macqueen and the Wallabies. The regular international rugby season was forced to finish earlier than usual and a short tour of Europe planned for late in the year would come after a ten-week layoff for the Australian squad. Having already lost the core of his management team, Macqueen had other problems. During the Tri Nations tournament several key players had asked if they could break their contracts after the final match against South Africa rather than continue to the end of the calendar year which meant an additional three more Test matches in Europe. The player of the World Cup tournament, Tim Horan, his centre partner Jason Little, and flanker David Wilson had received lucrative offers to finish their careers in England, while veteran front-rower Richard Harry wanted to retire for business reasons. Important decisions had to be made and quickly. Macqueen's mind went back to the beginning of the year when he'd spent time with the coaches of other Australian sporting teams who'd achieved long-running success. Jeff Miller was putting a succession plan in place and together with Macqueen was planning the future of the Wallabies.

In looking to the future we needed as much information as possible on how to maintain a high level of success. I had several enjoyable discussions with Wayne Bennett, coach of the Brisbane Broncos, and the most professional rugby league coach in Australia. I'd also seen Ric Charlesworth who'd managed an unbelievable string of tournament victories with our women's hockey team, the Hockeyroos. I wanted to get an idea of how they had handled ongoing success and how they had maintained the intensity of their players. Wayne Bennett had one key piece of advice. He told me it was always better to make a decision on the future of a player a year earlier than a year later. That stayed with me and immediately came to mind during our talks in the middle of the Tri Nations series. Knowing we could lose four of the team's most important players before heading into rugged Test matches against France, Scotland and England, we realised it was finally time to make some hard decisions.

Everyone's acknowledged goal was to retain the World Cup which Australia would host in 2003. But at the same time no-one wanted to risk losing the three European Test matches. And there was another factor to be taken into account. First up the following year the Wallabies would take on a visiting touring side, the British and Irish Lions, traditionally the toughest to come out of Europe. It was a side comprising the best players from England, Ireland, Scotland and Wales and held the enviable record of being undefeated on Australian soil.

I had discussions with Jeff Miller, John O'Neill and the board. It was with some trepidation, but with a firm understanding of what we were doing, that we agreed to let those four players go. It was time to think of the long term, to bring young players in and give them their opportunity at Test level. I am constantly reminded of the situation where you hire a young businessman who has come straight from university with a degree with all the necessary qualifications and full of enthusiasm. But there's no substitute for time spent in the workplace getting an understanding of what it's all about. The same thing applies to rugby. It doesn't matter how much time you spend on the training field or how often you play in general competition, there is absolutely no substitute for playing at Test level where you are playing with and against better players.

We had made the hard decisions. We could have retained our older, experienced players through to the end of the year to try and ensure victory, but we decided to rebuild for our long-term goal, the 2003 World Cup. The answer had been tough but simple. New blood was needed in the side and it was time to let go of the players who wanted to retire or go overseas. Horan, Little, Wilson and Harry had already done a wonderful job with the Wallabies both on and off the field. For those wanting to play in England it meant excellent money for the last of their playing years and the wonderful experience of living overseas with their families. We felt it was time they were rewarded for their contribution to Australian rugby. It was also time for us to look to the future.

A tour for all reasons

When selection of the touring side began, new problems arose. The team's dynamic scrum base duo, George Gregan and Stephen Larkham, were both injured and out of contention indefinitely. In fact when it finally arrived in Europe, the team would contain only seven of the Wallabies who had helped win the World Cup twelve months earlier. But the decision to blood new players had already been made and, once selected, the new squad had a special chemistry, a high level of excitement, and a great deal of enthusiasm. It was almost as though the young players who had been given an opportunity to impress were breathing new life into the remainder of the side which had carried all before it.

A warm-up match against a Japanese fifteen developed some cohesion which blossomed into strength and character to forge an impressive win in the first Test match against the French in Paris. Another victory against Scotland, in appalling weather, set the scene for a tough confrontation with England, a side that was well-prepared and desperate to defeat the world champions.

In front of a frenzied English crowd the Wallabies' winning run came to a sad end. Although they felt they had the game well under control at half-time, a bizarre series of events late in the match resulted in two Wallabies being sent to the sin-bin with only minutes to go. Trailing by only a few points, the English kicked through and scored a controversial try in the last few seconds of injury time to snatch victory.

The Australian touring party that had begun its rebuilding program with such promise returned home. With three victories and a one-point loss to England the expectations of the new-look touring party were probably surpassed, however there was still the disappointment of falling at the final hurdle. But on their return they were accepted and embraced by a public who over the past two years had enjoyed and shared in the greatest riches international rugby could offer.

With one season remaining of his four-year term Macqueen was determined to adhere to his principle of placing a time span on his tenure.

I have always liked being in control of my own destiny, putting a time limit on achieving the goals required, whatever the project. This way you are not continually using excuses and looking for more time to succeed. It also means you are mindful of your successor and able to assist in preparing the structures and path to take over that role. I believe, as a coach, there comes a time when fresh ideas and new blood are needed.

As usual Macqueen would not walk out and leave the house of Australian rugby in disorder. Succession planning was already well underway. Achieving the ultimate goal is the most difficult of all feats —until it is done. Retaining it can be even harder.

Chapter 24

Revolution not Evolution

Poor surfing conditions on Queensland's Sunshine Coast in January 2001 led to a serious discussion about the future coaching of the Wallabies. During a family Christmas holiday Rod Macqueen met with his friend and rugby confidante, Paul McLean, for a surf at Kings Beach, Caloundra. With the lack of waves making bodysurfing impossible, the pair ended up standing chest-deep in water debating the contentious issue of when and how the Wallaby coach should hand over control to his successor. Given Macqueen's lifetime involvement in surf lifesaving and rugby it was an eminently suitable location.

Choosing the appropriate time for me to retire was a difficult one. At that time a decision still hadn't been made on who would take over the coaching position. Recruiting overseas coaches was not considered an option, for two reasons: there was now such a big difference between club and provincial rugby we needed to improve the standard of local coaching by elevating those able to perform at the next level; and by bringing in coaches from other countries we would lose the intellectual expertise which had taken so long to develop and was the reason for the Wallabies' success. The advent of professionalism and the big money it provided already meant that several of our top coaches had been lured overseas.

Paul McLean, who by now was president of the Queensland Rugby Union, was sympathetic. Macqueen had achieved more than anyone had thought possible and no one in Australian rugby would stand in his way if he wanted to step aside. However, there were major issues conflicting with his personal priorities which McLean helped him talk through. 'Rod was most concerned that the successful structure he had helped put in place didn't disintegrate when he left. If he stopped at the beginning of 2001 there would be not only a new Wallaby coach but, as it happened, three new provincial coaches as well. Not a good situation for Australian rugby. He was also concerned about a new coach coming in cold and experiencing what he had when he took over at the end of 1997. Back then he inherited a team he knew very little about and a structure into which he'd had no input whatsoever, which made it a real struggle. What made it even more galling for Rod was the similarity between the upcoming Lions tour and the problems he had at the start of his second year with the Waratahs in 1992. Once again many of the arrangements had been made without his knowledge or input. The visitors would have six lead-up matches to get their team right and the Wallabies would have just one. It would be a tough start to a very tough year. Rod was agonising over what to do but I think even at that time he knew he would have to stay on to the end.'

The final decision would have to be made in a matter of weeks. Macqueen's dilemma would be resolved in the same way all such things had been done since he had taken over as Wallaby coach—in a relaxed conversation with John O'Neill and confirmed with a handshake.

During my four years as Wallaby coach only one contract was ever signed and that was halfway through the season, well after I had reached an agreement with John. I think that reflects the trust and respect we had for each other.

Now Macqueen had to reach an agreement, not on the terms of his future with the ARU, but on the timing of his departure. It was over another lunch, a long one, with John O'Neill. By the time early afternoon had changed, unnoticed, into early evening, Macqueen had agreed to stay with the Wallabies until the end of the Tri Nations series.

The three-dimensional leader

Another person with whom Macqueen had established a strong personal relationship and great mutual respect was John Eales. Towards the end of the 2000 season, for the first time ever, Macqueen was hearing criticism of the captain from within the squad. Some players had started calling him 'Jellyback,' a nickname referring to the fact that he was considered to be enforcing the views of team management rather than listening to the players. It was a complete turnaround from when Macqueen took over as Wallaby coach, when Eales was regarded as a virtual mouthpiece for the players. But much had changed over the years. Because of his own extraordinary ability and natural leadership qualities, Eales had always been an excellent captain, but Macqueen believed that the experience acquired during those years had made him the ultimate leader.

John was able to speak to both sides and then assess the right way to go. And once that decision was made he didn't back down, he stood by it, and this was what some of the players perceived as a weakness. In fact it was the ultimate strength. Having the courage of your convictions, making the right decision, and standing by it even though it mightn't be the most popular decision for some individuals. John Eales understood what the Wallaby ethos was all about. It wasn't a game that was just played to make money. It was far more complicated than that. It was understanding that you were the custodians of a game that had been played for one hundred years. As the late Sir Donald Bradman stated so eloquently, 'The custodians of the game of cricket are the players. It is their responsibility to pass on the game to the next generation of players in a better state than how they found it.' This applies to the international game of rugby as much as it does to cricket. Not only how you play the game, but how you behave on and off the field has a marked effect on the future of the sport.

John Eales not only came to understand this but he supported and contributed to the many initiatives introduced within the team to promote this ideal. As a result he wasn't always popular, but that's what makes a good leader. At times there were disagreements between John and myself, but we always overcame them.

He has many natural attributes which make for a great Wallaby captain. John would be the last person left at training signing autographs for the kids, he would be the one caring if someone had a family member who was sick, remembering their name and inquiring about them. John recognises more than most the importance of behaviour and the responsibilities that go with wearing the Wallaby jersey. I often wondered how many members of the Wallaby squad actually understood the importance of the standards he was setting and what it meant for the future.

The custodians of culture

During his time as Wallaby coach Macqueen was heartened by the great number of letters he received from people impressed by the behaviour and demeanour of the players. Some wrote to express pride in the humility shown in victory and the respect given to the opposition. Others, who had approached individual players after games or met them in public places such as hotel lobbies, were thankful for the time they took to talk about the game and sign autographs. For Macqueen there was always much more to being a Wallaby than winning rugby matches. Being a role model and fulltime ambassador for your country was equally important.

However, Macqueen believes there are several important issues that could affect the direction of Australian rugby in the future.

When professional rugby came into existence, a Rugby Union Players Association (Rupa), was formed to protect the elite players' interests. Recently, a new collective bargaining agreement was produced and agreed on, which carried a number of important initiatives including; player education, insurance, working conditions and measurements of financial rewards. However, the agreement doesn't appear to contain anything about the Wallaby ethos. There doesn't seem to be anything about the pride of wearing the Wallaby jumper, the importance of tradition and the significance of personal standards. All of these things will be left in the hands of the Wallabies themselves and management teams of the future. Surely there needs to be some kind of written guidance. If we consider that the very essence of our sport, the heart of its success, is the culture and standards, then why aren't they mentioned in the agreement? I believe it leaves a fine line between success and failure in the future.

Including all stakeholders

Perhaps the final issue concerning Macqueen was the role of the International Rugby Board. When the IRB held its special conference just one month after the World Cup to discuss the future direction of the game, coaches, administrators and players from countries all around the world were invited to attend. Macqueen was looking forward to open discussion on the many problems which he believed had been highlighted during the competition. He had heard a lot about the so-called old men of rugby who controlled the game. He was also aware of the infamous remark of former England captain, Will Carling, who criticised them for being out of touch and referred to them all as 'old farts'.

I must admit that my first impressions were that perhaps some of his thoughts were correct. We were given an agenda for the three-day conference and the heading on the first page read, 'The law makers are the custodians of the game.' Before I could read any further I had bells ringing in my ears, I just couldn't get past this statement. The more I looked at it the more I realised it was totally upside-down. In fact the players and supporters should be the custodians of the game. After that the coaches and administrators should be there to make the appropriate laws.

As in any business, the customers should dictate the end product. The managing director is there to ensure that the customers get what they want, so that at the end of the day he gets the profits that he wants. The people in charge of international rugby seemed to have the whole concept turned on its head. At the first opportunity I pointed out that there seemed to be a huge anomaly. We needed a vision to work towards, a vision of the way the game should be played. Something that everyone agreed on and which provided us with a checklist and the direction in which to go. Only after this vision of the game is realised can we success-fully identify the laws necessary to ensure the game is played that way.

It was the first time that all coaches came together and it was quite remarkable that we all had similar ideas on the future of the game. The coaches were now able to be part of the decision making process.

I believe the most important initiative that has come from the confer-ences since the World Cup has been the recommendation that changes to the laws would now come from a committee representing not only the administrators, but all stakeholders of the game, players and coaches and spectators as well. The concern now is whether the IRB will continue to honour this new administrative process in the future.

Future of the game

There is no argument that in recent times rugby has evolved into a faster, more exciting game of football, played at a greater pace for much longer periods of time. The level of attacking and defensive skills has developed immeasurably due to the amount of time professional players are now able to spend on their preparation. As a result, this more entertaining, continuous style of play has attracted many more spectators to the game, especially in Australia where great inroads have been made into the traditional support base of the other major codes—rugby league, Australian rules and soccer. But despite the many innovations Macqueen believes the core value of rugby hasn't changed.

There is always a genuine contest for possession at the various parts of the game starting from the kickoff and continuing through to the scrums, lineouts, 22 restarts and of course at the tackle. Because of this, unlike some other football codes, rugby will always need different types of players with a variety of unique skills. Due to the importance of winning the ball from so many different areas of play, we still need to retain the different body shapes to play the game. Every team needs its skillful ball players and fast runners but now these team members must also be multi-skilled, with a high level of fitness, power and strength so they can contest the ball at the breakdown. Quite simply, rugby has developed into a great game and is getting better all the time.

The only remaining area of concern is the breakdown where there are so many different laws involved that a penalty can be given either way at virtually any time depending on the interpretation of the referee. This leads to a definite lack of consistency and this makes it confusing for everyone including players, coaches, spectators and the referees themselves. Pressure has to be taken off the referees by introducing new guidelines but the last thing we should do is add more laws to the game, making it even more complicated. Its time to sit back and think outside the square to come up with a solution that suits everyone. So many great improvements have already been made, I think the perfect game is not far away.

Rivalry and friendship

Seeing an international coach threaten to storm out of a press conference because of intimidating questions was always great entertainment for supporters. So too was the bitter rivalry between coaches. The sniping, the personal attacks, the accusations. Where has it all gone? Members of the media openly bemoan what seems to be a new code of gentlemanly conduct where polite restraint tends to be the order of the day. For Macqueen though, despite his fierce competitiveness, nothing has changed. Throughout his coaching career, from the very earliest days, he has enjoyed his association with the coaches from other sides, at all levels; those in Australia and the various characters who motivate the leading teams from around the world.

It's not only a busy and stressful life but the old saying, 'It's lonely at the top' really does hold true. I always tried to make a point of meeting my adversaries and keeping a healthy relationship going. By doing this I was not only able to compare notes and learn things along the way, but I was able to resolve problems and fast-track decisions, bypassing the various levels of administration which tangle the game in red tape. Some of these relationships have been very special. Over the years I have spent a lot of time swapping ideas in particular with John Hart from New Zealand; and with Ian McIntosh and Harry Viljoen, my old friends and adversaries from South Africa. People may find this strange. But for me, giving away some of my thoughts constantly forces me to come up with new ideas; keeping everything to myself can lead to tunnel vision and predictability. Ian McIntosh successfully coached Natal and later had a great input in South Africa's victory in the 1995 World Cup. I still remember the quote he wrote on the conference agenda in Durban back in 1993. 'How deaf is a man— who does not want to hear?' I must admit that in hindsight I was somewhat guilty of that. I wish that during that period I had spent more time listening to Mac's thoughts. All have remained close friends and as families we continue to enjoy each other's hospitality.

Following our victory in the final game of the 2000 Tri Nations series in South Africa, Harry Viljoen and Magda joined Liz and me at a private game park. On one of the game drives we came across five big ugly water buffalo. Harry joked that next year's Springbok pack would be just as big. I couldn't resist the comeback line that they'd have a similar combined IQ. We both had a good laugh but, later that night over a few drinks, he told me he had been approached to coach South Africa the following year. Knowing I would soon be ending my contract with the Wallabies he suggested I join him as a freelance consultant. The amount of money mentioned was huge. Later, discussing the possibility with Liz, it was an easy decision to make. As much as I saw Harry as a friend and would have enjoyed working with him, there was no way I could help coach one of our greatest rivals to try and defeat the Wallabies. Harry is an innovative coach with a proven success record and I was sure he would take South Africa to a new level.

Some months later it was revealed that Tim Lane, Macqueen's assistant coach during the World Cup campaign, had accepted the position of assistant coach to the South African team. He had managed to negotiate a release from his contract in France to take up a lucrative offer from Harry. Macqueen didn't regard this recruitment by Viljoen as a betrayal of their friendship, rather the actions of a professional coach doing everything possible to ensure the success of his team. He knew the Springbok coach was also seeking information and key personnel from leading teams in other countries.

Macqueen's main opponents as Wallaby coach had been New Zealand's John Hart and South Africa's Nick Mallet, because of the fierce competition during the Tri Nations series.

Despite the tension surrounding the big games there was always a great rapport between us. The many games of golf Liz and I played with John and his wife Judy were a welcome escape from all the media attention and the hype that surrounds world rugby. I'm sure many people don't understand this and never will. But life is bigger than winning and losing sporting fixtures. We've all been on the losing end and on most occasions make a point of seeking each other out and putting things into perspective after each game. The loneliest place in a room crowded with people is the area surrounding the losing coach.

I value the ongoing association and friendships that I have made, not only with my coaching predecessors in Australia, but with the many coaches I have met throughout the world.

One last victory

After winning the World Cup in 1999 and collecting every other available trophy in 2000 there was another achievement which interested Macqueen. It was one over which he had no direct control, but a strong emotional link: victory for an Australian team in the Super 12 competition. The side which had come closest was the ACT Brumbies, the team to which he and Liz had contributed so much. Since their inception they had shown the way with new ideas and skills that had thrilled spectators and baffled opposition teams throughout the competition.

On the evening of 26 May 2001 under the fine leadership of Eddie Jones the Brumbies were again in the final and were favourites to defeat the Sharks from South Africa. Rod and Liz Macqueen were present in the capacity crowd at Bruce Stadium.

Liz and I experienced something very special as we were walking towards the stadium, hearing the kids in the street singing the old Brumbies' song and seeing the huge crowd of supporters, who were as parochial and passionate as ever. The Brumbies had played well all year and it was obvious that they desperately wanted to win this game. Watching the game unfold and seeing many of the original players out there brought back many fond memories. Towards the end when the score line showed they couldn't lose we realised that the Brumbies had finally achieved the ultimate goal. They had played great football all year, and that evening were justified in winning comprehensively 36-6. Liz and I slipped out early and went back to our hotel, had a quiet drink at the bar and reflected on those first two years. When we first arrived in Canberra it was a big rugby league town; now, five years on it had embraced rugby union with a passion.

The continued success of the Brumbies has also helped promote the success of Australian rugby when combined with the contributions from both NSW and Queensland. When Macqueen took over as national coach in 1997 he introduced a structure that encouraged communication between the provinces and a core vision for Australian rugby with provision to allow for individual ideas and creativity. In 1998 Macqueen and his management team incorporated the best from the three provinces and developed a style of play second to none. When the players then returned to their respective provinces, the Super 12 coaches used these skills and made their own changes and improvements which in turn came back to the Wallabies. To complete the cycle, the Wallabies once again took the best and with further innovations raised the game to yet another new level.

The rugby revolution Macqueen began with the ACT was now responsible for the dramatic evolution of Australian rugby. With this vital infrastructure now in place the Wallabies have the opportunity to continue improving and maintaining their dominance of the modern game.

Chapter 25

The Measure of the Man

As I made clear when appointed to the Brumbies and the Wallabies, rugby is not my whole life. My wife Liz and I set out on a journey and we have enjoyed every part of it. It is now time for a new coach to come in and guide the Wallabies to their next goal.

With these words Rod Macqueen officially announced his retirement at a media conference on 4 May 2001. It was news that surprised many rugby supporters who were sure the Wallaby coach could have been persuaded to stay in the position for as long as the team kept on winning, as others before him had done. But as Macqueen had continually stressed—to those who would listen—four years was the maximum he believed he could remain on top before it was time to move on to other things.

I was happy that there were now good people in place to take over, who could bring new enthusiasm and ideas. The Wallabies undoubtedly accomplished great things and Liz and I shared this success and the fun and excitement that came with it. We had travelled the world, made many new friends and seen individuals achieve greater things than they could ever have imagined. We were proud to be part of this and I guess the most important thing was that we managed to smell the roses along the way.

That part of Macqueen's life which didn't involve rugby would soon take precedence. Greater involvement in Advantage Line which was continuing to expand and explore new directions; consultancy opportunities with a number of national and international corporations; a chance to take up numerous invitations to address business functions and private boardroom conferences, where his successful application of the same principles to sport and business had generated enormous interest. Also there would be time to help guide his children in their individual careers—Jacqui in childcare, and Scott who had just joined the team at Advantage Line (with a guarantee of no favouritism) as a promising young industrial designer. And there would be more time to spend with Liz. Living back in Beach Road, at the Basin, where Macqueen spent his childhood days, they would have a greater opportunity to enjoy the company of family, close friends and neighbours.

Of course it would be naïve to assume the thought of dabbling in rugby would disappear completely. Tempting offers were constantly arriving from rugby nations and rugby clubs in all parts of the world. Regardless of whether he wanted to retire or not, Macqueen's coaching record seemed to demand otherwise.

Time for family and friends

After winning the 1999 World Cup, followed by retaining the Bledisloe Cup, then victory in the Tri Nations series in 2000, Macqueen's place in rugby coaching history was assured. Now the unbiased assessments and unashamed compliments flowed freely. They came in many forms from many different people and covered not only the contribution and changes he had made to the game of rugby, but the changes it had made to him.

Family and friends see numerous subtle differences in Macqueen's personality and general approach to life. He has a more rounded outlook and greater confidence in the public arena. His characteristic intensity has given way to a more balanced and reasoned approach. At the same time his easygoing relationship with family and friends remains the same, although there seems to be a new urge to spend more time with those who are close. Long-time friend John Nolan believes the World Cup victory germinated yet another side to the man he first met as a wild young footballer more than thirty years ago. 'It was something important to him that gave him great satisfaction. But he doesn't need to hang on to it. Instead he has moved on to the next phase of his life, which I think is unique. He has the satisfaction of having achieved something exceptional but, interestingly enough, doesn't talk about it much and in fact is quite humble. He is a much more thoughtful person who recognises there is reward in guiding others to achievement.'

Edwin Zemancheff, the Sydney lawyer who jokes he was only recruited as manager of the NSW Waratahs because he could provide free secretarial services and prestigious boardroom facilities, has a similar view. He has since become Macqueen's personal and company legal advisor and, like so many other rugby associates, a good friend. 'Rod is certainly more confident now in everything he does, but at times I feel sad because of the demands placed on his time and the pressure placed on his personal life. Because of this I think he is more guarded towards many people. Perhaps he's wary they are trying to get close to him for reasons other than it appears on the surface. I for one will be almost glad when his time as Wallaby coach is over so we can have more opportunities to relax and enjoy each other's company.'

How does an eleven-year-old boy feel when he asks his uncle to turn up at school as part of his latest class project, and the uncle agrees? The answer is 'Overwhelmed'! Especially when Uncle Rod happens to be coach of the world champion Wallabies. According to Macqueen's sister Katy Jenkins, her son Matt was the envy of all his mates when he produced, in the flesh, the 'Famous Person' on whom he had based a major project. A person who then, at the request of the headmaster, gave a short speech to the school assembly in which he stressed to the children how they should strive to enjoy all aspects of their life, including of course, rugby and in particular, he spoke of respecting the opposition. Katy says her brother rearranged his busy schedule on twelve hours' notice to be at the school. 'Despite the enormous pressures on him he really puts himself out when it comes to helping members of the family. I was very proud of him, but when I thanked Rod for taking the time to come he virtually took offence. He told me it was extremely important for him to do all he could to be a part of the family and explained how much he enjoyed doing that sort of thing.'

In the trenches

Finding someone who will say something negative about Macqueen isn't easy. Former Wallaby turned rugby journalist Peter FitzSimons, who detested the strict training regime and unbending discipline imposed on players, gives glowing tributes on several fronts. He notes the enormous amount of time Macqueen gives to speak at charity and fundraising events for a variety of causes, not only taking the stage as speaker, but happily walking through a crowded auditorium holding up rugby memorabilia to be auctioned to raise money for a struggling club or for young men crippled in accidents, on or off the field. FitzSimons makes several observations. 'Once he reached celebrity status after the World Cup he did not rush out to cash in. There has never been an ounce of sport's notorious, "Show me the money", attitude about him. And he has continued to do the post he holds enormous honour.'

FitzSimons also makes the often-repeated comment about Macqueen's application of business techniques, but adds a twist. 'Most people say, "These are the golden rules for success in sport and this is how you can apply them in business." In my view the reason the Wallabies have been such a success is that Rod has done the reverse. He has applied the rules of business to sport and run the Wallabies like a business. But there is more to it than his planning and management skills. There is an old Australian expression, "He'd be a good man to be in the trenches with." In the case of Rod Macqueen, if I was in the trenches he would be the one I would choose to blow the whistle telling us when to charge. He is a natural leader, and a good man, who has great care for his people.'

One person who has spent more time than most in the rugby trenches with Macqueen is John Eales. He too believes the greatest contribution was organisational skills and a business structure that took pressure off the players and gave them direction. The selection of troops was another crucial factor. 'Without a shadow of a doubt, and I think Rod would be the first to say so, he couldn't have done it singlehandedly. The importance of the people he put in place will never be fully documented and can never be overestimated. That is one of his strengths, to find those people who gave him such enormous support over that time. As a person he's a lot more sensitive than most people in the street would believe. He's never liked showing off, or strutting around, and that's an important part of his character. That side of him also showed through in his philosophy of involving family with the team and the setting up of a permanent base camp, which was sensational. In many ways that in itself was probably one of the best things that has happened to Australian rugby in the past four years.'

The Wallaby family

The importance of spending time with family is a subject raised by most players. The hefty financial rewards of professionalism don't always fully compensate for the stress placed on personal relationships, a factor appreciated by 'Player of the World Cup Tournament', Wallaby centre Tim Horan. 'Life at Caloundra really did create a Wallaby family. With a wife and children, I appreciated being able to have them with me for long periods of time enjoying barbecues and other group get-togethers. It allowed them to see what we were doing and understand why we were away from home for such a long time. After we had won the World Cup I was proud to be able to show it to my daughters who could then see it as the reward for all our hard training, and for the time our family had spent apart.'

Contrary to the observations of some people at the time, Horan doesn't believe Macqueen's insistence on adhering to a strict game plan restricts individual brilliance. 'His game plans always revolve around the different strengths of the players and once the organisational skills are in place, we're free to roam about the field as individuals. His organisation and preparation off the field can be time-consuming and at times annoying, but it's rarely questioned. For a coach to be successful he needs the respect of the players, and Rod earned that from each and every one of us very early on. He always kept us fully informed of what our goals were so we knew what we were doing, and why we were doing it.'

Raising the standards

Already Australia's most successful rugby coach, Macqueen would leave behind much more than an impressive list of statistics in the record books. Jeff Miller, his assistant coach during the World Cup campaign, echoes the sentiments of other members of the management team. 'From the time he started he was concerned about the future of Australian rugby. He looked at succession planning and how to bring players through. His other legacy from Australia's point of view is that there is now a unity of purpose between the states and the relationships are much stronger than they were previously. From an overall perspective in my opinion he's revolutionised the game. Most other countries are still trying to copy the same style of team management and structure.'

Not surprisingly the thoughts of Macqueen's fellow selector and now close friend Paul McLean, are all complimentary. But the man who has always been available to offer support and advice on rugby matters believes Macqueen has made a much greater contribution. 'During his time Rod has raised the standards and ideals of the position. He has conducted himself extremely well in public in everything he has said and done. For someone in a high-pressure position under intense scrutiny, he has not left himself open to any major criticism, which has been a wonderful benefit to the game. Equally, his commitment to the ongoing success of Australian rugby is exemplified by his passion to filter his knowledge and expertise through to clubs and schools throughout the country. He has built an infrastructure that will continue to work well after his retirement. Rod's influence on not only the rugby landscape but also the sporting landscape of Australia has been indelible.'

Similar observations are made by former Wallaby coach and national radio broadcaster Alan Jones, who says Macqueen's achievements and contribution to rugby cannot be overstated. 'Rod's success is derived from several sources. At the personal level he is a planner and an organiser. If he doesn't know he'll find out. And this disposition has led him to build a team of staff who have complemented one another in attitude, knowledge and skill. Rod is also a people person—a gentle but firm individual always willing to place the players' interests at the centre of his quest for team results. It is no coincidence that his Australian teams have advanced dramatically Australia's rugby interests as a direct consequence of the coach's own ambition to secure the best for all things Australian.

'I shall remember Rod Macqueen's control of the reins of Australian rugby for the dignity with which the job was done. And for the superb way in which his players, by performance and personal presentation, always placed the interests, image and traditions of the game in the vanguard of what they were doing. Those of us who love the game of rugby are more than grateful for that.'

Big picture thinking

'He is uncompromising. Something I believe is a prerequisite for any successful person.'

These are the words of ARU chief executive, John O'Neill.

'He would continually say to me, "Let's be obsessive about the Wallabies winning." That approach was surely endorsed by victory in the 1999 World Cup. The way the team performed, the planning and the execution—it was a great victory for all concerned. I think Rod's biggest contribution is as a strategist. He is a big picture thinker, and bringing business practices and discipline to the job of coaching has been one of the key factors in his success.'

It's hard to find any form of criticism of Macqueen, even amongst his archrivals across the Tasman. Former New Zealand coach John Hart has become firm friends with Macqueen and, like other international coaches, offers genuine praise—even though his previously all-conquering All Blacks were firstly subdued then repeatedly beaten by Macqueen's Wallabies. 'Rod's appointment as Wallaby coach signalled a significant change in the approach and, more particularly, attitude of the Wallabies. Prior to that I always felt we had the measure of Australian teams which I thought tended to do much of their talking off the field.

'I first came into contact with Rod in 1996, during my first year as All Blacks coach, when he was in charge of the Brumbies. His professionalism and deep thinking impressed me and it is those attributes that have become hallmarks of his success with the Wallabies. When he became Australian coach I immediately sensed a more professional approach in terms of PR and media off the field, and certainly a far more hardnosed approach to the game on the field. While the Wallabies deserved their World Cup success I do not necessarily believe they were the most skilled team in the competition. Their success was built on foundations of excellent shared leadership—both on and off the field—mental toughness and the ability to make decisions under pressure.

'Rugby today is in many ways a game of physical chess, and the Australians have adapted to the requirements quicker than most. Rod faces a huge task in his final season, with three Tests against the Lions followed by the Tri Nations series. But regardless of the outcomes he has already shown he is one of the great thinkers and coaches in the modern game.'

A great ambassador

Most Australian political leaders have been dedicated followers and supporters of their nation's sporting talent, and Prime Minister John Howard is no exception. Apart from hosting Macqueen's Wallabies at an official dinner following the World Cup, he has also enjoyed several dressing room celebrations after notable victories. Away from the usual media presence, he has enthusiastically joined the traditional circle and, with arms draped around shoulders, sung the national anthem. John Howard is another who believes the achievements of Macqueen and the Wallabies reach further than the playing field. 'I found Rod to be a charming man and one who is professional and successful in his endeavours. He is an outstanding rugby coach and a good motivator, able to get the best out of his players. Rod has also been a great ambassador for Australia. Every time I had the pleasure of meeting the Wallabies under his leadership they were an impressive group of men.'

Chapter 26

The Ultimate Compliment

In the final analysis, Rod Macqueen's contribution to rugby and how it came about can, with the help of a misguided personal attack, be readily understood.

Perhaps the defining moment in his career as a coach occurred towards the end of the 2000 season. It came in an unusual and totally unexpected way. During an off-the-record private conversation with a rugby journalist from one of Australia's leading newspapers, Macqueen was asked about claims being made privately by one of the fringe Wallabies. Appearing slightly embarrassed, the reporter told Macqueen that the player believed he and the other team members, along with the assistant coaches, did most of the work and came up with the majority of ideas, that Macqueen 'did very little'. In other words, without his support team and regular input from the players, the Wallabies would not be world champions. To the journalist's surprise, instead of being insulted Macqueen relaxed into a wry smile. Even more confusing, he appeared to be pleased by the accusation.

He obviously didn't realise that he had just paid me the greatest compliment possible. At that moment I knew it had all come together. As a businessman my absolute aim was to have a company that was able to run itself. In rugby my aim was to reach the level where the players believed they were capable of running the show with the help of the assistant coaches. Then I would have achieved my ultimate goal.

At the end of the World Cup, I honestly believed we had virtually reached that goal, and that allowed us to go to another level. I was now looking not from the inside out, but from the outside in. I was able to keep control and still make final decisions within the team while seeing where we were in our world. It was possible because I was operating on the periphery, not having to be involved in the day-to-day business. It was the ultimate example of being in the best position to look at the big picture, allowing me to have a greater vision for the future. This gave us an obvious advantage and a new dimension.

The planning, the philosophies, the experience, the selection of players and the coaching staff, the structures, the meetings, the research that goes into achieving all this is something perhaps many people are unaware of. But for Macqueen it was the culmination of what he had learned and developed from childhood. Lessons observed and knowledge absorbed. Refined, combined and put into practice. It had been a journey of discovery and achievement highlighted and illuminated by many personal beacons:

The new dominance of the Collaroy surfboat crews, transformed from easybeats to national title contenders by discipline, courage and commitment;

The spirit and tradition of the Warringah Rats, firmly established by victory in the Club Championship during only his second year as club coach;

Triumph on the faces of the NSW Waratahs in 1991 after sweeping through the season undefeated, aided by a professional structure and dedicated staff assembled against the apathy of amateurism;

Elation at the end of the Brumbies' first year, when seven players, discarded or rejected by other states, deservedly won the coveted Wallaby jumper;

The quiet, unspoken fatherly pride of Ian Macqueen, when Exhibition Displays was reinvented and then surged ahead on a wave of innovation and goodnatured enthusiasm;

Plaudits and personal friendships flowing from senior company executives in Australia and around the world as Advantage Line set new benchmarks and charted new directions for point-of-sale merchandising;

The William Webb Ellis Trophy. The Bledisloe Cup. The Tri Nations Cup. Numerous other international trophies firmly ensconced in the display cabinet of the Australian Rugby Union, all fought for and delivered by a new breed of players and management who set unequalled standards both on and off the field.

Each project—the surf club, rugby or business—was built around special people with special skills. This was Macqueen's unique gift. With an uncanny vision, he was able to identify the talent required and recognise the people who had it. This enabled him to create an environment where everyone was able to work together harmoniously, and to ensure they had enough confidence and belief in themselves to make it all work. This is the ultimate proof of success.

The unnamed player in his boasting observation to the journalist had unwittingly confirmed to the outside world what Macqueen already believed to be true. What he had established with his private company, he had also achieved with the Wallabies—a strong, well-balanced structure with personnel capable of operating independently on a daily basis.

All this was achieved by a man suddenly described as a person who 'did very little'. An assessment worthy of a wry smile indeed.

Epilogue
Ahead Before Kickoff

The Australian Rugby Union had a mission statement in place for the season 2001: 'To be an ongoing force in world rugby.' The first goal would be to defeat the touring British and Irish Lions recognised as the strongest rugby combination the northern hemisphere had to offer.

No one could argue with such a grand and laudable vision but it contained a fatal flaw, one that was immediately recognised by the man who would be responsible for putting it into action. It was a very focused Rod Macqueen who walked into the ARU boardroom in February to deliver a half-hour presentation. He was inwardly fuming as he outlined the facts to those present. Under the schedule presented to him, victory over the Lions would be virtually impossible. The proposed Wallaby preparation for the upcoming series simply didn't reflect the ARU's own mission statement.

As Macqueen told the board, the Lions would play six warm-up matches before the first Test, allowing them to develop and experiment with their squad of thirty-six players, giving them plenty of opportunity to forge a strong and cohesive Test XV. By comparison, the Wallabies had a disrupted preparation in place, with no lead-up matches scheduled and some Wallabies playing for their provincial side against the tourists. For a coach who had won so much by concentrating on every detail, the consequences seemed obvious. What he wanted was an unbroken block of preparation time for the whole Wallaby squad, at least one warm-up game, and a two-week break between the second and third Test matches. Macqueen concluded his presentation with a recommendation—either the board change the team preparation or re-write the ideals outlined in the mission statement. As it stood, it was a contradiction and one or the other needed to change.

The result was exactly what Macqueen hated most in business, 'the grey decision'; a compromise solution from a committee. It was decided that all players should go into camp with the Wallabies, but at the same time Queensland's Wallabies would still be allowed to play for their province against the touring side. In the final event, this compromise wouldn't help either Queensland or Australia. In addition, the touring schedule was so tight, there was time to squeeze in just one hastily arranged warm-up game. The board members admitted all this did not match their own mission statement and were in fact sympathetic to Macqueen's concerns. In fairness to them, negotiations on the itinerary had begun almost three years earlier, but had not included the actual Wallaby management until the previous year. Now little could be done to make the drastic changes all agreed were necessary.

Disappointed, Macqueen moved to counter this setback by putting even more effort than usual into the pre-camp build-up. On top of everything else, he was acutely aware of the changed personnel available to him both on and off the field. While the rugby public was earnestly talking up a contest featuring the World Cup champions, the Wallaby squad of twenty-two players included only twelve of those who had carried off the William Webb Ellis Trophy just two years earlier. In addition, out of Macqueen's original support staff of twelve, only three remained. As part of the ARU's vision for the future, the Australian side was in the midst of this rebuilding yet was now about to take on the combined might of the four Home Unions. Macqueen arranged a two-day management meeting with his staff, and given the limited preparation, he stressed that the Wallabies had to hit the ground running. To this end, the message on the detailed manual that he and team management always prepared for the players before any series was 'Ahead Before Kickoff'. The key element was to do the basic things extremely well against a team built around an English side that had conquered all before them. As Macqueen had continually emphasised to those who would listen, this team would be the best-prepared and most professional side to ever hit Australian shores.

Against such a powerful team there would be no margin for error on the basics. Macqueen consequently planned to double the time the Wallabies would spend on scrums, lineouts and restart skills. With no time to develop their own new moves, he decided to take the best of the existing Wallaby plays and add a blend of the most successful tactics used by the Australian Super 12 teams.

When the Lions finally arrived on Australian shores they came not so much as a touring rugby side, but an invading force. They were accompanied by a red-shirted army of around 15,000 supporters, which generated an atmosphere never seen before in Australia. Media interest was intense, fuelled by comments by team management and the accompanying Fleet Street journalists who, from the outset, made it clear they believed they were a better side than the world champions. It was a declaration of war.

In their early games, the Lions showed determination, the sharpest of skills and a single-mindedness that reinforced Macqueen's concerns. They rolled past the opposition, including a brutal 42–8 demolition of the best Queensland had to offer and a 41–24 win over the NSW Waratahs marred by numerous spiteful incidents. A clean sweep in these lead-up games was only prevented by an enthusiastic and committed Australia A side, which took an early lead and held on to win 28–25.

By the time the Wallaby squad came together, detailed research had been gathered on the Lions' style of play. All the information was broken down and made available to the players, using the now accepted CD technology. But there was an added twist. At almost every training session, they spent time running in opposition against a squad of reserve players dubbed the Leos (the Lions), suitably prepared by Jeff Miller and John Muggleton. Outfitted in red jerseys, they not only played the expected moves of the touring side but adopted the more aggressive style used by northern hemisphere teams at the break-down.

Additionally, in the reduced lead-up to the series, assistant coaches Ewen McKenzie and Glen Ella had been working overtime in assisting Macqueen to prepare a strategy which they believed would be necessary to beat the Lions.

As the first Test in Brisbane approached, Macqueen felt more and more uneasy with his side's limited preparation and the pressures it placed on him. Despite an encouraging win over a resilient Maori side, for the first time since he had taken over as Wallaby coach three and a half years before, each day was becoming an ordeal. The media pressure and high expectations of the public were generating stress he had never before experienced.

On the eve of the first Test, he and Liz shared a private meal at a Japanese restaurant as they always did. Macqueen had made a decision and his wife was the first to hear the words that would later shock Australian, and indeed world rugby. He planned to step aside. The Lions series would be his last as Australian coach and he would not remain for the Tri Nations and Bledisloe Cup series. They had discussed the notion several times before and Liz agreed with the decision. Both knew the pressures were making him uncomfortable and he had always said he would know when it was time to go. The moment had come. Macqueen knew it was the right decision for both him and the team. His nominated successor, Eddie Jones, was already working in tandem and had been part of the team's selection and planning that season. He felt Jones was ready to take over and at that point had more to offer the Wallabies, who would need lifting to defend their formidable record against the Springboks and All Blacks. After further discussion with Liz only one more decision had to be made: the timing of the announcement. But that would come after consultation with key officials and of course, the first battle against the Lions the following day.

'It wasn't a game, it was a shame,' was the opening line in the *Sydney Morning Herald*'s scathing report on the match. The Wallabies appeared slow and complacent as the Lions attacked with speed and aggression, making numerous midfield breaks to secure a 29–13 victory. Australia's limited backline opportunities were constantly crushed by bruising defence. Whenever the Australians threw the ball wide, they played into the hands of the opposition, which was trained to rush forward in close and then slide across field to shut down any such moves. At halftime Macqueen looked at his players and was disturbed. For the first time in his experience, they appeared to be in shock, overwhelmed by the physical confrontation of the Lions and the deafening support of the red army that seemed to outnumber the locals two-to-one. It appeared the British media's predictions of northern hemisphere dominance were worryingly accurate as the Lions pressed home their advantage to the final whistle.

Macqueen didn't need to tell the players that a massive reversal was needed. The team had one week to reprogram and counter the passionate touring side. In the meantime, unknown to the outside world, he had other matters to deal with.

Macqueen arranged with Jeff Miller to discuss with Eddie Jones whether he was ready to take over. Macqueen then met with Australian Rugby Union chief John O'Neill, who reluctantly supported his decision saying he was more than confident that Jones could take up the reins. It was agreed that his retirement would be made public immediately after the second Test in Melbourne, regardless of the result.

Before the game, Macqueen took Eales and Gregan into his confidence and also quietly mentioned his decision to relatives, close friends and team manager, John McKay, but no one else. It was a bold move before a game that would have a monumental impact on the public memory of his coaching career. If they lost, stepping aside immediately afterwards would look like an admission of defeat and inevitably tarnish his amazing record and rugby legacy.

However, the build-up to the second Test was different. Macqueen noticed a stronger resolve among the players without words being spoken. It was obvious they were determined to level the series. Within themselves, they knew the Lions were not invincible and this was supported by their game analysis which once again revealed statistics that would be crucial to the Wallabies' success. It was noted that after holding possession for more than two or three phases, the Lions seemed to run out of attacking options and either kicked or made mistakes. In contrast, the longer the Wallabies held the ball the more fragile the Lions' defence became. With a revamped front row the Wallabies trained to put pressure on the opposing scrum and direct more attacks through the forwards.

The Australian Rugby Union had also learnt a belated, but valuable, lesson: the value of massed enthusiastic support. Australian spectators were deliberately seated together in large blocks and yellow scarves were freely distributed in a bid to counteract the wall of red that had so dominated the stands in the first Test. The music and general pre-game hype at the stadium was also deliberately more parochial to help stir the local supporters.

This time the Wallabies played to their true potential. Although the crowd and millions of television viewers around the world believed the Wallabies were barely in the match when they left the field at half-time trailing 11–6, in the dressing room the environment was one that Macqueen was accustomed to. Without exception, everyone was calm and quietly confident. They felt they had the measure of the opposition and it was a matter of maintaining pressure around the rucks and mauls and the opportunities would come. The breaks came earlier than expected. Two tries in the first seven minutes of the second half by winger Joe Roff sparked a vintage performance from the rest of the side, who out-muscled the Lions to secure a special 35–14 victory. For the first time on the tour, the singing and chanting of the Australian crowd also gave them a points victory over the visitors. There was controversy too, with three late shoulder charges on playmaker Larkham, which went unpunished by the referee and created almost as much comment as the result. All this was soon overshadowed at the after-match press conference when Macqueen, as planned, announced his retirement.

The scene was set for a monumental showdown at Sydney's Stadium Australia the following Saturday night. The series would be decided, as would Macqueen's place in history. After securing every other prize in international rugby, he now had the opportunity to finish by achieving what no other Australia coach ever had before.

Although unintended, Macqueen's announcement of an early departure gave new impetus to the Wallaby build-up. In contrast, the Lions' preparation was racked by internal bickering and embarrassing public statements which damaged team morale and embarrassed tour officials. Members of the Wallaby squad were astounded when several high profile opposition players wrote columns in British newspapers in which they were critical of each other and the way in which the tour was being handled. Under the Wallaby code of behavior, such problems would not have arisen in the first place. Under Macqueen's 'We not me' selection criteria, players with such an attitude problem would not have been selected in the squad. The disruption was a sad reflection on many of those in the touring side whose attitude, strangely enough, contrasted sharply with the behaviour of their many thousands of supporters. While members of the red army may have been rowdy and parochial, they brought with them a lively sense of humour and passion for the game that was openly welcomed and appreciated by everyone with whom they came in contact.

If media hype over the first two Tests had been unprecedented, it would be impossible to describe the intensity surrounding the third and deciding match. Rarely had a single sporting event in Sydney aroused such public interest. Of concern to the Australian camp were injuries to second-rower David Giffin, who had aggravated a hamstring injury at training, and five-eighth Stephen Larkham, who had not recovered from his severe battering in the previous match. The experienced Elton Flatley came into the all-important position of flyhalf and an aggressive, no nonsense player from the Brumbies was selected in place of Giffin. For Macqueen, it was one of the most enjoyable tasks of the past few months. He had great pleasure in telling 'Googie' Harrison he was about to play his first Test for the Wallabies.

The moment was made even more special when Harrison recalled their first meeting when he was reprimanded for playing the clown.

Throughout the Lions' series the Wallabies had, as usual, invited a Classic Wallaby to present the captain's jersey before each game. So too had they invited a speaker to offer some words of motivation to the team. The most moving and inspirational address came from John Coutis, whose courage and endurance had helped him survive being born with withered and crippled legs. After constant bullying during early schooldays, he chose to have his legs amputated. Speaking to the Wallabies, he explained his positive approach to life and the strength of 'self-belief'. His emotional speech gave the team the message they were looking for to take in to the final game: 'Believe in Yourself.'

The focus for the team was to maintain continuity and along with that a continuing call to the players from John Eales to 'never be satisfied'. After every facet of play, he would call for more and more improvement. As usual, they ran onto the field knowing they had a comprehensive game plan; this time one that would constantly pressure and challenge the Lions. They knew too that they were better prepared defensively following intensive sessions with John Muggleton throughout the week.

The red and gold crowd of 84,188 was a world record for a Lions match and the vocal support from the competing spectators at times drowned out the public address system. As the match swung back and forth, the booming chant of 'Lions . . . Lions . . . Lions was equally countered for the first time by 'Wallabies . . . Wallabies . . . Wallabies' and outbursts of 'Waltzing Matilda'. At half-time, the match was very much in the balance with the Wallabies leading 16–13. Despite the evenness of the contest, there was again a clear confidence and composure among the Wallabies in the dressing room and the usual calm discussion over the play required in the second half. All were well aware of the enormous significance of the occasion and how hard ultimate victory would be. There was no change to the game plan and Macqueen sent them back out with a stern reminder, 'This will be the hardest forty minutes of football you'll ever play in your life.'

His words were no overstatement. With fifteen minutes remaining and the scores locked at 15–all the stadium fell strangely silent. So absorbing was the contest it seemed supporters from both sides were almost afraid to barrack for their side. The deadlock was broken by two penalty goals from Matthew Burke, but the game produced the ultimate ending to the ultimate confrontation. Throughout the game, newcomer Harrison had secured crucial ball from kickoffs and lineouts. Finally, with two minutes remaining and the tourists with a lineout only metres from the Australian line, young 'Googie' Harrison leapt high to steal a crucial throw directed to Lions captain Martin Johnson. A clearing kick relieved the pressure and the Wallabies held out a dramatic last-gasp attack after the final whistle to secure victory 29–23.

It was the finish Macqueen had worked towards and deserved. Post-match celebrations on the field were even more emotional than they were after the World Cup final. The coach and players embraced more warmly than ever before with many noticing a tear in Macqueen's eye, including the niggle king Owen Finegan who couldn't resist a parting shot as he pointed this out to those around.

Macqueen's normally reserved feelings later overflowed during a short impromptu speech when he heard himself tell spectators at the ground, and the millions watching the worldwide television broadcast, 'It's bloody good to be Australian.' When Eales held aloft the Tom Richards Cup, it was an action that signified the close of an historical chapter in Australian, and world, rugby.

The raucous celebrations continued in the dressing room with the team joined by the Australian Prime Minister John Howard, who once again linked arms to sing the national anthem. Macqueen made a passionate farewell speech in which he firstly thanked John O'Neill for his support saying how significant he had been in the success of the Wallabies. Then he turned to the players, telling them what a pleasure it had been coaching the side for the last four years, thanking them and wishing them well for the future. He assured them they could go onto yet another level under new coach Eddie Jones.

When the team finally arrived back at their hotel, Rod and Liz Macqueen joined in the celebrations and were quickly surrounded by a small group of familiar faces. They were people who had waited patiently to share in this moment of final glory. Coincidentally, the group represented virtually every stage and aspect of Macqueen's life, ranging from close family members to friends who had been present at so many other special occasions—from Collaroy Surf Club, Warringah and NSW rugby, his company Advantage Line, local neighbours and new friends from Caloundra. Fittingly, it was a get-together that allowed those who had contributed and shared the journey, to also share in the finale.

Macqueen's place in history was finally secured. Victory over the touring British and Irish Lions meant he had achieved a feat matched by no other rugby coach in the modern era. Teams under his control had won every competition and trophy available in the international arena.

However, at the end, the trophy that meant more to Macqueen than any other wasn't made from silver, gold or crystal but woven gold fabric, adorned with the stars of the Southern Cross. After the final victory over the Lions, Eales made a special presentation to his coach on behalf of the players. It was a Wallaby player's jersey, on this occasion embroidered below the coat of arms with Australia v The Lions, Sydney 2001. Such jerseys are traditionally produced before each Test match especially, and only for the players. For Macqueen, who had never played for Australia, it was a gesture of great emotional significance. Until now he had always celebrated victories alongside the team but not as one of them. Finally, the players had made him one of their own.

Rod Macqueen Biography

Date of Birth: 31 December 1949

Family: Married in 1971 to Elizabeth

Children: Jacqueline (1973) Scott (1975)

Surf lifesaving career
- Won three NSW surfboat titles with Collaroy in 1977, 1978, 1984.
- Twice second in the national surfboat championships in 1979, 1980.
- Third in one mile surfboat race at world championships in Hawaii in 1983.
- Represented NSW five times, on three occasions as captain, with the team winning each time.
- Won Australian masters rowing competition in 1989, 1990.
- Won over-35 state surfboat championship in 1990.
- Two years captain of Collaroy Surf Club and subsequently awarded honorary life membership.

Playing career
- Eleven seasons as a forward with Warringah and two with Eastwood between 1969 and 1981.
- Entered Warringah's first grade at 18 years of age. Played more than 200 first grade games, 173 of them with Warringah and had five seasons as Warringah captain.
- Warringah's Best and Fairest Player in first grade in 1969, 1973, 1974, 1976 and also awarded the President's Trophy in 1973.
- Played for Sydney and Australian Barbarians in 1973 and following year in Australian Possibles-Probables trial.

Coaching experience
- Started aged 19 with Warringah junior representative sides.

- Took Warringah second grade to the final in 1985.
- In 1986, appointed Warringah's club and first grade coach, with the club fielding six grade and four colts teams. During the four-year period 1986–89, Warringah won the NSWRU club championship and minor premiership in 1987 and competed in the first grade grand finals in 1987 and 1988. In 1987, all ten grades reached the semi-finals.
- Coached Sydney in 1987, NSW B in 1988, NSW Waratahs in 1991–92, Australian XV in 1995, ACT Brumbies in 1996–97.
- Australian coach from September 1997 until his retirement after the Lions series in July 2001.
- Coached Australia against 14 different countries.

Australian selector
- 1992, 1994–95, 1997–01.

Records/achievements
- In 1991, NSW Waratahs were undefeated in 10 games under his coaching, including wins over Argentinean and New Zealand provincial teams, Queensland (twice), England and Wales. The 71–8 victory over Wales in 1991 was a record score. Altogether, he guided the Waratahs to 14 wins and a draw from 19 games.

- ACT Brumbies never beaten on home soil when Macqueen was coaching and in 1997, their second year in the competition, were finalists against Auckland Blues in Super 12 in which they were defeated 35–12.

- Macqueen assumed the role of national coach after Australia suffered a 61–22 defeat at the hands of South Africa in Pretoria on 23 August 1997.
- On 6 November 1999 the Wallabies defeated France 35–12 in Cardiff to capture the Rugby World Cup, after an undefeated run through their pool games, then the quarter and semi-finals.
- Macqueen's Wallabies played before a world record rugby crowd of 109,874 when beaten 39–35 by New Zealand at Stadium Australia on 15 July 2000. They also attracted 107,042 to the same venue when they defeated New Zealand 28–7 on 28 August the previous year.
- Vodafone Wallabies received International Team of the Year Award at the 2000 Australian Sports Awards in Adelaide. Other finalists in the international teams category included the Hockeyroos and

the Australian cricket team. Macqueen also a finalist in Coach of the Year category.
- Macqueen's record as national coach: Tests 43, won 34, drawn 1, lost 8. Unbeaten ratio: 81.4 percent. Non-Test match record: played 5, won 5.
- The Wallabies had never beaten the Lions in a series until they did so under Macqueen in 2001.

Cups Won
- Cook Cup (v England) 1998/1999.
- Bledisloe Cup (v NZ) 1998/1999/2000.
- Hopetoun Cup (v Scotland) 1998, 2000.
- Lansdowne Cup (v Ireland) 1999.
- World Cup 1999.
- Puma Trophy (v Argentina) 2000.
- Mandela Challenge Plate (v South Africa) 2000.
- Tri Nations Trophy 2000.
- Trophee des Bicentenaries (v France) 2000.
- Tom Richards Cup (v British & Irish Lions) 2001.

Record Scores
- 76–0 (v England), Brisbane 1998. This was the highest score ever against any nation and the biggest winning points margin.
- 53–6 over Argentina in Brisbane in 2000.
- 66–20 over Fiji in Sydney in 1998.
- 46–10 over Ireland in Brisbane in 1999.
- 57–9 over Romania in Belfast in 1999 (World Cup).
- 45–3 over Scotland in Sydney in 1998.
- 44–23 over South Africa in Melbourne in 2000.
- 74–0 over Tonga in Canberra in 1998.
- Longest winning streak (10): 28 August 1999–15 July 2000 and 29 August 1998–17 July 1999.

Macqueen's Test Record

DATE	COUNTRY	VENUE	SCORE
1997			
1 Nov	Argentina	Buenos Aires	23–15 W
8 Nov	Argentina	Buenos Aires	16–18 L
15 Nov	England	London	15–15 D
22 Nov	Scotland	Scotland	37–8 W

1998

6 Jun	England	Brisbane	76–0	W
13 Jun	Scotland	Sydney	45–3	W
20 Jun	Scotland	Brisbane	33–11	W
11 Jul	New Zealand	Melbourne	24–16	W
18 Jul	South Africa	Perth	13–14	L
1 Aug	New Zealand	Christchurch	27–23	W
22 Aug	South Africa	Johannesburg	15–29	L
29 Aug	New Zealand	Sydney	19–14	W
18 Sep	Fiji	Sydney	66–20	W
22 Sep	Tonga	Canberra	74–0	W
26 Sep	Samoa	Brisbane	25–13	W
21 Nov	France	Paris	32–21	W
28 Nov	England	London	12–11	W

1999

12 Jun	Ireland	Brisbane	46–10	W
19 Jun	Ireland	Perth	32–26	W
26 Jun	England	Sydney	22–15	W
17 Jul	South Africa	Brisbane	32–6	W
24 Jul	New Zealand	Auckland	15–34	L
14 Aug	South Africa	Cape Town	9–10	L
28 Aug	New Zealand	Sydney	28–7	W

World Cup matches

3 Oct	Romania	Belfast	57–9	W
10 Oct	Ireland	Dublin	23–3	W
14 Oct	United States	Limerick	55–19	W
23 Oct	Wales	Cardiff	24–9	W
30 Oct	South Africa	London	27–21	W
6 Nov	France	Cardiff	35–12	W

2000

17 Jun	Argentina	Brisbane	53–6	W
24 Jun	Argentina	Canberra	32–25	W
8 Jul	South Africa	Melbourne	44–23	W
15 Jul	New Zealand	Sydney	35–39	L
29 Jul	South Africa	Sydney	26–6	W
5 Aug	New Zealand	Wellington	24–23	W

26 Aug	South Africa	Durban	19–18 W
4 Nov	France	Paris	18–13 W
11 Nov	Scotland	Edinburgh	30–9 W
18 Nov	England	London	19–22 L

2001

30 Jun	British & Irish Lions	Brisbane	13–29 L
7 Jul	British & Irish Lions	Melbourne	35–14 W
14 Jul	British & Irish Lions	Sydney	29–23 W

Category guide

Many of the subheadings from this book have been grouped into a broad range of categories to provide easy reference for anyone wishing to access information they may find relevant or helpful in the future.

Photo credits

Picture section 2:

Pg 8:   Macqueen wins flag competition, News Ltd.

Picture section 3:

Pg 6:   Brumbies early training session.
Pg 7:   Owen Finegan in bonnet.
       Space cadets.
       Seven Brumbies.
Pg 8:   Brumbies celebrating in the dressing room.
Pg 8:   Final on field in Auckland.

Courtesy of Andrew Dawson, Brumbies Rugby Magazine.

Picture section 4:

Pg 3:   Camp Wallaby, Courier-Mail.
Pg 5:   Australian team with Bledisloe Cup, Allsport/Getty Images.
Pg 5:   Wallabies fans, News Ltd.
Pg 6:   John Williamson, News Ltd.
Pg 9:   Australian World Champions on ground, Allsport/Getty Images.
Pg 10: Assistants and Rod with World Cup, Allsport/Getty Images.
Pg 11: Rod with World Cup, Allsport/Getty Images.
Pg 12: Australian World Champions at Sydney Town Hall, News Ltd.
Pg 13: Australian team with Tri Nations trophy, Allsport/Getty Images.
Pg 15: A personal farewell between Macqueen and Eales, News Ltd.
Pg 15: Macqueen and Eales waving, Allsport/Getty Images.

Chapter 14

Style of Play

Before the Brumbies' first scheduled Super 12 match, Macqueen organised a short tour of Japan. The trip to one of the weaker rugby nations was a deliberate choice designed to deflect attention from Australian and international media over the fledgling team's performance. Macqueen wanted the team to experiment and get to know each other outside the glare of publicity, which their formation had already attracted.

Our four-match tour of Japan was critical to our preparation for the Super 12. While we had been training for two months, our matches in Japan would give us the opportunity to test our playing patterns against reasonable opposition. The tour would also build unit skills and develop the forwards and backs into a harmonious and competitive outfit.

But Macqueen was anxious for the Brumbies to develop their own culture as much as their own playing style. They were still constantly branded by the media as the team of rejects and no-names from other states.

We needed to establish our own identity. As it turned out, the playing style of the Japanese themselves was very beneficial for us. They were basically trying to keep the scores against them to a minimum and so played very negatively. At every breakdown they threw eight players onto the ground to kill the ball. It was very frustrating at times because to be successful we had to be innovative to overcome their negative play while still developing our own skills. Although it wasn't planned that way, it certainly helped us to develop our style. We had to find ways to stop them killing the ball because our whole style of play was based on retaining possession and mounting attacks from different phases of play.

Judging standards

The Japanese tour proved a success for the two purposes Macqueen had sought. They had developed a distinct pattern of play and just as importantly, bonded together and created their own team culture. A great deal of the latter could be attributed to the rules and regulations players had set for their own behaviour. Before embarking on the trip Macqueen had suggested they come up with their own set of standards, which was put together by a small group headed by Brett Robinson and Pat Howard. The night before they left all members of the squad were given a typed booklet detailing what was expected, ranging from the various modes of dress for different occasions to rules of behaviour. At any one time all members of the party would be wearing the same uniform. When travelling by aircraft and at all official functions, they were to wear suit and tie. At any other time in public they were to wear the team shorts or long pants with appropriate belt, shoes, socks and team shirt. Even at breakfast the minimum dress was team shorts and shirt with collar. The penalty for any offender was levied by a 'Court Judge', usually Brett Robinson or Owen Finegan. It was a system used several years before with the Wallabies and one which worked well, with players going to great lengths to catch each other out. The rules applied to everyone including Macqueen, who was notoriously vague and absentminded. He claims he was inevitably preoccupied with ensuring that every last detail had been double checked and was therefore easy prey. At the end of the tour he was the first one to admit he was the greatest and most punished offender, to the delight of team members.

The fines levied depended on the seriousness of the offence and the person who committed them. They were usually announced during the traditional team 'happy hour' following a match or at the end of a normal day. The usual minimum penalty was to skol, or drink in one gulp, at least one large beer. For non-drinkers the consequences were worse: they were ordered to eat something they were known to dislike. Unfortunately, Macqueen often found himself confronted with a row of full glasses. After spending so much of his life as a player and then a coach he accepted it in good humour. Joining in the happy hour was one of the few times he could relax and genuinely enjoy the company of the players. Other members of the management team consistently say Macqueen was able to walk the fine line between being 'one of the boys' and maintaining his position of authority. Any coach who stays out late at night drinking and arguing with his players finds it hard to make the difficult decisions that can make or break a player's career, but Macqueen seemed to know instinctively how far he could go without losing their respect.

After returning from Japan, Macqueen was confident he had a side that could compete with the established clubs in Super 12 competition. They had only two weeks to prepare for their first match but the competition draw could not have been kinder: their first three matches were on home turf at the Bruce Stadium in Canberra. The historic first game for the ACT Brumbies would be on 5 March 1996, against the strong South African side from Transvaal. With a large component of Springboks, this team was known for their uncompromising forward play.

Answering the questions

As the Brumbies ran on the field they were surprised and heartened by a deafening roar of support from a vocal crowd of more than 8000. A turn-up like this of rugby union supporters was unheard of in Canberra, but something that was to become a feature of all home games to follow. The support was unashamedly parochial. Any refereeing decisions in favour of the Brumbies were widely cheered, any decision in favour of the visitors loudly booed. It seemed the Brumbies could do no wrong and as the game progressed the support for the home team became even greater.

The game itself was hard and tightly fought. The Brumbies' aggressive defence negated the Transvaal attack while their innovative backline moves, although not always successful, continually confused the visitors. Perhaps most significantly was the confusion the Brumbies created in the lineouts by constantly moving their men into different positions in the line at the last moment. The Transvaal players continually complained to the referee that the Brumbies were playing illegal tricks, but they simply couldn't understand the tactics: they were legal and they worked, frustrating not only the South African forwards, but providing a wealth of possession.

The final result was a 13–9 victory for the Brumbies.

It was a great relief to have won that first game. Valuable lessons had been learnt and solidarity strengthened. It was an important stage in the building of our team. We proved to ourselves that our different tactics were effective. We won the lineouts by confusing the opposition with some innovation and for the first time we showed a new brand of aggressive defence. To me it showed we had a very strong bonding within the side that could only develop further.

The right ingredients

So, from the very first game people in the rugby world were shown the strengths, traditions and style of play that would become synonymous with the Brumbies.

One person watching that game from the Brumbies' private box was in a better position than most to appreciate exactly what had been achieved. As president of the ACT Rugby Union, David Lewis had observed the preparation at close hand. He had been involved in rugby for the past twenty-six years and more recently had been the manager for the Australian under 21s and the emerging Wallabies. Lewis knew it was far more than just winning a game of football. He was impressed. 'Macqueen had three months to get them ready. NSW and Queensland had months, years, but he had three months and he did it. I mean that's rarely been publicised, exactly what he did in that three-month period. He had the vision to be able to identify what the problems were. He identified what the goals were. He identified the personnel that he needed to achieve it, and he just went about it.'

Most members of our management team had not worked together before which made for an exciting start. As time went on I began to appreciate the skills that everyone brought with them. Apart from Bill James who had worked with me in the past, there was Phil Thomson, a policeman with an easy and friendly demeanour who brought respect to the team and constantly overcame everyday problems without fuss or difficulty. Stuart Livingston was one of the most professional fitness trainers I had ever come across and added something extra with his impromptu guitar-playing sessions. Our hard-working physio Gavin Malouf was another valuable member of the team, as was Doc Hughes, the ultimate profes-sional with a great sense of humour and a liking for the odd beer. Jake Howard, a former Wallaby and the father of our centre, Pat Howard, also played a prominent part during these first two years and developed a great rapport with the players. I learned a lot from Jake and appreciated